"Tragedy" has been understood in a variety of conflicting ways over the centuries, and the term has been applied to a wide range of literary works. In this book, H. A. Kelly explores the various meanings given to tragedy, from Aristotle's most basic notion (any serious story, even with a happy ending), via Roman ideas and practices, to the Middle Ages, when Averroes considered tragedy to be the praise of virtue, but Albert the Great thought of it as the recitation of the foul deeds of degenerate men. Professor Kelly demonstrates the importance of finding out what writers like Horace, Ovid, Dante, and Chaucer meant by the term, and how they used it as a tool of interpretation and composition. Referring to a wealth of texts, he shows that many modern analyses of ancient and medieval concepts and works are oversimplified and often result in serious misinterpretations. The book ends with surveys of works designated as tragedies in England, France, Italy, and Spain.

D1209926

CAMBRIDGE STUDIES IN MEDIEVAL LITERATURE 18

Ideas and forms of tragedy
from Aristotle to the Middle Ages

CAMBRIDGE STUDIES IN MEDIEVAL LITERATURE 18

This series of critical books seeks to cover the whole area of literature written in the major medieval languages – the main European vernaculars, and medieval Latin and Greek – during the period *c.* 1100–*c.* 1500. Its chief aim is to publish and stimulate fresh scholarship and criticism on medieval literature, special emphasis being placed on understanding major works of poetry, prose and drama in relation to the contemporary culture and learning which fostered them.

Illuminated frontispiece from a fourteenth-century manuscript of
Nicholas Trevet's commentary on Seneca's tragedies (Vatican MS
Urbinas lat. 355, fol. 1v), illustrating an imagined performance of
Hercules furens.

Ideas and forms of tragedy
from Aristotle to the Middle Ages

HENRY ANSGAR KELLY

Professor, Department of English, University of California, Los Angeles

CAMBRIDGE
UNIVERSITY PRESS

CAMBRIDGE UNIVERSITY PRESS
Cambridge, New York, Melbourne, Madrid, Cape Town, Singapore, São Paulo

Cambridge University Press
The Edinburgh Building, Cambridge CB2 2RU, UK

Published in the United States of America by Cambridge University Press, New York

www.cambridge.org
Information on this title: www.cambridge.org/9780521431842

First published 1993
This digitally printed first paperback version 2005

A catalogue record for this publication is available from the British Library

Library of Congress Cataloguing in Publication data
Kelly, Henry Ansgar, 1934–
Ideas and forms of tragedy from Aristotle to the Middle Ages /
Henry Ansgar Kelly.
p.   cm. – (Cambridge studies in medieval literature: 18)
Includes bibliographical references and index.
ISBN 0 521 43184 0
1. Tragedy.   2. Literary form.   I. Title.   II. Series.
PN1891.K45   1993
809.2'512–dc20   92-24353   CIP

ISBN-13 978-0-521-43184-2 hardback
ISBN-10 0-521-43184-0 hardback

ISBN-13 978-0-521-02377-1 paperback
ISBN-10 0-521-02377-7 paperback

For Robert Looker

All words are pockets into which
now this, now that is put,
and sometimes many things at once.
Nietzsche, *The Wanderer and his Shadow*

ERRATA

Kelly: *Ideas and forms of tragedy from Aristotle to the Middle Ages*

ISBN 0 521 43184 0 hardback

p. 28, line 25: *profitemu* to read *profitemur*

p. 36, n. 1: *Origine* to read *Origines*

p. 38, line 10: Carmine quo to read Carmine qui

p. 41, 2 lines up: *pulpitam* to read *pulpitum*

p. 59, n. 107: egentes to read agentes

p. 64, line 6: *vocabulus* to read *vocabulis*

p. 69, n. 6: emunerabantur to read remunerabantur

p. 73, n. 18: lectus to read luctus.

p. 89, n. 100: quidem to read quid[a]m

p. 89, n. 101: fol. AD 1101. to read for AD 1101.

p. 90, n. 109: Shakleton to read Shackleton

p. 130, n. 80: *antigua* to read *antiqua*

p. 157, n. 178: *supez* to read *super*

p. 159, n. 183: Atikinson to read Atkinson

p. 175, n. 11: Berger to read Bergen

p. 205, n. 123: elegre to read alegre

p. 208, n. 139: Santillana account to read Santillana's account

p. 223, line 4: A. Grudeman to read A. Gudeman

p. 223, line 30: Shakelton to read Shackleton

p. 224, line 6: *super librio Boethii* to read *super libris Boethii*

p. 224, line 17: *Translatio Antiquior* to read *Translatio Antiquior*

p. 227, line 25: (1989) to read (1899)

p. 232, line 11: *In Artem Donati minorem commentum* to read *In Artem Donati majorem commentum*

p. 232, line 12: *In Artem Donati minorem commentum* is a new subentry

p. 236, line 7: *Romantic Reviews* to read *Romanic Review*

p. 240, line 26: *Annali del Corso di Lingue Letterature* to read *Annali del Corso di Lingue e Letterature*

p. 241, line 13: l'*Ecerinis* to read l'*Eccerinis*

p. 242, line 4: *Studie* to read *Studi*

In the Index, references to pages between 88 and 109 sometimes need to be advanced to the next page; for instance, under Accursius, read 107-08 for 107; under Berengar, read 90 for 89-90; under Brito, read 103 for102.

Contents

Contents

Preface

In this book I have set myself the task of examining the various ideas that were associated with the Greek word τραγῳδία and the Latin *tragoedia* (or *tragedia* in its later medieval spelling) and its vernacular "reflexes" in Antiquity and the Middle Ages up to the time of the Italian prehumanists. My primary emphasis is upon medieval understandings and practices, and my treatment of the classical period in chapters 1 and 2 is designed principally as background for the later material. In these early chapters, after a brief look at Aristotle's *Poetics*, I examine the theories and applications of tragedy in classical Rome. In chapter 3, I analyze the conjectures made by Isidore of Seville and others in the early Middle Ages about the nature of ancient Roman tragedy, and in the next chapter I deal with the more enlightened views of twelfth-century writers. The fifth chapter takes up the thirteenth and fourteenth centuries. First, I study early reactions to Aristotle's *Poetics* and to Seneca's newly discovered tragedies. Next, I examine Dante's subject/style notion of tragedy (noblest subjects, highest style), and the narrative idea of tragedy (beginning in tranquillity and ending in horror) set forth by his mystified commentators. Then I survey the various meanings of tragedy in French translations of Boethius and other Latin works. In the sixth chapter I summarize the situation in England in the fourteenth and fifteenth centuries, look at some French manifestations of the idea of tragedy as lamentation, note the latter-day Latin tragedies composed in Italy in imitation of Seneca and Mussato, and finally examine at some length developments in fifteenth-century Iberia: Castile, Portugal, Valencia, and Catalonia.

My reasons for conducting this review are, beyond enlarging our knowledge of the changes that have been rung on the most famous of all genre terms, first, to correct some faulty preconceived ideas about classical notions and practices, and, second, to alter received opinion about the nature and scope of medieval viewpoints. I will demonstrate that the rather limited number of writers in the Middle Ages who use the word "tragedy" vary widely on the meanings they attach to it. Most of them, however, consider it to refer to an obsolete genre, one practiced only by poets of classical Antiquity. Only a few authors think of tragedy as a current variety of literature, and fewer still think of themselves as composers of tragedies. This is a much different picture from that usually presented in scholarly studies of the subject, according to which it is assumed that tragedy, usually understood in the light of one of Geoffrey Chaucer's definitions, was an active genre, well known and widely practiced, Boccaccio's *De casibus virorum illustrium* being unusual only in that it was a collection of tragedies. In fact, Boccaccio did not consider his accounts of falls to be tragedies. But Chaucer did, and went on to write tragedies of his own, to be imitated later by John Lydgate and Robert Henryson. This was such a revolutionary and important development in the history of tragedy that I will devote a separate study to it, to be called "Chaucerian Tragedy."

I have titled the present volume *Ideas and Forms of Tragedy*. The various forms of tragedy will, of course, be very prominent in the first chapters, since they deal with times when tragedies were frequently written and performed. In the later chapters, the main emphasis will be on ideas of tragedy, that is, on interpretations of the word, since actual instances of compositions considered to be tragedies are rare and abortive.

It should be clear by now, but I shall make it clearer, that my enterprise differs radically from the more usual undertaking of writers who begin with a characterization of what they think tragedy is, or should be, and then attempt to see what literary or dramatic works of the past fit this classification, or live up to their notion of "the tragic spirit." I wish rather to see what authors of the past meant by the word as a literary or dramatic term, and, for those who considered their own works to be in the genre of tragedy, to see what requirements or restrictions this notion placed on their manner of composition.

I also distinguish my enterprise from more general efforts of developing theories of genres in which tragedy is given a role, as in Northrop Frye's theories of myths and modes in his *Anatomy of Criticism*, and other general systems as outlined by Alastair Fowler in *Kinds of Literature: An Introduction to the Theory of Genres and Modes*. I do not mean to deny the stimulating nature of many of these systems, but simply to note that my goals are different and my area of operation is in a different sphere. I should point out, however, that generic theories sometimes make unwarranted assumptions about the nature of generic thinking in the past, and I offer my researches as providing new data for a more accurate application of theory to historical circumstances.

The word "tragedy" is badly misused in most modern discussions of "the nature of tragedy," especially when dealing with dramatic forms. The chief offenders are commonly those who claim to draw on an Aristotelian definition of tragedy. The usual fault is to transform Aristotle's analysis of the *best kind* of tragedy in chapter 13 of the *Poetics* (the fall of a good man through some flaw) into a definition of the *only kind* of tragedy. Aristotle did not mean to eliminate from the genre of tragedy plays which did not have such a plot. This would have meant excluding almost the whole body of ancient Greek tragedy. How would one fit in, for example, the plays that have Medea as the protagonist? Here we have the story of a thoroughly vicious woman who moves from adversity to triumph by means of the most unspeakable crimes. Another protagonist, Iphigenia, fortunately refrains at the last moment from sacrificing her brother Orestes, and the story ends quite pleasantly. In chapter 14 of the *Poetics*, Aristotle praises Euripides's version of this story as containing the best kind of tragic action.

It is clear that many self-proclaimed Aristotelians not only read Aristotle selectively, but also employ a double standard in their use of the term "tragedy." They seem willing enough to use a simple generic meaning of the word when speaking of ancient tragedies: that is, they accept as tragedy any play designated as tragedy. But when it comes to postclassical works, they restrict the term to mean "great tragedy," in accordance with their own definition of tragedy.

Aristotle himself, as we shall see in the first chapter, defined tragedy, or rather the tragic genre, so broadly as to take in narrative as well as dramatic works, and inept as well as effective works. His understanding of the genre would clearly have included the modern everyday definition, "any sad story," which is close to both Chaucer's and Shakespeare's understanding of the term. But Aristotle went so far as to include in his generic definition "any serious story."

I shall, then, be using the word "tragedy," in keeping with my classical and medieval sources, primarily as a generic term of literary taxonomy, with no presupposition as to the artistic success of works so designated. This will not, of course, prevent my discussing the artistic merits and demerits of such works.

For the purposes of this study, in sum, the name of tragedy is both a necessary and a sufficient condition for tragedy. That is, every work considered by its author to be a tragedy is a tragedy; and only those works considered by their authors to be tragedies are tragedies. As for works considered to be tragedies by other ancient or medieval writers (that is, by writers other than the authors of the works in question), they come under the category of ideas of tragedy rather than forms of tragedy.

I wish to thank the UCLA Friends of English and the Center for

Medieval and Renaissance Studies at UCLA for supporting the publication of this study.

When quoting both edited and unedited sources, I use my own punctuation and capitalization. I follow the old-fashioned convention of capitalizing the first word of each line of verse.

A note on my citations of Latin texts: when quoting classical texts in a classical context, I avoid the letters *j* and *v* and use only *i* and *u*, thus *iucundus* rather than *jucundus*, and *uult* rather than *vult*. But in texts of the fourth century onwards, including later quotations of classical texts, I use *j* and *v* in order to reflect the change in pronunciation from semivowels to consonants – though without meaning to assert a fixed and uniform practice by the fourth century, and even though in actual orthographic practice (as opposed to pronunciation) the restriction of the letters *u* and *i* to vowels, and *v* and *j* to consonants, did not occur in either Latin or the European vernaculars until the seventeenth century.

My treatment of the classical diphthongs *ae* and *oe* is somewhat different. Even though they had lost their diphthongal nature by the fourth century (again, approximately), and were pronounced simply as *e*, they continued to be spelled in the old way through the eleventh century or so. I therefore use the simple spelling of *e* only in texts of the twelfth to the fifteenth centuries, even when the printed editions that I use give classical spellings.

One of my objectives is to discourage the classical pronunciation of medieval Latin. Or, to put it more positively, I wish to encourage the classical pronunciation of classical Latin, and to promote medieval pronunciations of medieval Latin. The general rule is simple: medieval Latin was pronounced in the same way as the vernacular of the user. For more on this subject, I refer to my essay, "Lawyers' Latin: *Loquenda ut vulgus?*"

Abbreviations

CCL   Corpus Christianorum, series latina (Turnhout, Belgium)
CCM   Corpus Christianorum, continuatio mediaevalis (Turnhout)
CSEL   Corpus scriptorum ecclesiasticorum latinorum (Vienna)
ITS   *Index thomisticus, Supplementum* (Stuttgart 1980)
LCL   Loeb Classical Library (Cambridge, Mass.)
MGH   Monumenta Germaniae historica (Berlin)
PG   Patrologiae graecae cursus completus, ed. J. P. Migne (Paris)
PL   Patrologiae latinae cursus completus, ed. J. P. Migne (Paris)

1

Greek and Roman poetics

In any modern discussion of tragedy, Aristotle almost always has some role to play, whether on center stage or whispering from the wings. But the *Poetics* was not known to Latin Antiquity, and it was badly misunderstood or neglected when it finally came to light in the thirteenth century.[1] And since our present enterprise is primarily concerned not with what we think about tragedy (or with what we think Aristotle thought about tragedy), but rather with what was thought about tragedy in the Middle Ages, we shall not have to be much concerned with Aristotle's views.

But there are, I think, good reasons for taking a brief look at the contents of the *Poetics*: first to dispel widespread misapprehensions of Aristotle's generic views on tragedy, and second to provide ourselves with a basis of comparison with Latin poetic theory. We shall, in fact, be able to see that Aristotle's broadest characterization of tragedy was transmitted to the Latin world by his disciple Theophrastus, as witnessed explicitly by the grammarian Diomedes.[2]

ARISTOTLE ON THE TRAGIC IN GENERAL

In the second chapter of the *Poetics*, Aristotle introduces the epithets *spoudaion* and *phaulon*, which are essential to his definitions of tragedy and comedy. The terms may be given in English form as "spudean" (rhyming

---

[1] H. A. Kelly, "Aristotle–Averroes–Alemannus on Tragedy: The Influence of the *Poetics* on the Latin Middle Ages"; see chap. 5 below.

[2] See A. Philip McMahon, "On the Second Book of Aristotle's *Poetics* and the Source of Theophrastus' Definition of Tragedy," and "Seven Questions on the Aristotelian Definitions of Tragedy and Comedy." McMahon claims that Theophrastus is drawing on a lost dialogue of Aristotle, *On Poets*, rather than on the extant *Poetics*. But I believe that there is an adequate basis for Theophrastus's definition in the *Poetics* (see the discussion of Diomedes below). Aristotle died in 322 BC, and Theophrastus, who had been his principal collaborator, succeeded him as head of his school (called the Peripatos, from the covered walk in the buildings that Theophrastus set up); he died around 287 BC. He was best known in the Middle Ages for his *Characters*, and for an antimatrimonial treatise preserved by St. Jerome in his *Adversus Jovinianum* 1.47. See Charles B. Schmitt, "Theophrastus in the Middle Ages."

with "Judean") and "phaulic." For the purposes of artistic imitation, men are either spudean (above the average, of high character, good, superior, noble, heroic) or phaulic (below the average, of low character, inferior, bad, ignoble). Homer's characters are spudean, and so are those of dramatic tragedy, whereas the persons who appear in comedy are phaulic: that is to say, comedy tends naturally to imitate men worse (*cheirous*) than average, and tragedy to imitate men better (*beltious*) than average.[3]

These distinctions are taken up again in chapter 5, where, however, tragedy itself is termed both spudean and phaulic, in the sense of good and bad (artistic and inartistic).[4] As usual, Aristotle here restricts the term "tragedy" to drama, but he clearly considers epic to be tragic as well, for he says that epic and tragedy are alike in being large-sized imitations of spudean matters (men or events) in verse; and whoever knows about spudean and phaulic tragedy knows about epics, for all the properties of epic are possessed by tragedy.[5]

In classifying epics, in effect, as nonactable forms of tragedy, Aristotle was following in the footsteps of Plato in the *Theaetetus*, where Socrates remarks that the chief poets in the two kinds of poetry are Epicharmus in comedy and Homer in tragedy. That Plato is thinking chiefly of Homer's *Iliad* is clear, since he has Socrates quote a line from it.[6] But Aristotle explicitly names the *Odyssey*, as well as the *Iliad*, as pertaining to the tragic genus.[7]

Aristotle's formal definition of tragedy comes in chapter 6 of the *Poetics*. Its primary characteristic is that it is "an imitation of an action that is spudean." In addition to the qualities of completeness, magnitude, and language that it shares with epic, tragedy is acted rather than narrated. So far, the definition fulfills Aristotle's introductory statement that it follows from his previous discussion. The final clause gives the purpose or effect of tragedy: by pity and fear, it brings about the catharsis of these and similar passions.[8]

Since the last clause contradicts the introductory assertion (that the definition follows from the above discussion), we must conclude either that something about the effects of tragedy was originally contained in the first part of the treatise and subsequently lost, or that it was added later, perhaps in light of Aristotle's subsequent discussion. But the concept of catharsis, which has so bemused critics since the Renaissance, finds no further mention in the rest of the *Poetics*, and nothing like it is to be found in later

---

[3] Aristotle, *Poetics* 2.48a1–18 (i.e., chapter 2, Bekker p. 1448a1–18). I follow the edition of D. W. Lucas. For a recent translation, see Stephen Halliwell, *The Poetics of Aristotle: Translation and Commentary*, to be distinguished from his larger study, *Aristotle's Poetics*.
[4] Similarly, in 9.51b35–37, poets who are *phauloi* are contrasted with those who are *agathoi* (good).
[5] *Poetics* 5.49b9–20.   [6] Plato, *Theaetetus* 1:152e.
[7] See *Poetics* 4.48b38–49a (taken up below) as well as the following discussion.
[8] *Ibid.* 6.49b24–28.

classical or medieval notions of tragedy.[9] But most later definitions do insist even more than Aristotle upon the presence of pitiable, fearful, and pathetic events, especially in the outcome of the story. For Aristotle, however, a serious play or epic that does not end catastrophically is not for this reason to be excluded from the genus of tragedy, though it might be considered "untragic" to a greater or lesser degree: that is, as lacking in the desired tragic effects.

In his listing of possible plots for tragedy in chapter 13, Aristotle characterizes the example of a bad man going from bad to good fortune as the most "atragic" of all. He does not bother to consider the case of a good man going from bad to good fortune, but it goes without saying that he would find it almost as objectionable. Clearly, then, the move from good to bad fortune is to be preferred. But Aristotle has already rejected one such plot: namely, of the wholly virtuous man suffering a bad turn; and he proceeds to reject another, the fall of an evil man, even though it might satisfy one's "philanthropic" impulses.[10] He gives his full approval to only one kind of fall – that of a man not thoroughly good falling because of some defect (*hamartia*). He gives the cases of Oedipus and Thyestes as examples, without specifying Sophocles's *Oedipus rex* or any other specific dramatization of their stories.[11] What most modern simplified reports of the *Poetics* leave out of consideration is that Aristotle is here speaking not of the plot that all tragedies *must* have in order to be classified as tragedy, but only of the sort of plot that the best (*kallistē*) tragedy should have.

When Aristotle himself simplifies his doctrine later in the same chapter, he names only the unhappy ending as the prerequisite for the best tragedy: it is right (*orthon*) for Euripides to end his plays in misfortune, and in so doing he is the most tragic of poets.[12] Aristotle contrasts such plays with those that have a double ending, in which the good characters end happily and the evil ones unhappily. He cites the *Odyssey* as having this kind of plot. And though he notes that some people of his day consider these double-plotted tragedies to be the best, he himself judges them to be only second best. The reason is that the pleasure derived from them is more appropriate to comedy than to tragedy.[13]

---

[9] In Averroes's *Middle Commentary on Aristotle's Poetics*, as rendered into Latin by Herman Alemannus around 1256, the clause is translated, but not discussed: the imitation of the action is said to produce "self-moderating" passions. See p. 120 below.

[10] What we would call "poetic justice." This was the ideal form of tragedy for Sir Philip Sidney and other English theorists in Shakespeare's time. See Kelly, "Chaucer and Shakespeare on Tragedy," p. 198.

[11] *Poetics* 13.52b28–53a22.   [12] *Ibid.* 13.52a23–30.

[13] *Ibid.* 13.53a30–36. He describes the sort of comedy he has in mind: one in which the main characters, such as Orestes and Aegisthus, make friends at the end. He seems to take it for granted that comedy can feature the spudean characters of tragedy.

In chapter 14, however, Aristotle produces yet another ranking of tragic plots, in which certain plays with happy endings are declared to be best. The plots are discussed in the following order:

1 The protagonist intends a heinous deed and commits it
2 The protagonist commits such a deed and only later realizes its heinousness
3 The protagonist intends to commit such a deed but realizes its heinousness in time to refrain from action
4 The protagonist intends to commit such a deed, well aware of its heinousness, but does not (for some reason) commit the deed

Of these possibilities, Aristotle declares the third to be the best, and the fourth the worst. As an example of the third and best type of play, he cites Euripides's *Iphigenia among the Taurians*, in which Iphigenia is about to sacrifice her brother Orestes, but recognizes him as her brother at the last moment: whereupon all is well. But what Aristotle says of the fourth and worst mode would seem to apply as well to the third and best: "It is not tragic, for it is *apathes*."[14] That is, it has no *pathos*, in the sense of "disastrous occurrence."

I do not wish to stress the contradictoriness of Aristotle's text[15] so much as the nature of the tragedies that he was dealing with. Whether Euripides was right to end a particular tragedy in misfortune or good fortune, Aristotle could not avoid the fact that more than a third of Euripides's tragedies ended happily.[16] And no matter how he rated their effectiveness, he could not deny them the name of tragedy. He was also unwilling, at least at times, to exclude the happily ended tragedy from the ranks of good tragedy.

Doubtless it was Aristotle's devotion to Homer as much as anything else that was at the bottom of his ambivalent attitude towards the fortunate outcome of tragedy. Though at one point, as we have seen, he admitted that the outcome of the *Odyssey* was more fitting for comedy than for tragedy, he makes no such remark when he deals with the epic form in its own right at the end of the *Poetics*. He praises the unity of plot in both the *Odyssey* and the *Iliad*, in that only one or at most two tragedies can be made from each of them.[17] And Homer properly shows, he says, that the kinds

---

[14] *Ibid.* 14.53b38.

[15] On this point, see *ibid.*, ed. Lucas, p. 155.

[16] See *ibid.*, p. 147, commenting on *Poetics* 13.53a25, where Aristotle seems to say that most of Euripides's plays end unhappily. From this remark one might expect to find a lower proportion of happy endings in Euripides's plays than in those of Sophocles, but such does not seem to have been the case (based on our admittedly fragmentary knowledge). One count gives Euripides twenty-four happy endings and forty-six unhappy ones, whereas the figures for Sophocles are sixteen and forty-three respectively.

[17] *Poetics* 23.59a30–b7.

4

and parts of epic ought to be the same as in tragedy.[18] But he commends the *Iliad* for its pathetic quality: it is dominated by the tragic deed and unhappy ending. The *Odyssey*, on the other hand, is primarily ethical: it is dominated by character and the receipt of just deserts.[19] In effect, Aristotle is saying that Homer produced two kinds of tragic plots, both of them admirable.

Later authors can also be found who apply the distinction between *pathos* and *ēthos* to the difference between tragedy and comedy,[20] and the sad or happy ending will be the dominant criterion, but for Aristotle the broadest defining criterion was the spudean subject matter, which overrode even the requirement of producing the passions of pity and fear. To classify the *Odyssey* as anything other than tragic would not, I believe, have occurred to Aristotle, and it would have been unthinkable for him to have ranked it with the phaulic baseness of comedy, even though he could admit at one moment that its effect was more appropriate to comedy than to tragedy.

When Theophrastus defined tragedy as representing the critical fortunes of heroes, without further qualification, he can be said to have captured the essence of Aristotle's doctrine of the spudean. Later in this chapter we shall examine the relics of the Theophrastian tradition handed on by the fourth-century grammarians Diomedes and Donatus. In chapter 5, we shall see what sense or lack of sense was made of tragedy in Herman Alemannus's Latin translation of Averroes's commentary on the *Poetics*, and also note the almost complete neglect of William of Moerbeke's Latin translation of the original Greek text of Aristotle's treatise. We shall also look at the passing references Aristotle makes to tragedy in some of his other works and see how they were translated into Latin and interpreted by commentators.

THE ROMAN TRADITION

The chief surviving theorist of tragedy in ancient Rome is Horace in his *Ars poetica*. In this work, an apparent hodgepodge of literary observations that he addresses in an epistle to the Piso family,[21] Horace purports to be speaking of all poetry; but, like Aristotle, he spends most of his time dealing with dramatic poetry. Horace is more allusive than specific, and is generous of exceptions to his rules. For instance, we are not explicitly told

---

[18] *Ibid.* 24.59b8–17.
[19] *Ibid.* 24. See Gerald F. Else, *Aristotle's Poetics: The Argument*, pp. 531–32, 594–95.
[20] McMahon, "Seven Questions," pp. 112 and 124 ("Longinus" and Quintilian).
[21] A word frequently used by classical scholars about the *Ars poetica* is "puzzling." It is not certain who the Pisones (father and son) were whom Horace was addressing, nor when he wrote his epistle (it was published probably around 13 BC), nor how original his ideas were, nor how relevant his comments on the drama and epic would have been for his own day.

what the difference is between tragic and comic styles and subject matters, but only that they should not be mixed, except when appropriate:

> Uersibus exponi tragicis res comica non uult;
> Indignatur item priuatis ac prope socco
> Dignis carminibus narrari cena Thyestae.
> Singula quaeque locum teneant sortita decentem.
> Interdum tamen et uocem Comoedia tollit,
> Iratusque Chremes tumido delitigat ore;
> Et tragicus plerumque dolet sermone pedestri
> Telephus et Peleus dum, pauper et exsul, uterque
> Proicit ampullas et sesquipedalia uerba,
> Si curat cor spectantis tetigisse querella.[22]   (89–98)

(A comic matter does not call to be set forth in tragic lines; likewise, the dinner of Thyestes suffers indignity if told in domestic verse almost worthy of comedy. Let everything keep its allotted and befitting place. Nevertheless, even Comedy raises her voice at times, and Chremes when angered quarrels with bloated mouth; and often the tragical Telephus and Peleus mourn in ordinary speech when, in poverty and exile, the one and the other throw away their big jugs and overgrown words, if they hope to have touched the heart of the spectator with their complaint.)

The word "private" will figure heavily in later definitions, and in fact Horace's use of the term, in speaking of *priuata carmina* (vv. 90–91), is thought to be a direct allusion to the Greek definition quoted later by Diomedes.[23] Whether it is true or not, we can at any rate deduce a general rule from Horace: that comedy deals with private people and affairs, and tragedy with public. But there is nothing here about what kind, or kinds, of story line makes the best or most usual kind of tragedies. However, it is significant, as G. K. Hunter points out, that "the balanced Horace chose *cena Thyestae* as his type of the tragic episode."[24] We remember that Aristotle singled out the story of Thyestes as one of his two examples for the best tragic plot in chapter 13 of the *Poetics*, but Horace goes further and focuses on the climactic scene, one of the most horrible in all dramatic or narrative literature, in which Thyestes is unknowingly fed the flesh of his sons, and then told.

The last line cited in the above passage indicates, to some extent at least,

---

[22] Chremes is a typical comic figure, an old man who appears in Terence's *Andria* (*Lady of Andros*) and *Heauton timorumenos* (*Self-Tormentor*). Telephus, whom Horace designates as *pauper*, was the subject of a lost tragedy by Euripides; he was wounded by Achilles's spear, but finally healed by its rust. Peleus, "the exile," was the protagonist of a lost play by Sophocles; he was driven from Aegina for murdering his half-brother. For a full commentary on the *Ars poetica*, see the edition and commentary of C. O. Brink, *Horace on Poetry*.

[23] Brink, *Horace*, 1:98 n. 3. For Diomedes, see below.

[24] G. K. Hunter, "Seneca and English Tragedy," p. 175 n. 3.

the purpose of tragedy: it is to "touch the heart," to make the audience sympathize with the sufferings they witness.

The passage gives particular attention to style, which in the literary and rhetorical theory of Horace's time was often divided into categories such as grand, polished, and plain.[25] For instance, the anonymous *Rhetorica ad Herennium* (*c.* 80 BC) names the three stylistic "figures" as *grauis, mediocris,* and *extenuata* (or *adtenuata*).[26] The early rhetorical treatises do not illustrate the oratorical styles by referring to literary genres, though at one point the *Ad Herennium* contrasts the lowest of the three "tones" of oratory, *sermo remissa,* with the tone of tragedy.[27] When writers did come to make stylistic comparisons, tragedy was an obvious candidate for the most exalted rank,[28] and it is clear that this is Horace's choice. However, it was left for the grammarian Placidus, who wrote around the turn of the sixth century, to arrive at the "classic" formulation that tragedy is to be written in *stilus altus.* But whereas Horace clearly classifies the *sermo pedester* of comedy with the lowest of the three styles, Placidus assigns the *stilus mediocris* to comedy, even though it deals with *personae humiles.* His statement can be rendered as follows: "Tragedy is a genre of poetry in which poets describe the grievous falls of kings and unheard-of crimes, or the affairs of the gods, in high-sounding words; comedy is a genre that encompasses the affairs of private and lowly persons, not in such a high style as in tragedy, but in one that is middling and pleasant."[29]

Taking the *stylus,* or "pen," to mean "style" is found in the fifth-century

[25] Brink, *Horace,* 1:264 and 2:109–13, commenting on *Ars poetica* 26–28.

[26] *Rhetorica ad Herennium* 4.8.11. I use the edition and translation of Harry Caplan, LCL (1954).

[27] There are three kinds of *mollitudo* or flexibility of voice: *sermo* (conversational tone); *contentio* (tone of debate); and *amplificatio* (tone of amplification). *Sermo* is "oratio remissa et finitima cotidianae locutioni" ("relaxed and very close to daily speech"), and is subdivided into four kinds: the dignified; the explicative; the narrative; and the facetious (*iocatio*). The dignified tone must have a certain *gravitas* and *remissio* of voice (3.13.23); the voice is full-throated, calm, and subdued, but we must not move from the fashion of the orator to that of the tragedian: "ita tamen ut ne ab oratoria consuetudine ad tragicam transeamus" (3.14.24). For the possible influence of these passages on discussions of comedy and tragedy in fourteenth-century commentaries on Dante's *Comedy,* see Kelly, *Tragedy and Comedy from Dante to Pseudo-Dante,* p. 29.

[28] For instance, Victorinus in the fourth century distinguishes the three styles of tragedy, satire, and comedy, in Heinrich Keil, ed., *Grammatici latini,* 6:81. See Franz Quadlbauer, *Die antike Theorie der Genera dicendi im lateinischen Mittelalter.* I draw also on his paper, "Die poetischen Gattungen und die rhetorische Theorie der drei Genera dicendi."

[29] Placidus, *Glossae,* S 21 *scaena,* ed. J. W. Pirie and W. M. Lindsay, p. 34: "Tragoedia est enim genus carminis quo poetae regum casus durissimos et scelera inaudita vel deorum res alto sonitu describunt; comoedia, quae res privatorum et humilium personarum comprehendit, non tam *alto* ut tragoedia *stilo,* sed mediocri et dulci." This definition is repeated among dubiously Placidian glosses in the *Glossaria Ansileubi,* T 17 *tragoedia* (*ibid.,* p. 50). (Note that Placidus the glossographer here cited is to be distinguished from another grammarian, Lactantius Placidus, who seems to have lived in the sixth century and to whom are attributed scholia on Statius's *Thebaid.*) The tradition of associating comedy with the middling style is traced in Quadlbauer's paper.

scholiast Pseudo-Acron, who interprets Horace as saying that Tragedy (personified) does not wish to be expounded in common meanings, that is, in comic style.[30] Earlier still, Aelius Donatus, drawing on Evanthius, notes the "humbleness of argument and style" in a certain kind of comedy.[31] The word "style" was perhaps first associated with tragedy by Suetonius, who says that Octavian began to write a tragedy, *Ajax*, with great energy, but destroyed it because the style was not successful ("non succedenti stilo").[32]

Horace holds up Homer not only as the model for writing on martial themes in hexameters,[33] but also as the exemplar when writing for the stage.[34] We cannot be sure whether he considers tragedy and epic to belong to a single supergenus, as does Aristotle, but it is likely that he does. The same may be true of Ovid, especially in the opening poem of the third book of the *Amores*, where a personified Elegeia and Tragoedia appear to him. That is to say, Tragoedia may be urging Ovid to abandon the distichs of frivolous love-elegies and to apply himself, not to creating more stage-tragedies like his *Medea*, but to composing a serious work of epic proportions in hexameters: that is, his *Metamorphoses*.[35] But however he understands tragedy here, Ovid says explicitly that it consists of *sublimia carmina*, in contrast to the lighter forms of elegy;[36] and it goes without saying that such poetry must be written in a sublime style. He makes this explicit in the *Tristia*, where he says that tragedy surpasses every kind of writing in seriousness.[37] Here he seems clearly to be distinguishing tragedy from epic. He has just shown how themes of love figure in Homer's works, and now he goes on to show that the same holds true in tragedy, the most solemn of all literary forms. A bit later in the *Tristia* he makes an undoubted reference to his *Medea*, which he calls a "kingly writing" given to the tragic buskins, containing the sort of words that the grave buskin requires.[38]

[30] *Pseudacronis scholia in Horatium vetustiora* on *Ars poetica* 91, ed. Otto Keller, 2:325: "Tragoedia non vult communibus sensibus exponi, idest comico stilo."

[31] *Aeli Donati Commentum Terenti* 4.1, ed. Paulus Wessner, 1:21: "tabernarias ab humilitate argumenti ac stili." Cf. 3.7 (1:20). For a more recent edition of the material attributed to Evanthius, see Cupaiuolo's edition of *De fabula*. Both grammarians are discussed below.

[32] Suetonius, *Augustus* 85.

[33] *Ars poetica* 73–74: "Res gestae regumque ducumque et tristia belli / Quo scribi possent numero monstravit Homerus" ("In what measure the exploits of kings and captains and the sorrows of war may be written, Homer has shown," LCL).

[34] *Ibid.* 140–42, where he commends the beginning of the *Odyssey*, as does Aristotle, *Poetics* 24.60a5–11.

[35] This interpretation is suggested by Ulrich Fleischer, "Zur Zweitausendjahrfeier des Ovid," pp. 44–47. See the comments on Fleischer's theory by Friedrich Walter Lenz in his edition of the *Amores*, summarized by Kelly, "Tragedy and the Performance of Tragedy in Late Roman Antiquity," p. 38 n. 71.   [36] Ovid, *Amores* 3.1.39–42.

[37] Ovid, *Tristia* 2.381: "Omne genus scripti gravitate tragoedia vincit."

[38] *Ibid.* 2.553–54:

> Et dedimus tragicis scriptum regale cothurnis,
> Quaeque gravis debit verba cothurnus habet.

8

The *gravitas* that Ovid has in mind for tragedy may correspond to some extent to the category of the spudean that Aristotle takes to be the essential prerequisite of tragedy. There may be an even closer correspondence with the *seueritas* that Seneca attaches to tragedy in an offhand remark that he makes to Lucilius in one of his epistles: he characterizes the Roman plays known as *fabulae togatae* as having something of severity or seriousness in them, and therefore as standing midway between comedies and tragedies.[39]

Let us look now at the more formal discussions of tragedy in the grammarians Diomedes and Donatus, both of whom lived in the fourth century but drew upon earlier material. Diomedes, to begin with, is thought to have used as his main source Suetonius (second century), who in turn may have drawn largely on Varro (first century BC); but Diomedes also cites Varro directly. He attributes his definition of tragedy, however, to neither of these authorities, but to Aristotle's successor, Theophrastus: "Tragoedia est heroicae fortunae in adversis comprehensio; a Theophrasto ita definita est: '*Tragōidia estin hērōikēs tuchēs peristasis.*'"[40] Before I attempt a translation of Diomedes's definition, I must discuss the meaning of Theophrastus's terms and Diomedes's understanding of them.

I have already suggested that Theophrastus's "heroic fortune" or "fortune of heroes" corresponds to Aristotle's criterion of spudean characters and events. We may also take it to mean that the traditional myths were the source of tragic subject matter. Aristotle himself said that the best tragedies drew on the histories of a few families, and the examples he gives of Alcmaeon, Oedipus, Orestes, Meleager, Thyestes, and Telephus[41] could well be summarized as pertaining to the heroic age. In addition, according to Albin Lesky, the definition set a standard of social distinction as a *sine qua non* of tragedy.[42] Or, if this is assuming too much of Theophrastus's words, it is true at least of Diomedes: as we shall see below, he expands the *dramatis personae* of tragedy to include leaders and kings as well as heroes.

It has been suggested that Theophrastus's term *peristasis* is the equivalent of Aristotle's *peripeteia*, so that his definition would mean "a reversal of heroic fortune." But those who interpret the term in this way are making

---

[39] Seneca, Epistle 8.8: "Non adtingam tragicos nec togatas nostras; habent enim hae quoque aliquid seueritatis, et sunt inter comoedias ac tragoedias mediae." Pseudo-Acron also speaks of the *seueritas* of tragedy, contrasted with the *lenitas* of comedy, with the *satyrica fabula* taking a position between these two extremes (scholion on *Ars poetica* 236, *Scholia in Horatium*, p. 349).

[40] Diomedes, *Ars grammatica*, book 3, ed. Keil, *Grammatici latini* 1:487. Little is known about Diomedes, except that he flourished in the late fourth century AD, and is thought to have borrowed material from his African contemporary, Flavius Sosipater Charisius.

[41] Aristotle, *Poetics* 13.53a17–22.

[42] Albin Lesky, *Greek Tragedy*, p. 8.

9

the mistake (or making Theophrastus responsible for the mistake) of limiting the definition of tragedy to one of Aristotle's formulas for the best kind of tragedy. *Peristasis* ("a standing around") is clearly a much broader word than *peripeteia* ("a falling around"), and may signify nothing more than its neutral meaning of "circumstances," "situation," or "state of affairs." If so, the definition adds nothing to the spudean norm. But the word may have its meaning of "difficult position" or "crisis," and reflect Aristotle's expanded notion that tragedy deals with pity and fear. I assume that Diomedes took the word in this sense because of his phrase *in adversis*.

Diomedes's definition can therefore be translated: "Tragedy is an encompassing of heroic fortune in adverse circumstances." We must be careful not to make too much out of his word *comprehensio*, which I have rendered as "encompassing"; "arrangement" or "presentation" might do as well. *Comprehensio* is the general term used by Diomedes and others, including Cicero and Quintilian, to mean "a collection of units." A syllable, for instance, is a comprehension of letters; a period, of clauses; an epic, of divine, heroic, and human matters.[43] In the last-named case, *descriptio* would be an acceptable synonym for *comprehensio*, and the same would be true in the cases of tragedy and comedy. The virtual equivalence of the terms appears in Placidus's definitions: "tragoedia est genus quo poetae *describunt*," while "comoedia *comprehendit*."[44]

Diomedes's definition of comedy will help us to understand his notion of tragedy: "Comoedia est privatae civilisque fortunae sine periculo vitae comprehensio. Apud Graecos ita definita: '*Komōidia estin idiōtikōn pragmatōn akindunos periochē.*'"[45] That is: "Comedy is an encompassing of private and civil fortune without danger to life. The Greeks define it thus: 'Comedy is an encompassing of personal deeds without danger.'" He goes on to give a list of explicit differences between comedy and tragedy which in some ways resembles that given later by Placidus, cited above. Diomedes says:

Comedy differs from tragedy in that heroes, leaders, and kings are introduced into tragedy, but humble and private persons into comedy. In tragedy there are lamentations, exiles, and slaughters, whereas in comedy we have stories of love and the abductions of virgins. Finally, tragedy frequently and almost always has sad outcomes to joyful affairs and the recognition that one's children and former good fortunes have taken a turn for the worse. [In comedy, on the contrary, sad affairs are succeeded by more joyful outcomes].[46]

[43] Diomedes, *Ars grammatica*, pp. 427, 465, 483–84.
[44] See above, p. 7.   [45] Diomedes, *Ars grammatica*, p. 488.
[46] *Ibid.*: "Comoedia a tragoedia differt, quod in tragoedia introducuntur heroes, duces, reges; in comoedia, humiles atque privatae personae. In illa, luctus, exsilia, caedes; in hac, amores, virginum raptus. Deinde quod in illa frequenter et paene semper laetis rebus exitus tristes, et liberorum fortunarumque priorum in peius agnitio; [in hac tristibus laetiora succedunt]."

The two forms therefore differ in three ways: the quality of the characters, the nature of the subject matter, and (usually) the endings. He continues:

Therefore, they are distinguished by different definitions, for the one is called an *akindunos perioche* and the other a *tuches peristasis*; that is to say, sadness is proper to tragedy. Hence it was that Euripides, on being asked by King Archelaus to write a tragedy about him, refused, and expressed the hope that Archelaus would never experience anything appropriate to tragedy. He thereby demonstrated that tragedy is nothing more than a presentation of miseries.[47]

These distinctions between comedy and tragedy are almost entirely descriptive and hardly prescriptive at all. Perhaps the statement that sadness is proper to tragedy could be taken as an admonition against cheerful tragedies; but it would be only a faint echo of the sort of advice that Horace gives on the appropriateness of diction and character-portrayal. And granted that tragedies are meant to be sad, is one kind of sadness more effective than another, and can the means for achieving it be formulated? There is no sign here of the sort of critical assessment that Aristotle ventured upon, however tentatively, in the *Poetics*.

We do not know whether Diomedes or his Latin sources reflect the doctrine of Theophrastus beyond the definition of tragedy (though presumably the Greek definition of comedy comes from him as well). In the definition itself, there is no general commitment of tragedy to an unhappy ending, as there is in Diomedes's subsequent explanation. One can undergo crises, experience hard times, and even run the risk of death without coming to final disaster. We need only think of Orestes's adventures in *Iphigenia among the Taurians*. It is true that unhappy endings are more plentiful in Greek tragedy than happy ones, but it is not true that "almost all" tragedies end this way, and Diomedes gives a distorted impression of Euripides's *opera omnia* when he has him deliver such a gloomy assessment of the genre. Placidus is closer to "reality" when he says that tragedy can deal not only with the falls of kings and with unspeakable crimes, but also with the affairs of the gods.[48] Donatus, however, who hands on a doctrine in many ways similar to that of Diomedes, puts even greater stress upon the unhappy ending as a distinctive and virtually inevitable trait of tragedy.

Donatus deals with tragedy as well as with comedy in his commentary on the comedies of Terence. The first portion of his treatise seems to have been

---

[47] *Ibid.*: "Quare varia definitione discretae sunt. Altera enim *akindunos perioche*, altera *tuches peristasis* dicta est. Tristia namque tragoediae proprium; ideoque Euripides, petente Archelao rege ut de se tragoediam scriberet, abnuit, ac precatus est ne accideret Archelao aliquid tragoediae proprium, ostendens nihil aliud esse tragoediam quam miseriarum comprehensionem."

[48] See above, p. 7.

taken from the work of Evanthius, another grammarian of the time.[49] On the question of endings, we recall that for Plato, Homer was the chief poet in tragedy, and that Aristotle considered both the *Iliad* and the *Odyssey* to be tragedies, though at one point he recognized that the effect of the *Odyssey* was more proper to comedy.[50] Following later tradition,[51] Donatus goes all the way in the latter direction, and considers Homer the father of both tragedy and comedy on the basis of these two epics. After mentioning the traditional founders of tragedy (Thespis) and old comedy (Eupolis, Cratinus, and Aristophanes), he says: "Nevertheless, Homer, who is the most abundant source of nearly every kind of poetry, gave examples for these kinds of poems as well, and set down as it were a kind of law for them in his works; for one can see that he made his *Iliad* to be like a tragedy, and the *Odyssey* after the fashion of a comedy."[52] Donatus (still drawing on Evanthius) explains the difference between the two forms later:

Many things distinguish comedy from tragedy, especially the fact that comedy involves characters with middling fortunes, dangers of small moment, and actions with happy endings, whereas in tragedy it is just the opposite: imposing persons, great fears, and disastrous endings. Furthermore, in comedy what is turbulent at first becomes tranquil at the end; in tragedy, the action is just the reverse. Then too, tragedy presents the sort of life that one seeks to escape from, whereas the life of comedy is portrayed as desirable. Finally, all comedy is based on invented stories, whereas tragedy is often derived from historical truth.[53]

[49] See McMahon, "Seven Questions," pp. 126–28. Evanthius seems to have been the grammarian who, according to St. Jerome, died in Constantinople in AD 358. His commentary on the comedies of Terence is lost except for the introductory treatment that was incorporated into the beginning of Donatus's commentary. Donatus, one of Jerome's own teachers, flourished in the middle of the fourth century. He was most famous in the Middle Ages as the author of the *Ars grammatica minor* and the *Ars grammatica major*. His commentary on Terence survived only as compiled in the sixth century from glosses in manuscripts of the plays.

[50] See above. Aristotle does consider Homer as the originator of comedy, but only in the epic farce *Margites* (no longer attributed to Homer), in *Poetics* 4.48b34–49a2: "But, as in the serious line [*spoudaia*] Homer was most truly a poet, since he alone not only wrote well, but composed dramatic imitations, so likewise he was the first to outline the main form of comedy, by giving us a drama, and not one of invective but of the laughable; for the *Margites* stands in the same relationship to our comedies as the *Iliad* and the *Odyssey* to our tragedies" (tr. Else, *Aristotle's Poetics*, p. 143; for unexplained reasons, Else considers the mention of the *Odyssey* here to be a non-Aristotelian interpolation).

[51] See Margarete Bieber, *The History of the Greek and Roman Theater*, pp. 2–3: she analyzes a relief by Archelaus of Pirene (second century BC), now in the British Museum, which shows Homer flanked by the personifications of the *Iliad* and the *Odyssey*. He is paid homage by Historia, Poiēsis (Lyric Poetry), Tragōidia, and Komōidia. We may presume that Tragedy looks principally or solely to the *Iliad* and Comedy to the *Odyssey*.

[52] Donatus–Evanthius, *Commentum Terenti* 1.5, ed. Wessner, 1:14–15: "Quamvis igitur retro prisca volentibus reperiatur Thespis tragoediae primus inventor et comoediae veteris pater Eupolis cum Cratino Aristophaneque esse credatur, Homerus tamen, qui fere omnis poeticae largissimus fons est, etiam his carminibus exempla praebuit et velut quandam suorum operum legem praescripsit: qui *Iliadem* ad instar tragoediae, *Odysseam* ad imaginem comoediae fecisse monstratur."

[53] *Ibid.* 4.2 (ed. Wessner, p. 21): "Inter tragoediam autem et comoediam cum multa tum imprimis hoc

The division of styles between comic and tragic is not stressed in the above account, except by inference: since comedy does not deal with "great fears" but only with "minor attacks" and "middling fortunes," it follows that the text is composed accordingly. In fact, before giving these distinctions, Donatus–Evanthius praises Terence for keeping to the practice of writing straight comedy and moderating its passions so that it does not jump over into tragedy – which Plautus and the other great comic authors failed to do. Terence's adherence to the mean keeps him from rising to the heights of tragedy and from descending to the cheapness of mime.[54] Decorum in this view, it seems, is more important than "comic effect"; whereas Horace is willing to let comic characters rant in tragic tones, presumably for the humor it produces. But most theorists of comedy never discuss humor or mention it as one of the features or goals of comedy. When Donatus at one point, in commenting on the *Andria*, notes that the "catastrophe" of this play is almost tragic, he is not talking about humorous incongruity, but about plot movement, for he notes that turmoil suddenly gives way to tranquillity.[55]

Plautus himself professed to see a combination of tragedy and comedy in one of his plays, when he called the *Amphitruo* a "tragico-comedy." But it was not because the play resorted to elevated style, but rather because it introduced characters proper to tragedy (kings and gods), as well as those proper to comedy (slaves).[56] This, of course, is a criterion specifically mentioned by Donatus–Evanthius, but it is one that is implicitly underplayed, since the *Odyssey* is taken as a stellar example of comic form. It seems that some criteria are more important than others, and that the happy ending is the most important of all, since in other respects the *Odyssey* has the characteristics of tragedy. The very exercise of contrasting the plots of comedy and tragedy undoubtedly had the effect of down-playing or eliminating the notion of humor from comedy, since if comedy was

---

distat, quod in comoedia mediocres fortunae hominum, parvi impetus periculorum, laetique sunt exitus actionum; at in tragoedia omnia contra: ingentes personae, magni timores, exitus funesti habentur. Et illic prima turbulenta, tranquilla ultima, in tragoedia contrario ordine res aguntur. Tum quod in tragoedia fugienda vita, in comoedia capessenda exprimitur. Postremo quod omnis comoedia de fictis est argumentis; tragoedia saepe de histori[c]a fide petitur" (I follow Cupaiuolo in reading *historica* for *historia*). Cf. 5.2 (ed. Wessner, p. 23), a non-Evanthian section: comedy is named from the Greek word for village, "hoc est ab actu vitae hominum qui in vicis habitant ob mediocritatem fortunarum, non in aulis regiis, ut sunt personae tragicae." Note that the term *personae*, which originally meant "masks," had come to be used not only for characters on the stage, but also for persons in real life (not to mention the persons of the Trinity).

[54] *Ibid.* 3.5 (ed. Wessner, pp. 19–20): "Ejus fabulae eo sunt temperamento ut neque extumescant ad tragicam celsitudinem neque abjiciantur ad mimicam vilitatem."

[55] Donatus on *Andria, ibid.* 1.5 (ed. Wessner, pp. 35–36): "Hic *protasis* subtilis, *epitasis* tumultuosa, *katastrophē* paene tragica, et tum repente ex his turbis in tranquillum pervenitur."

[56] Plautus, *Amphitruo* 58–63, 88–96; see McMahon, "Seven Questions," p. 119.

supposed to end in joy or tranquillity and tragedy was supposed to begin the same way, the joy or tranquillity should be more or less of the same kind, and it seems that, in theory at least, the serious atmosphere of tragedy won out over the frivolous setting of comedy. The same was true of the disastrous circumstances that were to begin comedy and end tragedy: humor was drained from the notional comic plot rather than added to the paradigmatic tragic plot. This analysis in turn produced a distorted view of tragedy, that is, of the actual tragedies that survived from Latin Antiquity; namely, the ten Senecan plays. That is to say, these plays are said to begin pleasantly and end horribly, but in fact none of them really does begin pleasantly, or at least not for long.[57]

It is noteworthy that our grammarians in the texts cited do not designate a clear purpose for comedy or tragedy. A general moral has been seen in the Donatus–Evanthius phrase, *fugienda vita*: namely, "the lesson expressed in tragedy is the rejection of life"; and the expression *capessenda [vita]* has been made to yield the lesson that life should be embraced.[58] But, as is evident from my translation above, I regard the life spoken of not as "life in general," but rather as "the sort of life depicted in the play." In other words, it is the characters in the tragedy who wish to flee from their life. It goes without saying, of course, that the audience would also wish to avoid that kind of life; but it does not follow that they are meant to conclude that no life is worth living.

Aristotle considered tragedy to be aimed at moving the emotions, probably for both moral and esthetic purposes (this is a much-argued question, which I shall not enter into). Horace wanted it to touch the heart; and he named delight or instruction, or both, as the goals of all poets:

> Aut prodesse uolunt aut delectare poetae,
> Aut simul iucunda et idonea dicere uitae. (*Ars poetica* 333–34)

Taken together, Horace's purposes match the threefold aim of *docere*, *mouere*, and *delectare* set forth in classical rhetorical theory and imitated in poetic theory.[59]

Donatus, it turns out, does enter into this sort of consideration, but only when he puts Evanthius aside (if indeed it was Donatus and not some later editor or compiler who introduced Evanthius's treatise into Donatus's Terence commentary) and starts to discourse on comedy from other sources. After giving a Greek definition of comedy similar to the one in Diomedes, he quotes another definition, this one attributed to Cicero,

[57] See Kelly, *Tragedy and Comedy*, pp. 20–21. See p. 132 below for a discussion of Seneca's beginnings.
[58] J. V. Cunningham, *Woe or Wonder*, reprinted in *The Collected Essays of J. V. Cunningham*, p. 30.
[59] Brink, *Horace*, 2:352.

which sets the art a goal beyond that of mere entertainment: it is "the imitation of life, the mirror of custom, the image of truth."[60] There is no comparable statement of purpose for tragedy; but Cicero's declaration could serve just as well for the whole dramatic art, as it would in Elizabethan England. It is the basis of Hamlet's definition of the purpose of playing: "to hold, as 'twere, the mirror up to Nature, to show Virtue her own feature, Scorn her own image, and the very age and body of the Time his form and pressure."[61]

To summarize, the Romanized Theophrastian tradition of tragedy accentuated Aristotle's stress on the unhappy ending, to the virtually absolute exclusion of other kinds of stories. But the plot structure is not further described or defined, whether in terms of the generality of tragedies, or in terms of quality or effectiveness. We may perhaps infer that good tragedy should aim at its proper effect, sadness; but we are not told what kind of sadness is most proper, or how it is best achieved, or what further effect the sadness is meant to have on the audience – that is, what reaction beyond compassion the sadness of the characters is meant to provoke.

The remarks of Horace and Placidus may also reflect the teaching of Theophrastus, but they differ from Diomedes and Donatus in stressing the importance of style. All of these authorities provide summary views of the thematic subject matter of tragedy, but we shall deal at length with this point, and with the physical forms of Roman tragedy, in the next chapter.

---

[60] Donatus 5.1 (ed. Wessner, p. 22): "Comoediam esse Cicero ait imitationem vitae, speculum consuetudinis, imaginem veritatis." Donatus goes on to quote or paraphrase Cicero further: "Comoedia autem, quia poema sub imitatione vitae atque morum similitudine compositum est, in gestu et pronuntiatione consistit" (5.3). "Aitque esse comoediam 'quotidianae vitae speculum,' nec injuria: nam ut intenti speculo veritatis liniamenta facile per imaginem colligimus, ita lectione comoediae imitationem vitae consuetudinisque non aegerrime animadvertimus" (5.5). See chap. 2 below.

[61] Shakespeare, *Hamlet* III.ii. 24–27. See McMahon, "Seven Questions," p. 190.

2

Modes and subjects of Roman tragedy

In the first chapter, we looked primarily at theoretical questions of plot structure, generic content, and style, and only secondarily, or not at all, at the actual forms in which tragedy could appear, and the kinds of themes that it could deal with. Our interest in these latter questions must be focused upon the practices and opinions of late Roman Antiquity, for the Latin Empire was the principal channel of classical traditions to the medieval West.

WAYS OF PERFORMING TRAGEDY

When speaking of ancient tragedies nowadays, one tends to think only of the full-length dramas represented by the surviving plays of Aeschylus, Sophocles, and Euripides among the Greeks, and the ten Latin plays ascribed to Seneca the Younger.[1] But by the beginning of the Christian era, the staging of such dramas seems to have become quite rare in the Roman world – though how rare is not clear. But poets continued to write full-scale tragedies, and probably never altogether gave up hope of seeing them produced in the old fashion. They could more optimistically have hoped that their plays would be excerpted or adapted for one of the other kinds of stage production that I shall detail below. But the sort of production that these poets could most clearly and confidently expect would be one organized and performed by themselves – namely, a public recitation. Finally, they would want their plays to be enacted in another old-fashioned way: in the theater of the mind, by being read in private, in their published form, like any other kind of literature.

There were three kinds of theatrical adaptation of tragedy current in Imperial times: the pantomime ballet, or danced tragedy; the sung concert

---

[1] I will speak of these plays as by Seneca Moralis, even though it is certain (to me, at least) that he did not write *Octavia*, which deals with contemporary Roman events and in which he himself appears as a character and his future fate is accurately predicted, and even though his authorship of the Greek-myth plays is not beyond doubt.

tragedy; and the citharedy. The first two genres were often spoken of simply as "tragedy," and the third, in which the performer sang a tragic aria and accompanied himself on the lyre, was unavoidably associated with tragedy.

First let us look at danced tragedy, *tragoedia saltata*. This genre consisted of a tragic story told in silence by the gestures and balletic movements of a single pantomime artist. He would normally wear a mask with no mouth aperture, so that he could not convey meaning or emotion by facial expression, except for his eyes. To play another character in the same tragedy, the dancer had only to change his mask.

One can see how almost any kind of story could easily be conveyed in this way, especially if the basic plot was known beforehand, whether from traditional plays or from some other literary source. But it is also clear that in itself the pantomime performance could be quite limited. However, there were many ways in which the dancer's activities could be supplemented. Sometimes there were two dancers of the sort described above,[2] or there could be many dancers, without masks.[3] There was usually, or perhaps always, a chorus, which could consist of a single singer,[4] or many. We do not know how extensive or "informative" the libretto or *fabula saltica* sung by the pantomime chorus was, or could be, but such texts were no doubt more than mere program notes, and there is some sign that care was taken in their composition. The poet Lucan is said to have written fourteen of them for pantomime tragedy.[5]

In addition to the choral singers, actors could play roles in pantomime tragedies and deliver spoken or chanted speeches. Lucian speaks of the actor's "euphony" during the course of the tragedy,[6] and indicates that the actor could also serve to introduce the drama to the audience and perhaps deliver an epilogue as well.[7] St. Augustine reports that in Carthage, before his time, a herald would describe to the audience the story that the pantomimist was about to enact, whereas in his own day, the spectator was left on his own.[8]

Most of our information about the other two forms of tragic stage-show, the concert tragedy and the citharedy, comes from accounts of the Emperor Nero, especially those by Suetonius (*c.* AD 120) and Dio Cassius (*c.* 220). Nero was an assiduous performer of both of these genres. Another

---

[2] Quintilian, *Institutio oratoria* 6.3.65.
[3] Apuleius, *Metamorphoses (The Golden Ass)* 10.19–34.
[4] *Greek Anthology* 9.542 and 16.287.
[5] Reported by the sixth-century grammarian Vacca in his *Vita Lucani*, p. 336, perhaps drawing on Suetonius. See Kelly, "Tragedy and the Performance of Tragedy," p. 28 n. 22.
[6] Lucian, *The Dance* 68; cf. 83.   [7] Lucian, *The Mistaken Critic* 19; cf. 27.
[8] Augustine, *De doctrina christiana* 2.38.97. I shall give the text in the next chapter, p. 45.

well-known performer in the field was St. Augustine; among the numbers he sang was *The Flying Medea*.[9] But Nero not only performed tragedies and citharedies, he wrote the lyrics and music for them as well, and, as can be imagined, his pieces enjoyed a certain vogue, at least during his lifetime. According to Philostratus, a drunken citharedian used to go about Rome and entertain diners with songs from the emperor's tragic works, including his *Oresteia* and *Antigone*, and if his auditors failed to show the proper appreciation or pay for the privilege, he would threaten to charge them with *lèse-majesté*. Philostratus also reports that a certain tragedian who had not dared to compete with Nero in the Grecian contests featured the emperor's melodies while on tour in Spain.[10]

As I have indicated above, the citharedy was, so far as we know, a one-man performance, whereas in the concert tragedy, as in the pantomime tragedy, the protagonist was assisted by other performers. The citharedian could easily demonstrate his arts outside the theater, as Nero is said to have done during the burning of Rome when he sang, appropriately enough, *The Destruction of Troy*. His citharedic costume, which he wore on this occasion as well as in his more formal appearances in the theater, included the cothurn or tragedian's boot (buskin), which may have been more elevated than that used in concert tragedy, where acting was required.[11]

The concert tragedian's main task, like that of the citharedian, was to sing an aria, but the musical accompaniment was supplied by others. Furthermore, he used, or could use, other actors to help him set the scene. During one performance, when Nero was playing *The Mad Hercules* and was being bound in chains by his fellow-performers, a novice guard rushed to the assistance of his emperor.[12] On another occasion, we are told, Nero fumbled his scepter and was afraid that the judges would disqualify him from the competition, until he was assured by a *hypocrita* who was performing with him that no one had noticed because of the cheers of the audience.[13]

It is unlikely, on the face of it, that the acted parts of the concert tragedy would have been performed in dumbshow, since the *hypocrita* used his voice even in the pantomime genre. We should assume, that is, that the protagonist of *tragoedia cantata* engaged in dialogue with the subordinate actors. We find this supposition confirmed by Dio Cassius, who characterizes Nero as speaking and listening, as well as acting, in his tragedies.[14]

[9] Augustine, *Confessions* 3.6; cf. 4.1–3.   [10] Philostratus, *Life of Apollonius* 4.39 and 5.9.
[11] Dio Cassius, *Roman History* 61.20.1–2; 62.18.1; 63.22.4.
[12] Suetonius, *De uita Caesarum, Nero* 21.3; Dio, *Roman History* 63.10.2.
[13] Suetonius, *Nero* 24.1. For mistaken interpretations of this passage, see Kelly, "Tragedy and the Performance of Tragedy," p. 34.
[14] Dio, *Roman History* 63.8.2; 63.9.6; 63.22.5.

Ways of performing tragedy

It seems, then, that the concert tragedy was, at least on occasions, simply a one-act tragedy: that is, a short version of the traditional full-scale tragedy, as far as the essential theatrical ingredients are concerned.

As for the public recitation of tragedies, what I said above about the flexibility of the citharedy is even truer of this easiest and most common method of performance. As with other kinds of literature, the circumstances of such readings of tragedies could range from an informal gathering of friends to the assembling of a large audience in an auditorium.[15] We can readily imagine tragedies being read as after-dinner entertainments, perhaps with the various roles taken by different speakers.[16] Finally, they could be recited in the theater, since even nondramatic poems were so presented. Nero once more comes forth as an example: according to Dio, he read some of his Trojan poems in the theater, and Suetonius says that he recited his poems not only at home, but also in the theater.[17] Quintilian reports the custom of hiring professional actors to perform such recitations.[18]

We see, then, that the normal way of performing tragedies differed in no way from the normal way of performing other kinds of poems, that is, by reciting them. The effect on an audience of the story of a tragic heroine like Medea was potentially the same whether delivered through Ovid's tragedy, *Medea*, or through his *Epistula Medeae Iasoni* from the *Heroides*, and the emotions of Dido would be rendered in a similar way whether one recited the fourth book of the *Aeneid* or Ovid's *Epistula Didonis Aeneae*.

Furthermore, we know from Lucian that the story of Dido and Aeneas, which was first treated by Vergil, was a suitable topic for pantomime tragedy.[19] It was not only the *subjects* of narrative poems that were adapted

[15] See especially Pliny the Younger, *Letters* 7.17.
[16] The late-antique comedy *Querolus* was designed to be presented in this way (see below). Suetonius, *Vita Terentii* 3, tells of an impromptu command-recitation of *Andria* by Terence at the dinner table. For discussions of postprandial *acroamata* (entertainments), see Cornelius Nepos, *De latinis historicis: Atticus* 14.1, and Pliny the Younger, *Letters* 6.31.13. Plutarch, a contemporary of Pliny and Suetonius (d. AD 120), has a character refer in a dialogue to a recent Roman practice of having slaves memorize Plato's dialogues and deliver them with the gestures and vocal modulation suitable to each of the speakers (*Table-Talk* 7.8.1 = *Moralia* 711B-C). The text does not make clear whether a different slave would be assigned to each of the parts, or whether the recitation and acting out (*hupokrisis*) of each dialogue would be performed by only one person taking on all the roles. Later in the same dialogue, another participant rejects various entertainments as unsuitable for banquets: for example, tragedy, with its elaborate acting out of deeds (*pragmatōn hupokrisis*), and the Pyladic ballet, which is *poluprosōpos* (requiring many masks or characters). Old Comedy is also rejected, but New Comedy is admitted, and Menander is said to be traditional at banquets (7.8.3 = 711E-12B). Plutarch confirms this last point in his introduction to the fifth book of *Table-Talk* (673B), and in his essay on Aristophanes and Menander (854B).
[17] Dio, *Roman History* 62.29.1; Suetonius, *Nero* 10.2.
[18] Quintilian, *Institutio oratoria*, 11.3.4.
[19] Lucian, *Dance* 46.

for stage-tragedies of one form or another, but the poems themselves. Ovid has this to say:

> Carmina quod pleno saltari nostra theatro,
> Uersibus et plaudi scribis, amice, meis,
> Nil equidem feci – tu scis hoc ipse – theatris,
> Musa nec in plausus ambitiosa est.[20]

That is:

You write to me, my friend, that my poems are being danced to in the crowded theater, and my verses applauded. But, as you yourself know, I composed nothing for the theaters, and my Muse is not eager for applause.

Let us consider some of the possible implications of Ovid's statement in the light of what we have seen of the various kinds of theater performances available for serious works in the Roman Empire. His denial of having done anything for the stage has been taken as categorical – inclusive, therefore, of his tragedy *Medea*.[21] This would mean that his statement about dedicating it to the buskins must be taken figuratively.[22] He could also be referring to it by the word *carmina*, which sometimes denoted tragedy. Vergil, for instance, speaks of poems worthy of the Sophoclean buskin.[23] It is possible, therefore, that Ovid is saying here that the *Medea* has been adapted as a pantomime ballet (*saltatio*), with some of its verses sung by the chorus or chanted by the protagonist's supporting actors; or that it was performed both as a pantomime tragedy and in its original form, or else excerpted as a concert tragedy or a citharedy; or, finally, he may mean only that it was recited in the theater. But it is much more likely that Ovid was referring not to the *Medea*, but to parts of the *Heroides* or *Metamorphoses* which were adapted for the ballet, and perhaps also for citharedy or concert tragedy. He speaks earlier in the *Tristia* of his *poemata* being presented in ballet form before the emperor.[24]

Let us analyze another passage, this one written some three centuries later, by the Christian Lactantius.[25] In his *Divine Institutions* (completed by the year 313), after expounding at length on the sinfulness of witnessing the

[20] Ovid, *Tristia* 5.7.25–28.
[21] E. F. Watling, Introduction to *Seneca: Four Tragedies and Octavia*, p. 21.
[22] Ovid, *Tristia* 2.553–54 (text quoted on p. 8 above).
[23] Vergil, *Eclogue* 8.10: "Sola Sophocleo tua carmina digna cothurno."
[24] Ovid, *Tristia* 2.519–20 (I quote the text below, p. 30).
[25] Lucius Caecilius Firmianus Lactantius was an African who was appointed *c.* 300 as a teacher of rhetoric by the emperor Diocletian at his new capital of Nicomedia (about fifty miles east of Byzantium), where he became a Christian. He was forced to resign his office at the beginning of the persecution of the Christians in 303, and wrote the *Diuinae institutiones* between 304 and 313 while continuing to live in Nicomedia in straitened circumstances. A few years after the Edict of Milan in 313, Lactantius, now an old man, was summoned by the emperor Constantine to Gaul to tutor his son Crispus.

brutal manslaughter of the gladiatorial games, he goes on to wonder whether attendance at shows in the theater is not even more deleterious to one's character:

> In scaenis quoque nescio an sit correptela uitiosior. Nam et comicae fabulae de stupris uirginum loquuntur aut amoribus meretricum, et quo magis sunt eloquentes qui flagitia illa finxerunt, eo magis sententiarum elegantia persuadent; et facilius inhaerent audientium memoriae uersus numerosi et ornati.
>
> Item tragicae historiae subiciunt oculis parricidia, et incesta regum malorum et cothurnata scelera demonstrant.
>
> Histrionum quoque inpudicissimi motus quid aliut nisi libidines et docent et instigant? Quorum eneruata corpora et in muliebrem incessum habitumque mollita inpudicas feminas inhonestis gestibus mentiuntur.
>
> Quid de mimis loquar, corruptelarum praeferentibus disciplinam, qui docent adulteria dum fingunt, et simulacris erudiunt ad uera?[26]

I translate as follows:

> And as for the stages, their power of corruption is for all I know still worse. For even the comic plays speak of the defilement of virgins and the loves of whores. And the more eloquent the authors who have dreamed up these villainies, the more persuasive they are in the elegance of their sentiments, and their skillfully metered and polished verses can be more easily retained in the memory of the audience.
>
> Likewise, the tragic histories bring parricides before one's eyes, and set forth the unclean and incestuous deeds of wicked kings, and buskined crimes.
>
> Then there are the histrions and the utter shamelessness of their movements: what do they teach or inspire except lustful desires? Their enervated and softened bodies, as they walk like women and dress like women, give a lying impression of shameless females with their lascivious motions.
>
> What shall I say of the mimes, who excel in teaching corrupt ways? They give instruction in adultery as they act it out, and by presenting imitations show what is to be done in real life.

The last category of stage-show that Lactantius deals with presents the fewest ambiguities. The loquacious and bawdy mime is not to be confused with the masked pantomimist and his silent distillation of tragic events; instead, the mime set forth a debased version of comedy. E. K. Chambers describes him thus: "Clad in a parti-colored *centunculus*, with no mask to conceal the play of facial gesture, and *planipes*, with no borrowed dignity of sock or buskin, he rattled through his side-splitting scenes of low life, and eked out his text with an inexhaustible variety of rude dancing, buffoonery, and horseplay."[27] The mime's act seems originally to have been a

---

[26] Lactantius, *Diuinae institutiones* 6.20.27–30, CSEL 19:560–61. For the term *scelus* in connection with tragedy, see Livy, *Ab urbe condita* 1.46.3: "Tulit enim et Romana regia sceleris tragici exemplum," that is, "The royal house of Rome also produced an example of a tragic crime." He is presumably likening the way in which Tarquinius Superbus became king to the stories of Atreus and Oedipus.

[27] E. K. Chambers, *The Medieval Stage*, 1:5.

monologue, but as time went on he was provided with various straight-men, *stupidi* and *parasiti*, and he himself became the *archimimus*. Chambers likens their performances to the shows of the burlesque or vaudeville stage in his own time (he was writing in 1903). Lactantius's account does not quite jibe with this picture, mainly perhaps because he does not see any humor in the theatrical world, either in the mime-shows or in the comedies.

As far as the comedies go, Lactantius is clearly thinking of verse dramas of the kind that Plautus and Terence wrote. Perhaps he means to say that those old-style comedies were still being performed, or even that there were new ones being written and performed. The only late comedy that has come down to us is *Querolus* (*The Grouch*), which dates from the fourth or fifth century. It is, however, not written in verse, but in rhythmic prose, and, according to the author or authors, it was intended to be presented as a dinner-entertainment.[28]

The thought must inevitably cross our minds that Lactantius the strict moralist was not fully aware of what went on in the theater, and that he may have acquired his knowledge of comedies only from reading the published *fabulae* of the comic poets, or from hearing about them. But in his comment on tragedies, he does seem to indicate firsthand experience of performances. True, he does not speak in terms of hearing eloquent speech – though he may have meant his remarks on the artistry of comic authors to apply to the tragic poets as well – nor is there any mention of music, which would be the focal point of the citharedy and also of the concert tragedy. He does, however, emphasize the visual: the audience sees the crimes committed. Perhaps, then, he is speaking of pantomime tragedy, even though the crimes are "buskined." He may be using the term *cothurnata* figuratively, or he may be referring to the subordinate actors in the pantomime plays, who did in fact wear buskins, while the effeminate pantomimists, so well suited in his view to acting the roles of lecherous women, did not. More likely, I think, he is contrasting concert tragedy, where all of the players, including the protagonist, wore buskins, with the pantomime play, acted by the *histriones*. The term *histrio* could be applied to any stage-performer, from tragedians to mimes, but Lactantius seems to reserve it for the pantomimists, especially in their acting out of female roles. However, his description of their mincing ways calls to mind the figures of comedy rather than the sterner females of tragedy.

Perhaps Lactantius knew exactly what he was talking about, perhaps he

---

[28] *Querolus, sive Aulularia*, p. 33: "Nos fabellis atque mensis hunc librum scripsimus" (literally, "We have written this book for plays and tables"). The argument of the play, called *materia* in the Dedication, is termed *fabella* by the Prologus, who refers to the play as a *fabula* which he and the other players are going to act (*acturi*) (p. 35).

did not. His ideas, however, had at least some correspondence to reality. But his words could easily mislead someone with no experience of the live stage at all: someone, say, like Isidore of Seville. We shall see that many of Isidore's strange notions of dramatic performance can be traced to a distorted understanding of this passage.

TRAGEDIES READ, TRAGEDIES LIVED

The private enjoyment of tragedies and comedies through reading has a long tradition. In his discussion of whether tragedy is superior to the lyric, Aristotle noted that tragedies could be read like epics.[29] We have seen that Ovid speaks of tragedy as the most serious kind of writing,[30] and, of course, the most immediate correlative of writing is reading. When he goes on to describe the contents of what he calls "the Roman book,"[31] he includes the tragic dramatist Ennius as well as Lucretius and Catullus. In his *Dialogue on Orators*, Tacitus describes how he and some friends found Curiatius Maternus reading his tragedy *Cato* to himself, on the day after he had recited it in public.[32] St. Augustine remarks that boys are compelled to read comedies and tragedies as part of their liberal education.[33] And Donatus, who explains comedy in the context of its Ciceronian goal as a poem in which gesture and pronunciation are combined, says that we can perceive the imitation of life and morals by reading comedy.[34]

Now let us consider some "applied" uses of the term "tragedy." It is natural enough that actions or stories considered apt for tragedies, whether in life or literature, should be called tragedies in themselves. Lucian, for example, when running through the various topics of pantomime drama, includes "the whole tragedy in the realm of Hades."[35] And just as Maternus referred ironically to the histrionic methods of orators,[36] Cicero called bouts of rhetorical bombast tragedies,[37] and St. Jerome used the same expression of an adulterer's escapades.[38] Just as St. Paul said that he had become a "theater" for angels and men (1 Corinthians 4:9), Dio spoke of the murder of Agrippina by her son Nero as a tragedy,[39] and thought of Nero at the end of his life as finally playing himself in a tragedy, rather than playing others.[40]

[29] Aristotle, *Poetics* 26.62a11–13.   [30] Ovid, *Tristia* 2.381.   [31] *Ibid.* 2.422.
[32] Tacitus, *Dialogue*, chap. 3.
[33] Augustine, *De civitate Dei* 2.8; I give the text below, p. 31.
[34] Donatus, *Commentum Terenti* 5.3, 5. For the text, see p. 15 above.
[35] Lucian, *Dance* 60.   [36] Tacitus, Dialogue 25, 29.   [37] Cicero, *De oratore* 1.51.219.
[38] Jerome, Epistle 147.11, CSEL 56:327–28. See below, p. 31.
[39] Dio, *Roman History* 61.13.3: "But the sea would not endure the tragedy that was to be enacted upon it" (tr. Earnest Cary, LCL).
[40] *Ibid.* 63.28.4, on Nero's attempt to escape in disguise: "Such was the *drama* that Fate [*to daimonion*] now prepared for him, so that he should no longer play the roles [*hypokrinētai*] of other matricides

Modes and subjects of Roman tragedy

The Palestinian Eusebius, writing at the turn of the fourth century, compares the story of Herod and his wife and children to tragedy: its shadows are darker than any tragic dramaturgy.[41] Elsewhere, he says that Christian soldiers were accused of Thyestean feasts and Oedipean incests.[42] That is, their crimes were falsely said to be worse than those of tragedy.

Even the martyrdom of a saint could be called a tragedy, as we read in the account of St. Romanus given a century later by the poet Prudentius: "They say the governor reported all the facts to the emperor, with a series of scrolls in which he laid out in order all the details of this great tragic drama [tanta tragoedia], the oppressor cheerfully entering all his own wickedness in packets of records on sheets that were meant to last."[43] Later on, at the beginning of the sixth century, Boethius was to use the same phrase, tanta tragoedia, in his treatise against Eutyches and Nestorius to characterize the solemn circumstances of Christ's incarnation: "But if flesh had been formed new and real and not taken from man, to what purpose was the tremendous tragedy of the conception?"[44] But Ennodius, also writing in the sixth century, agrees with Prudentius in applying the designation of tragedy to suffering, though in this case it was not terminal. He is addressing Laurence, bishop of Milan: "I do not wish to remain overlong in sadness, I do not wish to open the tragedy of that evil time; I willingly omit some details of your glorious actions, lest in describing them I force you to endure anew what you have suffered."[45] In the previous

and beggars, but only his own at the end; and he now repented of his past deeds of outrage, as if he could undo any of them. Such was the tragic part that Nero now played [*etragōidei*], and this verse constantly ran through his mind, 'Both spouse and father bid me cruelly die' " (LCL). Suetonius, *Nero* 46.3, cites a similar line as the concluding verse of *Oedipus exsul*, the last *fabula* that Nero sang in public.

[41] Eusebius, *Historia ecclesiastica* 1.8, PG 20:101B. For Rufinus's Latin translation, see p. 55 below.

[42] *Ibid.* 5.1, PG 20.413C.

[43] Prudentius, *Peristephanon liber* 10.1111–15 (tr. H. J. Thomson, LCL). Prudentius, who spent most of his time in his native Spain, was writing around the year 400. The deacon Romanus was martyred at Antioch in 303.

[44] Boethius, *Contra Eutychen et Nestorium* 5.86–87 (tr. H. F. Stewart and E. K. Rand, LCL ed. 1). The Latin runs: "At si nova veraque non ex homine sumpta caro formata, quo tanta tragoedia generationis?"

[45] Magnus Felix Ennodius, *Dictio in natale Laurenti Mediolanensis episcopi*, in *Opera*, ed. Friedrich Vogel, p. 3: "Nolo diutius tristibus immorari, nolo tragoediam maligni temporis aperire, libens de inlustri conversatione tua aliquanta praevolo, ne te narrando cogam denuo sustinere quae passus es." St. Ennodius (c. 473–521) was born in Arles but reared in northern Italy. He taught rhetoric in Milan before becoming bishop of Pavia around 514. He has another figurative use of *tragoedia* in a letter to a religious woman named Speciosa, who may have been his former fiancée (see *Opera*, pp. vi–vii): he speaks of being called away from epistolary speech to tragedy ("de epistolari alloquio ad tragoediam") (Epistle 2.3.2, *Opera*, p. 36) – apparently taking the term to mean "unpleasant duties." In another letter, when speaking of his distress over a friend's troubles, he says that neither epistolary forms nor the constraints of speech are sufficient to explain his heart's tragedy (Epistle 5.18.3, *Opera*, pp. 194–95). He also uses *nomen tragicum* to mean, seemingly, "an opprobrious name" (*Opera*, p. 177 line 7; cf. p. 50 line 16).

24

century, some years after Prudentius wrote his versified account of St. Romanus's martyrdom, Nestorius himself gave the title *Tragedy* to the work in which he explained the reasons for the convocation of the Council of Ephesus (AD 431), and his friend Irenaeus used the same title for the book he wrote in honor of the patriarch.[46]

Whereas Dio Cassius saw incidents in Nero's life in a theatrical light, a matter almost of nature imitating art, Prudentius spoke of tragic matter recorded in literary form: not as verse drama, however, but as historical narrative. So too Ennodius, in speaking of "opening" the tragedy of St. Laurence's martyrdom, seems to have thought of the saint's suffering recorded in a book as a drama rather than as a history. Nestorius and Irenaeus went a step further and applied the name of tragedy to actual historical narratives.

It is easy to see how various kinds of poems might have the name tragedy applied to them, because they contained narratives of the sort used in tragedies, or because they were adaptable, or had actually been adapted, to tragedies. Aristotle comes close to characterizing Homer's epics as tragedies, and so does Orosius when he says that it was the *Iliad* that Nero sang during the burning of Rome while dressed in *tragic* garb.[47] I have spoken of the possibility that Ovid considered Romana Tragoedia to be the "Muse" of his *Metamorphoses*. Nearly two centuries after Ovid, Apuleius wrote another *Metamorphoses*, otherwise called *The Golden Ass*, in which he says at one point that the reader is now starting in on a tragedy rather than continuing with a comedy, and is ascending from the comic sock to the tragic buskin: "Lector optime, scito te tragoediam, non fabulam, legere, et a socco ad cothurnum ascendere."[48] The story he refers to deals with a wicked and abominable deed ("scelestum ac nefarium facinus"): a certain woman, "whether naturally shameless or impelled to the great misdeed by fate," falls in love with her stepson; and when he rejects her advances, her love turns to hatred. We have here, of course, a basic plot of classical

[46] See Eduard Schwartz in the preface to his edition of Rusticus's *Synodicum*, p. xiii and n. 3. Among the letters that Rusticus (writing after AD 565) translates from Irenaeus's *Tragōidia* is one sent by the bishops of Tyana and Tarsus to Pope St. Xystus III (AD 423–40), which lists an abundance of evils worthy of Jeremiah's Lamentations and surpassing every tragedy: "scientes quod horum malorum nimietas non solum Jeremiae Lamentationibus digna sit, sed et universam tragoediam superaverit" (no. 205.7, p. 148). I should note that the tragedy *Christus patiens*, formerly attributed to St. Gregory of Nazianzus (d. *c.* 390), actually dates from the eleventh or twelfth century (Altaner, *Patrology*, p. 348). It presents the Incarnation and Passion of Christ in the form of a Euripidean tragedy (PG 38: 131–338).
[47] Paulus Orosius, *Historiae adversum paganos* 7.7.6: "Laetusque flammae ut ajebat pulchritudine, tragico habitu *Iliadem* decantabat." Orosius undertook his history in 417 at the request of St. Augustine.
[48] Apuleius, *Metamorphoses* 10.2. Though Apuleius here uses the term *fabula* for comedy as opposed to tragedy, the usual sense of the word in its dramatic acceptance (that is, short for *fabula scaenica*) is "play," and includes tragedy. See Wilhelm Cloetta, *Komödie und Tragödie im Mittelalter*, p. 7 n. 1.

tragedy, one that was set forth in Euripides's *Hippolytus* and Seneca's *Phaedra*. But, apart from the fact that the *tragoediae personae* are private persons, without the public and legendary stature of Phaedra, Hippolytus, and Theseus, there is a great difference: for the boy's deceived father, unlike Theseus, is prevented from bringing about his son's death, thanks to the fortune of Providence ("famosa atque fabulosa fortuna providentiae divinae").[49] In his playful characterization of this story as a tragedy, Apuleius makes the same sort of figurative application of the term as those who see tragedies in real life, but at the same time he shows that the idea of literary nontheatrical tragedy could easily suggest itself.

Towards the end of the fifth century, when Blossius Aemilius Dracontius of Carthage told the story of Medea in dactylic hexameters, he noted that the story was usually spoken without words by Polyhymnia (the Muse of dance), or told in tragic iambs by the bellowing Melpomene on her high buskins, but that now these two Muses requested Calliope to do the honor.[50] However, when he tells the story to Orestes, though he requests Melpomene to descend from her buskins and let the iambics rest while the dactyl resounds, he asks her help in recording a son's praiseworthy crime:

> Te rogo, Melpomene, tragicis descende cothurnis
> Et pede dactylico resonante quiescat iambus:
> Da valeam memorare nefas laudabile nati.[51]

The poem ends happily for its protagonist, thus going counter to the general norms of the grammarians for dramatic tragedy, but it is in keeping with respectable Greek precedents like Aeschylus's *Oresteia*.

The title of Dracontius's poem in one manuscript is *Orestis tragoedia*, that is, *The Tragedy of Orestes*.[52] It is disputed whether Dracontius himself was responsible for the title,[53] but it is beyond question that someone, a copyist at least, considered the work a tragedy. It is a quite natural development, similar to that recorded by Placidus: one of the meanings of "scene" is any poem fit to be performed with tragic exclamations in the theater.[54] Presumably Placidus is speaking of reciting rather than acting the poems since he uses the word *agere*, whereas when he speaks of the

---

[49] Apuleius, *Metamorphoses* 10.12.

[50] Dracontius, *Medea*, part 10 of *Romulea*, lines 16–28, in *Opera*, pp. 180–81. Lines 20–21 read: "Vel quod grande boans longis sublata cothurnis / Pallida Melpomene, tragicis cum surgit iambis."

[51] Dracontius, *Orestis tragoedia* 13–15, in *Opera*, p. 197. See also the edition of Emanuele Rapisarda, *La tragedia di Oreste*.

[52] Another text gives it as *Horestis fabula*.

[53] See Cloetta, *Komödie*, pp. 4–8, and Rapisarda, ed., *Orestis tragoedia*, p. 37.

[54] Placidus, *Glossae*, S 21 *scaena*: "Item scaena vocatur compositio alicujus carminis quae digna [sit] agi in theatro exclamationibus tragicis."

acting of plays, in connection with his definition of scene, as a room on the stage, he uses *actitare*.[55] But in any case, poems can be called scenes whether or not they are actually produced in the theater: it is enough if they are "worthy" of such employment. The word *carmen*, which Placidus uses, could, as we have seen, refer to dramatic verse: in other words, to tragedies, or parts of tragedies, in traditional form. But it seems more likely that Placidus is using the word in its more general sense, and means it to designate nondramatic poetry.

RASH GENERALIZATIONS OF TRAGIC THEMES

So much for the forms of tragedy. Now let us look at the subject matter. I am not so much interested, at this point, in what kind of stories were actually dealt with in the several kinds of tragedy, as in various general impressions of their contents. What kinds of things, in the opinions of the ancients, did tragedies usually concern themselves with? It is this sort of characterization that was to have the most importance for the formation of medieval notions of tragedy, until Seneca's plays were discovered at the turn of the fourteenth century. We have already looked at several generalizations as to the content of tragedy, but they require a closer examination. Let us begin with Aristotle's remark that the best tragedies of his time deal only with characters like Alcmaeon, Oedipus, and others "to whom it befell to suffer or commit terrible things."[56] In the simplest terms, protagonists can be guilty of crimes or be the victims of crimes, and can be deserving or undeserving of suffering. Most summary statements manage to stress one or other of these dichotomies rather than giving a balanced view. When Placidus names *casus durissimi regum* and *scelera inaudita*, it could easily give the impression that the kings have fallen so resoundingly because they themselves have committed unheard-of crimes. When, on the other hand, Diomedes lists *luctus*, *exsilia*, and *caedes*, and characterizes tragedy as a *comprehensio miseriarum*, the protagonists naturally seem the innocent victims of malignancy rather than the perpetrators; and the same is true of Donatus's *magni timores, funesti exitus*, and *fugienda vita*.

When Horace gives the example of *cena Thyestae*, it would depend on one's knowledge of the story whether Thyestes is to be thought of as more sinned against than sinning. Aristotle, we recall, named him, along

---

[55] *Ibid.*: "Scaena est camera hinc inde composita quae inumbrat locum in theatro in quo ludi actitantur."

[56] Aristotle, *Poetics* 13.53a17–22.

with Oedipus, as fitting the characterization of a good man who falls because of a *hamartia*. But it is clearly the pitiable aspect of the more obscure characters Telephus and Peleus that Horace elicits when he terms them, respectively, *pauper* and *exsul*, rather than any sense that they have received their just deserts. This impression is confirmed in the glosses of the fifth-century scholiast, Pseudo-Acron. After noting that "tragedy always sets forth sorrows,"[57] he explains Telephus as having been wounded and then cured by Achilles, whereas Peleus was exiled because he killed his mother and brother through madness.

Diomedes singles out *amores* and *raptus virginum* as the subjects of comedy, as if they do not enter into tragedy, and Ovid gives the same impression in the *Amores*. In one of the last poems of the second book, Ovid contrasts himself with a friend, Macer, who is writing a *carmen* on wrathful Achilles and the Trojan War, whereas he himself is lingering in the shade of Venus, and Amor always breaks up his grand enterprises. He finds himself summoned away from the taking up of arms in order to sing of deeds done at home and his own wars. He goes on to say that in spite of these impediments he began to work on tragedy:

> Sceptra tamen sumpsi, curaque Tragoedia nostra
> Creuit, et huic operi quamlibet aptus eram.
> Risit Amor pallamque meam pictosque cothurnos
> Sceptraque priuata tam cito sumpta manu.
> Hinc quoque me dominae numen deduxit iniquae,
> Deque cothurnato uate triumphat Amor.
> Quod licet, aut artes teneri profitemu Amoris –
> Ei mihi, praeceptis urgeor ipse meis! –
> Aut, quod Penelopes uerbis reddatur Ulixi,
> Scribimus, et lacrimas, Phylli relicta, tuas.[58]

(None the less, I did begin to sing of scepters, and through my effort Tragedy grew in favor, and for that task no one more fit than I. But Love laughed at my pall and painted buskins, and at the scepter I had so promptly grasped in my unkinglike hand. From this ambition, too, the worshipful will of my lady drew me away – for she liked it not – and Love triumphant drags in his train the buskined bard. What I may, I do. I either profess the art of tender Love – ah me, I am caught in the snares of my own teaching! – or I write the words Penelope sends her Ulysses, and thy tearful plaint, abandoned Phyllis.)

That is, Ovid finds himself prevented from writing either epic or tragedy, and constrained instead to write the rules of the *Ars amatoria* or the letters of the *Heroides*. He goes on to mention the letters sent to Paris (from

[57] Pseudo-Acron on *Ars poetica* 95 (*Scholia*, 2:325): "*Et tragicus plerumque dolet*: quia tragoedia semper dolores exponit."
[58] Ovid, *Amores* 2.18.13–22 (tr. Grant Showerman, LCL).

Oenone), Macareus (from Canace), Jason (from Hypsipyle and Medea), Hippolytus (from Phaedra), Theseus (from Ariadne), Aeneas (from Dido), and Phaon (from Sappho). He ends the poem by referring to the letters written in response to these heroines and delivered by his friend Sabinus: a cheering reply from Ulysses to Penelope and from Phaon to Sappho, discouragement from Hippolytus to Phaedra, bad news from pious Aeneas to the wretched Dido, from Jason to Hypsipyle, and from Demophoon to Phyllis – if she is still alive.

At the beginning of the third book of the *Amores*, where, as we have noted before, Tragoedia and Elegeia appear to Ovid, all love-themes are sponsored by Elegeia, whereas Tragoedia urges him to sing not of women but of men: "Cane facta uirorum!"[59] But we need only think of his own tragedy *Medea* to realize that tragedy is very much taken up with love, and Ovid is at pains to make this point in the *Tristia*, where, writing from exile, he attempts to defend his poetry to the emperor Augustus. I have cited before Ovid's remark that tragedy is the most serious form of writing; in the accompanying pentameter he says that it also constantly deals with love:

> Omne genus scripti grauitate tragoedia uincit:
> Haec quoque materiam semper amoris habet.[60]

He details the love-themes of tragedy, which he calls tragic fires, *tragici ignes*, and points out that the genre even contains lewd laughter and many words of past shamelessness:

> Est et in obscenos commixta tragoedia risus,
> Multaque praeteriti uerba pudoris habet.[61]

He gives the example of Achilles, who became *mollis* (weak, effeminate, or tender) for love.

Much later, at the turn of the fifth century, the great Vergilian commentator Servius noted that the story of Dido and Aeneas in the fourth book of the *Aeneid* was based in large measure on the treatment of Medea in the *Argonautica* of Apollonius Rhodius. He goes on to remark that the fourth book deals almost entirely with "affection," except for the pathos at the end, where Aeneas's departure causes sorrow. It is all taken up in plans and subtleties, almost after the fashion of comedy – which is not surprising, he says, since the subject matter is love.[62] Servius's comment on Vergil's

---

[59] Ovid, *Amores* 3.1.25.   [60] Ovid, *Tristia* 2.381–82.   [61] *Ibid.* 407, 409–10.

[62] Servius, *In Vergilii carmina commentarii*, introduction to *Aeneid* 4, ed. Georg Thilo and Hermann Hagen, 1:459: "Apollonius *Argonautica* scripsit, et in tertio inducit amantem Medeam: inde totus hic liber translatus est. Est autem paene totus in affectione, licet in fine pathos habeat, ubi abscessus Aeneae gignit dolorem. Sane totus in consiliis et subtilitatibus est; nam paene comicus stilus est: nec mirum, ubi de amore tractatur." The longer version is the same, except "nam paene comicum stilum habet." See the Harvard Edition, *Serviani in Vergilii carmina commentarii*, 3:247.

comic *stilus* (he is speaking of content rather than style)[63] has been taken to mean that love was thought to be an unsuitable subject for tragedy; but this is not quite the point that he is making. He is referring to the "courtship" phase of the love story where the concerns are quite similar to those of the typical comedy. If he is saying anything about tragedy at all, it is (we can infer) that the typical love tragedy (say, of Medea) begins the action at a later stage and concentrates not on the origins of a love relationship, but on its disastrous breakup and aftermath.

Ovid speaks of love-themes not only in the old-style scripted tragedies, but in the danced tragedies as well. He first points to the *scaenica adulteria*, the scandalous and flippant treatments of love that are tolerated on the stage in mime plays. What if he had written of mimes with their lewd jests ("Quid si scripsissem mimos obscena iocantes")?[64] Would he have been safe from censure? In fact, he goes on to say, some of his own poems were adapted for the theater in another genre, the *saltatio* or pantomime tragedy, and had often been presented to the people, and often to the emperor himself:

> Et mea sunt populo saltata poemata saepe,
> Saepe oculos etiam detinuere tuos.[65]

We know from other sources that themes of love figured largely in the pantomime tragedy. Ovid himself says so in another context, in the *Remedies of Love*: one should avoid the theater, where *ficti amantes* are assiduously danced.[66] Of Ovid's poems, it would be the love stories of the *Heroides* and *Metamorphoses* that would doubtless have been used for this purpose.

St. Augustine confirms that the tragic theater of his day dealt with much the same subjects. We have observed that he himself chose to sing about Medea in a citharedy or concert tragedy.[67] He deals with pantomime tragedy earlier in the *Confessions*, when he attempts to analyze why people enjoy going to the theater and sorrowing over mournful and tragic events that they would clearly not wish to experience themselves. The subjects of these productions are characterized most generally as disasters that have befallen people (*calamitates hominum*). But Augustine says that he was most moved by stories of lovers: he rejoiced when they enjoyed themselves in their sinful passions (*per flagitia*), and was full of pity and sorrow when all was lost – yet even this he found to be a pleasurable experience.[68]

It is easy to see from Augustine's analysis of pantomime tragedy how the

---

[63] See chap. 1 above, for *stilus* as denoting style. [64] Ovid, *Tristia* 2.497.
[65] *Ibid.* 519–20. See also 5.7.25–28, analyzed above, p. 20.
[66] Ovid, *Remedia amoris* 755. [67] See p. 18 above. [68] Augustine, *Confessions* 3.2.

Church Fathers could regard the theater in the main with disapproval.[69] The tragedies of love that he describes clearly presented shameful actions in a sympathetic light, and thereby gave encouragement to vice. This was most clearly the case, of course, with the farcical and licentious mime plays, and less true of the pantomime plays, or even of the full-scale comedies and tragedies which were still read in the schools. Augustine says that these latter are more tolerable than many other kinds of stage plays; for though the action often touches on moral turpitude, there is no obscenity in the dialogue.[70] Though he might agree with Ovid that the plays sometimes give rise to obscene laughter, Augustine does not have Ovid's worry that elegance of language makes vice all the more dangerous.

St. Jerome, who, by the way, had been tutored by Donatus, the Terence commentator, has a predictably more dour view of tragedy than his contemporary Augustine. I noted earlier Jerome's sarcasm in referring to an adulterous affair: he reminds Sabinianus of "those tragedies of yours" when the husband arrived on the scene and he had to flee from Rome.[71] This is precisely the same sort of story, on a more serious level, that Augustine said he used to enjoy in the theater at Carthage.

In one chapter of his intemperate treatise *Against Jovinian*,[72] Jerome produces this bald summary: "All of the tragedies of Euripides are curses against women." He gives an example from the *Andromache* of a woman who herself was the victim of wicked women: "Malarum me mulierum decepere consilia" ("The counsels of wicked women have deceived me"). He then extends his generalizing to all tragedies ("Quidquid tragoediae tument ..."), that is, "Whatever is contained in the swelling passions of tragedies, and whatever subverts honor, cities, and kingdoms, is connected with disputes over wives and whores. The hands of parents are armed against their children, unspeakable meals are prepared, and because of the abduction of one light woman Europe and Asia fight a ten-year war." (Presumably, Homer's *Iliad* would convey this theme as well as tragedies about the Trojan War.) As an example of the sad lot of husbands, Jerome cites the case of Philip of Macedon: he it was against whom Demosthenes thundered his *Philippics*, and yet, when his angry wife shut him out of the bedroom, he could only console himself with a tragic verse. On Jerome's

---

[69] See Werner Weismann, *Kirche und Schauspiele: Die Schauspiele im Urteil der lateinischen Kirchenväter unter besonderer Berücksichtigung von Augustin*; Heiko Jürgens, *Pompa diaboli: Die lateinischen Kirchenväter und das antike Theater*.

[70] Augustine, *De civitate Dei* 2.8: "Et haec sunt scaenicorum tolerabilia ludorum, comoediae scilicet et tragoediae, hoc est, fabulae poetarum agendae in spectaculis, multa rerum turpitudine, sed nulla saltem, sicut alia multa, verborum obscenitate compositae; quas etiam inter studia quae honesta ac liberalia vocantur pueri legere et discere coguntur a senibus."

[71] Jerome, Epistle 147.11.

[72] Jerome, *Adversus Jovinianum* 1.48, PL 23:292.

assessment of tragedy, Philip would have had no trouble choosing an appropriate line or two to match his situation.

We have seen Lactantius's rather similar view of tragedy in the *Divine Institutions*: family murders, incest, and other crimes of wicked kings; and perhaps we should include also the shameless histrionics of the effeminate pantomimists that he denounces. He clearly considers the stage to be filled with bad examples that encourage vice rather than caution against it. Just before his indictment of the theater, however, he himself cited Oedipus (who was, needless to say, frequently represented on the stage) as a warning against abandoning children, even from the motive of giving them a better future as foundlings.[73] But although a good lesson can be gained from witnessing such spectacles, it is no excuse for exposing oneself to the attendant dangers. Presumably, Lactantius would apply to tragedies the argument he used against watching the gladiatorial games: even though the participants in the contests are convicted criminals and deserve to die, taking pleasure in their death contaminates the conscience.[74]

In another treatise, Lactantius speaks of real-life tragedies that arise from unbridled passions: persons who do not know the boundaries of right and wrong use sexual desire for corruption and pleasure, and use wrath and passion to injure even those who have done no offense; because of this, monstrous crimes are committed daily, and tragedies often occur ("hinc quotidie ad immania facinora prosilitur, hinc tragoediae saepe nascuntur").[75] He is still thinking to some extent of the vicious aspects of the tragic, but he may also have in mind the sufferings that the innocent must bear because of criminal behavior. This latter feature is certainly uppermost in his thought when he describes the way in which two innocent and virtuous pagan women were, through the connivance of the emperor Maximinus, falsely convicted of a charge of adultery and executed. He says of the event, "This tragedy was acted at Nicea."[76]

In this last passage, Lactantius illustrates a general tendency, noted by Werner Weismann, that when the Fathers use public shows for the purposes of comparison, they see them in a positive light.[77] The same was true when Prudentius termed St. Romanus's martyrdom a tragedy, and true also of Irenaeus's "Tragedy of Nestorius," if not of Nestorius's "Tragedy of Ephesus." Similarly, when Boethius, in opposition to Nestorius, calls Christ's begetting in human form a great tragedy, he is

---

[73] Lactantius, *Diuinae institutiones* 6.20.23, CSEL 19:559.
[74] *Ibid.* 6.20.10, CSEL 19:557.
[75] Lactantius, *De ira Dei* 18.11, CSEL 27:117.
[76] Lactantius, *De mortibus persecutorum* 40: "Agebatur haec tragoedia Nicaeae."
[77] Weismann, *Kirche und Schauspiele*, p. 111.

clearly thinking of the genre in favorable terms. And if he considers Christ's incarnation and passion to involve a fall of sorts – "tanta humilitas divinitatis" – yet it had the happy result that many were taken up into the Godhead.[78]

Earlier in the same treatise, Boethius gives a straightforward account of how the word *persona* developed from the meaning of "mask" used in tragedies and comedies, and gives two examples of tragic heroines, Hecuba and Medea.[79] His attitude toward them as characters is simply neutral. But when he comes to deal with tragedy in another work with a much different context, his global concept of the genre is not the same.[80] In the *Consolation of Philosophy*, he portrays himself in a discouraged state while Lady Philosophy attempts to reason with him. She asks him to listen to Fortune explaining her own nature, and Fortune, in the course of her monologue, asks: "What else does the clamor of tragedies bewail but Fortune overthrowing happy kingdoms with an unexpected blow?"[81] We must note that there is still no sign of the usual patristic disapproval of the content of tragedies here, no stress upon the wickedness of either protagonist or antagonist. Rather, the emphasis is on disasters and misfortunes that are undeserved and unforeseen; and if there is any fault implied, it is simply the mistake of not recognizing the nature of the goods of this world.

Like Jerome, Boethius draws on Euripides's *Andromache*, but not with the same animus: Philosophy first identifies the author as Tragicus, "the tragic poet," and cites him on the deceptiveness of glory.[82] Then she calls him "my Euripides," and approves his sentiment that a person with the misfortune of having no children is actually happy.[83]

Quite clearly, the urbane Boethius has no hostility to the ancient dramas, and he reacts to tragic disasters with a certain sorrow rather than indignation. He is thinking more of a Hecuba than of a Medea. But he does not approve of mindless sympathy. He opens the *Consolation* with a self-lamentation inspired by the Muses. Philosophy comes and drives them away, calling them *scaenicae meretriculae*.[84] By this term, Philosophy may simply mean "backstage harlots," theatrical camp-followers; or she may be referring to the lecherous female characters that appeared on the stage in various kinds of plays. But at the same time she could be dismissing the excessive and pointless clamors of tragic poetry.

---

[78] Boethius, *Contra Eutychen et Nestorium* 5.   [79] *Ibid.* 3.

[80] For a good explanation of Boethius as author of Christian theological treatises and a philosophical work without Christian references, see Brian E. Daley, "Boethius' Theological Tracts and Early Byzantine Scholasticism."

[81] Boethius, *De consolatione Philosophiae*, book 2, prose 2: "Quid tragoediarum clamor aliud deflet nisi indiscreto ictu Fortunam felicia regna vertentem?"

[82] *Ibid.*, book 3, prose 6.   [83] *Ibid.*, book 3, prose 7.   [84] *Ibid.*, book 1, prose 1.

The patristic hostility to tragedy, mainly in its Lactantian form as passed on by Isidore of Seville, will be joined to the Boethian context by commentators on the *Consolation*; but Geoffrey Chaucer, with the help of a knowledgeable glossator, will separate it again from Boethius's more neutral view, and Jerome's treatise, which will prove to be of great influence in some of his works, will not affect his view of tragedy.

Let me add a word on how the stories of tragedy were thought to relate to reality in late Antiquity. The context of Fortune's reference to tragedy in the *Consolation of Philosophy* indicates that she is referring to historical rather than to imaginary events. Yet there was another tradition that considered the events of tragedy to be not only untrue, but unlikely. According to the *Rhetorica ad Herennium*, there are three kinds of narratives based on events: the *fabula* or legendary tale, which contains events neither true nor probable, such as those handed down in tragedies; the *historia*, which deals with actual events of the distant past; and the *argumentum*, which recounts an imaginary event which nevertheless could happen, like the arguments of comedies.[85] It is curious that "true and recent events" are left out of this scheme.

At first glance, the doctrine of Evanthius, passed on by Donatus, would seem to be directly contrary to that of Herennius's rhetorical instructor: every comedy is about fictitious arguments, whereas tragedy is often faithful to history.[86] But Donatus goes on to repeat Cicero's characterization of comedy as being true to reality (the imitation of life, mirror of custom, image of truth). Similarly, Lactantius speaks of comic authors feigning their vicious plots, while he calls the events of tragedy *historiae*, and cites the case of Oedipus as factual. But at the same time he worries about the lifelikeness of comedy, alleging in effect that the plays hold up a mirror to nature in a bad sense, instructing the audience in the practice of vice.

It is conceivable that Donatus and Lactantius agree with the *Ad Herennium* on the nature of comedy: it has no bearing on historical truth, but aims at present-day verisimilitude. There does remain, however, a serious disagreement on the content of tragedy. For the *Ad Herennium*, tragedy conveys neither truth nor verisimilitude, whereas for Lactantius it conveys

---

[85] *Rhetorica ad Herennium* 1.8.13; the same distinctions are found in Cicero, *De inuentione* 1.19.27, but rather than mentioning tragedies in general as transmitters of *fabulae*, he cites a line from a single tragedy, Pacuvius's *Medus*. The *Ad Herennium* goes on to characterize narratives based on persons; he does not subdivide them into genres, but simply lists the attributes that all should have, including a variety of characters and a variety of events, such as *fortunae commutatio* (change of fortune), *insperatum incommodum* (unexpected misfortune), *subita laetitia* (sudden joy), and *iucundus exitus* (happy end).

[86] See chap. 1 above, p. 12.

the sordid facts. Donatus perhaps takes a middle position: if tragedy is *often* factual, it follows that it must *sometimes* be fictitious. Factual tragedies certainly have more claim to verisimilitude than nonfactual comedies, but the same may be true of nonfactual tragedies, for they too can present the *imago veritatis*, even though they are fictitious.

We must, clearly, be careful with the notion of fiction. When Ovid characterizes the lovers of the pantomime stage as *ficti*, he is, of course, not denying them verisimilitude. Furthermore, he is saying nothing about the historical reality or nonreality of the characters, but only pointing out their present nonreality: they are not experiencing love in their own persons, but only acting out a love story (which may or may not be based on fact). To use Lactantius's terms, in the theater we see *simulacra* rather than *vera*.

When St. Augustine characterizes the subjects of pantomime tragedy as *aerumna aliena et falsa*, he may mean that all of the sorrows depicted belong to others who are purely imaginary; or he may mean that only some of the characters are imaginary, whereas others are real. The latter interpretation would seem to fit his alternative characterization, *calamitates illae hominum vel antiquae vel falsae*: the disasters either happened long ago, or not at all; or, in Donatus's words, some of them are derived from historical truth.

We have seen that at the close of the classical period, tragedy was a sad and serious business that could occur or be presented in a number of grave or sublime ways, which could be regarded with pity or contempt or admiration. Many of the passages we have examined, and others of a similar nature, will be mined by the writers of the Middle Ages and put to use in quite new contexts. I hope that I have provided enough of the original context to illustrate how and why some of these metamorphoses took place.

3

Early medieval clues and conjectures

Most of the authorities we have studied from classical times were familiar with the conventions of the stage, and assumed that their readers shared this knowledge. But later generations of readers were totally in the dark about the most elementary characteristics of what went on in the theaters, and were understandably puzzled or misled by writings that took firsthand, or at least hearsay, experience for granted. We shall be dealing chiefly with lexicographers and commentators, who produced brief explanations of particular words or piecemeal glosses rather than sustained and coherent discourses.

ISIDORE OF SEVILLE

By far the most important encyclopedist–lexicographer of the early medieval period was St. Isidore, bishop of Seville from 599 to 636. His most important work, *Etymologies*, or *Origins*,[1] attempts to cover all areas of learning. It is made up of short entries arranged in various categories. Isidore often starts out by attempting to give the root meaning of the word under consideration, which sometimes results in a small-scale history of the development of an institution or practice. But for the most part he reveals a quite static and simple view of his subjects.

Many modern-day scholars of drama who have used Isidore's work attribute more knowledge to him than he actually possessed. It is vital that we face the hard facts from the beginning.

In the first place, all the theatrical activity of the ancient world had come to an end by Isidore's time. This was a point made firmly by E. K.

---

[1] See the edition of W. M. Lindsay, *Etymologiae, sive Origine*, which was designed to be used with the annotations of Faustino Arévalo's edition in PL 82. I have also consulted the edition of José Oroz Reta and Manuel-A. Marcos Casquero, with general introduction by Manuel C. Díaz y Díaz, *Etimologías: Edición bilingüe*, which reproduces Lindsay's Latin text, without variants but with some emendations, a Spanish translation, and valuable note – which, however, must still be supplemented by Arévalo's.

Chambers, who adds: "An alleged mention of a theater at Barcelona in Spain during the seventh century resolves itself into either a survival of pagan ritual or a bull-fight. Isidore of Seville has his learned chapters on the stage, but they are written in the imperfect tense, as of what is past and gone."[2] We shall see, however, that Chambers's summary statement is a bit misleading on two points. First, the physical structures of the theaters were still around to be seen, and Isidore's information is quite accurate. Second, he does not always write in the imperfect or past tense. But when he uses the present tense, our first hypothesis must be not that he is reporting something from his own knowledge, but rather that he is quoting verbatim from one of his authorities.

The next point concerns Isidore's authorities. It was not only classical drama that had disappeared from view, but most classical literature as well. We get some notion of Isidore's lack of direct contact with the ancient authors when we see him name Juvenal and Persius as authors of new comedies. Jocelyn Hillgarth sums up Isidore's reading scope thus: "Of the great pagan poets Isidore may possibly have made direct use of Ovid, more probably of Vergil, Martial, and Lucretius. It is possible that he had direct access to parts of Cicero and of Sallust, and it is certain that he used Quintilian. Apart from these authors, and even normally then, Isidore's use of the pagan classics is indirect."[3] We shall see that some of Isidore's comments bear a resemblance to material passed on by Diomedes and Donatus. But the indications are that he did not use even these late authors directly, and it is even more unlikely that he used an earlier common source like Suetonius.[4]

Finally, we must not readily assume that Isidore had a unified idea of tragedy or of drama in general – that he remembered what he (or his source) said about tragedy as poetry in book 8 when he came to write about tragedy in the theater in book 18, or when he wrote elsewhere about the masks or the footwear used on stage. Furthermore, we must not expect that anyone using the *Etymologies* would have dug out all the pertinent entries on a given subject like drama and coordinated them: the alphabetical index was not to be invented for a long time.[5]

Isidore usually avoids the terms *tragoedia* and *comoedia* and deals instead

---

[2] Chambers, *Medieval Stage*, 1:21–22.

[3] J. N. Hillgarth, "The Position of Isidorian Studies: A Critical Review of the Literature since 1935," p. 34. See also Katherine Nell MacFarlane, *Isidore of Seville and the Pagan Gods (Origines 8.11)*; Nicolò Messina, "Le citazioni classiche nelle *Etymologiae* di Isidoro di Siviglia," pp. 208–09, 218; and Díaz y Díaz's general introduction to the *Edición bilingüe*, pp. 189–200.

[4] On Diomedes, see Paulus Wessner, "Isidor und Sueton," p. 292 (quoted by McMahon, "Seven Questions," p. 134); on Donatus–Evanthius, see Friedrich Leo, "Varro und die Satire," p. 72 n. 3.

[5] It is noteworthy, however, that in book 10 of *Etymologiae* Isidore arranges words alphabetically, but only by their first letters.

37

with the practitioners of tragedy and comedy. The most important entries come in book 8, in the section on poets, and in book 18, on the theater and public shows.

In book 8, after discussing poets in general, he takes up the various kinds of poets, beginning with the lyric and proceeding to the tragic and the comic. In accord with Diomedes, who cites Varro on the point,[6] Isidore derives "tragic" from the Greek for "goat" (an etymology accepted by modern lexicographers). The entry is as follows:

Tragoedi dicti quod initio canentibus praemium erat hircus, quem Graeci *tragos* vocant. Unde et Horatius: "Carmine quo tragico vilem certabit ob hircum" [*Ars poetica* 220]. Jam dehinc sequentes tragici multum honorem adepti sunt, excellentes in argumentis fabularum ad veritatis imaginem fictis. (8.7.5)

(Tragedic [poets] were so called because in the beginning they sang for the prize of a goat: the Greek word for goat being *tragos*. This is also confirmed by Horace: "Who competed with a tragic poem for a cheap goat." Then after that time the following generations of tragic [poets] acquired much honor for the skill with which they composed the arguments of their stories in the image of truth.)

Elsewhere, Isidore follows Servius in defining *carmen* as any composition in meter (1.39.4).[7] According to Diomedes, it was *actores tragici* who competed for the goat, but Isidore characterizes the contestants as *canentes*, whom he identifies with *tragoedi*, by which he seems to mean the early authors of tragedies, as opposed to the later *tragici*. In classical Latin, *tragoedus* always referred to an actor of tragedy, whereas *tragicus* as a substantive could mean either a playwright or an actor. If we reflect on the various kinds of tragic performances treated in chapter 2 above, we might be inclined to think that Isidore had read something about the practice of tragic poets reciting their works to an audience, and that he merged this notion with that of an acted performance. But Isidore does not speak in book 8 of reciting or of acting, but only of singing. He may well, therefore, have been drawing instead on a report of concert tragedians and citharedians like Nero, who sang tragic arias of their own composition.

When Isidore characterizes the contents of tragic poems, his language is closest to what Donatus says not of tragedy, but of comedy, in reporting the *ficta argumenta* of Evanthius and the *imago veritatis* of Cicero. But tragedy deals with history, as we shall see in Isidore's discussion of the differences between comedy and tragedy (8.7.6), and in fact all poetry is said to be based on actual events, but transformed into modes different from history (8.7.10). It would seem, then, that in the chapter under discussion *ficta argumenta* means "stories composed in accord with fact."

---

[6] Diomedes, *Ars grammatica*, p. 487.   [7] Drawing on Servius on *Aeneid* 3.287.

As for the term *fabula* which Isidore uses, we saw earlier that in classical usage it could be elliptical for *fabula scaenica* and used as a synonym for "drama," or "the text of a play," with no overtones of "the fabulous" about it. No doubt this was the meaning of the word in the source that Isidore was using at this point. But earlier in his work, in the chapter *De fabula*, he gives a more general definition based on the word's etymology (a correct one, by the way) from *fari*, "to speak": fables are not facts, but only fictions created by speech (1.40.1). He follows St. Augustine[8] in giving three purposes for fables: to entertain; to show the nature of things; and to illustrate human conduct. As an example of the first purpose, he mentions the sort of fables composed by Plautus and Terence (1.40.3).[9] He also draws upon the rhetorical tradition witnessed by Cicero and the *Rhetorica ad Herennium*: histories deal with facts, arguments with what could happen, and fables with what could not happen because they are contrary to nature (1.44.5). But, whereas the *Ad Herennium* gives the example of tragedies,[10] Isidore is probably thinking mainly of beast fables.[11]

Isidore goes on in book 8 to speak of comedic and comic poets. Like Diomedes,[12] he says that *comoedia* comes either from the Greek *kōmē*, "village," or the Latin *comisatio*, "feast." In other words, he says, comedic poets were named either from the places where they performed (*agebant*), or from the times when people came to hear them, namely, after dining. He then characterizes the differences between comic and tragic poets, speaking now in the present tense:

Sed comici privatorum hominum praedicant acta; tragici vero res publicas et regum historias. Item tragicorum argumenta ex rebus luctuosis sunt; comicorum ex rebus laetis.

(8.7.6)

(The comic speak out on the deeds of private men, the tragic on public affairs and the histories of kings. Moreover, the arguments of tragic poets come from sorrowful things, those of the comic from joyful.)

In this chapter, Isidore is clearly drawing on sources that distinguish between the acting of comedians (*comoedi agebant*) and the description of deeds by comic poets (*comici praedicant acta*). But he himself is aware of no such distinction, it seems. And his use of the word *praedicare*, "preach," for both comic and tragic poets may indicate that his source reflects the context

---

[8] Augustine, *Contra Faustum* 20.9, PL 42:374.
[9] See Jacques Fontaine, *Isidore de Séville et la culture classique dans l'Espagne wisigothique*, 1:176–79; 3:1051.
[10] See p. 34 above.   [11] See his whole treatment in 1.40.1–7.
[12] Diomedes, *Ars grammatica*, p. 488.

of poetry recitals rather than of theatrical performances. Other terms (*reges,
privati homines, luctus*) and the lack of any opprobrious reflection on the
nature of tragic events may indicate a source related to Diomedes.

Isidore then distinguishes between the old comic poets, for instance,
Plautus, Accius (probably a mistake for Maccius Plautus), and Terence, and
the new comic poets, who are also called *satirici*. The examples he gives of
the latter are Flaccus, Persius, and Juvenal. He adds that they are painted
naked because they denude the vices they describe (8.7.7).[13] It is doubtful
whether he identified the Flaccus named here, and the Horace cited earlier,
as the same poet: Quintus Horatius Flaccus. No doubt Donatus was one
ultimate source of Isidore's confusion: he compares the Greek New
Comedy and the old Latin dramatic mode or *satura*.[14] This word, which
after the classical period was spelled *satira* and *satyra*, is not connected
etymologically with the Greek *Saturos* (Latin *Satyrus*, "Satyr") or dramati-
cally with the Greek Satyr-play; rather *satura* comes from *satis*, "enough,"
and originally referred to a mixture of foods, and was then used to
designate staged miscellanies.[15] By Horace's time, *satura* had come to be
applied to didactic poetry, that is, "satiric" verse. Thus there were
abundant possibilities for confusion in a later age, when the poetic forms
discussed were no longer available for inspection.

Further on in his discussion of poetry, Isidore designates the mode of
tragedies and comedies as dramatic. He says: "There are three characteristic
ways of speaking among poets. In one, only the poet speaks, as in Vergil's
Georgics. Another way is the dramatic form, in which the poet never speaks,
as in comedies and tragedies. The third is a combination of the two, as in the
Aeneid, where not only the poet speaks but also the introduced persons"
(8.7.11). But it is unlikely that Isidore is thinking of the theatrical nature of
tragedy and comedy at this point. By dramatic he only means that the poem
is written entirely in the dialogue of characters, the *personae introductae*. He is
drawing here on Servius's commentary on Vergil, which repeats the
teaching of Diomedes; in both of these accounts the dramatic mode is
illustrated not only by tragedies and comedies, but also by Vergil's eclogues
consisting entirely of the speech of shepherds.[16] When St. Bede the
Venerable, a century or so after St. Isidore, drew directly on Diomedes, he
changed his *tragicae et comicae fabulae* as illustrations of dramatic poetry, to
tragoediae et fabulae (noting that *fabula* is the Latin for *drama*); other examples,
he says, are Vergil's ninth eclogue, and, "among us," the Song of Songs,

---

[13] See n. 144 below.   [14] Donatus–Evanthius, *Commentum Terenti*, 2.6.
[15] On the dramatic *satura*, see Livy, *Ab urbe condita* 7.2.7–8, and see below, pp. 43–44.
[16] Servius on *Eclogue* 3, *In Vergilii carmina Commentarii*, ed. Thilo and Hagen, 3:29; cf. Diomedes, *Ars grammatica*, p. 482.

where Christ and the Church speak without a narrator's intervention.[17]

In book 18, Isidore again takes up tragedy and comedy from at least partially different sources and in a different context: the public theater. He doubtless had to guess how plays were performed and how the various parts of the theater were used; but he may well have been able to see with his own eyes how theaters were constructed. If any had been built in the regions of his acquaintance, they were probably still standing – some Roman theaters in fact are reasonably intact to this day – and there may have been a theater in Seville itself. According to the (perhaps dubious) testimony of Philostratus in his *Life of Apollonius of Tyana* (written around AD 220), the city of Ibola had a stage in the time of the emperor Nero. But if there was a stage, there was probably a theater; and if Ibola is to be identified with Hispalis, it was at Seville. However, Philostratus says that the local people had never seen a tragedy before a certain tragedian came to give a demonstration of Nero's works; he threw the audience into a panic because of his strange costume and unusually high buskins; and "when he lifted up his voice and bellowed out loud, most of them took to their heels, as if they had a demon yelling at them."[18] If this account is true, we must conclude either that the stage was not designed for such plays, or else that the staging of tragedies had died out and vanished from memory by the first century of the Christian era.

No doubt we are to take Philostratus's imputation of Spanish backwardness with a grain of salt. The province had been colonized by the Romans in the first century before Christ; Cordova had produced Seneca the Elder, his son Seneca the Younger (Nero's counselor and the reputed author of the extant Latin tragedies), and his grandson Lucan. At Mérida, Agrippa had built a lavish theater, completed in 18 BC, which was renovated by Hadrian in AD 135. From its remains we can see that it had much the same kind of structure as the theaters of Rome.[19]

But whether or not Isidore supplemented his written sources with personal observation, his accounts of theatrical structures are fairly accurate. He is right to take the term *scena* to refer primarily to the large roofed building at the rear of the open-air Roman theater, thus being more accurate than Placidus a century earlier, who calls it simply a room (*camera*) providing shade for the stage.[20] Isidore is also right to include the stage within the meaning of *scena*, though by itself the stage was called the *pulpitam*. Isidore use the masculine form, *pulpitus*, to refer to the stage, as well as the term *orchestra*. The latter word usually designated the flat floor

[17] Bede, *De arte metrica*, ed. Keil, 7:259. On discussions of dramatic form in the Song of Songs, see A. J. Minnis, *Medieval Theory of Authorship: Scholastic Literary Attitudes in the Later Middle Ages*, pp. 57–58.

[18] Philostratus, *Apollonius* 5.9 (tr. F. C. Conybeare, LCL). See chap. 2 above, p 18.

[19] Bieber, *History*, pp. 202–03, and figs. 680–84.   [20] See pp. 26–27 above.

area and the first few rows of semicircular bleachers just in front of the stage, where the senators and other magnates sat. In identifying the orchestra with the stage, he may simply have been relying on the Greek meaning of the word: it was the "dancing-place" where the members of the chorus went through their motions in Greek theaters.[21] Or he may have been drawing on a traditional usage. Festus seems to identify the orchestra as a place on the stage formerly reserved for certain actors,[22] while for Dio Cassius the term refers to the stage without qualification.[23]

The theater, Isidore says, is a semicircular structure containing the scene and providing standing room for the spectators: "Theatrum est quo scaena includitur, semicirculi figuram habens, in quo stantes omnes inspiciunt" (18.42.1).[24] His entry on the scene begins as follows:

Scena autem erat locus infra theatrum in modum domus instructa cum pulpito, qui pulpitus orchestra vocabatur, ubi cantabant comici, tragici, atque saltabant histriones et mimi.[25]

(The scene was a place within the theater built like a house with a stage, and the stage was called the orchestra. It was here that the comic and tragic singers performed, and where the histrions and mimes danced.)

He provides more information in a separate definition of the orchestra:

Orchestra autem pulpitus erat scenae, ubi saltator agere posset, aut duo inter se disputare. Ibi enim poetae comoedi et tragoedi ad certamen conscendebant, hisque canentibus alii gestus edebant. (18.44)

[21] According to Vitruvius, *De architectura* 5.7.2, this was still the usage in his time (he wrote before 27 BC): the Greeks have a wider orchestra and shallower stage, because only the main characters of tragedy and comedy act on the stage ("tragici et comici actores in scaena peragunt"), and the chorus stays in the orchestra ("reliqui autem artifices suas per orchestram praestant actiones").

[22] Sextus Pompeius Festus (second century AD), *Epitome* of Marcus Verrius Flaccus's *De verborum significatu*, p. 297: "Orc[hestra: locus in scaena], in quo antea qui nunc pla[nipedes dicuntur agebant, in quem] non admittebantur [histriones nisi tantum inte]rim dum fabulae ex[plicarentur quae sine ipsis] explicari non potera[nt]." That is, the barefooted actors used to act in this place on the stage, and the *histriones* did not use it unless they were needed to set forth the story. Diomedes, *Ars grammatica*, p. 490, identifies the *planipedes* with the mimes; they were so called either because they entered the stage (*proscaenium*) with bare feet, wearing neither the *cothurni* of the tragic actors nor the *socci* of the comic; or because they formerly did not use the platform of the stage, but acted on the flat part of the orchestra where the props were set out ("sive quod olim non in suggestu scaenae sed in plano orchestrae positis instrumentis mimicis actitabant"). W. Beare, *The Roman Stage*, p. 154, says that both Festus and Diomedes "appear to be thinking in terms of the Greek theater, which had a large orchestra, suitable for interludes." However, in spite of the corrupt text, it is quite certain that Festus is speaking of the stage itself, for Paul the Deacon abbreviates him thus: "*Orchestra*: locus in scaena" (*Epitome*, p. 297).

[23] Dio, *Roman History* 61.17.3; 62.29.1; 63.22.4. See Kelly, "Tragedy and the Performance of Tragedy," p. 30 n. 36.

[24] Cf. 18.52.2; 15.2.35. See Dino Bigongiari, "Were There Theaters in the Twelfth and Thirteenth Centuries?" pp. 205–06, on the possible sources (namely Tacitus or Livy) of Isidore's idea that the audience stood in the theater. In 10.253, Isidore identifies *theatrum* and *scaena*; see Mary Hatch Marshall, "*Theatre* in the Middle Ages: Evidence from Dictionaries and Glosses," p. 9.

[25] *Etymologiae* 18.43.

(The orchestra was the platform of the scene, where the dancer could act, or where two persons could hold a disputation. For it was the orchestra that the comedic and tragedic poets ascended for their competitions, and while they were singing, others made gestures.)[26]

It is clear from these passages and from those that follow that in book 18 tragic and comic poets are identified with tragedic and comedic singers, as in book 8. But the nature of their performances in competition with one another is not further described. It seems unlikely that Isidore thinks of two poets mounting the stage at the same time for a chanted debate. Therefore, the two disputants must refer either to a nondramatic oratorical contest, or, more likely, since he does not go on to include such rhetorical activity among "scenic offices,"[27] to the gesticular disputes of the actors who match their movements to the poets' words.

In his listing of the offices, or rather officers, Isidore would seem to imply that the *histrio*, *mimus*, and *saltator* have separate functions, and they do have different etymologies, but in effect he identifies them all with the *pantomimus*, a nonspeaking actor–dancer. We have already seen that the *histrio* and *mimus* dance, and that the *saltator* acts.

Isidore appears, therefore, to think of ancient drama as a dumbshow dubbed by a single singer. We shall see that later writers share this view, which John Cunliffe calls a "curious error," perhaps inspired by a mistaken reading of Isidore, but not shared by Isidore himself. Like most historians of the theater, Cunliffe believes that Isidore had greater access to the ancient authors than in fact was the case. He assumes, for instance, that the chapter on the orchestra reflects knowledge of classical plays and may be distinguishing between the iambic dialogue of the actors and the lyric *cantica* of the chorus.[28]

It has sometimes been suggested that Isidore took his ideas at least in part from Livy's account of the origins of the Roman theater, where he tells of Livius Andronicus, the first to abandon the musical medleys or *saturae* and to compose a play with a plot ("argumento fabulam serere"); and, like everyone else in those days, he was the actor of his own poems ("idem

---

[26] Allardyce Nicoll, *Masks, Mimes, and Miracles: Studies in the Popular Theatre*, p. 208, comes to conclusions quite similar to mine, but only by silently doctoring Isidore's texts. He runs the first part of 18.43 together with the middle of 18.44 to form a single passage (I insert the proper references and mark his cuts with asterisks): "Scena autem erat locus infra theatrum in modum domus instructa cum pulpito, qui pulpitus orchestra vocabatur, ubi cantabant comici, tragici, atque saltabant histriones *** [18.43]. *** Ibi *** poetae comoedi et tragoedi ad certamen conscendebant, hisque canentibus alii gestus edebant [18.44]." He gives a translation on p. 208 and a slightly different translation of the same merged text on p. 146. Millard Meiss, *French Painting in the Time of Jean de Berry*, part 2: *The Limbourgs and Their Contemporaries*, 1:51, 442 n. 201, takes over both text and translation from Nicoll's p. 208.

[27] "Officia scenica: tragoedi, comoedi, thymelici, histriones, mimi, et saltatores" (18.44).

[28] John W. Cunliffe, *Early English Classical Tragedies*, pp. xiv–xv.

scilicet, id quod omnes tum erant, suorum carminum actor"). Livy then goes on to recount that, because of his failing voice, Livius eventually started the practice of having a boy sing the words of the *canticum* while he himself acted it out. From that time on, Livy says, the *histriones* began to use singers to accompany their hand-gestures, reserving only the dialogue (*diverbia*) for their own voices.[29]

Though Livy's account has some interesting parallels with Isidore, it also differs on important points. According to Isidore, the poet sang the whole piece while others gesticulated, with much the effect perhaps of a puppetmaster supplying voices for his puppets, or an "actor" like Mel Blanc for animated cartoons. Or we might think of the Japanese silent movies of the 1920s, when a narrator (*benshi*) supplied commentary, or speakers pronounced dialogue from behind the screen.[30] But of course Isidore's poet–singer was on full view. However, according to Livy, the poet–singer was also a speaker–actor: the one man did everything – that is, until Livius had the idea of letting someone else do the singing. But even then the poet continued to act out all the roles himself, and to deliver all the spoken lines in a pseudo-dialogue (until such time as separate actors were assigned to individual roles). The poet therefore employed someone else's voice only for the sung portions. There are many modern examples of the same thing, especially in the cinema; for instance, Larry Parks "sings" with Al Jolson's voice in *The Jolson Story*, but uses his own voice to play Jolson in spoken dialogue.

We shall find closer parallels to Isidore's presentation by looking not at the origin of Roman drama, but at the forms of tragedy in the age of decline. I have already noted the similarity of his account of tragic and comic poets in book 8 to Neronian concert tragedy. In book 18, he seems to have combined concert tragedy with pantomime tragedy. His chapter *De mimis* is particularly instructive:

Mimi sunt dicti graeca appellatione quod rerum humanarum sint imitatores. Nam habebant suam auctorem qui antequam minum agerent fabulam pronuntiaret.[31] Nam fabulae ita componebantur a poetis ut aptissimae essent motui corporis.

(18.49)

(Mimes are so called from a Greek word because they are imitators of human things. For they had their author who would speak the story before they

---

[29] Livy, *Ab urbe condita* 7.2.9–10. See Vincenzo Rotolo, "*Cantare ad manum*: Ancora su Liv. 7.2.10."

[30] See the *Oxford Companion to Film*, p. 364; cf. Donald Richie, *Japanese Cinema: Film Style and National Character*, pp. 6–7.

[31] Lindsay mistakenly emends *pronunciaret* to *pronunciarent*, thereby making the mimes themselves (rather than their author) first pronounce the words before acting them out, or while acting them out. He assumes that Isidore knew about mimes with their speaking roles, whereas I argue that he identified mimes with the silent pantomimists.

performed their imitation. For the stories were composed by the poets in such a way that they would correspond closely to bodily movement.)

For "antequam mimum" one text reads "hoc primum" and another "hoc quam primum" (perhaps for "hoc quum primum"). The meaning may be, "as soon as," or "while," the mimes acted, the author set forth the story. This interpretation would bring the passage into line with the account of comic and tragic poets singing while others acted. But as the passage reads in the established text, it bears a close resemblance to an account of the pantomime theater given by St. Augustine in his *Christian Doctrine*:

Illa enim signa quae saltando faciunt histriones, si natura, non instituto et consentione hominum, valerent, non primis temporibus saltante pantomimo praeco praenuntiaret populo Carthaginis quid saltator vellet intellegi. Quod adhuc multi meminerunt senes, quorum relatu haec solemus audire. Quod ideo credendum est, quia nunc quoque si quis theatrum talium nugarum imperitus intraverit, nisi ei dicatur ab altero quid illi motus significent, frustra totus intentus est.[32]

(As for those signs that actors make in their dancing, if they were evident by nature rather than by the institution and consent of men, in former days when a pantomimist danced, a herald would not have announced beforehand to the people of Carthage what it was that the dancer wanted to be understood. Many old people remember this practice up to the present time, and we often hear them speak of it. It is quite believable, because even now if someone unfamiliar with these trifling conventions were to enter the theater and not be told by someone else what those movements signified, the whole meaning would be lost on him.)

Isidore may also have been drawing on reports of poetry recitals, whether in or out of the theater, since he speaks here of "pronouncing" rather than of "singing." Quintilian, one of the classical authors that Isidore was able to use, speaks of *scaenici actores* adding grace to even the best poets when they are heard in the theaters rather than simply read.[33] As for *fabulae quae ad scaenam componuntur* (that is, tragedies and comedies), they were not only heard but seen, and the various masks used by the actors helped to convey the dominant emotions.[34]

Isidore may have read other accounts of the late antique theater that mention speaking or singing roles in pantomime productions, some of which we have seen in chapter 2 above. Something of the sort may also lie behind his explanation of the *thymelici*:

Thymelici autem erant musici scenici qui in organis et lyris et citharis praecanebant. Et dicti thymelici quod olim in orchestra stantes cantabant super pulpitum, quod *thymele* vocabatur.   (18.47)

(The thymelicians were the theater's musicians, who sang along with organs, lyres,

---

[32] Augustine, *De doctrina christiana* 2.38.97.   [33] Quintilian, *Institutio oratoria* 11.3.4.
[34] *Ibid.* 11.3.73–74.

and cithers. They were called thymelicians because they originally stood on the orchestra and sang above the stage, which was called the *thymele*.)

He seems to be a bit uncertain here about the identification of the *pulpitus* with the *orchestra*. In the early Greek theater, the *thumelē* was the platform in the middle of the orchestra on which the altar stood, that is, it was the sacrificial step on the altar; or it could designate the altar itself. Later it was taken to be the whole orchestra.[35] Isidore's source may have specified that the term first referred to singers and then to instrumentalists, and it may be that Isidore's term "praecanebant" does not refer to singing, but to the musical accompaniment of singers. But there may also be some idea present of performers, like citharedians, who accompanied their own singing.

Whether or not Isidore drew upon St. Augustine for his account of the theater in book 18, he did use his works elsewhere in the *Etymologies*. We have seen that in book 1 he relies on Augustine's *Contra Faustum* for his discussion of fables; and in his discussion of music in book 3 he draws on *De ordine* when he says that vocal modulation "is proper to comedians, tragedians, choruses, and all others who sing with their own voice" (3.20.1).[36]

Isidore's clearest debt to a patristic author in book 18 comes in the following set of chapters:

De tragoedis. Tragoedi sunt qui antiqua gesta atque facinora sceleratorum regum luctuosa carmine spectante populo concinebant. (18.45)

De comoedis. Comoedi sunt qui privatorum hominum acta dictis aut gestu cantabant, atque strupra virginum et amores meretricum in suis fabulis exprimebant. (18.46)

De thymelicis ... (18.47)

De histrionibus. Histriones sunt qui muliebri indumento gestus impudicarum feminarum exprimebant; hi autem saltando etiam historias et res gestas demonstrabant. Dicti autem histriones sive quod ab Histria id genus sit adductum, sive quod perplexas historiis fabulas exprimerent, quasi historiones. (18.48)

(*Tragedians*. Tragedians are those who sang in poetry of the ancient deeds and sorrowful crimes of wicked kings while the people looked on.)

(*Comedians*. Comedians are those who sang of the affairs of private men, in their speech or gestures, and they set forth in their stories the defilements of virgins and the loves of whores.)

(*Thymelicians* ...)

(*Histrions*. Histrions are those who imitated the movements of shameless women

[35] Bieber, *History*, pp. xiv, 55, 59.
[36] Drawing on Augustine, *De ordine* 2.14.39. See Jürgens, *Pompa diaboli*, p. 227 n. 1.

by dressing in female clothes. They also by means of dancing set forth histories and past events. They were called histrions whether because that type of actor came from Istria, or because they presented stories made up of histories, and were therefore "historions.")

A glance at the passage from Lactantius's *Divine Institutions* analyzed in the last chapter[37] will show where Isidore got at least some of his ideas. It will also indicate the danger of trying to separate personal experience from documentary sources in Isidore's definitions. One scholar, for instance, thinks that the remark about female impersonators may be based on Isidore's own knowledge of contemporary folk festivals.[38] Another thinks that Isidore's expressions indicate a speaking role for the histrions.[39] But, apart from the fact that he names dancing and costuming as the modes of expression, Isidore is simply rewording an earlier report of another time and place. Still another scholar thinks that the present tense in the definition of histrions and mimes indicates their continued existence;[40] but even in instances where Isidore does not move to the imperfect tense (as he does here), he is likely to be simply quoting a source verbatim. Such is the case with his warning to avoid the shows of the scenic arts because of their association with the pagan deities: "You should hate this spectacle, O Christian, as you hate its authors," imitating the words of Tertullian.[41] The same is true of his warning against the circus: "Whence you should take notice, O Christian, that unclean deities possess the circus" – though here he has converted Tertullian from perfect to present: Tertullian says, "*how many* unclean deities *have possessed* the circus."[42]

Just as there is nothing in the above-cited chapters of Isidore to suggest that the *histriones* speak, there is no need to think that he presents the *tragoedi* and *comoedi* as anything but the singing poets treated earlier. At first glance, his description of the *comoedi* might make us think not only of the archmimes of old, who composed their own lines on scandalous and bawdy material and sang them in appropriate musical-comedy melodies, while silent stooges reacted accordingly; but it might also put us in mind of modern stand-up comedians who often act out their own gags. However, the expression *acta dictis aut gestu cantabant* undoubtedly does not mean that

[37] Lactantius, *Diuinae institutiones* 6.20.27–30.
[38] J. D. A. Ogilvy, "*Mimi, Scurrae, Histriones*: Entertainers of the Early Middle Ages," p. 605.
[39] Marshall, "*Theatre* in the Middle Ages," pp. 10–11.   [40] Nicoll, *Masks*, p. 146.
[41] *Etymologiae* 18.51: "Quod spectaculum, Christiane, odere debes, quorum odisti auctores," drawing on Tertullian, *De spectaculis* 10.9, CCL 1:237: "Oderis, Christiane, quorum auctores non potes non odisse."
[42] *Etymologiae*, 18.41.3: "Unde animadvertere debes, Christiane, quod circum numina inmunda possideant"; Tertullian, *De spectaculis* 8.7, CCL2:234: "Animadverte, Christiane, quot numina inmunda possederint circum."

the comedians "sang in words or gesture." One always sings with words, and sometimes one uses gestures as well, but it would be hard to sing with gestures and not with words. Rather, *dictis aut gestu* must modify *acta*: the comedic poets sang of the activities (sayings or doings) of private men, which were simultaneously illustrated by the imitative actions of the histrions and mimes – for Isidore's account of the mimes is clearly also dependant on Lactantius. What Lactantius says about *mimi* would do nothing to disabuse Isidore's identification of them with *pantomimi*.

Isidore deals incidentally with the theater in two other places in the *Etymologies*: in his alphabetical vocabulary list in book 10, and in the chapter on shoes in book 19. In the latter he simply follows Placidus when he defines *cothurni*: they were the cloglike shoes of the sort worn by heroes, and were used by tragedians when about to speak and sing poems in a high and resounding voice in the theater.[43] Comedians for their part wore something called *baxeae*.[44]

Isidore's awareness that *tragoedi* and *comoedi* wore special shoes when performing in the theater need not have affected his idea of them as poets whose sole function was to sing their poems while others acted them out. His view might have been shaken if he had read of *tragoedi* and *comoedi* as wearing masks, which, of course, they traditionally did. But he deals with masks only when treating the term *hypocrita* in his word list in book 10. He explains the biblical sense of "pretender" from the appearance of *hypocritae* in spectacles. They cover their faces, either by painting them with different kinds of pigments, including blue and red, or by wearing masks made of colored stuccoed linen, sometimes with their necks and hands tinted to match, in order to deceive the people while acting in plays; at times they appear as men, at times as women, either old or young, with short or long hair.[45]

Isidore does not specify here what sort of *spectaculum* or *ludus* the hypocrites performed, whether of the gymnasium, circus, gladiatorial

---

[43] *Etymologiae* 19.34.5: "Cothurni sunt quibus calciabantur tragoedi, qui in theatro dicturi erant et alta intonantique voce carmina cantaturi. Est enim calciamentum in modum crepidarum, quod heroes utebantur, sed tale est ut in dextro et in laevo conveniat pede" (that is, it can fit either right or left foot). Cf. Placidus, *Glossae*, C 34 *cothurni*, p. 16.

[44] *Etymologiae* 19.34.6: "Baxeae calciamentum comoedorum erat, sicut tragoedorum cothurni." When he defines *socci* (19.34.12), he does not give the term a theatrical meaning, nor does he do so for *baxea* (plural of *baxeum*): they are women's shoes (19.34.20).

[45] *Etymologiae* 10.119: "Nomen autem hypocritae tractum est ab specie eorum qui in spectaculis contecta facie incedunt, distinguentes vultum caeruleo minioque colore et ceteris pigmentis, [vel] habentes simulacra oris lintea gypsata et vario colore distincta, nonnumquam et colla et manus creta perunguentes, ut ad personae colorem pervenirent, et populum dum in ludis agerent fallerent: modo in specie viri, modo in feminae, modo tonsi, modo criniti, anuli et virginali ceteraque specie, aetate sexuque diverso, ut fallant populum dum in ludis agunt." Note that at the end of this repetitious entry he shifts from the imperfect to the present tense.

arena, or theater;[46] but if he were thinking of the *ludus scenicus* and the *officia scenica* as he later defines them, he would no doubt connect them with the histrions and their *muliebre indumentum*, and with the mimes, who, according to his source passage in Lactantius, used *simulacra*.

In actual practice, of course, it was the *pantomimi* who usually used masks (as well as the *tragoedi* and *comoedi*), while the mimes covered their faces with cosmetics. St. Jerome warns Eustochium to avoid those women who outdo the parasites of the mimes in the rubbed-on redness of their faces ("Quae rubore frontis attrito parasitos vicere mimos").[47] The gypsum or stucco that stiffened masks was white, and was also used, as well as Isidore's chalk (*creta*), on the exposed parts of the body, especially by those who played female roles. Cicero, for instance, speaks of Medea as having hands thickly coated with gypsum (*manibus gypsatissimis*).[48] A Pseudo-Augustinian sermon has been named as the source of Isidore's description, but it is possible that the sermon itself depends on Isidore, since it has not been dated.[49]

The upshot of Isidore's central teaching on tragedy is as follows. In book 8, tragedy can be seen as a realistic poem dealing with the sad affairs of kings and countries. In book 18, it appears as a poem chanted in the theater to the mumming of actors; and the events it deals with are not simply large-scale misfortunes of the indistinct Boethian variety, but, specifically, *facinora sceleratorum regum luctuosa*, evil and sorrowful deeds of evil kings, like the *parracidia et incesta regum malorum et cothurnata scelera* denounced by Lactantius, or the *regum casus durissimi et scelera inaudita* named by Placidus. Or, according to one reading of Isidore's text, tragedy is not a *carmen* of *facinora luctuosa*, but a *luctuosum carmen* of *facinora*, a tradition that was encountered by some of Isidore's notable users, for instance, Nicholas Trevet in the fourteenth century.[50] Isidore's unfavorable attitude towards tragedy in the context of the theater – the "scene of the crimes," so to speak – is encapsulated, perhaps, by his note that another meaning of *theatrum* is "brothel."[51]

Because Isidore is simply passing on information from various sources

---

[46] See *Etymologiae* 18.16.3: "Ludus autem aut gymnicus est, aut circensis, aut gladiatorius, aut scenicus."

[47] Jerome, Epistle 22.29.4, CSEL 54:188. Jerome was writing in the year 384.

[48] Cicero, *Epistulae ad familiares* 7.6.1. See Bieber, "Maske," pp. 2073, 2082–83.

[49] Pseudo-Augustine, *Sermones supposliticii* 62.9, PL 39:1863, noted by Arévalo, PL 82:379, and Jürgens, *Pompa diaboli*, p. 220. The sermon's text, as printed in PL, differs in some ways from *Etymologiae* 10.120, for instance in having *niveo* ("snowy") instead of *minio* ("cinnabar-red") and in omitting *anuli et virginali.*

[50] See pp. 128, 130 below. Trevet follows the variant *luctuoso* instead of *luctuosa* in Isidore's chapter *De tragedis* (*Etymologiae* 18.45).

[51] *Etymologiae* 18.42.2: *theatrum* is synonymous with *prostibulum* and *lupanar*. Isidore's etymology of *lupanar* (from *lupa*, "she-wolf") comes from Augustine, *De civitate Dei* 18.23, and his description from Lactantius, *Divinae institutiones* 6.23.7. See chap. 4 below, p. 73.

about matters of which he has little or no personal knowledge, the question of how integrated his understanding of tragedy was is not of the first importance. More important is the question of how he will be understood by others who have little else to go on except one or other of his brief discourses.

REMIGIUS AND REMIGIANS

St. Remigïus, or Remi, of Auxerre, who flourished at the turn of the tenth century, was one of the most learned men of the Carolingian renaissance. He was not as original a thinker as his older contemporary John Scotus Eriugena, some of whose teachings he adapted and simplified for pedagogical purposes, but his knowledge of a wide range of sources allowed him to make occasional original syntheses of traditions in his various commentaries.[52] He uses Isidore (though without ever naming him) for most of his etymologies and scientific knowledge,[53] but he had a different understanding of the classics from that of the Spanish bishop three centuries earlier. In the commentaries and in his mythography (he has been identified as the Second Vatican Mythographer),[54] he provided an independent souce of learning to the later Middle Ages. Unlike Isidore, Remigius knew the poems of Persius and Juvenal, and could not mistake them for comedies, for he also knew the Pseudo-Plautine comedy *Querolus*, and probably Plautus's authentic works as well.[55] He was also able to identify Geta as a comic *persona*, that is, character, in Terence, saying that the character has become a byword for Mysian *joculatores* too much given to games.[56] His reading of Boethius's treatise *Against Eutyches and Nestorius* made it clear to him that there was no Isidorian division of labor between poets and actors in the performance of comedies and tragedies. In his commentary on the work,[57] Remigius explains that originally *histriones* mocked people in the theater with uncovered faces but later took to using masks. The masks were called

---

[52] Remigius was born around 841 and died around 908. He succeeded his master Heiric as head of the monastic school of Saint Germanus at Auxerre, and later taught at Reims and Paris. Heiric lived from 841 to 876/7, and Eriugena from *c.* 810 to *c.* 877.

[53] Pierre Courcelle, *La Consolation de Philosophie dans la tradition littéraire: Antécédents et postérité de Boèce*, p. 242; Diane K. Bolton, "Remigian Commentaries on the *Consolation of Philosophy* and Their Sources," p. 392.

[54] Courcelle, *La Consolation*, pp. 244–248.   [55] Courcelle, "La culture antique de Remi d'Auxerre."

[56] Remigius, *In Sedulii Paschale carmen*, CSEL 10:321, on book 1, line 19: "persona comica est apud Terentium. Getae ipsi sunt Mysii populi, joculatores lusibus nimium studentes." Mysians were held in contempt in Roman circles. I do not know what specific source Remigius is using.

[57] Remigius's commentary on Boethius's theological treatises was edited by Edward Kennard Rand, but attributed to Eriugena, in *Johannes Scottus*, pp. 30–80 (nos. 1–3, 5) and 99–106 (no. 4). See Courcelle, *La Consolation*, p. 248 (Bolton, "Remigian Commentaries," p. 386, says that Remigius is "probably" the author). Rand believed that Remigius was the author only of a shorter commentary represented by his MS F: Munich lat. (Freising) 6367, of the eleventh century (see *Johannes Scottus*, ed. Rand, p. 87 n. 2 and p. 98). This shorter commentary is now attributed to a disciple of Remigius.

personae because the histrions used them to represent the substances of individual men; he implies, therefore, that the meaning of "person" as "human being" came first. However, he then gives another reason that suggests the opposite: the masks magnified sound (*per se sonantes*). He adds that the histrions mocked the sayings and doings of the men they represented by means of *fabulae* and bodily movement. He concludes by saying definitely that the meaning "persons-as-men" came from "persons-as-masks."[58] He has a similar account in his commentary on the *Ars minor* of Donatus, where he gives the examples of Hecuba and Priam.[59] But in both passages he seems to treat tragedy and comedy together as satirizing living persons. Of Boethius's examples of dramatic characters he names Simo and Chremes as *comicae personae*, but gives historical identifications to Hecuba (*uxor Priami*) and Medea (*Colchica meretrix*).[60] Presumably, he guessed that they were *tragicae personae*, but he does not say so.

Even though Remigius seemingly had access to Isidore's complete statements on tragedic/tragic poet–singers, he is taciturn on the nature and content of tragedy. He repeats the etymology delivered by Isidore, and gives a similar one of his own (or from another source): "Tragedies are so called because it was a *tragos* or goat that tragicians received as a reward; or they also get their name from cheap little gifts called *tragemata* in Greek and *bellaria* in Latin."[61] When he comes to explain the *tanta*

---

[58] Remigius, *Commentum in Boethii opuscula* 5.3, p. 63: "*Personis*: id est, larvis. Apud enim antiquos mos fuit histrionum ut in theatris hominibus quibuscumque vellent nuda facie illuderent, sed hoc cum displicuissent, adhibitae sunt larvae, in quibus et major sonus propter concavitatem ederetur, et nulli aperte illuderetur. Hae ergo larvae personae dictae sunt, eo quod histriones in his singulorum hominum substantias repraesentabant. Unde et personae quasi 'per se sonantes' sunt dictae. Et sciendum quia eorum substantias repraesentabant, eorum dictis et factis fabulis et gesticulatione corporis illudebant. Ab his itaque personis, id est, larvis, translatum est ut omnium hominum substantiae individuae personae vocarentur." For the traditional use of *persona* to mean a character, see above.

[59] Remigius, *In Artem Donati minorem commentum*, p. 33: "Invenitur autem prisco tempore concessum fuit histrionibus ut quibuscunque in comoediis et tragoediis publice insultarent. Deinde volentibus aliquem irridere assumebant larvas et apponebant sibi ad faciem. Sic quaecunque volebant repraesentabant, Hecubam videlicet vel Priamum. Quod cum potentioribus quibusdam displicuisset, jussum est ut haec superstitio penitus abdicaretur."

[60] Remigius, *Commentum in Boethii opuscula* 5.3, p. 64.

[61] *Ibid.*, p. 63: "*Tragoediisque*: Tragoediae sunt dictae ab eo quod est *tragos*, id est, hircus, quem tragici pro munere accipiebant, sive dictae a vilibus munusculis, quae graece *tragemata* dicuntur, latine bellaria." Remigius gives a similar explanation in his gloss on the expression *tragico boatu* in Sedulius, *Carmen paschale* 1.18 (cited by Rand, p. 94). *Tragēmata* and *bellaria* usually referred to sweetmeats or fruit served for dessert after meals. A scholion to Priscian, following the derivation from *tragēmata*, defines tragedies as cheap poems: "Hinc et tragoediae sunt vilia carmina, quasi bellaria" (Keil, ed., *Grammatici latini*, 3:497, note to line 1). The *Commentum einsidlense in Donati Artem majorem* (ninth or tenth century), which has also been atributed to Remigius combines the goat-reward and cheap-gift explanations with an account of a tragedy, *Orestes*, by Terence which deals with Orestes's killing of his mother because she killed his father. Comedy also has its vile or cheap aspects: it is a "carmen villanum de vilibus et inanibus rebus compositum" (p. 236). I should note that at the beginning of the ninth century,

tragoedia of Christ's generation, he says:

Tragedies describe ludicrous and monstrous things. If therefore the flesh of Christ was not taken from the flesh of man, what Holy Scripture says of the birth of Our Lord and Savior will be like a tragedy. For what we say of "twin suns and a twofold Thebes" will not be more monstrous than what is to be read of Christ's begetting.[62]

Remigius interprets Boethius to mean that the biblical account of the Incarnation would describe a more unnatural event than those that are to be found in tragedies, for instance, Vergil's account of Dido's troubled dreams in the *Aeneid*: as Pentheus in his madness sees squadrons of Eumenides, twin suns, and a twofold Thebes, and Agamemnon's son Orestes flees about the stage in agitation from his mother, who is armed with torches and black snakes, while the avenging Furies wait at the stage doors.[63] These lines are the only place in the *Aeneid* where Vergil makes direct allusion to stage-plays. It is not self-evident that he is referring to tragedies, but this is made abundantly clear in Servius's commentary on the passage: he says of the double sun that Vergil is speaking tragically, imitating Euripides, and he cites Pacuvius's tragedies at length.[64] Since Remigius definitely used Servius elsewhere,[65] he may have been drawing on him here, and if so, he could have told us much more about the content of tragedies if he had so wished. He also knew something about tragic style, for in his commentary on Martianus Capella's *Marriage of Philology and Mercury* he defines "buskined" songs as "tragic and high-sounding."[66]

Let us now turn to Remigius's commentary on Boethius's *Consolation of Philosophy*.[67] When he comments on the *scaenicae meretriculae*, Remigius

---

Smaragdus, abbot of Saint-Mihiel, took Orestes as a poet who specialized in mournful verse ("qui carmine delectabatur luctuoso"), whose name became synonymous with tragedy, just as Eunuchus was a poet whose very name signified comedy. See Charles Thurot, *Notices et extraits des divers manuscrits latins pour servir à l'histoire des doctrines grammaticales au moyen âge*, pp. 67–68.

[62] Remigius, *Commentum in Boethii opuscula* 5.5, p. 72: "*Tragoedia*: Tragoediae res ludicras et monstruosas describunt. Si ergo caro Christi non est sumpta ex carne hominis, quasi tragoedia erit quicquid de domini salvatoris nativitate scriptura sancta refert. Neque enim magis monstruosum erit quod dicimus geminos soles duplicesque Thebas quam illud quodcumque de Christi generatione legitur."

[63] *Aeneid* 4.469–73:

> Eumenidum ueluti demens uidet agmina Pentheus
> Et solem geminum et duplices se ostendere Thebas,
> Aut Agamemnonius scaenis agitatus Orestes
> Armatam facibus matrem et serpentibus atris
> Cum fugit, ultricesque sedent in limine Dirae.

[64] Servius, on *Aeneid* 4.469–73 (*In Vergilii carmina commentarii*, 1:549–50).

[65] See Courcelle, *La Consolation*, pp. 247–48.

[66] Remigius, *Commentum in Martianum Capellam* 2.51.19, 1:163: "*Coturnatos cantus*, id est, tragicos et altisonos."

[67] There has been some discussion in recent years as to how original Remigius's commentary is. Fabio Troncarelli, "Per una ricerca sui commenti altomedievali al *De consolatione* di Boezio," pp. 367–80,

defines *scaenicae* as referring to the theater, and identifies the scene as the place where plays were performed and poems were recited.[68] In his commentary on Martianus Capella, he also has the poets reciting in the theater, but he connects *scaena* with the Greek for shadow, and interprets the scene as a shaded area or structure.[69] It is possible that Remigius conceived of nonacted (recited) as well as acted tragedies. He seems to think that it was the tragic poets (and also hunters, following Servius) who wore buskins; he says quite definitely that comic poets (rather than actors) wore the sock.[70] It is easy to see how such a conception could have arisen, since the footwear was often taken by metonymy for the poet. Ovid carries it a step further (so to speak) when he conceives of himself as wearing buskins while attempting to write tragedy.[71] For these footwear notions Remigius may have been drawing on a seventh-century commentator on Horace, whom I shall call the Lambda Scholiast below, who says much the same thing more clearly.[72] Remigius may have also taken the notion of the recitation of dramatic works from a Horatian scholiast, or perhaps from a Carolingian commentary on Terence, like the *Expositio* discussed by Remigio Sabbadini.[73] Here, as elsewhere, the Terentian editor Calliopius is interpreted as the poet's *recitator*, probably from misunderstanding

has discovered glosses in a ninth-century Vatican text of Boethius, MS lat 3363, similar to those found in the commentary attributed to Remigius, and she concludes that the commentary is therefore not by Remigius; but Bolton, "The Study of the *Consolation of Philosophy* in Anglo-Saxon England," pp. 33–78, reports the judgment of Joseph S. Wittig that most of the glosses in question are of a later date (p. 36 n. 25). She herself notes that they correspond most closely to glosses by one of Remigius's revisers, those found in Cambridge University Library MS Kk 3.21 (late tenth or early eleventh century). See also Wittig's article, "King Alfred's *Boethius* and Its Latin Sources: A Reconsideration," p. 160: "The Remigian commentary, like a good number of other works attributed to Remi, exists in various versions. One might wonder whether Remi did more than give his particular stamp to glosses which originated as the common teaching of a whole school, for instance at Rheims or at Paris, much of which material antedated a specific course of lectures given by Remi or a commentary written down under his direction."

[68] Remigius, *In Boethii Consolationem Philosophiae commentum* 1, prose 1, among excerpts edited by Edmund Taite Silk, *Saeculi noni auctoris in Boetii Consolationem Philosophiae commentarius*, p. 316: "*Scenicas*: theatrales. *Has scenicas meretriculas* appellat Musas quia earum carmina in scenis recitabantur. Est enim scena locus ubi exercebantur ludi et carmina recitabantur." He gives another explanation based on the meaning of *scena* as "perfume" used by whores to entice their lovers.

[69] Remigius, *Commentum in Martianum Capellam* 2.51.19: "*In scenis*, id est in theatris; *scea* grece, 'umbra'; hinc scena umbraculum ubi poetae recitabant."

[70] Ibid.: "*Et sueta ferre soccum comicum*: Soccus genus est calciamenti quo comici poetae utebantur. Coturnus calciamentum tragicum vel venatorium utrique pedi aptum." See Servius on *Aeneid* 1.337 (*In Vergilii carmina commentarii*, 1:119).

[71] Ovid, *Amores* 2.18; see chap. 2 above, p. 28.

[72] *Scholia Lambda* on *Ars poetica* 80, ed. Botschuyver, *Scholia in Horatium λφψ*, p. 428: "Soccus genus calceamenti est quo utebantur comici, ut Terentius et Plautus. Cothurnus autem genus calceamenti est utroque pedi aptum, quo genere calceamenti proprie utebantur tragoedii. Posuit autem hic soccum pro comicis, cothurnum vero pro tragoediis, qui pede iambico sua carmina componunt."

[73] Remigio Sabbadini, "Biografi e commentatori di Terenzio," pp. 289–327. Sabbadini says (pp. 326–27) that the *Expositio* uses the grammarian Vergil (seventh century), and that it is used in

"Calliopius recensui" ("I, Callopius, edited the above") to mean "Calliopius recitavi" ("I, Calliopius, recited the above").[74] The *Expositio* interprets *recitator* as synonymous with *declamator*.[75] In another commentary, in which Calliopius also figures as Terence's reciter, the word *agere* is interpreted as *recitare*.[76]

As for the idea of *scena* or *scaena* (both spellings were used in Antiquity) coming from the Greek for shade, Remigius undoubtedly got it from Servius's commentary on Vergil. Servius says that in early times, when the theatrical scene did not have proper walls, shade was provided by foliage; later on, boards (*tabulata*) were used.[77] A gloss to Priscian also interprets *scaena* as shade, and says that it was set up in the amphitheater, and that games or plays took place in it. It was built first of branches, then of *tabulae*, and finally also of stones.[78]

In Boethius's *Consolation*, just after Fortune characterizes tragedies as bewailing the sudden overthrow of happy kingdoms, she goes on to speak of Jupiter's two tuns. Remigius explains this reference as being found in Pacuvius,[79] whom he would have known to be an author of tragedies from Servius, if not also from other sources. These contexts do not fit very well with his understanding of tragedy as dealing with the monstrous and the ludicrous, and in one copy of his commentary there is no gloss on tragedy.[80]

turn by Papias (pp. 326–27), who, as we shall see, was writing around 1045. Sabbadini dates the commentary to the ninth century ("Biografi," p. 320). The introduction, beginning with the Terentian *vita* no. 5, and the commentary on the prologue of the *Andria*, are edited by Friedrich Schlee, *Scholia terentiana*, pp. 163–73, under the title *Commentarius recentior*; on pp. 173–74, Schlee edits the glosses to some of the *scaenae* of *Andria*.

[74] Sabbadini, "Biografi," p. 323.

[75] *Expositio in Terentium, Scholia terentiana*, p. 165.

[76] *Scholia terentiana*, pp. 140–41; cf. p. 79. This commentary, which Schlee calls the *Commentarius antiquior*, appears in a ninth-century manuscript.

[77] Servius on *Aeneid* 1.164 (*In Vergilii carmina commentarii*, 1:67): "*Scaena*, inumbratio. Et dicta scaena *apo tēs skias*. Apud antiquos enim theatralis scaena parietatem non habuit, sed de frondibus umbracula quaerebant. Postea tabulata componere coeperunt in modum parietis."

[78] *Glossa Leidensia* to Priscian, ed. Voss, p. 37, cited by Georg Goetz, *Corpus glossariorum latinorum*, 1:179–80: "Scena umbra interpretatur, et in ampitheatro fiebat; quae barbare louba dicitur; in qua ludi exercebantur; et primo ramis, deinde tabulis, postremo etiam lapidibus aedificabatur."

[79] Courcelle, "Culture," p. 251, treats this passage accurately, but in *La Consolation*, p. 106 n. 1, he mistakenly says that Remigius's allusion to Pacuvius is explanatory of *Quid tragediarum*, and that Remigius is referring to the quotation from Pacuvius in *Rhetorica ad Herennium* 2.23.36 (which Courcelle gives on p. 131 n. 4).

[80] Vatican MS Pal. lat. 1581 (tenth or eleventh century), fol. 13v. Courcelle, *La Consolation*, p. 405, lists this manuscript as containing a very complete text of Remigius's commentary, but the opening gloss on *Carmina* ("Festiva jucunda, quia carptim pronuntiet[ur], carmen dicitur. Unde lanam quam discerpunt purgantes carminare dicimus," fol. 2, gloss b) is different from that given by Courcelle ("Carmen dicitur eo quod carptim pronunciatur, unde hodie lanam quam discerpunt purgantes carminare dicimus"). Troncarelli, "Per una ricerca," p. 371, notes other different or missing glosses. I have also looked at Vatican MS Regin. lat. 1433 of the twelfth century, which contains scattered glosses from Remigius's commentary. There is no gloss for *Quid tragoediarum* in the noted passage,

However, in one or more copies of Remigius's commentary, tragedy is explained in Isidorian fashion as a mournful poem, with the added note that tragedies consist of examples of dead men and bewail the miseries of men.[81] This explanation came from, or else inspired, a gloss on Eusebius's *Ecclesiastical History*, which also includes the observation that the base word means goat.[82] Related glosses define tragedy as "war song" (or "war story") or "goat song" (or "goat story").[83] One version of Remigius's commentary, allegedly revised by a disciple, says that tragedies are based on *battles* of the dead, rather than examples, that is, putting *ex praeliis* rather than *exemplis*.[84]

Eusebius said that the shadows at the end of Herod's life were darker than any tragic dramaturgy. In the Latin translation by Rufinus he is made to say: "It would be too long if I told how the prosperities of his rule which he had enjoyed until that time were overshadowed by domestic slaughters. If I were to describe the ignominy of his marriage, the deaths of his children (of which he was the parricide), and the slaughter of his sister and all of his relatives, it would seem that I composed a tragedy rather than a history."[85] It is clear that Rufinus considers it appropriate for tragedies to begin in prosperity and end in horror. Pope Nicholas I was probably inspired by Rufinus's phrase in a letter of the year 867: he will give the history – "if it should not rather be called a tragedy" – of two bishops who refused to send an adulteress back to her husband.[86] But in this case the tragic circumstances are scandalous rather than horrible. More in line with the Eusebian tradition, perhaps, is Ekkehard of St. Gall (*c.* 980–*c.* 1036), the fourth of that name at the Swiss abbey; several times in his chronicle he speaks of real-life tragedies, which involve hardship and destruction. At one point he says it must suffice to have touched on the tragedy of Waldo's time and on his greatness; for if he were to run through all the misery

---

fol. 12, but *tragicus* in book 3, prose 6 is glossed "poeta tragediarum" (fol. 26).

[81] "Carmen luctuosum; tragoediae sunt carmina, quae constant exemplis mortuorum (hominum) et deplorant miserias hominum," given by Hans Naumann, *Notkers Boethius*, p. 41, drawing on Trèves MS 1093 (eleventh century) and Maihingen MS I 2 lat. 4 no. 3 (tenth century).

[82] See Goetz, *Corpus glossariorum*, 5:426 and 7:360, from MS Ambros. M 79 (early eleventh century) under the rubric *De Eusebio*: "Tragoediae sunt carmina quae constant exemplis mortuorum hominum et deplorant miserias; *trago* enim hyrcus."

[83] *Ibid.* 7:360: "Tragoedica: bellica cantica vel fabulatio vel hircania; *trago* enim ircus."

[84] Vatican MS lat. 4254 (fourteenth century), fols. 1–80. See Courcelle, *La Consolation*, p. 406. On fol. 17v, above *Quid tragediarum*, is the gloss, "tragoediae sunt carmina quae constant ex praeliis mortuorum et deplorant miserias hominum."

[85] Eusebius, *Historia ecclesiastica* 1.8.4, ed. Mommsen, p. 65: "Longum est si prosperitates imperii ejus, quibus ad illud tempus usque pollebat, domesticis referam cladibus obscuratas. Ignominiam matrimonii, funera liberorum (quorum tamen ipse extiterit parricida), sororis etiam propinquiorumque omnium si exsequar cladis, tragoedia magis quam historia texi videbitur." See above, p. 24.

[86] Nicholas I, letter of 31 October 867, MGH Epistolae 6:341: "Ordinamur ergo historiam Theutgaudi et Guntharii, si tamen non tragoedia potius sit dicenda."

suffered because of the Saracens, he would fill a volume.[87]

Ekkehard was a student of Notker Labeo, whose commentary on Boethius draws on Remigius and other sources. Notker is one of the few medieval authors to note that comedy dealt with laughter; he is more usual in specifying sorrow as the specialty of tragedy.[88] He defines tragedies, following Isidore, as mournful poems. They are what Sophocles wrote among the Greeks, concerning the overthrow of kingdoms and cities. They are contrary to comedies, which have a joyful and happy end (echoing the happy ends, *laeti exitus*, of Donatus–Evanthius). He does not know whether there were any Latin tragic authors, whereas there is a good supply of Latin comic authors.[89]

One of Remigius's disciples, commenting on the treatise *Against Eutyches*, recorded the fanciful idea that tragedies were named from goats because men killed goats to clean their swords, marking on their weapons the number they had killed.[90] Another, or the same, Remigian, in revising the master's commentary on the *Consolation of Philosophy*, sees the "scene" as something more closely related to the brothel than to the theater. We recall that according to Isidore, "theater" came to be another word for "brothel" because men lay with whores after going to the theater. In our gloss, *scenica* is interpreted as "voluptuous" or "shady," and *scena* as the place in the theater where men lie with whores.[91] A further explanation is added at the end of the gloss, similar to the addition found in another manuscript which normally follows the unrevised text (that is, Trèves 1093). The scene, we are told, was the place in the old days where the people came to watch, for various games or plays were put on there. But they defiled themselves among these women, who were called scenic because they came there for

[87] Ekkehard IV, *Casus Sancti Galli* 15, MGH Scriptores 2:137–38; cf. chap. 3, 2:103, 107.

[88] Notker, *Boethius de consolatione Philosophiae*, ed. E. H. Sehrt and Taylor Starck, p. 13 ad v. *skenicas meretriculas*: "héizet er skenicas musas, álso comediae uuáren, únde tragoediae die óuh mánne scádotôn, uuánda comediae ráhtôn ímo risum, tragoediae luctum." See also the edition of Petrus W. Tax, *Die Werke Notkers des Deutschen*, 1:9–10.

[89] *Ibid.*, on Fortune's question in book 2, prose 2: "Tragoediae sínt luctuosa carmina; álso díu sínt díu Sophocles scréib apud grecos de euersionibus regnorum et urbium; únde sínt uuíderuuártig tien comoediis, án dien uuír io gehórên letum únde jocundum exitum. Uns íst áber únchúnt úbe dehéine latini tragici fúndene uuérdên sô uuír gnùoge findên latinos comicos" (Sehrt and Taylor, p. 70; Tax, 1:52).

[90] Rand, *Commentum in Boethii opuscula*, p. 94, citing MS F, fol. 99: "Tragoediae sunt dictae ab hircis. Nam hircos homines occidebant ad emundandum suum gladium; quot enim occidebant homines, illum numerum ponebant occisorum in sua spata." The second *homines* could also be taken as accusative, meaning perhaps that each time a person used his sword to kill a man, he would mark the number and then clean the sword by killing a goat!

[91] Vatican MS lat. 4254 fol. 5v on *Consolatio*, book 1, prose 1: "*scenicas* scilicet voluptuosas, id est umbraticas. Scena dicitur locus in theatro, viz. ubi cumbant cum meretricibus. Et meretriculae dicuntur septem artes liberales cum quibus delectabatur homo sapiens sicut cum meretricibus. Et dicitur scena unguentum quo unguntur ipsae propter fragrantiam odoris. Et ipsae dicuntur meretrices."

the purpose of lying with those who wished it, or of charming the people with their songs.[92] But later *scena vitae* is explained as the shade under which the plays of Fortune were performed.[93] Another manuscript glosses this passage thus: "Here he calls this world the scene in which Fortune enacts her plays, humiliating some and exalting others. 'Scene' is used for the variety of this world."[94]

NON-REMIGIANS, SENECANS, HORATIANS, AND LATER ISIDORIANS

Let us now look at some more treatments of tragedy that fall outside the wide circle of Remigius's influence. We saw above, in speaking of glosses to Rufinus's translation of Eusebius, an example of a reference to tragedy that came into Latin by adapting the text of a Greek Father. Another instance can be seen in the homilies of Paul the Deacon (d. 801), chancellor of Desiderius, last king of the Longobards. Where John Chrysostom said that the Syro-Phoenician woman tragedized (*exetragōidei*), that is, tragically narrated, her calamity to Jesus, Paul says that she enlarged upon her tragedy.[95] But what he understands by tragedy remains to be conjectured.

Paschasius Radbertus, writing at about the same time (before 831), but in the northern abbey of Corbie near Amiens, also uses the term "tragedy." He is probably drawing on anti-literary remarks of the Latin Fathers when he complains that some persons study Holy Scripture with less diligence than they labor over the carping criticism (*neniae*) of tragedies and the figments of poets in their desire to win applause through the theatrics of mimes. He, however, will not deal with Vergil's *arma virumque* in its Greek brine of fables, but rather with divine letters. He will not seek to soften the reader with tragic piety or saddle him with the burden of the comic authors ("neque tragica pietate permulcemus lectorem aut comicorum sagmate

[92] *Ibid.*: "Et scena dicebatur antiquitus locus quo populus ad spectandum veniebat, ubi enim ludos exercebant diversos; sed inter has mulieres stuprabantur. Inde scenicae illae mulieres dicebantur quae ad hoc veniebant ut concubitum volentibus preberent, vel cantibus suis populum demulcerent." For the similar gloss of the Trèves MS, see Silk, *Saeculi noni auctoris*, pp. 316–17. Remigius's name appears on fols. 115v and 146 of this MS. See Courcelle, *La Consolation*, p. 405. Silk, *Saeculi*, p. 306n., says, "The fact that the scholia of Trev. 1093 are fragmentary is most unfortunate, since that manuscript usually offers a better text than K [Maihingen MS I 2 (lat) 4to. 3, fols. 60–112 (tenth century)]."
[93] Vat. lat. 4254 fol. 19v on book 2, prose 3: "*in hanc presentis vitae scenam*: umbraculum sub quo ludi Fortunae fiebant."
[94] Vatican Regin. lat. 1433 (see above), fol. 13v: "Hic autem vocat hunc mundum scenam. In quo Fortuna ludos suos agit, quosdam humilians, quosdam exaltans. Scena pro varietate hujus mundi [ponitur?]."
[95] Paulus Diaconus, *Homiliarius* 81, PL 95:1235A: "Rogat mulier, obsecrat, deprecatur, deflet casum suum, auget tragoediam, ennarat passionem." Cf. John Chrysostom, *Commentary on Matthew* 15.21–22, homily 52, PG 58:519.

onerare cupimus"), but will use simple speech according to his ability.[96] He borrows the phrase *tragica pietas* from Fulgentius;[97] and since he seems to have the *Aeneid* so much in mind, perhaps he sees it as a tragedy, or *pius Aeneas* as a character from a tragedy. That is, we may well be jumping to the wrong conclusion if we think that his censure proves that Seneca's tragedies were being read by his contemporaries.

Some use was made of Seneca's plays during this period, of course, though doubtless mainly from florilegia. Aldhelm, for instance, writing in England in the seventh century, cites two lines from the *Agamemnon*,[98] Theodulf of Orleans at the turn of the ninth century quotes a line from *Hercules oetaeus*,[99] and the Neapolitan Eugenius Vulgaris at the beginning of the tenth century draws extensively on the plays.[100] But it is difficult to determine how even Eugenius understood tragedy as a form, except that it dealt with misfortunes. His *Metrum parhemiacum tragicum*, beginning "O tristia saecla priora," comes after his *Species comicae*, featuring the singing of birds.[101]

Let us now turn to two early medieval commentators on Horace's *Ars poetica*, the Lambda-Phi-Psi and Aleph-Beth Scholiasts, or Lambda and Aleph for short, to name them from the manuscripts in which their commentaries are preserved.[102] I have already cited Lambda, who, as

---

[96] Paschasius Radbertus, Preface to book 3 of the *Expositio in Matheo*, ed. Paulus, 1:233–34; PL 120:181–84. Paulus gives *sagmatae* in the text, but notes that the form is *sagmate* in various MSS, and notes also that Paschasius often writes *ae* for *e* (1:234).

[97] Fulgentius, *Mythologiae* 1 (Preface), *Opera*, p. 9: "aut satyra luseram aut comedico fasmate delectabam aut tragica pietate mulcebam aut epigrammatum brevitate condibam." Perhaps Paschasius's reading *sagmate* should be preferred to *fasmate*; other editors have emended Fulgentius's text to *plasmate* and *phantasmate*. Fulgentius wrote around the turn of the sixth century. The idea that he is the same person as Fulgentius, bishop of Ruspe, is rejected by Church historians, but favored by some classicists. See Bertold Altaner, *Patrology*, p. 588, and F. J. E. Raby, "Fulgentius, Fabius Planciades."

[98] *De metris et enigmatibus*, MGH Auctores antiquissimi 15:194.27. For this and other citations of Seneca, see Giorgio Brugnoli, "La tradizione manoscritta di Seneca tragico alla luce delle testimonianze medioevali," p. 215; Brugnoli, "Le tragedie di Seneca nei florilegi medioevali." See also Peter Lebrecht Schmidt, "Rezeption und Überlieferung der Tragödien Senecas bis zum Ausgang des Mittelalters," pp. 12–73; Winfried Trillitzsch, "Seneca tragicus – Nachleben und Beurteilung im lateinischen Mittelalter von der Spätantike bis zum Renaissancehumanismus."

[99] Theodulf, *Carmina* 28.375, MGH Poetae latini 1 (1881) 503, citing line 607, not noted by the editor, Ernst Dümmler. See Brugnoli, "Tradizione," pp. 215–16. Otto Zwierlein, "Spuren der Tragödien Senecas bei Bernardus Silvestris, Petrus Pictor, und Marbot von Rennes," pp. 195–96, notes that Theodulf's citation corresponds to the E (Etruscus or Italian) tradition, and judges that he was drawing on a florilegium based on it.

[100] Eugenius Vulgarius, *Sylloga*, pp. 406–440. See Max Manitius, *Geschichte der lateinischen Litteratur des Mittelalters*, 1: 433–36; Brugnoli, "Tradizione," pp. 216–22.

[101] *Sylloga*, pp. 430–33. In a letter to Pope Sergius III, pp. 416–17, he draws on many Senecan phrases to describe the miseries of the world.

[102] *Scholia Lambda*, ed. Botschuyver, *Scholia in Horatium* λφψ; *Scholia Aleph*, ed. Botschuyver, *Scholia in Horatium* אב .

noted, dates to the seventh century.[103] He made some use of the *Etymologies*,[104] but his ideas of tragedy and theater are pretty much independent of Isidore's work. Tragedy is written in high speech (*altus sermo*),[105] and deals with the *scelera* committed by the descendants of Tantalus, who gave his son Pelops to the gods to rear. Pelops's sons were Atreus and Thyestes, one of whom violated the other's wife, and the other killed the violator's son. Atreus (not Agamemnon, we note) was the father of Orestes, who killed his mother.[106] The fable to be recited in the scenes should not have more or less than five acting persons (that is, those about whom the fable is narrated), and no more than three speaking persons who narrate the fable.[107] It is not clear whether the acting persons are only described, or whether they are silent actors on (or in) the scene. Lambda does not explain what the scene is, but he seems to mean by it some sort of platform or raised structure, since *pulpita* is interpreted as the steps by which one ascended into or onto the scene.[108]

The Lambda Scholiast interprets Horace as saying that the poet who originally wrote tragedy, to be remunerated with a goat, abandoned the form as vile and started to write satire, which was considered more noble.[109] Tragedy should be composed in accord with morality, since it deals with moral and modest subjects, in contrast to satire, which publicly condemns the vices of others.[110]

But in spite of the fact that tragedy now is supposed to deal with *honesta* (rather than, say, with *scelera*), Horace is interpreted as saying that the tragic poems were sung by drunks with haughty speech and inflated mouth. Hence it is said that the word "tragedy" comes from *tryga*, "dregs"; hence, too, Terentian pictures in comedy or tragedy are painted with turgid and inflated mouth.[111] The scholiast has apparently seen wall paintings or

---

[103] On the date, see *Scholia Lambda*, p. ix; *Scholia Aleph*, pp. vii–viii.

[104] *Scholia Lambda*, pp. ix, 184.

[105] *Scholia Lambda* on *Ars poetica* 89, 94 (pp. 428–29).

[106] *Ibid.* on line 89.

[107] *Ibid.* on line 189 (p. 436): "Dicit ergo quia fabula quae recitanda est in scaenis non plus deberet habere personas egentes (id est, de quibus fabula narratur) quam quinque neque minus; loquentes vero (id est qui ipsam fabulam narrent) non amplius quam tres"; *ibid.* on line 192: "Quia tres personae loquentes tragoediam et comoediam narrant." Cf. Pseudo-Acron on *Ars poetica* 192 (*Scholia in Horatium vetustiora*, 2:341): "Loquentes vero, id est qui ipsam fabulam narrent, non amplius quam tres."

[108] *Scholia Lambda* on *Ars poetica* 215 (p. 437): "Pulpita erant gradus per quos ascendebatur in scenam."

[109] *Ibid.* on *Ars poetica* 223 (p. 438): "Dicit quia ille poeta qui antea carmen scribebat ut hirco mereretur remunerari, relicta tragoedia quasi viliore, contulit se ad saturam scribendam, utpote nobiliorem."

[110] *Ibid.* on line 232 (p. 439): "Tragoedia honeste debet esse composita, honesta tractans et quasi verecunda, ad comparationem saturae, quae publice aliorum vitia redarguit."

[111] *Ibid.* on line 276 (p. 442): "Dicit autem quia ora peruncti, id est, ebrii, decantabant eadem poemata tragica. Unde dicitur tragoedia quasi *tryga* quod sonat latine 'faecem,' quod faece tenus potato vino ea decantarent fastuoso sermone et inflato ore. Quapropter Terentianae imagines in comica vel

manuscript illuminations of actors in masks,[112] but he did not recognize the masks for what they were. He knows that masks, called *personae*, were used, having been invented by Aeschylus, but he assumes that the purpose of the masks, and also of the large cloaks or *syrmata*, was to disguise the reciters so that they would not be recognized by those whose vices they criticized; they may also have hoped that the "honor" of the masks would prevent them from being demeaned.[113]

The Aleph Scholiast, who relied more heavily on Christian writers, has been tentatively identified as Heiric, the teacher of Remigius.[114] According to him, *comici* used the sock as a sign that there was humble speech about humble persons in comedy. *Tragoedi* used the high buskin, because tragedy was high speech, *alta oratio*, and dealt with great persons. For tragedy is not composed of anything but the *magna miseria magnarum personarum*, like the kings Telephus and Peleus.[115] So far one cannot tell whether the scholiast is speaking of poet or actor. However, when he goes on to say that the *comici* and *tragoedi* did not invent the iambic meter but got it from Archilochus,[116] it is clear that he is speaking of poets or poet–reciters, if not poet–actors.

A high voice is becoming to tragedy, but sometimes the *tragicus*, or *tragicus recitator*, grieves with a humble voice, as when he leads on (*inducit*) the speaking Telephus and Peleus.[117] *Tragici* must be identical with *tragoedi*, for they are said to wear buskins because of the altitude of their matter, just as *comici* wear socks because of the humility of their matter.[118] Telephus is identified as the king of the Mysians.[119] Remigius, we recall, says that Mysians were called Getas, from Terence's character, because of their devotion to games or plays.

With Aleph, as with Lambda, it is hard to tell whether he envisages real mute actors responding to the reciter's voice, or simply thinks of the *introductae personae* of a narrative. He has a curious interpretation of the spectator whose heart Telephus and Peleus are to touch. It is not someone watching the recitation, but rather someone within the tragedy: Telephus is to move the heart of the watching Achilles, and Peleus the heart of the

---

tragoedia turgida et inflato ore pinguntur." The suggested etymology from *truga* is reported by Pomponius Porphyrion (early third century), *Commentarius in Horatium Flaccum*, p. 354, and also by Diomedes (*Ars grammatica*, p. 487) and by Donatus–Evanthius 1.2 (*Commentum Terenti*, 1:13).

[112] See p. 79 below for discussion of the Carolingian manuscripts of Terence.
[113] *Scholia Lambda* on *Ars poetica* 278 (p. 442): "*Personae pallaeque repertor honestae Aeschylus*: ostendit Aeschylum repertorem fuisse personarum, id est larvarum, et syrmatum palpitorum quoque et cothurnorum; quia ne cognoscerentur ipsi recitatores ab illis quorum vitia carpebant, vel etiam honestate personae ne vilescerent, larvas ponebant in capite et induebant syrmata, hoc est, vestimenta prolixa."
[114] *Scholia Aleph*, pp. ix–x. [115] *Scholia Aleph* on *Ars poetica* 80 (p. 461). [116] *Ibid.*
[117] *Ibid.* on lines 92 and 96 (pp. 462–63). [118] *Ibid.* on line 280 (p. 475).
[119] *Ibid.* on line 96 (p. 463).

watching Ceyx.[120] He has nothing to say about the number of persons involved in a drama, or about the scene, the pulpits, or masks.

I will conclude this section with an account of two later writers, Lambert of Hersfeld and Bernard of Utrecht, both of whom can be considered Isidorians, at least in spirit. Lambert has an interesting figurative use of theatrical tragedy in his *Annals*. He tells of the clergy of Bamberg in the year 1075 who were willing to accept Henry IV's appointee as their bishop, even though they did not like him. They preferred him to another candidate against whom they had appealed to the Holy See. He notes that they had also "promulgated a lugubrious tragedy on the life and morals of this person, intended to be sung to the whole theater of this world."[121] When he tells of the synod convoked by Henry against Pope Gregory VII at Worms in January 1076, Lambert says that Hugo Blancus, the deposed cardinal who presided, "brought with him such-and-such a tragedy, with scenic figments, of the pope's life and career, telling where he was born, his behavior as a youth, the perverse way he acquired the Holy See, and the incredible crimes he committed before and after becoming a bishop."[122] (We shall see in the next chapter that Henry IV would come to regard his own life, or rather the account that he gives of it in a letter, as a tragedy.)

Lambert's basic idea of tragedy is quite Isidorian: it was sung in the theater, it dealt with crimes, and was mournful. Whether he considers it a form that passed away with the ancients, or one still current, is not clear. He makes two metaphorical applications, characterizing pseudo-historical written accounts, containing false charges of misconduct, as tragedies to be performed, one in the world at large, which is likened to a theater, and the other on the "stage" of the synod.

Bernard of Utrecht was an Isidorian of another fashion. He wrote an introduction to Theodulus's *Eclogue* sometime during the last quarter of the eleventh century: he dedicated it to Conrad, bishop of Utrecht from 1076 to 1099.[123] Bernard explains that Theodulus's poem is named *Eclogue*, which means "goat-discourse," either because it deals with shepherds, or because it reprehends the filth of vice that is designated by the goat.[124] He

[120] *Ibid.* on line 97 (pp. 463–64).

[121] Lambert of Hersfeld, *Annales*, p. 240: "Cujus vitae institutionisque lugubrem tragoediam toto mundi hujus theatro decantandam vulgaverant."

[122] *Ibid.*, p. 253: "deferens secum de vita et institutione papae scenicis figmentis consimilem tragoediam: scilicet unde oriundus, qualiter ab ineunte aetate conversatus, quam perverso ordine sedem apostolicam occupaverit, quae ante episcopatum, quae post acceptum episcopatum memoratu quoque incredibilia flagicia commiserit."

[123] Bernard of Utrecht, *Commentum in Theodulum*, ed. Huygens, pp. 55–69. Bernard's work exists in six MSS of the twelfth century, one of the turn of the thirteenth century, and one of the fourteenth century (see Huygens's Introduction, pp. 7–9).

[124] Bernard of Utrecht, *Commentum in Theodulum*, p. 60: "Egloga a capris tractum est, quasi diceret *egle*

distinguishes between a title and prologue: the latter is prefixed to comic and prosaic books.[125] He identifies Theodulus's work as bucolic, and then proceeds to list various kinds of poems.

The first type of poem he mentions is the comic, in which the deeds of private men are represented through persons. The name comes either from the word for village, because of where it originated or because of the rustic persons introduced in it, or from the word for meal, because it was recited after eating, or from *como, comis*, referring to the ornate speech of the comic poets who were given socks because of the smoothness of their words. Their form of poem is called comedy, which contains scenes; for this sort of poem was recited in (or on) scenes.[126] By representation through persons, Bernard probably means not acting, but simply the dialogue of characters in a poem. When he takes up the three modes of poetry later on, he seems to be drawing on Bede. Instead of Bede's example of tragedies and fables for the dramatic mode (in which only persons speak), he cites Terence; but though he omits the Vergilian eclogue, he follows Bede in naming the Song of Songs.[127] He probably knew Terence's plays at first hand, and a commentary as well. The *Expositio* spoken of earlier gives the examples of Sallust and Terence as authors with prologues to their works, and it also refers to the sections of Terence's plays as scenes.[128] Bernard may also be drawing on it later when he says that comedies consist of arguments, which he defines as lifelike fictions, but both authors may have gone directly to Cicero, whom Bernard cites explicitly,[129] and to the *Rhetorica ad Herennium*. The second category of poem that Bernard lists is the tragic, in which public affairs and the crimes of the powerful are depicted; the name comes from another word for goat, since a goat was given to tragic poets because of the filthiness of vice that was to be expressed. Later on, buskins were also given to them because of the gravity of their words. The tragic poets' poem is the tragedy. Its parts are called *hori*, the Greek word for mountains, because they are like mountains in their declamatory and swollen vastness,

logos, id est, caprinus sermo, aut quia de pastoribus agit, aut quia foeditatem viciorum, quae per hoc animal designatur, reprehendit."

[125] *Ibid.*, p. 61.

[126] *Ibid.*: "Est enim comicum, quo privatorum facta per personas repraesentantur, dictum a *comos*, id est villa, qua fiebat, aut a rusticanis quae ibi inducuntur personis; aut a commessatione post quam recitabatur, vel a *como, comis*, quod ornate loquantur comici, quibus ob verborum lenitatem socci dabantur. Horum opus comoedia dicitur in qua sunt scenae: in scenis enim hujusmodi recitabatur carmen." For *como* and *comis* as connected with *ornare*, see Goetz, *Corpus glossariorum*, 4:220.25, 27; 4:497.42; 5.297.5; 5:495.12.

[127] Bernard, *Commentum in Theodulum*, p. 65. For Bede, see above, pp. 40–41.

[128] *Expositio in Terentium*, pp. 165, 173–74.

[129] Bernard, *Commentum in Theodulum*, p. 63: "diffinit Tullius, 'dubiae rei fidem faciens'"; *Expositio in Terentium*, p. 167: "argumentum ratio rei dubiae faciens fidem." Cf. Cicero, *Topica* 2.8: "argumentum autem rationem quae rei dubiae faciat fidem."

as Horace says in his *Ars poetica*: "Indignatur item privatis ac prope socco/Dignis carminibus narrari cena Thyestae."[130]

Bernard's citation of Horace may be an indication of the source of some of his ideas. He may have seen Horace's discussion of the dramatic *chorus*, which somehow got read as *horus*, and noted that Terence's comedies did not have such units, or he may have seen Horatian scholia to this effect.[131] The *Vita Horatii* that appears in the Pi Scholiast, a relative of Lambda, says specifically that the songs in tragedies are called *ori*, the Greek word for mountains, because they contain declamations of great things.[132] In a summary statement added by another hand the term is given as *hori*,[133] and in a similar statement given in the Phi and Psi texts of Lambda the form is *cori*.[134] The explanation of *horus* as Greek for mountain may be connected with Isidore's explanation of *corus* (a measure consisting of thirty *modii*) as based on the Hebrew for hill.[135] But in fact the Greek for mountain is *oros*, and *horus* is one of the ways it appears in the Carolingian glossaries.[136]

The *res publicae* and *scelera* of tragedy are perhaps also echoes of Isidore. Bernard may have been influenced by Horace's *vilis hircus*, but I know of no precedent for taking the goat's vileness in a moral rather than a monetary sense, and seeing its stench as a symbol of the fetid vices dealt with in tragedy. But Isidore in two places does note the fetid nature of goats.[137]

Bernard also interprets *oda* as "praise" rather than "song." He does so not in conjunction with *tragoedia* or *comoedia*, which may already have been spelled *tragedia* and *comedia* in his day, but with the next category of poem in his list, namely, the satiric. Satiric poets ironically praise what should be vituperated, and vice versa. The poem itself is called a satire and is made up

---

[130] Bernard, *Commentum in Theodulum*, pp. 61–62. "Est tragicum, quo publicae res et potentum scelera depinguntur, tractum a *tragos*, id est hirco, qui ob viciorum foeditatem exprimendam dabatur tragicis. Quibus et coturni ob verborum gravitatem postmodum dati sunt. Horum opus est tragoedia, in quo sunt *hori*, quod graece sonat montes, eo quod instar montis declamativam et turgidam habet magnitudinem, teste Horatio in *Poetria*," citing *Ars poetica* 90–91.

[131] Horace treats the chorus in lines 193–205. None of the scholia I have seen make this point. Both Donatus–Evanthius (3.1) and Diomedes (p. 491) explain that the chorus disappeared from Latin comedies.

[132] *Scholia Pi*, ed. Botschuyver, *Scholia in Horatium πυγ*, p. 4: "Notandum autem quod carmina in lyricis dicuntur odae, in tragoediis ori, eo quod ibi declamationes magnarum rerum fiant; graece enim ori montes vocantur ... In comoediis scenae carmina dicuntur, quia videlicet in conviviis et festivitatibus recitabantur, in bucolicis eclogae nuncupantur."

[133] *Ibid.*, pp. 4–5: "In tragoediis hori vocantur carmina, in comediis coene, in saturis saturae, in lyricis odae, in bucolicis eclogae."

[134] *Scholia Lambda*, p. 2: "In tragediis chori [ψφ cori] vocantur carmina, in comediis scenae [φ coenae]," and so on.

[135] *Etymologiae*, 16.26.17.

[136] Goetz, *Corpus glossariorum*, 3:78.11 (ninth century). See 6:709–10 for other references.

[137] *Etymologiae* 10.146: "Ircosus, quia sudore corporis foetido putet"; 11.1.65: armpits are called *subhirci*, "propter quod in plerisque hominibus hircorum foetorem reddant."

of *odae*, a word that means "praises."[138] This interpretation may be based on the discussion of comedy in the *Expositio* on Terence, where *oda* is explained as "laus sive cantus."[139]

Isidore of Seville was the great pioneer not only of the encyclopedia, but also of the dictionary, since book 10 of the *Etymologies*, called *De vocabulus*, is a roughly alphabetized glossary of select words. The lexicographical movement culminated in our period in the *Elementarium doctrinae rudimentum*, composed in Italy in the 1040s[140] by a learned authority who gave himself the name of Papias, "the Guide."[141] He names some of his authorities at the beginning, including not only Isidore and Remigius, but also Horace and Cicero.[142] One of his anonymous sources was the *Liber glossarum*, put together between 690 and 750 by a compiler in Spain, who drew heavily but creatively on Isidore, not just on his glossary, but on the rest of the *Etymologies* as well.[143] An example of this indebtedness can be seen in the successive accounts of "new comedy."[144] Another of Papias's unnamed sources is the Carolingian *Expositio* on the plays of Terence. Seneca is named in the body of the dictionary, in at least one of its versions, as the author of tragedies, with a reference to his "first tragedy."[145]

---

[138] *Commentum in Theodulum*, p. 62: "Est satiricum, quod communiter vicia reprehendit ... Satirici enim yronice laudant vituperanda et vituperant laudanda. Horum opus dicitur satira, in qua sunt odae, id est, laudes."

[139] *Expositio in Terentium*, p. 163.

[140] Violetta De Angelis in the edition of letter *A* of the *Elementarium*, 1:ii: she gives the *terminus ante quem* as 1045. For my main text of Papias, I use a manuscript of the beta tradition, Vatican Ottob. lat. 2231 (first half of the twelfth century), in consultation with the fourth edition of Bonino Mombrizio. Mombrizio uses the more defective alpha tradition.

[141] According to Silvio Giuseppe Mercati, "Intorno al titolo dei lessici di Suida-Suda e di Papia," pp. 14–19, "Papias" does not designate the author's proper name or identify him as a resident of Pavia, but refers to the function of the book or author: it is the Greek common noun *papias*, meaning "porter," "conductor," or "guide."

[142] See Goetz, *Corpus glossariorum*, 1:172–84, and, for sources used in the first letter, De Angelis's edition. See also her "Indagine sulle fonti dell' *Elementarium* di Papias, lettera A." For an edition and translation of his prologue, see Lloyd W. Daly and B. H. Daly, "Some Techniques in Mediaeval Latin Lexicography."

[143] Goetz, *Corpus glossariorum*, 5:xx–xxii, 159–255. See T. A. M. Bishop, "The Prototype of the *Liber glossarum*."

[144] *Etymologiae* 8.7.7: "Novi [comici], qui et satirici, a quibus generaliter vitia carpuntur, ut Flaccus, Persius, Juvenalis, vel alii. Hi enim universorum delicta corripiunt"; 18.46: "Comoedi sunt qui privatorum hominum acta dictis aut gestu cantabant." *Liber glossarum*, Goetz, *Corpus glossariorum*, 5:181, 6:241: "Postea [comoedia] civiles vel privatas aggressa materias in dictis atque gestu universorum delicta corripiens in scaenam proferebat." Papias under *comoedi*: "Postea aggressi gesta universorum et delicta corripientes in scena [proferebant]" (the last word is added from Mombrizio's text). For the whole entry, see Kelly, *Tragedy and Comedy*, p. 8 n. 30.

[145] Papias under *rabula*, which Manitius, 2 (1923) 722 n. 1, cites from Mombrizio's 1496 edition: "etiam patronus causarum: ut dicit Seneca in prima tragoedia: 'Hic clamosi rabiosa seri jurgia vendens

Papias's definition of comedy presents a startling mixture of sources:

Comoedia est quae res privatorum et humilium personarum comprehendit, non tam alto stilo ut tragoedia sed mediocri et dulci, quae saepe etiam de historica fide et de gravibus personis tractat. (*Elementarium*, under "Comoedia")

(Comedy comprehends the affairs of private and humble persons, not in such a high style as tragedy, but in a middle and sweet style, and it often deals as well with historical fact and important persons.)

The first part is taken from Placidus, but the rest is a botched summary of Donatus–Evanthius, in which Papias attributes to comedy what Evanthius specifies as proper to tragedy. Evanthius says that tragedy differs from comedy in dealing with *ingentes personae* rather than *mediocres fortunae*, and he ends by saying: "Postremo quod omnis comoedia de fictis est argumentis; tragoedia saepe de historica fide petitur" ("Finally, all comedy is based on invented stories, whereas tragedy is often derived from historical truth").[146] We have in Papias the ultimate source for Dante's unusual notions of comedy in *De vulgari eloquentia* (it uses a middle or low style) and in the *Inferno* (in contrast to Vergil's high tragedy, his poem is a comedy, even though it deals with historical events and important persons).[147]

And yet, even though Papias or his source has mangled the letter of Donatus–Evanthius, he has caught the spirit and made it explicit. For in considering the *Odyssey* to be modeled upon comedy, Donatus in the Evanthian section of his introduction to Terence admits in effect that at least sometimes, if not often, comedy could deal with serious characters based on accepted fact. Donatus confirms this impression later on when ostensibly discussing comedy, but reports peculiarities in the stage appearance of Ulysses, Achilles, and Neoptolemus.[148]

Papias does not report any of the Donatian points of difference between comedy and tragedy, but he does add the notion of comic plot movement contained in the description of the four parts of comedy (*prologus, protasis, epitasis, katastrophē*). Papias says that the epitasis is the development of troubles, whereas the catastrophe brings the troubles under control and produces the happy outcomes.[149] Perhaps Papias's explanation is based on

---

improbus iras et verbo locat.' " Cf. *Hercules furens* 173–75. No such entry appears in the Vatican MS of Papias.

[146] Donatus–Evanthius, *Commentum Terenti*, 4.2. [147] See chap. 5 below.

[148] Donatus, *Commentum Terenti* 8.4–5 (Wessner, ed., p. 29). Ulysses always has a *pilos* ("Ulixen pilliatum semper inducunt"); the masks of Achilles and Neoptolemus have diadems, even though they do not hold regal scepters. In "Tragedy and the Performance of Tragedy," p. 24, I suggested that Ulysses's skullcap may have eliminated the need for false hair; perhaps more likely it was used to portray him as bald.

[149] Papias: "Comoedia in quattuor par[tes dividitur] ... Epitasis est incrementum processusque turbationum. Catastrophe est custodia turbationum ad jocundos exitus." Cf. Donatus–Evanthius

the beginning of Donatus's commentary on *Andria*, where, as we have seen, he says that the epitasis is filled with tumult, and the catastrophe is almost tragic but suddenly moves from turbulence to tranquillity.[150]

In his treatment of tragedy, Papias relies entirely on Isidore. He defines *tragoedi* by drawing on book 18 of the *Etymologies* for the subject matter (they sang of the old deeds and crimes of wicked kings while the people watched), and on book 8 for the etymology. He adds the point that *tragici* won honor for the arguments of their *fabulae*, but omits the point about verisimilitude, and he does not give Isidore's two differences between comedy and tragedy.[151] He does, however, note one of these differences in his entry under *comici*: he says that comics describe joyful things, whereas tragics describe arguments from mournful things (omitting Isidore's point that comics speak out on the deeds of private men, and tragics on public affairs and the histories of kings).[152] He characterizes tragedy as a poetic genre of the past: tragedy was whatever the men of old wrote or described in mournful poems. A tragedian was a singer of tragedies, a kind of writer who used buskins.[153]

Papias has in effect eliminated the mumming aspect of Isidorian tragedy, but he does reproduce Isidore's understanding of *histriones* and *mimi* as silent actors when he takes up the words alphabetically. An insightful reading of Donatus would have shown Papias that comedy at least used *histriones* who spoke *deverbia*, referring to the *diverbia* or dialogue of Livy's account; but the meaning of this word was not self-evident, and the variants *de umbia* and *de umbra* appear in manuscripts.[154] And, as we have already seen, Papias or his source did not follow Donatus faithfully or fully.

Papias indicates that the prologue is either by the poet or the *rector*, or by someone else speaking for them. The *protesis* is the first act and beginning of the *dragma* (a synonym for *fabula*), and the *persona* who opens it does not appear afterwards.[155] In a modification of Placidus, he says that comedians

---

Commentum Terenti 4.5: "Epitasis incrementum processusque turborum ac totius, ut ita dixerim, nodus erroris. Catastrophe conversio rerum ad jucundos exitus, patefacta cunctis cognitione gestorum."

[150] See p. 13 above. For other entries of Papias dealing with comedy, see Kelly, *Tragedy and Comedy*, p. 8.

[151] Papias: "*Tragoedi* sunt qui antiqua gesta et facinora sceleratorum regum concinebant populo spectante. Dicti tragoedi quia in initio canentibus praemium erat hircus, quem Graeci *tragos* vocant. Sequentes vero tragici multum honorem adepti sunt, excellentes in argumento fabularum."

[152] Papias: "*Comici* res laetas, traici [Mombrizio: "tragici"] argumenta ex rebus luctuosis describunt." For the rest of this entry, see Kelly, *Tragedy and Comedy*, p. 8, n. 31.

[153] Papias: "*Tragoedia* erat quidquid luctuosis carminibus describebant antiqui. *Tragoedus* vero [cantor] tragoediarum; genus describentium erat qui coturnis uteba[n]tur" (*cantor* is supplied from Mombrizio's text). Cf. *Etymologiae* 8.7.6; 18.45; 19.34.5.

[154] Donatus, *Commentum Terenti* 8.9: "Deverbia histriones pronuntiabant" (p. 30).

[155] Papias under *Comoedia in quattuor*: "Prologus est praefatio fabulae in qua licet absque argumento aliquid ad populum loqui ex comodo poetae vel rectoris. Protesis est primus actus et initium

criticized faults in (or on) the scene;[156] but his entries under *scena* do not include any clear reference to the acting of comedy or tragedy. After defining it as *theatri locus*, he first draws on Remigius in defining the scene as the shade where poets recited. He adds definitions from Placidus, but omits the point about the acting of plays and performing with tragic exclamations. He then repeats what Isidore says about the scene (a house in the theater with a pulpit called an orchestra where comics and tragics sang, and histrions and mimes danced). But he does not give Isidore's subjoined definition of the orchestra, which specified that others acted while the comedic and tragedic poets sang.

Papias's treatment of *persona* is abbreviated from Remigius's commentary on the *Ars minor*; he limits the use of masks to comedians.[157] His definition of *larva* is not enlightening ("an image worn over the face"), and his definition of *dragmaticon*, the type of poem in which only introduced *personae* speak, is illustrated by Vergil's first eclogue. Under *stili*, he does not illustrate the three styles by any reference to poetic genres.

This sampling of various "tradition-mills" in the earliest Middle Ages shows that there is some justification to the now unfashionable term "Dark Ages." Certainly as far as tragedy is concerned, the scholars of the time were largely working in the dark. They did manage to salvage some half-truths, however, and passed on at least the important idea that classical tragedy dealt with misfortune and sadness. But even this notion was not always to be associated with the word "tragedy" in the times that followed.

dragmatis, id est fabulae; cujus protesis persona postea non apparet in fabula, et semper aperit in principio maximam partem."
[156] In the entry on *comoedi* (see n. 144 above).
[157] Papias under *persona*: "Juxta diffinitionem soni dicta a concavitate larvarum quibus comedi utebantur." The whole entry is given in Goetz, *Corpus glossariorum*, 1:181.

4

The twelfth-century scene

In this chapter we shall be studying the ideas of tragedies that emerged during the "renaissance of the twelfth century." This rebirth of classical learning was not only short-lived, but also narrow-placed, being restricted mainly to France and England. Many of the advances made in literary knowledge did not survive as general knowledge through the next century, but some fragments did achieve a later resurrection. There were also some highly influential new formulations of older medieval ideas which were completely untouched by new acquaintance with the classics.

WILLIAM OF CONCHES AND THE COMMENTARIES ON BOETHIUS

Boethius's *Consolation of Philosophy* provided a particularly important channel for traditions of learning. Unfortunately, many of the medieval commentaries on Boethius remain unedited and even unsorted, so that whatever is said here on the matter must necessarily be provisional.

We have looked at versions of commentaries associated with Remigius of Auxerre around the beginning of the tenth century, and we have also examined Notker's translation. There were other Carolingian commentaries on the *Consolation*, but Remigius was by far the most important. Remigian commentaries continued to be copied and modified during the eleventh century, and they exerted influence on later efforts.[1]

Of the several new commentaries produced in the twelfth century,[2] the most important was that of William of Conches (*c.* 1090–*c.* 1155), written around the year 1125 when he had finished his own education at Chartres and begun his teaching career. He is most frequently discussed by scholars of our own day as a Platonist philosopher, and that is the aspect of his Boethian commentary that has received the most attention. But we must

---

[1] Courcelle, *La Consolation*, p. 301; Bolton, "Study," pp. 50, 60.
[2] Courcelle, *La Consolation*, pp. 302–06, isolates five commentaries, but there were also new combinations, or revisions of new and old commentaries, as we shall see in our discussion of William of Conches.

keep in mind that he was also a literary scholar, successor to the Christian humanist Bernard of Chartres so much praised by John of Salisbury; in fact, William was John's own Latin master (from around 1137 to 1140). He commented not only on Plato and Macrobius, but also on Martianus Capella, Priscian, and Juvenal.[3] It is, of course, the literary side of his commentary on Boethius that will most interest us here. The various forms in which Conches's commentary exists are still far from adequately analyzed, but for our purposes it will be enough to speak of a short version and a long version. The long version has sometimes been taken to be a second redaction by Conches himself, but it is more likely a revision by someone else; in any case, it draws heavily on Remigian material.[4]

In the short version of the commentary,[5] Conches glosses Fortune's rhetorical question on the contents of tragedies by observing that she has given Boethius historical examples demonstrating her mutability, and now she shows that the same thing can be seen in literature, for instance in tragedies. He then gives the following definition: "Tragedy is a writing dealing with great iniquities, which begins in prosperity and ends in adversity. And it is contrary to comedy, which begins with some adversity and finishes in prosperity. And it is called tragedy because its writers ['describers'] were remunerated with a goat, in order to point up the filthiness of the vices it contains." He ends by etymologizing tragedy as "goat-praise" or "goat-song."[6]

---

[3] See the biographical essay in Bradford Wilson's edition of William of Conches's *Glosae in Iuvenalem*, pp. 75–86; see also R. W. Southern, "Humanism and the School of Chartres," *Medieval Humanism*, pp. 78–81; Philippe Delhaye, *Christian Philosophy in the Middle Ages*, pp. 79–86.

[4] Courcelle's listing of manuscripts on pp. 409–10 of *La Consolation* is superseded for the present by that of Sylvie Lenormand, "Guillaume de Conches et le commentaire sur la *De consolatione Philosophiae* de Boèce," which was brought to my attention by A. J. Minnis. The long version is considered by J. M. Parent to be Conches's own second redaction (see *La doctrine de la création dans l'Ecole de Chartres*, pp. 123, 215), but in an essay by Minnis and Lodi Nauta in *Chaucer's* Boece *and the Medieval Tradition of Boethius*, ed. Minnis, it is shown to be a thirteenth-century up-dating of the commentary, which draws on works by Aristotle and his Arab commentators not available to Conches. Courcelle, *La Consolation*, p. 410, seems to consider the three manuscripts cited by Parent as separate, anonymous compilations of the commentaries of Remigius and William.

[5] I use Vatican MS lat. 5202, fols. 1–40v, dated by Courcelle and Lenormand as of the thirteenth century (Lenormand mistakenly calls it an Ottoboni MS). Similar texts, at least in the passages dealt with in this study, are found in Vatican MS Ottoboni 1293 (sixteenth century, according to Courcelle, who lists it as a compilation; it is not classified by Lenormand), and in Paris Bibliothèque Nationale MS lat. 14380 (fourteenth century; ascribed on fol. 100 to Linconiensis, that is, Robert Grosseteste).

[6] William of Conches, short text *Glose super Librum Boecii de consolacione*, book 2, prose 2, Vatican MS lat. 5202 fol. 13v: "*Quid tragediarum*. Ostendit exempla quibus poterat perpendere mutabilitatem Fortune. Modo ostendit quid in scriptis potuit perpendi, ut in tragediis. Tragedium [*lege* Tragedia enim] est scriptum de magnis iniquitatibus a prosperitate incipiens et in adversitate desinens. Et est contraria comedie, que ab aliqua adversitate incipiens in prosperitate finitur. Et dicta est tragedia quia descriptores illius ad designandum fetorem viciorum que in ea sunt hirco emunerabantur. *Tragos* enim hircus, *oda* laus vel cantus." As I noted in the Preface, I have used the classical spelling of *oe* and *ae* for the classical diphthongs up through the eleventh century, even though they had long since

For his symbolism of the goat, William may be drawing on Bernard of Utrecht, or a common source, explaining the purpose of tragedy: "ob vitiorum foeditatem exprimendam." Even closer is Bernard's explanation of that other goat-song, the eclogue, where he refers to the "foeditas viciorum quae per hoc animal designatur." Conches may also have seen Bernard's explanation of *oda* as *laus* in his discussion of satire, but the *laus sive cantus* of the Terentian *Expositio* is closer.

Another scholar writing about the same time as Conches definitely drew on Bernard: namely, Conrad of Hirsau in his *Dialogue on Authors*. But he merely says, of tragic poetry, that public affairs and the criminal deeds of the powerful are described in it.[7] He says later that the *tragedi, comici,* and other kinds of Roman authors were no longer studied because the Church did not approve of their false and vain teaching.[8]

No one before William of Conches, it seems, so clearly and unequivocally expressed a plot structure for tragedy and comedy. The closest, perhaps, was Diomedes on tragedy (*laetis rebus exitus tristes*) and Donatus–Evanthius on comedy (*prima turbulenta, tranquilla ultima*). At least, Conches's forms of expression seem completely original. His stress on the evils portrayed in tragedy may also have been inspired by Bernard, and perhaps also by Isidore's account of tragedical poets in the theater. But Conches in no way suggests anything of the theatrical context of tragedy. More surprising, he does not indicate the mournful nature of tragedy, even though the Boethian passage presupposes it. Furthermore, Fortune (or Philosophy) is not referring to tragedies that deal with great iniquities and vices, but rather to tragedies that deal with great misfortunes, such as those that Boethius himself suffered through no fault of his own (though perhaps through the wickedness of others).

In the long version of Conches's commentary,[9] the reviser may have noticed that the discussion of tragedy was rather at variance with the context of the *Consolation*, for he adds to it a paraphrase of Philosophy's meaning: "In this sort of poem [that is, tragedy], you could have taken to heart examples of kings and highly placed men brought down by Fortune's

ceased to be pronounced as diphthongs, to reflect early medieval usage. For texts written in the twelfth century and later, I use *e* for both, to reflect later medieval usage, which came into line with pronunciation.

[7] Conrad of Hirsau, *Dialogus super auctores*, p. 76: "tragicum quo publice res et gesta potentum scelerosa describuntur; *tragos* enim grece, latine hircus dicitur, qui recitatori carminum pro precio dabatur."

[8] *Ibid.*, p. 95

[9] For the long version, I use London British Library MS Royal B 3, fols. 1–143 (dated neither by Courcelle nor Lenormand). Gatherings have been lost between fols. 73 and 74 (book 1, prose 6 to meter 9), fols. 81 and 82 (book 3, prose 10 to prose 11), and at the end (interrupting book 5, prose 6). Also containing a long text for the most part (except at the end) is Vatican MS Ottoboni lat. 612, fols. 6–100 (not classified by Lenormand).

striking without discernment – that is, without expectation, because one knows neither the day nor the hour of one's miseries."[10]

Earlier in his commentary, Conches has an interesting explanation of the *scenice meretricule* (as he would have found it spelled, in high-medieval fashion). The scene, he says, was a certain part of the theater where "persons" were hidden and from which they issued. It was called a scene because the word means "covering" or "shade". But the poetic Muses are called scenic (that is, theatrical) because poets wanted nothing so much as to have their works heard in the theaters. Or they are called scenic in the sense of shady, because they are the shadow of knowledge rather than true knowledge, or because they shadow and becloud the hearts of men.[11] He seems to consider the scene to be a backstage area where actors or performers could wait their turn to appear before the audience. There is no stated connection between these persons and the poets whose works were heard in the theater.

For the reviser of the commentary, however, the scene was not a hiding place, but something that "persons" climbed upon and issued out of, and where the works of the poets were recited.[12] Moreover, as we shall see from another gloss, it was the persons who recited the poets' works. The reviser may honestly have mistaken *abscondebantur* for *ascendebant*, or he may have come across some version of Isidore's discussion of the theater. (Or, alternatively, the presence of the Isidorian concept may be an indication that the long text preserves the original version of Conches's commentary.) Isidore defined the scene as a place in the theater built like a house, with a pulpit called the orchestra which comedic and tragedic poets ascended (*conscendebant*). But though this text still has the persons coming out of the scene, it eliminates the "shady" meaning of the word from the theatrical

---

[10] William of Conches, long text *Glose super Librum Boecii de Consolacione*, book 2, prose 2, British Library MS Royal 15 B 3, fol. 39v: "*Quid tragediarum*, etc. Ostensis exemplis quibus Boethius potuit perpendere ... [continues much as in the short version]. In hoc carmine potuisti perpendere reges et provectos deprimi per Fortunam indiscrete percucientem, id est improvise, quia nescitur dies vel hora miseriarum." Cf. Matthew 25:13: "Vigilate itaque, quia nescitis diem neque horam."

[11] Conches, short text *Glose de consolacione*, book 1, prose 1, Vatican lat. 5202 fol. 5: "Scenice dicuntur quasi teatrales; scena enim dicebatur quedam pars theatri qua abscondebantur persone et exibant; unde dicebatur scena, quasi obumbratio. Scena enim est umbra. Poetice vero muse scenice, id est theatrales, dicuntur, quia ad hoc versabatur tota poetarum intentio, ut in theatris opera eorum audirentur. Vel scenice dicuntur quasi umbratiles, quia sunt umbra sciencie, non vera sciencia; vel quia obumbran[t] et obnubilant corda hominum."

[12] Conches, long text *Glose de consolacione*, book 1, prose 1, British Library Royal 15 B 3 fols. 8v-9: "Scenice vero dicuntur quasi theatrales. Scena enim dicebatur quedam pars theatri qua ascendebant persone et exibant, et ibi recitabantur opera poetarum. Ob hoc ergo dicuntur muse poetice scenice, id est theatrales, quia ad hoc erat sua tota intencio, ut in theatris recitarentur opera sua. Vel dicuntur scenice, id est umbratiles; scena enim dicitur umbra. Dicuntur ergo poetice muse scenice, id est umbratiles, quia sunt umbra sciencie et non vera sciencia, vel quia obumbrant vel obnubilant corda hominum."

context and introduces it only when it takes up the alternative meaning of scenic as obfuscating.

When the long text comes to Boethius's expression *hanc vite scenam*, it supplies a totally new gloss, where there is none in the short text. First, a nontheatrical meaning is suggested, and then a theatrical: "And note that she calls this life a 'scene,' that is a shade, because the life of this world is nothing but a kind of passing shadow. Or she calls it a scene because it is in the scene, that is, in the theater, that the recitation of persons takes place. Such recitation is a vain thing, for while it is heard it gives pleasure, but the pleasure quickly passes. This present life is called a scene by reason of this comparison, for it pleases while we are in it, but it quickly passes."[13]

The long Conches commentary probably took its notion of the recitation of poetry on the scene from Remigius of Auxerre's commentary, or from a commentary based on it. In addition to the commentaries considered in the last chapter, I wish to consider at this point two more Remigius-based texts – only one of which retains the notion of scenic recitation – for, even though both are largely or even entirely Carolingian in content, they came to light and were used in the twelfth century. We may call their authors the Erfurt Anonymous and the Heiligenkreuz Anonymous, from the manuscripts in which they are found.[14]

Both commentators gloss Fortune's question, *Quid tragediarum*, with a version of the "Eusebian" definition added to Remigius's commentary: tragedies are poems that bewail the miseries of men, whether based on "examples of dead men" (Erfurt),[15] or "battles of dead men" (Heiligen-

---

[13] *Ibid.*, book 2, prose 3, fol. 42v: "Et nota quod appellat istam vitam *scenam*, id est, umbraculum, quia vita mundi non est nisi quoddam umbraculum preteriens. Vel ideo dicitur scena quia in scena, id est, in theatro, fit recitacio personarum; et est res vana ista recitacio, quia dum auditur delectat, sed hujus delectatio cito preterit. Ad similitudinem hujus presens vita dicitur scena, quia dum sumus in ea placet, cito tamen preterit."

[14] The only complete copy of the commentary of the Erfurt Anonymous is contained in Erfurt MS Quarto 5 (thirteenth century), fols. 1v–82v. It was edited from three other manuscripts and dated to the ninth century by Edmund Taite Silk, *Saeculi noni auctoris in Boetii Consolationem Philosophiae commentarius.* Silk first believed that the commentary was written by John Scot Eriugena; he later conceded that it was not, but still held that it was Carolingian and predated Remigius's commentary. Courcelle, *La Consolation*, pp. 250–53, 304, summarizes the reasons for placing the author in the twelfth century. Silk's latest contribution on the subject is, "Was Pseudo-Johannes Scottus or Remigius of Auxerre a Plagiarist?"

The other commentary is contained only in Heiligenkreuz MS 130, an interlinear gloss that appears with Boethius's text on fols. 5v–76. It has been analyzed and partially edited by Nicholas M. Haring (Nikolaus M. Häring), "Four Commentaries on the *De consolatione Philosophiae* in MS Heiligenkreuz 130." Haring believes that the commentary may be by Eriugena; at least, he says, the author was familiar with Greek. The second commentary in the same manuscript is that of the Erfurt Anonymous (fols. 77–85v, and also mixed in with the first commentary). The other two are versions of Remigius (fols. 85v–92) and William of Conches (fols. 93–121).

[15] Erfurt Anonymous on book 2 prose 2 (Silk, *Saeculi noni auctoris*, p. 70): "Tragedie sunt carmina que constant exemplis mortuorum hominum et deplorant miserias hominum."

kreuz).[16] Later on, where Boethius cites Euripides as *tragicus*, the Erfurt author glosses the word as "a certain Greek philosopher."[17] Heiligenkreuz instead stitches together other definitions from the glossaries: Tragic poets are those who write tragedies. Tragedy is a poem named after the Greek for goat, which was given to those poets for a reward. "Tragic" signifies sorrow. Tragedy is a fabulous composition, or one that deals with hardship, or contains sorrowful narratives; or it is a warlike song or confabulation.[18]

The Heiligenkreuz Anonymous understands *scena* to refer primarily to a brothel.[19] He then adds the remarks that we found in revisions of Remigius's commentary: the scene was the place where people flowed together to the spectacle, where they engaged in various *ludi*, and defiled themselves with women. Next he traces the meaning of the word to the Greek for shadow, and then gives an abbreviation of Isidore's chapter *De scaena*: The scene was a place within the theater built like a house, in front of (*pro*) a pulpit which was called the orchestra; there comics, traics (*traici*), istrions, and mimes sang. Whether the commentator connected the *traici* with the *tragici* or tragic poets he defines later is not clear. He goes on to give Isidore's etymology of the word (from the Greek for house), and his explanation of the Jewish *scēnopēgia* or dedication of tabernacles.[20] He ends by attributing to the *scena* what Isidore says of the *theatrum* in its meaning of *lupanar* or "brothel": it was where the shame of unhappy women was advertised to the Greeks, and where both active and passive participants were held to ridicule.[21]

The Erfurt commentator's explanation of the "scenic little whores" is based largely on Remigius: the Muses are called scenic because their poems were recited in the scenes. The scene was a place in the theater where books

---

[16] Heiligenkreuz Anonymous on book 2, prose 2 (Haring, "Four Commentaries," p. 298): "Tragedie sunt carmina que constant ex preliis mortuorum et deflent miserias hominum."
[17] Erfurt Anonymous on book 3, prose 6 (Silk, *Saeculi noni auctoris*, p. 137).
[18] Heiligenkreuz Anonymous on book 3, prose 6 (Haring, "Four Commentaries," p. 300): "Tragici: poete tragedias scribentes; quod carmen ab hirco tractum est (qui grece *tragos* dicitur), qui pro mercede poetis dabatur. Tragicus, id est lectus Tragedia compositio fabulosa, vel cum asperitate; vel luctuose relationes; vel bellica cantatio vel fabulatio."
[19] *Ibid.*, on book 1, prose 1 (Haring, "Four Commentaries," p. 296): "Scena est proprie locus vel habitatio meretricum."
[20] Cf. Isidore, *Etymologiae* 18.43.
[21] Heiligenkreuz Anonymous (Haring, "Four Commentaries," p. 296): "Ibi enim Grecis pudor mulierum infelicium publicabatur, et ludibrio habebantur et hi qui faciebant et qui paterentur." Cf. *Etymologiae* 18.42.2: "Lupanaria enim a paganis constitua sunt ut pudor mulierum infelicium ibi publicaretur, et ludibrio haberentur tam hi qui facerent quam qui paterentur." The correct reading, evident from Isidore's source (Lactantius, *Diuinae institutiones* 6.23.7) should be "*quae* paterentur": the devil set up *lupanaria* and advertised the shame of unhappy women, to make a mockery both of these who do the deeds, and the women who must suffer them ("ut ludibrio haberet tam eos qui faciunt quam quas pati necesse est," CSEL 19:565).

were recited: "Est autem scena locus in theatro ubi libri recitabantur."[22]
This is clearly an abbreviated misreading of Remigius: "Est enim scaena
locus ubi exercebantur ludi et carmina recitabantur." But when Erfurt
comes to explain *hanc vite scenam*, he produces another explanation. He first
defines *scena* as "shade," but then says that it signifies the world because of
the scene's variety, in the way in which it was turned and moved about; for
as different tragedies were recited on it (or in it), corresponding figures
would be placed before the eyes of the seated audience, and they took a
delight in the diversity of the figures as well as in the diversity of the
tragedies. The scene was constructed of double tables. But when it was set
up on the periphery, the first tables would be drawn behind it, so that those
sitting there could take pleasure in the figures on the inside as well. Or it
was so managed that the figures concurred with the different "persons"
represented by the comics.[23]

I shall not attempt to visualize the author's fanciful picture of the theater,
for the necessary context of his ideas is lacking. He was perhaps inspired by
Servian accounts of how *tabulata* or *tabulae* came to be used in building the
scene. But it is clear that he considered tragedies to be poems that were
recited, with movable visual aids in the background. It is not clear who did
the reciting, or whether comic actors represented characters in the recited
tragedies, or whether comedies were acted and not recited, or acted as well
as recited, in contrast to tragedies.

Another prominent Boethian scholar was Gilbert of La Porrée, who
became bishop of Poitiers in 1142 (d. 1154). He succeeded Bernard of
Chartres as chancellor of Chartres in 1126, but he is mainly known for his
teaching career at Paris, where he taught logic and theology; John of
Salisbury was one of his students in 1141.[24] Gilbert commented not on the
Consolation, but on the theological treatises.[25] He therefore had the
advantage of knowing how histrions used masks in speaking and acting
tragedies and comedies. But he interprets the method of delivery as

---

[22] Erfurt Anonymous on book 1, prose 1 (Silk, *Saeculi noni auctoris*, p. 16). He adds another reason based
on a supposed verb, *scenare*, "to deceive," and then gives Remigius's alternative explanation for
scaena as perfume.

[23] *Ibid.* on book 2, prose 2 (Silk, *Saeculi noni auctoris*, pp. 76–77): "*In hanc scenam*, id est, in hoc
umbraculum vite. Scena per varietatem sui mundum significat. Erat enim versilis et ductilis, que ideo
vertebatur ut, sicut diverse tragedie in ea recitabantur, ita diverse figure oculis residentium
anteponerentur et ita varietate figurarum sicut diversitate tragediarum delectarentur. Que etiam
constabat duplicibus tabulis; ubi vero ducta fuisset in circuitu subducebantur priores tabule, ut
figuris quoque interioris ibi residentes delectarentur. Vel ideo agebatur ut diversis personis a comicis
ibi representatis ipse figure concurrerent."

[24] Southern, *Medieval Humanism*, pp. 67–72; for his philosophical teachings, see Delhaye, *Christian
Philosophy*, pp. 81–83.

[25] *The Commentaries on Boethius by Gilbert of Poitiers*, ed. N. M. Haring; given also in PL 64:1255ff.

recitation: "in recitandis comediis tragediisque."[26] In using this expression he may have been influenced by one or other of the *Consolation* commentaries. He speaks of the "comediarum tragediarumque recitandarum persone,"[27] which resembles the *recitatio personarum* of the expanded Conches commentary. But in Gilbert's case there is no doubt that he knows what he is talking about, at least to a certain extent, and the same is probably true of several of his followers or readers, or the readers of Boethius.[28]

Abelard, one of Gilbert's teachers, shows a less clear understanding. He cites Boethius on the "persons" of tragedies and comedies to support his notion that the persons of comedies are men who, by their gestures, represent deeds and words.[29] He seems to indicate that the actors of the comedies he mentions (perhaps referring to contemporary entertainments) do not speak. But he may simply be abbreviating Remigius.

Gilbert does not define tragedy, but he knows that Hecuba and Medea are characters in tragedy.[30] Perhaps he assumed it by the process of elimination, if he knew that Simo and Chremes were characters of comedy from their appearance in Terence's *Andria*. When he comes to explain the *tanta tragedia* of Christ's generation, he indicates his understanding of tragedy as some kind of "come-down," or loss of status. Boethius means, he says, "such a great humbling of so high a thing, that He whose generation was without time should be generated in time." But it also

---

[26] Gilbert on *Contra Eutychen* 3, section 19 (Haring, *Boethius by Gilbert*, p. 275).

[27] *Ibid.*, section 24 (Haring, *Boethius by Gilbert*, p. 276).

[28] See Marshall, "Boethius' Definition of *Persona* and the Mediaeval Understanding of the Roman Theater." One oddity in Gilbert's account is that he thinks of the performances as taking place in amphitheaters (section 26, Haring, *Boethius by Gilbert*, p. 277). See Marshall, "Boethius' Definition," p. 474. The same is true of Gilbert's disciple, Hugh of Honau, writing about 1180, in his *Liber de diversitate nature et persone proprietatumque personalium non tam latinorum quam ex grecorum auctoritatibus extractis* 13.2, ed. Haring, "The *Liber de diversitate naturae et personae* by Hugh of Honau," p. 138: "Personarum scenicarum ac theatralium que in amphiteatris in ludis imperialibus in comediarum et tragediarum representationibus introducebantur, principaliter et proprie fuit hoc nomen [i.e., persona]." But he also speaks of these productions as occurring in the theater, and he does not use the term *recitatio*. Rather, by speaking of the histrions' sonority of voice, he indicates that each actor spoke words appropriate to the characters represented – of which he gives several examples: "In quarum representationibus talis observabatur modus, ut hystriones larvis faciem suam obducerent ne cognoscerentur, et ut tam ordinabilis aptaque fieret tota larvalis dispositio – que et vulgo admirationem moveret et omnibus in theatro delectabile spectaculum preberet – atque tam assimilata in sonoritate vocis et forma larvali ejus qui representandus esset imitatio foret, et tam expressa pro suo cujusque modo et proprietate configurato, ut per eam certa sui fieret et ab omnibus aliis in scena representandis discreta cognitio: velut Achillis vel Hectoris in armis, Priami ad aram occumbentis, Hecube necem viri et nati plangentis, Symonis et Cremetis filii lasciviam aut servi dolos objurgantis" (*ibid.*).

[29] Abelard, *Theologia christiana* 3 (PL 178:1258D): "Personas etiam comediarum dicimus ipsos videlicet homines qui per gestus suos aliqua nobis facta vel dicta representant." The whole passage is in Marshal, "Boethius' Definition," p. 474.

[30] Gilbert, section 27 (Haring, *Boethius by Gilbert*, p. 277).

involved a cast of thousands, as it were: so many *persone*, from Abraham, or from Adam, until the time of Christ.[31] Of the commentaries on the tractates that survive from the circle of Theodoric Brito of Chartres (usually called by the modern French version of Theodoric, Thierry), who died around 1157, there survives only the one on the *Contra Eutychen*, or *De trinitate*, and that in fragmentary form.[32] In the discussion on masks, the commentator avoids mentioning or commenting on the terms "tragedy" and "comedy" and the characters named by Boethius. He says only that *persone* were masked men, *larvati*, who represented men, that is, who were brought into theaters to "represent people concerned," in other words, people whose representation is useful or profitable for the instruction of morals.[33] He calls the *larvati* at one point *theatrales*, and *histriones* are identified as "joculatores vel qui aliquid representabant."[34]

Thierry of Chartres himself mentions the word "tragedy" once in his commentary on the *Rhetorica ad Herennium* at the point where oratorical and tragical practices are contrasted. He says, "reciters of tragedy at times use an excessively loud voice in their recitations, and this mode of enunciation does not suit orators."[35] He seems to have nothing very classical in mind for tragedy. Another, somewhat earlier, writer of the time, Marbod of Rennes (1035–1123), knew that tragedians recited the sort of accounts related by poets and historians. In his *Book of Ten Chapters*,[36] he says in the chapter on "The Bad Woman" (which is balanced by the next chapter, "The Good Woman"):

---

[31] *Ibid.*, 5, section 52 (Haring, *Boethius by Gilbert*, p. 325): "*Quo*, id est, ad quid et cujus utilitatis causa tanquam rei facte ficta est. *Tanta*, id est, tot personarum vel ab Abraham vel ab Adam usque ad Christum. *Generationis* ejus *tragedia*, hoc est, rei adeo alte tanta humiliatio ut ille, cujus generatio erat sine tempore, generaretur in tempore."

[32] *Commentarius in Boethii librum contra Eutychen et Nestorium: Fragmentum londinense*, ed. N. M. Haring, *Commentaries on Boethius by Thierry of Chartres and His School*; it covers the very end of part 1, all of parts 2 and 3, and some of part 4. On Thierry himself, see Southern, *Medieval Humanism*, pp. 81–83, who calls him "the complete teacher of the liberal arts of his day" (p. 81).

[33] *Commentarius in Boethii* on part 3, section 5 (Haring, *Boethius by Thierry*, p. 236): "*Ex his scilicet personis*, i.e. ex larvatis, *que*, scilicet persone, *representabant*, i.e. adducebantur in theatris ad representandum, *homines quorum*, i.e. hominum, *interest*, i.e. quorum representatio utilis est, scilicet quos representare prodest ad instructionem morum."

[34] *Ibid.*, sections 7–8 (Haring, *Boethius by Thierry*, p. 237).

[35] Thierry of Chartres, *Commentarius super Rhetoricam ad Herennium*, ed. Karen Margareta Fredborg, *The Latin Rhetorical Commentaries by Thierry of Chartres*, p. 297, commenting on 3.14.24, "ne ab oratoria consuetudine ad tragicam transeamus" (see Kelly, *Tragedy and Comedy*, p. 29). His comment reads in the original: "Recitatores scilicet tragedie quandoque voce nimis grossa in recitationibus suis utuntur, qui modus pronuntiandi non competit oratoribus."

[36] Marbod of Rennes, *Liber decem capitulorum*, ed. Leotta. He wrote the work after becoming bishop of Rennes in 1096.

> Multas pretereo, quas commemorare poete
> Historieque solent, Eriphylen et Clytemestram,
> Belides et Procnen concertatamque decenni
> Terrarum bello Leda genitam meretricem,
> Quasque solent alias populo recitare tragedi. (3.40–44)

(I omit many whom poets and histories are accustomed to commemorate – Eripyle and Clytemnestra, the Danaids and Procne and the prostitute born of Leda over whom a ten-year world war was fought – and whom elsewhere [or: "and others whom"] tragedians are accustomed to recite to the people.)

Presumably the present tense that he uses for the tragedians refers no more to his own day than does the same tense applied to the poets and historians. There is a slight possibility that Marbod had some acquaintance with Seneca's tragedies or a florilegium of extracts.[37] Of the women mentioned, only Clytemnestra and Helen figure in the plays (in *Agamemnon* and *Troades*, respectively). Eripyle appears most prominently in the *Thebaid*, the Danaids in the *Heroides*, and Procne in the *Metamorphoses*.[38] There are no definite signs of knowledge of Seneca's plays – or extracts from them – until around 1200.[39] As a student of Ovid, Marbod is probably thinking of his discussion of the tragedies of love in the *Tristia*, which includes a reference to Clytemnestra ("the crime of Aegisthus and the daughter of Tyndareus"),[40] which is immediately preceded by a characterization of Helen in the *Iliad* as "adultera de qua/Inter amatorem pugna virumque fuit" ("an adulteress over whom there was a battle between her lover and her husband").[41] We remember that Ovid calls tragedy here a *genus scripti*, and refers to a *scriptum regale* of his own that he gave to the *tragici cothurni*, and says that his *poemata* were often *saltata populo*. Marbod's reference to the Belids or Danaids probably comes from a line in the next section of the *Tristia*,[42] and the final line cited is verbally indebted to a distich in *Ex Ponto* in which Ovid speaks of reciting his *scripta*.[43]

[37] See Zwierlein, "Spuren," 183–95.
[38] Statius, *Thebaid* 4.187–213; Ovid, *Heroides* 14; *Metamorphoses* 6.424–674.
[39] See E. R. Smits, "Helinand of Froidmont and the A-Text of Seneca's Tragedies," p. 326. Smits believes that the extensive quotations from the tragedies in the *Chronicon* of Helinand of Froidmont (*c.* 1160–after 1229) are taken from the complete plays ("Helinand," pp. 338–43). But Zwierlein, *Prolegomena zu einer kritischen Ausgabe der Tragödien Senecas*, pp. 153–54, believes that he was drawing on the florilegium that was the source of the extracts given by Vincent of Beauvais and others in the thirteenth century (see chapter 5 below). In any case, Helinand shows no interest in the term "tragedy," or in the way in which Seneca presents the action. The excerpts are edited by Smits in "Helinand," pp. 347–58.   [40] Ovid, *Tristia* 2.396.   [41] *Ibid.* 2.371–72.
[42] *Ibid.* 3.1.62: "Belides et stricto barbarus ense pater." See Leotta's note.
[43] Ovid, *Ex Ponto* 4.2.37–38: "Hic mea cui recitem nisi flavis scripta Corallis, / Quasque alias gentes barbarus Hister habet." Literally, this means, "To whom shall I recite my writings here except to the yellow-haired Coralli and whatever other races the barbarous Hister holds?" But Marbod could have read *quasque alias gentes* as parallel to *scripta*, and therefore as referring to the subject of his writings: "To whom shall I recite my writings and the various races of the barbarous Hister?" At any rate, he

The different meanings and nuances of the word "tragedy," whether explicit or implied, that we have seen in this section are interesting in showing the varied changes that can be rung on a term because of the diverse reading backgrounds of individual authors and their respective limited exposures to traditional usages. But, as noted at the beginning, it is William of Conches's formulations that are most significant in terms of their effect on posterity. In commenting on the *Consolation of Philosophy*, Conches negates Boethius's sympathetic presentation of tragedy as bewailing unexpected disasters befalling even the most blameless of persons and peoples. He ignores Isidore of Seville's neutral view in book 8 of the *Etymologies* (tragedy deals with the mournful aspects of republics and historical kings), which would have been in keeping with the Boethian context. Instead, he says that tragedy treats of great iniquities. This definition corresponds to Isidore's book 18, which incorporates the patristic animus against the genre (tragedians sing of the misdeeds of wicked kings). Conches does give the Horatian etymology of book 8, but he darkens it to accord with the iniquitous subject matter: the prize goat was given to underline the filthiness of the vices described in tragedy.

Conches's definition of tragedy as a *scriptum* beginning in prosperity and ending in adversity, which answers to nothing in Isidore or other available traditions, was to have an important future, along with its comedic converse. His characterization establishes the form as a purely narrative genre, and gives no hint of the dramatic aspects explained by Isidore in book 18.

METAPHORICAL TRAGEDY

So far we have seen no evidence that twelfth-century views of tragedy, or comedy, were affected by a fresh reading of the classics, except in the case of Marbod of Rennes. If it is true, as has been suggested, that William of Conches was the author of the *Moralium dogma philosophorum*, which draws heavily on Terence and Horace,[44] he may have written it, and read these authors, only after his commentary on Boethius. I should note that the title of his *Dragmaticon philosophie* refers not to drama but to dialogue.[45]

We can find an abundance of first-hand citations of the classics in the writings of the man best known for his learning in the twelfth century,

adapts the *quasque alias* to this construction in his own line.
[44] William of Conches, *Moralium dogma philosophorum*, ed. Holmberg.
[45] André Wilmart, "Préface de Guillaume de Conches pour la dernière partie de son *Dialogue*," note 2, points out that the work is titled in the manuscripts not only *Dragmaticon*, but also *Dialogus*, *Philosophia*, and so on.

John of Salisbury, in his *Policraticus*, which he finished in the year 1159. John has a fairly good understanding of how ancient drama was produced: histrions brought real or fictitious histories before the public eye by means of bodily gesture, and artful use of words and vocal modulation. Examples of the form, he says, can be found in Plautus, Menander, and Terence. He knows the difference between dramatic poets (*comici et tragici*) and dramatic actors (*comedi et tragedi*).[46] He does not, however, seem to know about the use of masks, though he was acquainted with at least some of the works and doctrines of Gilbert of La Porrée.[47] He was also directly acquainted with the plays of Terence, and might have seen the authentic illustrations of the masked actors which appeared in at least some of the Terentian manuscripts. The Carolingian tradition of classical illumination was continued through the twelfth century.[48]

John of Salisbury is famous for his metaphorical fugue on the subject of "all the world's a stage."[49] He was inspired by some lines from the *Satyricon* in which the activity of the multitude is seen as a mime-play on a stage, which is over when the page closes on their ridiculous parts.[50] He admires Petronius's "elegant simile," for it is true that almost everything that is done by the common crowd is more like a comedy than the *res gesta* of real life. He recalls Job's metaphor, that the life of man upon earth is a battle (*militia*), and says that if Job had foreseen John's day he would have called it a comedy in which each person is oblivious of himself and acts out another's role; and, what is worse, he enters so far into his comedy that he cannot get out of it. This secular comedy captures the minds of great men; the successive periods of time are acts in which the characters play out their parts until the roles in the play assigned to them by joking Fortune are finished.[51]

But the way in which Fortune casts the roles, for example by turning an orator into a consul and vice versa,[52] makes John think that the life of men is more like a tragedy than a comedy. We need not be surprised at his reason: because almost everyone's end is sad, while all the sweet things of the world, no matter how great they are, turn bitter, and (quoting Proverbs 14:13) mourning succeeds the extremities of joy: "In eoque vita hominum tragedie quam comedie videtur esse similior, quod omnium fere tristis est

[46] John of Salisbury, *Policraticus* 1.8, ed. Webb, PL 199:405AB. (I follow Webb in using the PL references.)
[47] See Haring, Introduction to *Boethius by Gilbert*. When John speaks of the persons of comedy as adapted to each other, he is referring to roles or characters. See below.
[48] Millard Meiss *et al.*, *French Painting in the Time of Jean de Berry*, part 2: *The Limbourgs and Their Contemporaries*, 1:45–46 and 2:figs. 173–74.
[49] See Ernst Robert Curtius, *European Literature and the Latin Middle Ages*, pp. 138–40.
[50] John of Salisbury, *Policraticus* 3.7 (488CD), citing Petronius, *Satyricon* 80.
[51] *Ibid.*, 3.8 (488D–489C). [52] *Ibid.*, citing Juvenal, *Satires* 7.197–98.

exitus, dum omnia mundi dulcia quantacumque fuerint amarescunt, 'et extrema gaudii luctus occupat.' " The wicked men whom Fortune serves according to their desires will in the end find themselves tripped up by her, and she will become as bitter as absinthe.[53]

We have encountered the notion of the world as a theater in which Fortune puts on plays, giving good fortune to some and bad fortune to others, in the Remigian tradition. If John knew of it, he translated these plays into two kinds, comedies and tragedies. It is clear that he considers the main feature of tragedy to be the mournful ending, and gives the specific case of the fortunate wicked who wind up in misfortune. He may have known William of Conches's definition of tragedy as an account of great iniquities beginning in prosperity and ending in adversity. As already noted, John had been Conches's student: he studied grammar under him at Chartres from 1137 to 1140. His emphasis on the tragic ending is illustrated later when he justifies the use of pagan fictions (like Fortune) to make the point that the end of all things is tragic.[54] But he does not argue with those who consider life to be a comedy rather than a tragedy, since they agree with Petronius that almost everyone plays the part of a histrion. The world is the theater in which this universal and indescribable tragedy or comedy can be acted out, and the *area* or stage on which the players act is as vast as the earth's globe.[55]

Not everyone, however, joins in the acting. The play has spectators as well, namely, men of virtue who refuse to partake in the madness. Their end is thought to be without honor (tragic, perhaps?), because they refrain from polluting the dignity of their nature with the costume of a worldly actor. From the high prospect of their virtues they look down with disdain on the theater of the world and the play of Fortune; and together with God and the angels they watch the actions of the worldly comedy and circus games.[56] John goes on to illustrate the interconnectedness of the roles in the *ludibrium* or playful mockery of Fortune by citing characters (*persone*) from Terence's *Andria*.[57]

Salisbury speaks of specific events, as well as life in general, in theatrical terms. As an example of what lack of moderation in feasting can lead to, he cites the banquets of Herod and Pharaoh, which resulted in a tragic end and

---

[53] *Ibid.* (489D).
[54] *Ibid.* (491A): "Ut ergo gentilium figmentis pium accommodemus auditum, rerum omnium tragicus finis est."
[55] *Ibid.* (491B).
[56] *Ibid.* 3.9 (394D–494A). Apuleius, *Metamorphoses* 6.23, speaks of a convocation of the gods "in the heavenly theater." Cf. Augustine, *Sermones* 51.1.2, PL 38:333, speaking of the games in which the martyrs were exposed to wild animals: "Alii vero, sicut et sancti angeli, spectant."
[57] *Policraticus* 3.10 (494AB).

the defilement of manslaughter.[58] He considers Cleopatra's death a fitting one; she who once had commanded kings became miserable but not pitiable; her end might have been tragic to her, but it was comic to the Roman Empire that she tried to subvert.[59] John was not the first to see the tragic dimension of her career. Lucian named the story of Cleopatra the Egyptian as the nether limit of the good dancer's tragic repertory: he must know everything from Chaos to Cleopatra.[60]

Salisbury calls Petronius, or his character Eumolpus, *tragicus* when relating a history or fable about the fickleness of women. Eumolpus, however, did not call his story of the Widow of Ephesus a tragedy, but simply said that he was not drawing on old tragedies or on names known to the ages, but on an incident that had happened in his lifetime.[61] At the end of his retelling of the story, John remarks that Petronius was not the only one to ridicule or display the defects of women, for, as St. Jerome pointed out, all of the tragedies of Euripides were maledictions against women.[62]

Another striking theatrical metaphor which seems to be informed by knowledge of the classics, or at least of Boethius, is found in the life of St. Prudentius, written by a learned Burgundian monk named Teobaud some time after 1124. One of the miracles that occurred in Teobaud's own times through the intercession of the saint was the restoration of a dead man to life. The mourning that followed upon his death is described thus:

Personant itaque tragedie muliercularum, singula (ut fit) mortui insignia in planctus revocantium.[63]

(Tragedies of the womenfolk sound forth, recalling in their complaints (as is usual) each of the dead man's outstanding qualities.)

The word *personant* may be a sign that Teobaud knew Boethius's discussion of *personae* in *Against Eutyches*. The first line of the widow's poetic lament that follows, "Ecce mesta cogor loqui Letho de convivio," draws on the first meter of Boethius's *Consolation*.[64]

Somewhat earlier in the twelfth century, the mysterious Honorius Augustodunensis used an interesting theatrical metaphor. In the *Gemma anime*, or *Jewel of the Soul*, which he wrote in England, he speaks of those

---

[58] *Ibid.* 8.9 (741B).

[59] *Ibid.* 3.10 (495B): "Profecto antea regibus imperaverat, postmodum misera nec miserabilis sibi forte tragicum, sed romano imperio, quod subvertere moliebatur, finem comicum fecit."

[60] Lucian, *Dance* 37.

[61] Petronius, *Satyricon* 110–12.

[62] *Policraticus* 8.11 (753B–755A). For Jerome, see p. 31 above.

[63] Teobaud, *Acta, translationes, et miracula sancti Prudentii martyris* 4.3.95, p. 376. On the author, see pp. 346, 377.

[64] Teobaud 4.3.96; cf. Boethius, *De consolatione*, book 1, meter 1, line 2: "Flebilis heu maestos cogor inire modos."

who used to recite tragedies in the theater and to represent the activity of combatants by their gestures. Just as, he says, the priest, *tragicus noster*, by his gestures represents the combat of Christ in the theater of the church. In Honorius's view, a tragedy can clearly have a triumphant end, for the priest as tragedian impresses upon the Christian people the victory of Christ's redemption.[65] Honorius's idea of comparing theatrical and ecclesiastical forms may have been partially inspired by the early Fathers.[66] For instance, Quodvultdeus contrasts the fictitious god Jupiter, whom spectators see in the theater committing adultery and thundering, with the true God of the Christians. The same Jupiter is shown to have Juno as both sister and wife, "whereas we preach holy Mary as both mother and virgin. In the theater, a man walks on a tightrope, whereas Peter walks on water. Chastity is violated in the theater through the turpitude of the mimes, whereas lust is restrained through the example of the chaste Susanna and Joseph. In the theater, the chorus and song of the pantomime attracts the ear, but overcomes sound affection, in contrast to our songs. In the theater one can admire the skill of the 'scandalists,' seeing children playing in the air and showing various histories, but we too have a play of infants: the story of how Rebecca's two sons fought in her womb."[67] There is no specific mention of tragedy in this or other suggested passages. St. Jerome makes such a link, but in a disapproving fashion: "one should not medicate one's throat after the fashion of tragedians, so that theatrical modulations and songs will be heard in church." His statement was included in the collection of canons made by Anselm of Lucca (d. 1086) and in Gratian's *Decretum* (*c.* 1140), where the text reads, "in tragediarum modum" ("after the fashion of tragedies").[68]

[65] Honorius Augustodunensis, *Gemma anime* 1.83, PL 172:570AB: "Sciendum quod hi qui tragedias in theatris recitabant, actus pugnantium gestibus populo representabant. Sic tragicus noster pugnam Christi populo christiano in theatro ecclesie gestibus suis representat, eique victoriam redemptionis sue inculcat."

[66] Bigongiari, 'Were There Theaters in the Twelfth and Thirteenth Centuries?" 212; Marshall, "Boethius' Definition," p. 471. A disapproving comparison can be found in the twelfth canon of the English Council of Clovesho, AD 746–47: "Priests are not to chatter in church after the fashion of secular poets, lest they corrupt or confound the composition and distinctiveness of the sacred words with a tragic tone, but rather let them use a simple and holy melody according to the custom of the Church" ("Ut presbyteri saecularium poetarum modo in ecclesia non garriant, ne tragico sono sacrorum verborum compositionem ac distinctionem corrumpant vel confundant, sed simplicem sanctamque melodiam secundum morem Ecclesiae sectentur"), in *Councils and Ecclesiastical Documents Relating to Great Britain and Ireland*, 3:366.

[67] Quodvultdeus, *De symbolo* 1.2.10–21 (CCL 60:308–09), cited by Marshall, "Boethius' Definition," p. 479 n. 5, as still attributed to Augustine, *De symbolo* 2.2.4 (PL 40:639).

[68] Jerome on Ephesians 5:19, *Commentum* 3.5, PL 26: 562A: "nec in tragoedorum modum guttur et fauces dulci medicamine colliniendas, ut in ecclesia theatrales moduli audiantur et cantica." Modified in the canon *Cantantes* in Gratian, *Decretum* 1.92.1, ed. Emil Friedberg, *Corpus iuris canonici*, 1:317: "Nec in tragediarum modum guttur et fauces medicamine liniende sunt, ut in ecclesia teatrales moduli audiantur et cantica." For Anselm of Lucca, see Friedberg, *Corpus iuris canonica*, 1:xlix.

But it is clear that Honorius's idea of tragedy is more medieval than classical. In another work, *De anime exsilio*, he says that there are four kinds of poetry, namely, tragedies, comedies, satires, and lyrics. He knows enough of the classics to give Persius as an example of a satirist, and Horace as a lyricist (a writer of odes, that is, poems in praise of the gods or kings). He even cites Terence as a writer of comedies – though he characterizes comedies as songs about marriages. But for tragedies he follows a glossarial definition: they deal with wars; and he gives Lucan as an example.[69] He is much closer to Isidore of Seville than to John of Salisbury. According to Isidore, poets are lyric, tragic, comic, new comic (or satiric), and theologic. Terence is offered as an example of the (old) comic poet, and Persius of the satiric. Lucan, however, is given as an example of a nonpoet who writes history instead of poetry.[70] Isidore seems to be following Servius on this last point, and reflecting also an opinion found in the *Satyricon*.[71]

An explanation for Lucan's association with tragedy can perhaps be found in the Tegernsee *Accessus ad auctores*, which exists in a mid-twelfth-century manuscript. The portion on Lucan is also be found in a manuscript of similar date from the Bavarian abbey of Benediktbeuern, which was closely associated with the abbey of Tegernsee.[72] The treatment of Lucan begins with a long account of Roman history, which concentrates on the strife between Julius Caesar and Pompey and its aftermath. Then there is a rapid listing of the first emperors: Augustus, Tiberius, Caligula, and Nero, but a description is given of Nero: "The wicked baldpate who killed his mother and polluted his sisters; who conquered Cordova, a city in Burgundy; there he seized Lucan and Seneca his uncle, whom he made his own pedagogue, and brought them to Rome. He, when he pondered upon the praise and usefulness of writers, entered upon a desire to write; for he was a very fine tragedian, being master of the grand style."[73] This last

[69] Honorius, *De anime exsilio et patria* 2 (PL 172:1243D): "Libri poetarum ... in quattuor species dividuntur, scilicet in tragedias, in comedias, in satyrica, in lyrica. Tragedie sunt que bella tractant, ut Lucanus. Comedie sunt que nuptialia cantant, ut Terentius. Satyre que reprehensiva scribunt, ut Persius. Lyrica que odas, id est, laudes deorum vel regum hymnilega voce resonant, ut Horatius."
[70] Isidore, *Etymologiae* 8.7.4–10. Isidore lists a good many more kinds of poems in his section on meters, 1.39.5–25.
[71] Servius on *Aeneid* 1.382; Petronius, *Satyricon* 118. See Eva Matthews Sanford, "Lucan and His Roman Critics," pp. 234–35.
[72] *Accessus*, ed. Huygens, p. 2, describing Munich MSS clm 19475 (T = Tegernsee) and clm 4593 (B = Benediktbeuern). Huygens says that the final part of the Lucan accessus is lacking in B, yet it is quoted by Sanford, "The Manuscripts of Lucan: *Accessus* and *Marginalia*," p. 285. For the date of the Tegernsee MS as *c.* 1150, see Peter Dronke, "A Note on *Pamphilus*."
[73] *Accessus ad auctores*, p. 42: "Augustus XL annos regnavit, post hunc ejus privignus Livie filius Tiberius Germanicus Claudius Nero Cesar, post hunc Gajus Cesar Galigula, post hunc Nero calvus nequam, qui matrem occidit, stuprum sororibus intulit; qui Cordubam civitatem Burgundie vicit; ibi Lucanum et [T: Senecam] avunculum [T: ejus], quem sibi pedagogum fecit, rapuit et Romam duxit. Hic cum scribentium laudem et utilitatem perpenderet, scribendi desiderium invadit: fuit enim

sentence would apply just as easily to Nero or Seneca as to Lucan, and I suggest that in the original source of this account it was Nero who was designated as a *tragoedus* (which he was in fact, as we have seen), though probably not in such favorable terms; and that the antecedent was later taken to be Lucan. Perhaps a similar explanation is at the root of the ascription of tragedies to Seneca, for it is by no means certain that Seneca the Younger was the author of the tragedies attributed to him.[74]

After a parenthetical discussion of tragedy (to which I shall return), the accessor notes that Lucan was accused before Nero of conspiring against him and was killed, as was Seneca after him. The matter of "this work" (that is, the *Pharsalia*, which has not yet been mentioned) is then discussed, and then its intention. One possible intention was to praise Nero through his "parents," that is, Julius Caesar and Augustus, of whose line he was; and this praise is rightly understood as vituperation.[75] Perhaps this notion was inspired by Vacca's report in his life of Lucan (which precedes the accessus in the Benediktbeuern copy)[76] that Lucan won a prize for reciting Nero's praises in the theater of Pompey, and thereby incurred Nero's anger.[77]

There follows a discourse on the three styles, *humilis*, *mediocris*, and *grandiloquus* (Lucan is later judged to be *grandiloquus*), and then an account of Lucan's meter, which is heroic: it deals with human and divine persons, and contains truth mixed with fiction. Of the three modes or styles of reciting, namely, the dramatic, the exagematic (narrative), and the mixed, Lucan's is the mixed, for both author and introduced persons speak. Lucan is said to be both *historicus* and *satiricus*, and the Benediktbeuern copy adds *heroicus*.[78] But there is no further mention of his being a *tragedus*.

The accessus explains tragedy as coming from the Greek for goat, which was given to the writers of tragedy as a prize. Tragedy dealt with regal persons, and had a joyful beginning and a sad ending. It differs from comedy, which means "village-song"; comedy has middle-level persons, a tearful beginning, and a joyful ending.[79] The language, particularly in the

optimus tragedus, stilo florens grandiloquo."
[74] See Kelly, "Tragedy and the Performance of Tragedy," 41 (n. 84) and 44.
[75] *Accessus*, p. 43.
[76] Sanford, "Lucan," p. 281.
[77] Kelly, "Tragedy and the Performance of Tragedy," p. 32 n. 40.
[78] *Accessus*, pp. 43–44, and Sanford, "Manuscripts of Lucan."
[79] *Accessus*, pp. 42–43, T text: "*Tragos* grece, latine dicitur hircus, inde *tragedia*, quia hircus scribenti tragediam dabatur in precio. Hec regales personas habens materiam, leto principio, tristi fine contexebatur. Differt ergo tragedia a comedia, quia *comos* est vicus, *ode* carmen; unde *comedia*, quia mediocres habet personas, flebile principium, letum finem." For "Hec ... contexebatur," MS B has "regales personas habens materiam. *Tragedia leto principio, tristi exitu contexebatur*" (the italicized words are written in the margin).

Benediktbeuern text, is closest to Diomedes in expressing the plot structure of tragedy: *laetis rebus exitus tristes*; but in speaking of the characters of comedy it recalls Donatus's *mediocres fortunae hominum*. There is, we note, no suggestion that tragedy dealt with evil in high places. The same is true of the explanation of tragedy in one of the accessuses to Ovid's *Amores* that appears in the Tegernsee manuscript, in which the figures of Tragedy and Elegy are discussed. Tragedy is the goddess of poetry dealing with the deeds of nobles and kings, whereas Elegy is the goddess of misery: for miseries and adversities also happen in love.[80]

Unlike Honorius, the author of the Lucan accessus does not speak of gestures in the performance of tragedy. But the sort of gestures that a reciter of the *Pharsalia* might use would not be much different from those of the priest at mass (which Honorius goes on to detail in the *Gemma anime*), and he may have had in mind the kind of performances given by minstrels in his own day.

There is a clear instance of the poetry recited by minstrels being identified or associated with tragedies in the *Speculum caritatis* of Aelred, or Ethelred, of Rievaulx. Writing in his Yorkshire monastery of Rievaulx[81] around the year 1142 at the request of his fellow Cistercian Bernard of Clairvaux, Aelred explains to a novice that the love of God is not to be judged in terms of the momentary emotion aroused by poetic fictions:

> For when in tragedies or vain poems someone is made out to be injured or oppressed and his lovable beauty, wonderful courage, and graceful affection are described, if a person who hears it sung or sees it recited is moved to tears by a certain affection, is it not absurd to try to form some opinion of the quality of his love from this empty pity – to say, for instance, that he loves this imaginary figure, when in fact he would not be willing to spend a modicum of his wealth to rescue him, even if it were all truly happening before his eyes?[82]

It is even more ridiculous, Aelred says, to suppose that God loves persons who easily weep empty tears, but do not reform their lives, more than He loves those who do His will. The novice agrees, and recalls his own experience of being aroused by fiction:

---

[80] *Accessus*, pp. 36–37: "Et sciendum est quod Tragedia dea est facti carminis de gestis nobilium et regum; Elegia autem dicitur dea miserie: contingunt etiam in amore miserie et adversitates."

[81] Rievaulx is situated in the valley of the Rye River and means "Rye Vale." Its traditional pronunciation, RIV-us, is closer to the Old French pronunciation than the spurious modern "spelling" pronunciation, ree-VOH (or REE-voh).

[82] Aelred of Rievaulx, *Speculum caritatis* 2.17.50, ed. A. Hoste and C. H. Talbot, *Aelredi Rievallensis opera omnia*, p. 90. "Cum enim in tragediis vanisve carminibus quisquam injuriatus fingitur vel oppressus, cujus amabilis pulchritudo, fortitudo mirabilis, gratiosus predicetur affectus, si quis hec vel cum canuntur audiens, vel cernens si recitentur, usque ad expressionem lacrymarum quodam moveatur affectu, nonne perabsurdum est, ex hac vanissima pietate de amoris ejus qualitate capere conjecturam, ut hinc fabulosum illum nescioquem affirmetur amare, pro cujus ereptione, etiamsi hec omnia vere pre oculis gerentur, nec modicam quidam substantie sue portionem pateretur expendi?"

For I remember being more than once moved to tears by popular stories made up about a certain Arthur. Hence I am not a little ashamed at my own vainglory, for if I manage to squeeze out a tear over what is piously read or sung or certainly over what is preached in public about Our Lord, I at once applaud myself for being a saint, just as if some great and unheard-of miracle has happened to me. And it is truly a sign of a vain mind to be puffed up in vainglory because of such emotions, when they happen to be aroused by pity, since the same feelings of compunction and sorrow used to be aroused by fables and lies.[83]

It is not certain that the publicly recited tragedies that Aelred speaks of are to be identified with the vernacular stories of Arthur mentioned by the novice, but it is likely. It must have been at a very early stage of such stories, of course, since Geoffrey of Monmouth had only recently given Arthur his historical context in his *Historia regum Britannie* (*c.* 1138).

We can characterize tragedy from Aelred's report as a narrative of the misfortunes of a sympathetic protagonist.

Aelred's account was imitated by Peter of Blois (*c.* 1135–1211). Peter had studied grammar and literature in Paris in his youth, perhaps with John of Salisbury, and later law at Bologna, and theology back at Paris; he eventually settled in England, around 1174. His discussion of Arthurian tragedies appears in his work on sacramental confession, which he wrote at the request of an unnamed bishop.[84] True penitence, he says, does not consist in momentary tears, and meritorious affection must proceed from the love of Christ:

Often in tragedies and other works of poets, and in the songs of jougleurs, there is described some man who is prudent, decent, strong, lovable, and graceful in all things; and then there are recited the acts of oppressions or injuries cruelly visited on him. Such are the fabulous accounts told by histrions of Arthur and Gaugan and Tristan; and when the audience hears about them, their hearts are struck and moved to compassion, and they feel such sorrow that they shed tears. Therefore, if you are moved to pity by the recitation of a fable, do you think you can say something about the love of God just because hearing something pious read about Our Lord squeezes tears out of you? You feel sympathy for God, but you feel sympathy for Arthur as well. You will therefore shed both sets of tears in vain if

[83] *Ibid.* 2.17.51: "Nam et in fabulis que vulgo de nescioquo finguntur Arthuro, memini me nonnunquam usque ad effusionem lacrimarum fuisse permotum. Unde non modicum pudet proprie vanitatis, qui si forte ad ea que de Domino pie leguntur vel cantantur, vel certe publico sermone dicuntur, aliquam mihi lacrimam valuero torquere, ita mihi statim de sanctitate applaudo, ac si magnum aliquid ac inusitatum mihi miraculum contigisset. Et revera vanissime mentis indicium est pro his affectibus, si forte pro pietate contingant, vana gloria ventilari, quibus in fabulis et mendaciis solebat compungi."
[84] See N. Iung, "Pierre de Blois." For his dependence on Aelred, see Peter von Moos, *Consolatio: Studien zur mittellateinischen Trostliteratur über den Tod und zum Problem der christlichen Trauer*, 2:213–14; cf. Chambers, *Arthur of Britain*, who does not know of Peter's indebtedness to Aelred (pp. 145–46, 267). On Peter's career, see Southern, "Peter of Blois: A Twelfth-Century Humanist?"; Elizabeth Revell, "Peter of Blois."

you do not love God, if you do not shed tears of devotion and penitence from the fonts of Our Savior, that is, hope, faith, and charity.[85]

We shall see in the next section that Peter of Blois knew of contemporary poetry that the author himself (namely, his brother William) designated as tragedy. But I take it that when he and Aelred use the term in connection with Arthurian romance, they are, consciously or unconsciously, going beyond the intentions of the authors, and perhaps deliberately employing a metaphor: these poems are like tragedies.

The metaphor of tragedy is applied to literature in various ways by Otto of Freising (*c.* 1114–58), so called because he was bishop of the Bavarian diocese of Freising from 1137 until his death. In the preface to his world-chronicle, which goes up to the year 1146, he tells the emperor Frederick that he wrote the history of the clouded past out of turbulence and bitterness of mind, and for this reason he set forth not so much the series, as the miseries of events (the play on words is in the original Latin) in the manner of tragedy. Accordingly he gave each of the first six books an unhappy ending. He did not do so for the seventh and eighth books, which he took to symbolize the repose of souls and the twofold resurrection.[86] He cites previous writers, including Eusebius, "in which the prudent reader can find not so much histories, as troublous tragedies of mortal calamities" ("in quibus non tam historias quam erumpnosas mortalium calamitatum tragedias prudens lector invenire poterit"). He finds in these events a purpose devised by divine providence: to cause men through the misery of this transitory life to turn from creatures to recognize the Creator. But he himself has not so much read of troubles (*erumpne*) of mortal men in books, as witnessed them in his own life, placed as he is at the end of time (*in fine temporum*).[87] By implication, perhaps, the whole world of time, or at least its recorded history, could be seen as a single great tragedy.

[85] Peter of Blois, *Liber de confessione sacramentali*, PL 207:1088C–89A: "Vera siquidem penitentia non in lacrymis momentaneis aut horaria compunctione consistit. Nulla etiam affectio pia meritoria est ad salutem nisi ex Christi dilectione procedat. Sepe in tragediis et aliis carminibus poetarum, in joculatorum cantilenis, describitur aliquis vir prudens, decorus, fortis, amabilis, et per omnia gratiosus. Recitantur etiam pressure vel injurie eidem crudeliter irrogate, sicut de Arturo et Gangano [*lege* Gaugano] et Tristanno fabulosa quedam referunt histriones, quorum auditu concutiuntur et ad compassionem audientium corda et usque ad lacrymas compunguntur. Qui ergo de fabule recitatione ad misericordiam commoveris, si de Domino aliquid pium legi audias quod extorqueat tibi lacrymas, nunquid propter hoc de Dei dilectione potes dictare sententiam? Qui compateris Deo, compateris et Arturo. Ideoque utrasque lacrymas pariter perdis, si non diligis Deum, si de fontibus Salvatoris, spe, scilicet, fide, et caritate, devotionis et penitentie lacrymas non effundis."

[86] Otto of Freising, *Chronica*, Dedicatory Epistle, 4: "Unde nobilitas vestra cognoscat nos hanc historiam nubilosi temporis quod ante vos fuit turbulentia inductos ex amaritudine animi, ac ob hoc non tam rerum gestarum seriem quam earundem miseriam in modum tragedie texuisse; et sic unamquamque librorum distinctionem usque ad septimum et octavum, per quos animarum quies resurrectionisque dulpex stola significatur, in miseria terminasse."

[87] *Ibid.*, book 1, Prologue (pp. 10–12).

At the same time that Otto was writing, Bernard of Cluny dedicated his famous poem, *De contemptu mundi* (beginning "Hora novissima, tempora pessima sunt, vigilemus"), to Peter the Venerable, abbot of Cluny (d. 1156).[88] In it he extends the comparison of tragedy to heaven and hell: in heaven, there is no tragedy,[89] but in hell there is, and that tragedy will last forever.[90] He also uses tragedy as a synonym for lamentation or protest: the complaint, or rather tragedy, of the chaste about the flourishing filth of the world reaches to the stars.[91] Perhaps tragedy is personified when he associates naked Tragedy with the tears befitting Religion.[92] Tragedy is clearly invoked later as a kind of Muse:

> Innumerabile, debile, labile, stat genus Eve,
> Dic, mea tibia, tolle, Tragedia, flebile "Ve, ve!"[93]

(The race of Eve is numberless, weak, fallible.
Speak, my pipe, raise up, O Tragedy, your tearful "Woe, woe!")

Otto of Freising was no doubt influenced by Rufinus's phrase in his rendering of Eusebius, "tragoedia magis quam historia texi videbitur." The same is true in the *Gesta Frederici* when Otto says of an episode, "Since everyone knows to what end the foresaid expedition came because of our sins, I leave it to others or to another time to tell of it, since I did not propose to write a tragedy this time but rather a cheerful history."[94] He does tell one incident, however, "so as not to cover in silence the Fortune of Frederick, for from his adolescence to the present day, even in grave dangers, she has never shown him a completely cloudy face."[95] This statement is revealing, both about Otto's notion of tragedy, and his notion of Fortune. A tragedy can be an account of a disastrous event from which the protagonist survives intact; and Fortune can be seen as a sort of private "genius," like a guardian angel or attendant demon, controlling the life of a single person.

---

[88] Bernard of Cluny, *De contemptu mundi*, ed. H.C. Hoskier, who calls the author "Bernard of Morval," but, as pointed out by André Wilmart, "Grands poèmes inédits de Bernard le Clunicien," his toponymic is uncertain, and it is best to refer to him by his religious profession.

[89] Bernard of Cluny, *De contemptu* 1.284: "Nulla molestia, nulla tragedia, lacrima nulla."

[90] *Ibid.* 1.621–22: "Illa tragedia durat in omnia secula, durat, / Cum dolor ubera, tortio viscera, flamma cor urat."

[91] *Ibid.* 2.427–28: "Ah, gemit omnia vivere turpia regula casta, / Hec querimonia, sive tragedia, clamat ad astra."

[92] *Ibid.* 2.170: "Nuda Tragedia, lacrima propria Relligionis."

[93] *Ibid.* 3.53–54.

[94] Otto of Freising, *Gesta Frederici*, 1.47, ed. G. Waitz, p. 65: "Verum quia, peccatis nostris exigentibus, quem finem predicta expeditio sortita fuerit, omnibus notum est, nos, qui non hac vice tragediam, sed jocundam scribere proposuimus hystoriam, aliis vel alias hoc dicendum relinquimus." This passage appears on p. 218 of the edition of Franz Josef Schmale.

[95] *Ibid.*: "ne Friderici principis . . . Fortuna, que ei ab adolescentia etiam in periculis gravibus usque ad presentem diem numquam ad plenum nubilosum vultum ostendit, silentio tegatur."

Otto may have been partially inspired in his use of the term "tragedy" by the example of his own grandfather, the deposed emperor Henry IV, who, in a letter written to the abbot of Cluny in 1106, pours out his woes, and calls the recital a tragedy: "Now it is time to put an end to so long a tragedy of our miseries, which, most beloved father, we have taken care to bewail to your piety, because in God and in you we have a great and singular hope of counsel and aid for our safety and liberty."[96] Otto makes no reference to this letter, but he does cite one that Henry wrote at the same time to the king of France.[97] Henry does not use the term tragedy of this even longer account of his troubles, but Otto does: he says that the letter contains "the tragedy of his miseries," and declares that it could soften even stony minds to contemplate and bemoan the sad conditions of the mutable world.[98]

Finally, Otto speaks of two other works written *ad modum tragedie*. One is a poem by "one of us" deploring the fall (*casus*) of human things after the death of many of the emperor Conrad's people.[99] The poem was characterized only as a *cantilena* by its author, as is obvious from its first two lines, which Otto gives ("Qui vocem habet serenam, / Hanc proferat cantilenam"). But it turns out to be on the death of the emperor himself (AD 1039), as can be seen from the text that Wipo gives at the end of his chronicle of Conrad, using the same expression, "one of us." Wipo himself was probably the author of the work, which he calls only a *cantilena lamentationum*.[100]

The other tragic work referred to by Otto is a report of how a group of travelers, including Themo, archbishop of Salzburg, was ambushed by the emperor Alexius and most of them killed. He perhaps refers to the account by Ekkehard of Aura, who, however, does not use the word "tragedy."[101] Otto says that one of the survivors wrote the history "miserably and excellently in the manner of a tragedy."[102]

---

[96] Henry IV, *Epistolae*, letter 37, p. 50: "Jam tempus est tam longe nostrarum miseriarum tragedie finem imponere, quam iccirco tue, pater amantissime, pietati deflere curavimus, quia in Deo et in te magna et singularis spes est nobis consilii et auxilii salutis et libertatis nostre."

[97] *Ibid.*, letter 39, pp. 52–58.

[98] Otto, *Chronica* 7.12 (p. 518): "Extat de hoc, inter ceteras ejus epistolas, ad regem Celtice, qui Francorum dicitur, seu Aquitanie ducem, epistola missa, que, miserarum ejus tragediam continens, saxeas quoque mentes ad mutabilium rerum erumpnas contemplandas ac deplorendas emollire posset."

[99] *Ibid.* 6.31 (p. 480): "Unde quidam ex nostris hunc rerum humanarum casum deplorans rhitmum in modum tragedie simplici stilo composuit."

[100] Wipo, *Vita Conradi Salici*, PL 142:1248C: "Pro quo quidem de nostris cantilenam lamentationum fecerat." The text of "these lamentations" appears on cols. 1247–50. Lammers, Otto's editor, assumes that the poem is by Wipo (p. 480 n. 109).

[101] Ekkehard of Aura, revising Frutolf of Michelsberg *Chronicon universale*, MGH Scriptores 6:220–21, fol. AD 1101.

[102] Otto, *Chronica* 7.7 (p. 510): "Quam hystoriam miserabiliter ac luculenter in modum tragedie quidam ex his qui se eidem expeditioni interfuisse testatur executus est."

Another author of the time who spoke of contemporary writings as tragic is Berengar of Poitiers in his attack on Bernard of Clairvaux. But here the intention is satirical.[103] Berengar criticizes Bernard for interrupting his sermons on the Song of Songs with a eulogy for his dead brother. Echoing Rufinus–Eusebius, he says it would seem that he had written a tragedy rather than a commentary.[104] He holds that such mourning is totally foreign to the nuptial context of the Song: tragedy destroys the laughter of marriage.[105] Perhaps Berengar is thinking of the characterization of comedy as celebrating *nuptialia*, recorded by Honorius. But Berengar is much more of a classicist than Honorius, and he is particularly well acquainted with Horace's *Ars poetica*. He is alluding to the same poet's satires when he says that it is "obvious to apothecaries and barbers" that Bernard was wrong to marry lamentations to an epithalamium.[106] He goes on to "speculate" about his tragic bellowing or lowing ("de ipso boatu tragico"), and says that he took the image of "cow calling to cow" verbatim from St. Ambrose.[107] The phrase *boatu tragico* would have been familiar to Berengar from Sedulius's *Carmen paschale*, which he cites earlier.[108] But since he goes on to refer to Bernard's *lugubris Musa*, he may also have known the poem of "Cato" on the nine Muses, of which the fourth line reads thus: "Melpomene tragico proclamat maesta boatu."[109] The poem was widely circulated in the Middle Ages; it appears, for instance, at the beginning of the Heiligenkreuz Boethian manuscript (to help explain the Muses that appear at the beginning of the *Consolation*).[110]

Finally, let me cite two historiographers who apply concepts of tragedy to the history of England, namely, Orderic Vitalis (1075–*c*. 1143) and William of Malmesbury (*c*. 1090–*c*. 1143). Orderic takes pains to dissociate his work from tragedy and comedy. Writing in the early 1130s, he vouches for the accuracy of his account of what the disposition of God manifested in the death of William the Conqueror. He says he has not written a fictitious tragedy for the sake of gain, nor does he foster cackling parasites with a verbose comedy, but rather he presents a true report of the various events for serious readers. He goes on to speak of the providential lesson in terms

---

[103] See von Moos, *Consolatio*, 1:279 and 2:159–60. Berengar's *Apologia* is edited by R. M. Thomson, "The Satirical Works of Berengar of Poitiers." It was written after July 1140, but before Abelard's death in 1142 (Thomson, "Satirical Works," p. 90).

[104] Berengar, *Apologia*, p. 120: "Possemus sane lucubrationibus diserti hominis acquiescere, nisi potius tragediam videretur quam commentarios texere."

[105] *Ibid.*, p. 121: "Tragedia risum proterit nuptiarum." Older editions read *profert* for *proterit*.

[106] *Ibid.*, p.123; cf. Horace, *Satires* 1.7.3.   [107] Berenger, *Apologia*, p. 123.

[108] *Ibid.*, p. 115. For Sedulius, see chap. 3 above, p. 51 n. 61.

[109] Cato (Pseudo-Cato), *Nomina Musarum*. For similar poems which also associate the verb *boare* with Melpomene, see *Anthologia latina*, part 1, 1:121 (no. 88; ed. Shakleton Bailey, 1:78, no. 76) and 2:135 (no. 644a).   [110] Haring, "Four Commentaries," p. 289.

reminiscent of William of Conches's tragic movement from prosperity to adversity: "In the midst of the prosperous, the adverse appeared, so that the hearts of earth-dwellers might be terrified."[111] He sums up what happened to William's body once he died. A powerful king, feared in many places, lay naked, despoiled by his own people, and was subjected to other shameful treatment.[112]

If anyone is to blame, according to Orderic's account, it is William's followers, and not William himself, whom Orderic greatly admired. His point is not that William was punished for any wrongdoing, but that all flesh fades like grass, and rich and poor alike must suffer death and decay. He implies that he could have distorted the truth about William's death by turning his account into a tragedy or a comedy for the sake of pleasing others. It is difficult to guess what he means, but perhaps he is thinking in terms of lamentation and panegyric. A bit later, Orderic recounts some of the quarrels that occurred in Normandy under William's weak successor, his son Robert, and says that similar sparks of evils sprang up everywhere and prepared vast raw material for tragic poets (*tragedi*).[113]

William of Malmesbury introduces the term "tragedy" in an entirely different context, when reporting the death of Prince William, the Conqueror's grandson, in a disastrous shipwreck that occurred in the year 1120 – an event that Orderic was also to treat at great length, even supplying a lamentation in elegiac distichs.[114] According to Malmesbury, after the drunken sailors had run the ship onto a rock, they tried to dislodge it, but Fortune resisted, reducing all their efforts to failure ("sed obsistebat Fortuna, omnes eorum conatus in irritum deducens"). Prince William managed to get into a lifeboat, but he returned to the ship to save his half-sister, and the boat was overwhelmed and sunk by a multitude of persons trying to get on board. Thus the poor young man died because of his merciful effort ("mortem misellus pro clementie teneritudine

---

[111] Orderic Vitalis, *Historia ecclesiastica* 7.16, 4:106: "Non fictilem tragediam venundo, non loquaci comedia cachinnantibus parasitis foveo; sed studiosis lectoribus varios eventus veraciter intimo. Inter prospera patuerant adversa, ut terrerentur terrigenarum corda." Orderic was born in England of a French priest and an English woman, and he spent his life in Normandy in the monastery of St. Evroult.

[112] *Ibid.*, pp. 106–08.

[113] *Ibid.* 8.5 (4:163): "Par equidem malorum fomes inter alios proceres undique per Normanniam pullulavit, et enormem tragedis farraginem preparavit."

[114] *Ibid.* 12.26 (6:294–306). He introduces the story thus: "In illa navigatione triste infortunium contigit, quod multos luctus et innumerabiles lacrimas elicuit" (p. 296). The poem has Leonine rhyming in each line, as can be seen from the opening couplet: "Accidit hora gravis, Thomeque miserrima navis; / Quam male recta terit, rupe soluta perit" (p. 302). He introduces it by saying that he does not wish to multiply useless threnodies, but he will give a short poem by just one outstanding metrist ("Inutiles trenos non curo multiplicare, unius tantum egregii versificatoris brevem camenam nitor hic annotare").

indeptus"). A great number of the nobility was lost; there was only one survivor, a rustic, who floated the whole night on a mast and in the morning related the act of the whole tragedy ("totius tragedie actum expressit"). There was never any ship of England of such great misery, and none whose fame so spread to the whole world. The difficulty of finding the corpses increased the calamity, and the death of the prince had a profound effect on King Henry.[115]

Malmesbury's reference to the *actum* would seem to indicate some knowledge of the theatrical context of tragedy, and thus, like Lambert of Hersfeld, he would be anticipating John Salisbury in using tragedy as a stage metaphor. The substance of the tragedy concerns a protagonist who comes to his ultimate misfortune not because of some crime, but because of an act of mercy.

TRAGIC STYLE AND NEW TRAGEDIES

Most of the accounts or ideas of tragedy that we have seen so far in this chapter are based mainly on the disastrous or lugubrious content of tragedy, rather than on any peculiarities of tragic style. The accessus to Lucan, however, does indicate that being a good writer of tragedy involves mastery of a grand style. Perhaps some stylistic criterion is involved in Berengar's analysis of Bernard's *tragicus boatus*, or Orderic's rejection of *fictilis tragedia*. But style is uppermost in Matthew of Vendôme's oneiric presentation of the species of poetry.

We have seen one notable discussion of the genres of poetry already, in the *De anime exsilio et patria* of Honorius Augustodunensis. But when he speaks of the four kinds of poetry, he is not thinking of different styles, but of different subject matters or purposes. The same is true of the *Isagoge in theologiam* (mid-twelfth century).[116] The author does seem to be aware of stylistic considerations, for he defines all poetry, in effect, as being in high style: "Poetry is the science that encloses grave and illustrious speech in meter. Through satire, poetry eliminates vices and sows virtues; through tragedy, tolerance of labors and contempt of Fortune. Commonly, however, every poem proposes examples of the brave and the cowardly."[117] He then gives a scheme for poetry embracing satire, comedy,

[115] William of Malmesbury, *Gesta regum Anglorum*, book 5, section 419, ed. Thomas Duffus Hardy, 2:653–54. William was the librarian of Malmesbury Abbey; he finished his *Gesta* in 1125.

[116] See the edition by Arthur Landgraf, *Ysagoge in theologiam*. See also Gilbert Dahan, "Notes et textes sur la poétique au moyen âge," p. 174 n. 13: it represents an ancient tradition of Latin origin antedating the diffusion of Aristotelian texts.

[117] *Isagoge*, book 1, p. 72: "Poesis autem est scientia claudens in metro orationem gravem et illustrem. Que per satiram vicia eliminat et virtutes inserit; per tragediam, tolerantiam laborum et Fortune contemptum. Communiter autem omne poema fortium et ignavorum exempla proponit."

and tragedy. This is his first mention of comedy, and he does not explain it. According to this presentation, then, tragedy would seem to deal with forceful, sympathetic – and successful – protagonists.

Honorius likens the four kinds of poetry to four villas belonging to the city of grammar, one of the cities of the soul's exile from its homeland of true wisdom, Holy Scripture.[118] Matthew of Vendôme in his *Ars versificatoria*, seemingly written around mid-century,[119] accepts a similar classification, but with elegy taking the place of lyric poetry. He describes a dream in which they are attendants upon Philosophy (a figure drawn in part from Boethius).[120] Tragedy is the first to be described, and she does not go well with the idyllic spring setting:

Inter ceteras boatu multiphario clamitans, Tragedia projicit ampullas et sesquipedalia verba, et pedibus innitens coturnatis, rigida superficie, minaci supercilio, assuete ferocitatis multiphariam intonat conjecturam.[121]

(Shouting among the others with multifarious bellowing, Tragedy hurls forth her jugs and eighteen-inch words. Towering on buskined feet, with rigid features and threatening brow, she intones multifarious criticisms with her accustomed fierceness.)

Matthew has converted Melpomene's mournful *boatus* to a ferocious roar,[122] and transformed the meaning of Horace's *proicit*. Tragedy does not humbly put aside her bombastic words, but uses them as projectiles.

The other generic ladies are almost as ill-suited to the setting as Tragedy, or at least to their ministerial posts at the side of Philosophy. Satire is garrulous, shameless, cross-eyed (testifying to her obliquity of mind), and wholly unembarrassed by her nudity.[123] Next to her Comedy creeps along in workaday clothes and bowed head, making no pretence of festive

---

[118] Honorius. *De anime exsilio* 2, 12 (PL 172:1243CD, 1245C).

[119] According to Matthew's editor, Franco Munari, *Mathei Vindocinensis opera*, 2:23–25, after Matthew studied at Tours under Bernard Silvester, he taught at Orleans in the epoch of Hugh Primas, at which time he composed the *Ars versificatoria*. He later transferred to Paris for about ten years, during which time he wrote his *Epistles* (in which he names the *Ars*, as well as *Milo* and *Pirimus et Thisbe*). After returning to Tours, he composed the *Tobias*, some time after *c.* 1180 and probably before 1187. Munari's edition of the *Ars* is in vol. 3. See also the earlier edition of Edmund Faral, *Les arts poétiques du XIIe et du XIIIe siècle*, pp. 109–93; Faral dates the work some years before 1175 (*Les arts*, p. 14).

[120] For other influences, see Winthrop Wetherbee, *Platonism and Poetry in the Twelfth Century: The Literary Influence of the School of Chartres*, pp. 146–51.

[121] Matthew of Vendôme, *Ars versificatoria* 2.5 (Munari, ed., *Opera*, 3:135), quoting Horace, *Ars poetica* 97. On the meaning of *conjectura*, compare what Matthew says of Philosophy: "Videtur ... multimodis conjecturis humane nature fragilitatem fastidire" (p. 134).

[122] Later, 2.17 (*Opera*, pp. 141–42), he uses the expression *boatu declamatorio* of an unskilled orator who tried to imitate another's forceful delivery and ruptured himself (citing Horace, *Epode* 1.19.15).

[123] *Ars verificatoria* 2.6 (p. 135).

delights.[124] The fourth lady, Elegy, at least has some vernal, if not philosophical, qualities. She "sings of quivered loves" (quoting Ovid),[125] with pleasing brow, welcoming eye, and flirtatious expression, and her lips full of sweetness seem to sigh for kisses. She limps, because one foot is shorter than the other, but this very defect enhances her charm, as Ovid says.[126]

In citing the *Amores*, Matthew makes clear that his picture of both Elegy and Tragedy is based on Ovid's account of the altercation between these two representatives of poetry. Matthew has the four ladies quarrel over who should have the "official epithet." Ovid, as we saw, did not make clear whether Tragedy was inclusive of epic, and whether her regular meter (in contrast to the uneven elegiac distich) was to be thought of as the dactylic hexameter as well as, or instead of, the iambic trimeter of dramatic tragedy. Matthew too is unclear about the meters of poetry other than elegy. He says only that he has used pentameters in his examples rather than hexameters so that the epithet might be given to Elegy, for she has sole rule over elegiac verse and pentameters.[127] Perhaps, then, Matthew assumed, in spite of his knowledge of Horace's *Ars poetica*, that the dactylic hexameter was the standard meter, or at least one of the standard meters, of tragedy. Tragedy, therefore, would include what we nowadays classify as epic, as it does implicitly for Honorius when he gives Lucan as an example of the genre. This kind of poem must after all fit somewhere in Matthew's four species of poetry, if these species are to be taken as inclusive of all poetry. Yet he would hardly assume that all poems written in hexameters, for instance, the *Ars poetica* itself, were tragedies.

As for comedy, there was a recent practice or tradition associating it with elegiac distichs. Around the middle of the twelfth century, Vitalis of Blois wrote two narrative poems, *Geta* (or *Amphitryo*) and *Aulularia*, in this meter. He calls the latter a comedy and says it is based on Plautus; it is in fact based on the pseudo-Plautine comedy *Querolus*. The *Geta* may also be based on a similar Plautine imitation; it is designated as a comedy in several manuscripts. Both works also resemble ancient comedies in having arguments and prologues.[128] William of Blois, Peter's brother, wrote a similar poem, *Alda*,[129] which he called a comedy and which he said was

[124] *Ibid.* 2.7 (*Opera*, p. 136). Wetherbee interprets the phrase, "nullius festivitatis pretendens delicias" to mean: "offering the delights of the everyday" (p. 147), but "humiliato capite" would seem to indicate the absence of delights.   [125] Ovid, *Remedia amoris* 379.

[126] Matthew, *Ars* 2.8, citing Ovid, *Amores* 3.1.10.   [127] *Ars* 2.40 (*Opera*, p. 160).

[128] Faral, "Le fabliau latin au moyen âge," pp. 325–26; Gustave Cohen, general ed., *La "comédie" latine en France au XII siècle*, 1:ix; 1:1–57 (*Geta*, ed. and tr. Etienne Guilhou); 1:59–106 (*Aulularia*, ed. and tr. Marcel Girard); Ferruccio Bertini, general ed., *Commedie latine del XII e XIII secolo*, 1:17–137 (*Aulularia*, ed. and tr. Bertini); 3:139–242 (*Geta*, ed. and tr. Bertini).

[129] William of Blois, *Alda* ed. and trans. Marcel Wintzweiller, in Cohen, *La "comédie,"* 1:107–51; new edition and Italian translation forthcoming in vol. 6 of Bertini, *Commedie*.

based on a Latin summary of a work by the *comedus* Menander; he probably acquired it when he was abbot of a Sicilian monastery, Sancta Maria de Maniaco in the diocese of Messina, in 1167–69.[130] Similar works of the same time, though not bearing the name of comedy, have been considered as such by modern scholars. Of particular interest is the *Pamphilus*, written around AD 1100, which is influenced by Terence and is entirely in dialogue form.[131] A crux-ridden gloss by Arnulf of Orleans in his commentary on the *Remedia amoris* has been taken as evidence that the *Pamphilus* was performed in public. Arnulf, a contemporary of Matthew of Vendôme, cites Pamphilus and other "persons" who are "induced" in a comedy as examples of the *ficti amantes* whom Ovid speaks of as danced (that is, Arnulf says, represented by leaps and gestures) in theaters.[132] But even if Arnulf is referring to the medieval *Pamphilus* and not to the characters named Pamphilus in Terence's *Andria* and *Hecyra*,[133] he may simply be alluding to the "introduced persons" in comedies and tragedies that we have seen Isidore and others speak of,[134] and imagining how such works were performed in Ovid's day. Or, if the reference is to contemporary productions, one cannot tell from his description whether the roles were acted out, or the words merely recited, with appropriate gestures, by several speakers, or by a single performer who took all the roles. The same questions are raised by Peter the Chanter's account of persons being picked to fit parts, not only in student plays, but also on the Feast of Fools, in comedies and tragedies and in similar amusements and mimic representations.[135] We

---

[130] Faral, "Fabliau," pp. 334–35; William of Blois, *Alda*, pp. 113–17.

[131] *Pamphilus*, ed. and tr. Eugène Evesque, in Cohen, *La "comédie,"* 2: 167–223; ed. and tr. Stefano Pittaluga, in Bertini, *Commedie*, 3:11–137. On the date, see Pittaluga, pp. 13–14, citing Dronke, "A Note on *Pamphilus*." Line 71, "Tunc Venus hec inquit," has been taken as a narrative statement, but, as Dronke points out ("A Note," p. 227, with Pittaluga concurring, p. 34), it could be interpreted as Pamphilus's report of what he hears Venus say. On *Babio* as a comedy, see below, p. 103.

[132] Bruno Roy, "Arnulf of Orleans and the Latin 'Comedy,'" pp. 259–60, with alternative readings of Arnulf's text in MS Wolfenbüttel Gud. lat. 4to 155, fol. 145, suggested by Dronke, "A Note," p. 226. Commenting on Ovid's *Remedia amoris* 755, "Illic adsidue ficti saltantur amantes" (see chap. 2 above), Arnulf says, in Dronke's reconstruction: "*Illic*, in theatro; *ficti*, sicut Pamphilus et sicut ceteri que in commedia inducuntur p[erson]e; inflammantur, quia quanto plus cernunt ludicra illa, tanto magis afflammantur amore earum; *saltantur*, per saltationes et gesticulationes representant." The passage still presents many problems. See the variants from other MSS given by Roy.

[133] A possibility considered by Roy, "Arnulf," p. 260 n. 20, and Dronke, "A Note," p. 226.

[134] Isidore, *Etymologiae* 8.7.11 (see chap. 3 above, p. 40).

[135] Peter Cantor, *Verbum abbreviatum*, chap. 61, long version, ed. John W. Baldwin, *Masters, Princes, and Merchants*, 2:144 n. 234: "Item si in representatione miraculorum sancti Nicholai vel alicujus sancti, licet jocose facta, tamen movente hominibus affectus, attenditur etas, ut personatum beati Nicholai dent simplici ac mansueto, personatum Abacuc seni, personatum Joseph discreto et eloquenti; vel si etiam in festo stultorum in comediis et tragediis et in hujusmodi ludicris ac mimicis representationibus representatur nobis quales in officiis singulis debeant persone eligi, quare in seriis, et exhibicione veritatis, in veris scilicet pastoribus ecclesie eligendis, non attenditur vel consideratur que persone debeant eligi vel quam mature etatis?" It is not clear whether the short version came before or after the long; if it came after, Baldwin dates the long version to *c.* 1191–92

should note that in the treatment of the *Pamphilus* which was added to the Tegernsee *Accessus ad auctores*, it is not called a comedy, but simply a book, *liber*, in keeping with its title, *Liber Pamphili et Galathee*.[136]

One of the narrative poems included in this class of medieval Latin comedies is by Matthew of Vendôme himself, *Milo*.[137] It is given the title of comedy in one of its two fourteenth-century copies, and in its second couplet it invokes Thalia, who is identified as the comic Muse in the Catonian verses and elsewhere. But Thalia was also the Muse of idyllic poetry, and she appears in Ovid as the Muse of elegy, or at least the Muse of the elegiac couplet;[138] and it may be that Matthew was simply appealing to Ovid's Muse, as was the author of another "elegiac comedy," the *Miles gloriosus*.[139]

When Matthew cites *Milo* in the *Ars versificatoria*, he does not call it a comedy, but simply *Versus de Afra et Milone*.[140] The poem's elegiac meter would seem to exclude it from the category of comedy, at least as he now understands it in the *Ars*, since Elegy is the only one who limps with unequal feet. A similar point could be made about Matthew's *Pirimus et Thisbe*, if he considered it a tragedy, and if his poem of this name is to be identified with any of the six extant poems on the subject, for all are in elegiac distichs.[141] One is ascribed to Matthew in the manuscript itself, and this attribution has been strongly supported. The opening couplet is as follows:

> Est amor amoris species et causa cruoris
> Dum trahit insanus in sua fata manus.[142]

(That love is only the appearance of love and the cause of bloodshed which insanely draws hands to one's own fate.)

The internal leonine-style rhyme in these lines, which is also to be found in the third couplet of *Milo*, would mark this poem as earlier than the *Ars*,

---

and the short to 1197, the year of Cantor's death (1:14–15). The short version, as given in PL 205:188C, reads: "Si etas personarum attenditur in representatione miraculorum quasi jocosa (tamen movente hominum affectus), si in comediis, et si in tragediis, cur non in seriis, et in exhibitione veritatis, in veris scilicet Ecclesie pastoribus eligendis?"

136 *Accessus ad auctores*, p. 53.
137 Matthew of Vendôme, *Milo*, in *Opera*, 2:57–72; also ed. and tr. Marcel Abraham, in *La "comédie,"* 1:153–77, and Paola Busdraghi, in Bertini, *Commedie*, 1:139–95.
138 Ovid, *Ars amatoria* 1.264: "praecipit imparibus vecta Thalia rotis." Cf. *Tristia* 4.10.56; 5.9.31; *Heroides* 15.84.
139 *Miles gloriosus*, in Cohen, *La "comédie,"* 1:179–210, line 2: "imparibus pange, Thalia, modis."
140 Matthew of Vendôme, *Ars* 3.43 (*Opera*, 3:185).
141 See Robert Glendinning. "Pyramus and Thisbe in the Medieval Classroom." Faral, *Arts poétiques*, p.10, gives details of five of the six Pyramus poems and edits one, *Consulte teneros non claudit tutor amantes*, on pp. 331–35. Cf. Cloetta, *Komödie*, p. 122, who eliminates two of the five poems as candidates for Matthew's authorship.
142 *Pirimus et Thisbe*, in *Opera*, 2:45, Munari, however, emends *amoris* to *ardoris*, in order to rectify the meter. Cf. line 35: "Crescit amor, nec amor, ymmo furor" ("Love increases, or rather not love, but madness").

since in the *Ars* Matthew ridicules leonine verse and all rhymes.[143] Furthermore, the couplet does not promise the level of bluster one would expect from Tragedy's appearance in the *Ars*, just as the *Milo* does not reflect the quotidian drabness of Comedy.[144] But then neither poem suits the flirtatious cheerfulness of Elegy, and it would be hard to maintain that Matthew now considers every poem in elegiac verse to be an elegy: for instance, the portrait-poems that he gives in his treatise.[145] It seems simply to be the favored form of verse. We note that it is Elegy who informs Matthew of the three components of metrical elegance.[146]

Matthew's early idea of comedy, which is operative in the *Milo*, may have had nothing to do with style (and certainly nothing to do with humor), but only with plot, and the same may be true of tragedy, if he thought of himself as writing tragedy. At the end of *Milo*, *dolor* gives way to *gaudia*,[147] and Milo and his wife Afra "rejoice to enjoy a more prosperous course of life."[148]

Other poems in elegiac meter that have been considered tragedies are the *Mathematicus* or *Patricida* of Bernard Silvester (early twelfth century), which is vaguely related to the Oedipus story, and the anonymous *Afra et Flavius*.[149] *Mathematicus* was not based directly on a tragedy, but on an oratorical exercise, a *declamatio pseudo-quintiliana*, also called *Mathematicus*.[150] A recent attempt to find traces of Seneca's tragedies in it has turned up several similarities (though only three lines from *Oedipus* are adduced).[151] But if they are taken to mean that Bernard knew the tragedies, or a florilegium based on them, one would have to conclude either that the parallels are simple reminiscences, conscious or otherwise, or the result of a deliberate effort to avoid direct quotation.

The only certain author of a tragedy in the twelfth century is William of Blois. But we know of his work only through the report of his brother

---

[143] Matthew of Vendôme, *Ars* 2.43 (*Opera*, 3:161–62); pointed out by Abraham, in Cohen, *La "comédie,"* p. 163.

[144] Glendinning, "Pyramus and Thisbe", p. 60, sums up Munari's arguments for Matthew's authorship of this Pyramus poem, specifically noting echoes in the *Ars versificatoria*, but he agrees with Bruce Harbert, "Matthew of Vendôme," pp. 232–33, that if the attribution is correct, it must be a very early work, finished before Matthew had perfected his techniques.

[145] Matthew of Vendôme, *Ars* 1.50–58 (*Opera*, 3:64–88).

[146] *Ibid.* 2.8–9 (*Opera*, 3:136–37).

[147] *Milo*, lines 243–44 (*Opera*, 2:71).

[148] *Ibid.* 251–52: "gaudent / Vite curriculo prosperiore frui."

[149] Cloetta, *Komödie*, pp. 113–22.

[150] *Declamationes xix maiores Quintiliano falso ascriptae*, no. 4: *Mathematicus* (pp. 60–84). The declamations went under Quintilian's name by the fourth century. For analyses of Bernard's *Mathematicus*, see Cloetta, *Komödie*, pp. 114–18, and Wetherbee, *Platonism and Poetry*, pp. 153–58.

[151] Zwierlein, "Spuren," pp. 172–78. Of the three authors whom Zwierlein searches for traces of Seneca, namely, Bernard Silvester, Peter Pictor, and Marbod of Rennes, only Marbod uses a word connected with tragedy, in the passage I cited above, p. 77.

Peter. In one letter, Peter speaks of William as having written comedies and tragedies,[152] until he convinced him to stop wasting his time. He may not have meant the plural literally, for when he lists William's literary works in another letter, dated 1170, he names only one of each, namely the tragedy *Flaura et Marcus* and the comedy *Alda*.[153] But it is possible that the first-cited letter is the later of the two, and that William did not give up writing profane poetry until he had added one item or more to each genre.

Like Vitalis of Blois, William of Blois definitely thought of himself as writing comedy. But both did so because they believed that they were imitating classical comedies. Perhaps William had a classical model for tragedy as well. Or perhaps he came to the conclusion that it was all a question of subject matter or style: if he had an acceptably serious story to tell, it could be termed a tragedy, even if it used elegiac meter. It is easy to see how Vitalis could have come to such as conclusion, if his remarks at the beginning of the *Aulularia* are a reflection of what Horace says about comedy and tragedy. He answers the possible objection that his comedy refers to fate and the stars and is too attached to high things – that he has ignorantly raised the humble style to grand affairs. He says first that he has only followed Plautus's example, and second that the subject matter justifies the high things.[154] He might have added that Horace allows it; and if one can follow Horace in writing a narrative comedy in elegiac distichs, one could do the same with tragedy.

Early in the next century, Geoffrey of Vinsauf says in the *Documentum de arte versificandi* that he will omit what Horace has to say about comedy, for it is obsolete; he will deal instead with humorous matter, *jocosa materia*.[155] In the *Poetria nova* he simply interprets Horace's *res comica* as *res jocosa*, and uses one of the examples he gave in the *Documentum*.[156] In another version of the *Documentum*, expanded after he had written the *Poetria*,[157] he tells us what he

---

[152] Peter of Blois, *Epistolae*, epistle 76 (PL 207:235A): "in scribendis comediis et tragediis." The full text is cited by Cloetta, *Komödie*, p. 77 no. 2, and Cohen, *La "comédie*," p. 113 no. 1.

[153] Peter of Blois, epistle 93 (PL 207:291–93). Peter congratulates William for resigning his abbacy in Sicily, and lists his writings that will bring him honor: "Nomen vestrum diuturniore memoria commendabile reddent tragedia vestra *De Flaura et Marco*, versus *De pulice et musca*, comedia vestra *De Alda*, sermones vestri, et cetera theologie facultatis opera, que utinam diffusius essent ac celebrius publicata" (col. 292D). Von Moos, *Consolatio*, 4:33, lists epistle 206 (PL 207:488), in which the writer speaks of his only brother Nicholas, as not by Peter.

[154] Vitalis of Blois, *Aulularia*, lines 17–22; text in Cloetta, *Komödie*, p. 159.

[155] Geoffrey of Vinsauf, *Documentum de arte versificandi* 2.3.162–63, ed. Faral, *Arts poétiques*, p. 317. Geoffrey taught rhetoric in England in the last quarter of the twelfth and early years of the thirteenth century. He studied in Paris and taught at "Hamton," thought to be Northampton. He is reported to have gone to Rome on one occasion on a mission for an English king, either Richard I or John.

[156] Geoffrey of Vinsauf, *Poetria nova*, ed. Faral, *Arts poétiques*, p. 255. See Faral, "Fabliau," pp. 375–78.

[157] See Traugott Lawler, *The Parisiana Poetria of John of Garland*, appendix 2: "The Two Versions of Geoffrey of Vinsauf's *Documentum*" (pp. 327–32); he gives excerpts of the longer version from Oxford, Bodleian MS Laud Misc. 707, fols. 81–83v.

means: Horace's rule that there must be five and only five acts in comedy is no longer in use.[158] Presumably, he also considered some of Horace's points about tragedy to be similarly obsolete, though he does not say so explicitly. He contrasts jocose matter, or comedy, which is about lasciviousness, with tragedy, which deals with grave persons ("ut si quis materiam jocosam vel comediam scriberet in qua partes deberent observari ad lasciviam pertinentes et transferret se ad partes tragedie, que sunt de gravibus personis et earum proprietatibus").[159] Later, he defines tragedy as a poem that deals with contempt of Fortune, showing the misfortunes of grave persons, and beginning in joy and ending in mourning ("Tragedia carmen est in quo agitur de contemptu Fortune, ostendens infortunia gravium personarum, et incipit a gaudio et finit in luctu"). We remember that the *Isagoge in theologiam* spoke of tragedy as teaching the "contempt of Fortune," but that was a case of the objective genitive, meaning "[our] contempt *for* Fortune." Vinsauf must intend the subjective genitive, "Fortune's contempt [for mankind]." He adds an explanation of the goat given to the *tragedus* to indicate the fetor of the matter. Another genre named for goats, the eclogue, featured fetid speech rather than fetid subject matter, though it concentrated on the deeds of vile persons: it included satire, or bitter reprehension, as practiced by Horace; bucolics, or the conversation of vile persons; and Theodulus's kind, where an honest person disputes against a vile person. Comedy, broadly speaking, is any jocose poem; strictly speaking, it is a rustic poem about humble persons beginning in sadness and ending in joy ("cantus villanus de humilibus personis contextus, incipiens a tristicia et terminans in gaudio").[160]

Elsewhere I have argued that Geoffrey himself did not name his work *Poetria nova*, but that the title was later bestowed on it to contrast it with Horace's *Ars poetica*, which, up to that time in the Middle Ages, had gone by the name *Poetria*. Henceforth it would be known, or thought of, as *Poetria vetus*.[161] But even though Vinsauf did not explicitly present his work as a replacement of, or even a supplement to, Horace's treatment, this was at least to some extent his purpose.

An interesting parallel to Vinsauf's discussion of humorous verse in place of Horace's treatment of comedy can be seen in Gervase of Canterbury's history of English kings (written around 1200), when he

---

[158] *Ibid.*, excerpt 4 (p. 332).
[159] *Ibid.*, excerpt 3a (p. 330): "as, for instance, if one were composing a joking piece or a comedy in which the elements ought to appear pertinent to lasciviousness, and were to shift to the elements of a tragedy, which deal with grave persons and their attributes."
[160] *Ibid.*, excerpt 4 (p. 332).
[161] Kelly, review of Marjorie Curry Woods, *An Early Commentary on the Poetria nova of Geoffrey of Vinsauf*.

distinguishes the historian from the chronicler, applying what Horace has to say about tragedy to the former, and what Vergil says in an eclogue to the latter: "Projicit historicus ampullas et sesquipedalia verba; cronicus vero silvestrem Musam tenui meditatur avena."[162] That is, "The historian throws forth great jars and oversized words, while the chronicler meditates on the sylvan Muse with his slender pipe." It is noteworthy that he, like Matthew of Vendôme, takes Horace's *proicit* to signify projection rather than rejection. Gervase's point is that the historian and chronicler have the same matter and the same intention (that is, to tell the truth about the past), but the *forma tractandi* differs; the historian proceeds in a diffuse and elegant manner, whereas the chronicler goes simply and briefly ("historicus diffuse et eleganter incedit, cronicus vero simpliciter graditur et breviter").

The last gasp of the twelfth-century literary rebirth, in university circles at least, can be seen in the *Parisiana poetria* of John of Garland, written around 1220 and revised ten or fifteen years later.[163] Interest in the classics had waned, and in spite of his own enthusiasm, Garland was probably little acquainted with the actual texts of the ancient authors.[164] He had somehow heard of Ovid's tragedy *Medea*, and was of the opinion that it was the only tragedy ever written in Latin before his time. It is not clear whether he believed that there had also been tragedies written in Greek, or whether he thought that the genre of tragedy had been established only in light of Ovid's unique entry. Or are we to think that Garland, like Aelred of Rievaulx and Peter of Blois, considered some vernacular poems to be tragedies? He knew nothing of William of Blois's Latin tragedy. He says simply that only two tragedies had ever been written in Latin: Ovid's *Medea*, now lost, and one of his own composition.[165]

Garland proceeds to present his tragedy to his reading public, first by stating its argument, then by giving its characteristics, and finally by copying out the poem itself, a narrative consisting of 126 dactylic hexameters. It tells the sordid story of a washerwoman and her soldier-lover, who are killed out of envy by a second washerwoman; the murderess then lets the enemy into the city in order to conceal her crime, and in the ensuing massacre all of the defending soldiers, including her own brother, are killed.[166]

---

[162] Gervase of Canterbury, *The Chronicle of the Reigns of Stephen, Henry II, and Richard I*, 1:87, citing *Ars poetica* 98 and *Eclogues* 1.2.
[163] See Lawler's edition and translation. Garland was born around 1195 and died around 1277.
[164] See Louis John Paetow, *The Arts Course at Medieval Universities with Special Reference to Grammar and Rhetoric*, p. 17.
[165] Garland, *Parisiana poetria* 7.4–6 (Lawler, p. 136). We should note, however, that Garland intends to inspire his readers to write tragedies of their own; see his Prologue, p. 2.
[166] *Ibid.* 7.11–23 (argument), 7.28–153 (text) (Lawler, pp. 136–42).

The three properties of this tragedy, he says, are as follows: it is written (described) in a grave style; it sets forth shameful and criminal deeds; and it begins in joy and ends in tears ("Hujus tragedie proprietates sunt tales: gravi stilo describitur; pudibunda proferuntur et celerata [i.e., scelerata]; incipit a gaudio et in lacrimas terminatur").[167] This fits with Garland's earlier characterization of tragedy as a poem in grave style with a joy-to-sorrow movement. Even though he lays claim to gravity of style, unlike many definers of tragedy he takes no thought for grave persons in high places. Comedy, in contrast to tragedy, is a jocose poem beginning in sadness and ending in joy ("Est differencia inter tragediam et comediam: quia comedia est carmen jocosum incipiens a tristicia et terminans in gaudium. Tragedia est carmen gravi stilo compositum, incipiens a gaudio et terminans in luctum"). Moreover, a perfect comedy has five parts, as Horace notes, to correspond to its five characters, whereas tragedy, like history, is divided according to deeds, with no set number of parts.[168] He also defines *tragedicon* as a historical narrative that begins in joy and ends in sorrow ("Item hystoricum aliud tragedicon, scilicet carmen quod incipit a gaudio et terminatur in luctum").[169] In these passages, and in other discussions of genres, Garland is clearly drawing on Vinsauf's expanded *Documentum*.[170] He accepts Vinsauf's collocation of jocosity with comedy, but the stress on joy rather than humor at the end might make us think that *jocosum* was assimilated to *gaudiosum* in the formation of the French *joyeux*. However, Garland proceeds to present a comedy that must be deemed jocose in any language. It consists of a short narrative in which an evil spirit informs a peasant that he is a cuckold. Garland gives it in two forms, first in prose, and then, "more ornately," in leonine hexameters.[171] The first version, which he calls the *materia* of the comedy, might seem more classifiable as an argument than a poem, though he does say at one point that poets can use prose.[172]

It is, perhaps, a waste of effort to look for consistency in Garland, since he also says that every comedy is an elegy.[173] He does not mean to say that comedy should be written in elegiac distichs, as has been assumed;[174] rather, he is speaking of elegy as a narrative genre: a poem of misery that contains or recites the sorrows of lovers.[175] Now if every comedy is a poem

[167] *Ibid.* 7.24–26.
[168] *Ibid.* 4.463–81 (pp. 80–82). Lawler implausibly takes "Idem dicitur de tragedia" (line 477) to mean that tragedy has five parts, referring it to lines 463–64 rather than to the immediately preceding discussion of the parts of history.   [169] *Ibid.* 5.365–66 (Lawler, p. 102).
[170] Lawler, *Poetria*, p. 327, finds such dependence only in Garland's chapter 5.
[171] Garland, 4.422–31 (prose) and 4.433–58 (verse) (Lawler, pp. 78–80).
[172] *Ibid.* 5.426 (Lawler, p. 106).
[173] *Ibid.* 5.371 (Lawler, p. 102): "Omnis comedia est elegia."   [174] So Lawler, p. 256.
[175] Garland, 5.366–67: "miserabile carmen quod continet vel recitat dolores amantium." Cf. 1.396–97 (Lawler, p. 24). Elegy was traditionally associated with misery. See Isidore, *Etymologiae* 1.39.14, and

about love and begins in sadness, one could see how at least the first part of every comedy is an elegy (it would make even more sense, of course, to say that every tragedy is an elegy, since sadness in that form has the final word). But Garland's own comedy fits these criteria very uncomfortably. It may be said to deal with the sorrows of one lover, but in a joking rather than a miserable way; the husband–protagonist does not end in joy, but in sadness, whatever glee the audience may feel at his plight.

I have gone slightly beyond the confines of the twelfth century not only to tell of Geoffrey of Vinsauf and John of Garland's theories of tragedy, but also to tell of Garland's practice of it. However, Garland is exhibited mainly as a curiosity, for his efforts had, perhaps not undeservedly, an unhappy end: he had no readers of note, and no imitators. The same, however, is true of many of his more talented and more learned predecessors, including Vinsauf in his expanded *Documentum*, while others of little merit succeeded; all of which goes to show that the *fortuna* of literature is as arbitrary as Lady Fortune.

Garland's reaction to Vinsauf's characterization of the genre of tragedy was to see it as an almost entirely theoretical category; he believed that it had only had one exemplification, which, since it was missing, he decided to replace. Vinsauf's own reaction is likely to have been the same as his reaction to comedy, namely, to conclude that it was obsolete; he did not find it worth even a mention in his *Poetria*. The other major rhetorician of this era, Matthew of Vendôme, had characterized tragedy as one of four genres, but it is not clear whether he considered it to be an active form, either in his own practice or in that of his contemporaries. The only certain self-addressed tragedy that we know of which was composed in the twelfth century is William of Blois's *Flaura et Marcus*, but we know nothing of its rationale or contents.

Tragedy for Vendôme was a matter of sesquipedalian polemics, but for Vinsauf it was a combination of elements. Like the anonymous author of the *Isagoge*, he considered it to deal with *contemptus Fortunae*, but not our contempt of Fortune, rather her contempt of us, and not for the elimination of vice and the sowing of virtue. Like William of Conches, Vinsauf links the goatish etymon of tragedy to the filth of the subject matter, and also agrees with him in seeing it as a progression from wellbeing to its opposite, in this case, from joy to mourning; and he adds that it deals with important persons. We shall see now that a similar combination was to be found earlier in the lexicographer Huguccio, who, unlike Vinsauf and Garland, had a fortunate *fortuna*.

Papias under *eligiacum* (for the texts, see Kelly, *Tragedy and Comedy*, p. 8 n. 32). We have seen it connected with the miseries of lovers in the Tegernsee accessus to Ovid's *Amores* (p. 85 above).

CONTINUING TRADITION: THE LEXICOGRAPHERS

We shall look at two twelfth-century dictionaries, the *Liber derivationum* or *Panormia* of Osbern of Gloucester (*c.* 1160?) and the *Magne derivationes* of Huguccio (*c.* 1165?); a thirteenth-century successor to the latter, the *Catholicon* of John Balbus Januensis, or John of Genoa (1286); and another late-thirteenth-century work, the metrical dictionary of William Brito.

Osbern has always been much in the dark, whereas Huguccio has been bathed in a very prominent light, having been identified with the famous canonist, Huguccio of Pisa, who afterwards became bishop of Ferrara. But now it seems that this has been a false light, and that the lexicographer cannot have been the canonist-bishop. According to Wolfgang Müller, we can only know about the lexicographer from his lexicon: Huguccio professes the position of master at Bologna; and he mentions the year 1161 in one of his entries.[176] There is such similarity between the works of Huguccio and Osbern that we must conclude that one used the other, or that both used the same source. Georg Goetz tends to think that Huguccio used Osbern and Papias, and added much of his own material from other sources. Yet he may have had a fuller copy of Osbern's work than we possess.[177] Müller suggests that Huguccio possibly stayed in Paris in the 1160s, where he could have used the *Panormia*, since so early a reception in Italy appears unlikely.

Osbern quotes a great deal from the plays of Terence and, especially, Plautus, and also draws on *Babio*, which must have been composed in England shortly before Osbern's time of writing – therefore between 1145 and 1160. *Babio* is entirely in dialogue form and is designated as a comedy in two of its manuscripts, one of the early thirteenth and the other of the fourteenth century.[178] But Osbern's treatments of comedy under the letter *C* are too laconic for us to tell how much his idea of the genre was influenced by these works. He defines comedy as a cheap song (*vilicus cantus*), comic as "facetious" (which need not mean humorous), *comedus* as a writer of comedy, and *comedicus* as delectable, citing a line from Plautus.[179]

---

[176] Wolfgang P. Müller, "Huguccio of Pisa: Canonist, Bishop, or Grammarian?" pp. 137–39. Huguccio the canonist published most of his great *Summa* on Gratian's *Decretum* around 1188–90 (p. 142), and makes use of the *Derivationes* of his Bolognese namesake (pp. 149–50).

[177] Goetz, *Corpus glossariorum*, 1:202–03; Müller, "Huguccio," p. 139 n. 80, says that the Vatican MS of Osbern used by Mai for his edition (see below) is defective. See R. W. Hunt, "The 'Lost' Preface to the *Liber derivationum* of Osbern of Gloucester," who notes that the *terminus ante quem* for Osbern's work is 1179, the death date of one of the dedicatees.

[178] See Andrea Dessì Fulgheri's edition of *Babio*, in Bertini, *Commedie*, 2:129–301, pp. 150–58, 240, 242.

[179] Osbern, *Liber derivationum*, ed. Angelo Mai, p. 111, citing Plautus, *Miles gloriosus* 2.2.60. The definitions on p. 143 are similar, except that for *comicus* he gives not only *facetus*, but also *urbanus* and *curialis*, which is how he defines *facetus* (*urbanus, curialis, urbanicus*, p. 239). Geoffrey of Monmouth,

Osbern defines tragedy at greater length, and contrasts it with comedy. Tragedy is a mournful poem because it begins in joy and ends in sadness; comedy is its contrary, for it begins in sadness and ends in joy.[180] The phrase *carmen luctuosum* is found in book 18 of Isidore's *Etymologies*, which Osbern cites fairly often. But his attitude towards tragedy and comedy is closer to book 8, where Isidore speaks of the *res luctuosae* of tragedy and the *res laetae* of comedy, and there is no suggestion of stress on moral evil, and no theatrical dimension. However, Osbern adds to Isidore the currently fashionable insistence on beginnings and endings. His account may be compared to the Lucan accessus, which, as we have seen, also avoids the subject of crime and talks of a *letum principium* and *tristis finis*.

Osbern has little to say on theatrical words. He does not define *scena*, except as a component of *scenofactorius* (meaning "shade"),[181] but he does say that *scenule* are "young whores who were prostituted in the little scenes,"[182] indicating a familiarity with Boethius.

Huguccio takes up the subjects of tragedy and comedy under the entry of *oda*, which he defines as *cantus* or *laus*.[183] The difficulty of looking up compound words like *comedia* and *tragedia* treated out of alphabetical order in Huguccio's dictionary was alleviated in some copies by the addition of *repertoria* listing the hidden words.[184] He first discusses comedy, which he says treats of rustic matters and is close to daily speech. His source here is the ninth-century *Expositio in Terentium*, or a derivative.[185] As for tragedy, it means literally "goatish praise" or "goatish song," with goatish taken in the sense of fetid. It deals with the cruelest of subjects, for instance, a person who has killed his father or mother and eaten his child, or the reverse. For this reason the tragedian was given a goat, that is, a fetid animal, not that he would have no other worthy prize, but to designate the filth of the subject matter.[186]

writing in the 1130s, attributes *facetia* to the chaste women of Arthur's court, *Historia regum Britannie* 9.13, where it seems to connote elegance and sophistication. But these ladies are not without a sense of humor, for they jokingly stimulate knights in tournaments to furious flames of love (9.14); in Wright's edition, section 157, p. 113. See H. A. Kelly, "The Varieties of Love in Medieval Literature According to Gaston Paris," p. 304.

[180] Osbern, *Liber*, p. 593: "*Tragedia*: carmen luctuosum, quia incipit a letitia et finit in tristitia; cui contrarium est comedia, quia incipit a tristitia et finit in letitia."

[181] *Ibid.*, p. 567: "*Scenofactorius*: a scena, id est, ab umbra, dicitur."

[182] *Ibid.*, p. 556: "*Scenule*: meretricule que in scenulis prostituebantur."

[183] Huguccio, *Magne derivationes*, fol. 124. The entire entry is given in Kelly, *Tragedy and Comedy*, pp. 6–7, n. 27.

[184] Daly and Daly, "Some Techniques," p. 235.

[185] *Expositio in Terentium*, p. 163: "*oda*, laus sive cantus, unde *comoedia*, villanus cantus, et qui sit affinis cotidianae locutioni." See chap. 3 above, pp. 53, 64.

[186] Huguccio, under *oda* (fol. 124): "Item *oda* in eodem sensu componitur cum *tragos*, quod est hircus, et dicitur *hec tragedia, -e*, id est, hircina laus, vel hircinus cantus, id est, fetidus; est enim de crudelissimis rebus, sicut qui patrem vel matrem interfecit, et comedit filium, vel e contrario, et hujusmodi. Unde

Huguccio then gives three differences between tragedy and comedy:

1 Subject matter: comedy contains the acts of private persons, tragedy those of kings and magnates
2 Style: comedy is written in a humble style, tragedy in a high style
3 Story movement: comedy begins in sad matters but ends joyfully, whereas tragedy is the reverse.

He elaborates the last point by saying, "Whence we are accustomed in our salutations to send and wish to friends a tragic beginning and a comic end, that is, a good and joyful beginning and a good and joyful end."[187] He also notes three forms of adjective, *tragedus*, *tragicus* and *tragedicus*. *Tragedus* as a substantive means a writer of tragedy ("tragedie scriptor"). *Tragicus* means the same as the adjective *tragedus*, or pertaining to *tragedus* as substantive. *Tragedicus* has the latter meaning.

Huguccio may have got some of his ideas from Horatian scholia. His examples of tragic subjects bear some resemblance to the crimes of Tantalus and his progeny listed by the Lambda Scholiast,[188] and the statement on style was anticipated by another commentator, who could be termed Pseudo-Acron the Younger, but whom I shall call the Gamma Scholiast.[189] We can take his interpretation of Horace's statement on *res comica* as a contradiction to Placidus's stipulation of *stilus mediocris* for comedy. According to Horace, an insignificant and comic affair should not be treated in a high and difficult manner, as are tragic subjects. Tragedy is "described" or written in a high style, comedy in a humble style.[190]

Huguccio could have reconciled Placidus's stipulation, which was repeated by Papias, with that of the Gamma Scholiast by noting what the Terentian *Expositio* says of Menander: Menander wrote two plays on a

---

et tragedo dabatur hircus, scilicet, animal fetidum, non quod non haberet aliud dignum premium, sed ad fetorem materie designandum."

[187] *Ibid.*, fol. 124r–v: "Et differunt tragedia et comedia, quia comedia privatorum hominum continet acta, tragedia regum et magnatum. Item comedia humili stilo scribitur, tragedia alto. Item comedia a tristibus incipit set in letis desinit, tragedia e contrario. Unde in salutacione solemus mittere et optare amicis tragicum principium et comicum finem, id est, principium bonum et letum, et bonum et letum finem."

[188] See chap. 3 above, pp. 58–59.

[189] *Scholia in Horatium*: *Scholia Gamma*, ed. Hauthal. Hauthal's edition of the older scholia of Pseudo-Acron was superceded by Keller's edition (see Bibliography under Pseudo-Acron), but Keller does not give the entries judged to be later. Hauthal, 2:574, names the best text of the Acronian commentary on the *Ars poetica* as that of Paris, BN MS lat. 7975 (eleventh century), which he and Keller both designate by the Greek letter γ. Hauthal also lists MS B (Paris 7971) dated to the tenth century (not mentioned by Keller), and the Roman *editio princeps* (before 1474), which may preserve the text of MS A (Paris 7900). This last-named manuscript, dated to the ninth century by Hauthal and to the tenth by Keller, has lost the portion on the *Ars poetica*.

[190] Gamma Scholiast on *Ars Poetica* 89 (Hauthal, 2:591): "Res, inquit, parva et comica non debet alte tractari et difficiliter, ut tragica. Tragoedia autem alto stilo describitur, comoedia vero humili (gaudet)." The Roman edition omits the *gaudet*, and, Hauthal says, rightly so.

similar subject, *Andria* and *Perinthia*; but one had graver speech (*oratio*) and a middle style, while the other had lighter speech and humble style.[191] The distinction between speech and style is not further elaborated. One commentator on Horace, the Vienna Scholiast, who is probably to be dated to the eleventh century or later since he mentions a liturgical play, *Cena Herodis* (*The Dinner of Herod*),[192] names three styles, humble, middle, and grave, and details three corresponding defects in their use, but does not systematically discuss tragedy and comedy in terms of these styles.[193] His treatment is, however, very interesting, and I will give some details here to contrast with Huguccio's approach. The scholiast says that heroic meter is used to describe war, while tragedy employs the unequal meter of hexameters and pentameters, since such verses deal with complain (*querimonia*).[194] But *comici* and *tragedi* started to use iambics, which are good for the questions and answers of alternate speech and for overcoming the noise of the people who come to hear the writings of poets. He cites the beginning of Horace's second epode as an example ("Beatus ille qui procul negotiis"). The *tragedi* are called *grandes* because tragedy should be narrated in a clamorous voice,[195] though sometimes the *ampulle*, that is, elated and inflated words, are cast away.[196] When Medea's acts of killing her children are recited, no person is to be introduced to kill them.[197] The play of Herod is given as an example of actions being both referred to and acted by introduced persons.[198] The scholiast's concept seems to correspond fairly well to the Isidorian notion of a single reciter with pantomime actors sometimes acting out the words. Five judges would review written poems before they were to be recited to the people, and Ovid was one such judge in his day.[199] The scholiast's commentary on the goat is fairly straightforward: a goat was the prize given to a zealous writer of tragedy, perhaps because it had the most lamentable voice of all animals, to denote that the poem was made of lamentable matter; later on, the writers received great praise for their works, but eventually it was necessary for them to add

---

[191] *Expositio*, p. 169: "Materia non est dissimilis, quamvis oratio sit dissimilis, quia in una gravior, in altera levior habetur oratio. Et stilus dissimilis est: in una enim mediocris, in altera humilis habetur stilus."

[192] *Scholia vindobonensia ad Horatii Artem poeticam*, ed. Joseph Zechmeister, pp. i–ii.

[193] Vienna Scholiast on *Ars poetica* 8 (*Scholia*, Zechmeister, p. 2); treated by Quadlbauer, "Die poetischen Gattungen."

[194] Vienna Scholiast on lines 73–75 (*Scholia*, Zechmeister, p. 8). He takes for granted that this meter is elegiac: he comments on the *elegos exiguos* of line 78 by saying the *elegi* are "versus de miseria factos," and that they are *exigui* in comparison to hexameters with six feet, since they have only five feet (pp. 8–9).

[195] *Ibid.* on lines 80–82 (p. 9).   [196] *Ibid.* on line 97 (p. 10).

[197] *Ibid* on line 185 (p. 20).   [198] *Ibid.* on line 182 (p. 19).

[199] *Ibid.* on line 268 (p. 33).

satire (which involves joking) in order to receive the prize; but the satire was not to be too debased, for otherwise it would be like seeing the person held in great honor in the tragedy (in which grave speech was used) being made to enter a tavern and use low speech.[200]

Though Huguccio is closer to Osbern in speaking of joy and sadness rather than of prosperity and adversity, he is closer to William of Conches in interpreting *oda* as praise, and in specifying evil deeds as the subject matter of tragedy. He also agrees with Conches in having the goat designate the fetor of the subject matter. His use of the term *tragedus* for the tragic poet who receives the goat, and also the phrase *privatorum hominum acta*, may show direct dependence on book 8 of Isidore's *Etymologies*.

Huguccio does not hint of any connection of tragedy or comedy with the theater. Comedy was recited around the *villa*, not in the theater. But he shows himself familiar with at least some aspects of Isidorian theatrics. For instance,

he describes the scene as a shade, that is, a shaded place in the theater covered with curtains, like the stalls of merchants. It may be, he says, that the word comes from the Greek for house, for the scene was constructed in the manner of a house. In this shaded structure, masked persons would conceal themselves and then issue forth to the voice of the reciter and make gestures.[201] He may have taken his houselike structure directly from Isidore's *in modum domus instructa*, and the hiding and issuing forth of persons from William of Conches's *abscondebantur persone et exibant*. His notion of *persone larvate* may have come from a Horatian, Terentian, or Boethian tradition, though he does not specifically associate these performances with comedy or tragedy.

When Huguccio likens the scene to the curtained sheds of merchants, he may well be drawing on his own observations. But he does not seem to be alluding to contemporary entertainments, for he speaks of the scenic activities in the past tense.[202] When, however, *scena* is defined in Accursius's Ordinary Gloss to Justinian's *Digest*, it is characterized in terms of horse-puppets operated by "jugglers" (*joculatores*). Though the scene is called a shade of curtains or cloths, the word is derived from the Greek for

---

[200] *Ibid.* on lines 220–29 (pp. 26–28).
[201] Huguccio, *Magne derivationes*, under *scenos* (fol. 164vb): "*Scena, -e*, id est, umbra, et *scena*, umbraculum, scilicet locus adumbratus in theatro et cortinis coopertus, similis tabernis mercennariorum que sunt asseribus vel cortinis operte; et secundum hoc posset dici a *scenos* quod est 'domus,' quia in modum domus erat constructa. In illo umbraculo latebant persone larvate que ad vocem recitantis exibant ad gestus faciendos." For the full entry, see Marshall, "*Theatre* in the Middle Ages," p. 25.
[202] According to Claudia Villa, *La lectura Terentii*, p. 249, such descriptions were common in Terence manuscripts, but she does not give any precise references or indications of dates.

rope, since the wooden horses were controlled by ropes.[203]

John Balbus Januensis uses most of Huguccio's definitions and explanations in his *Catholicon*, finished and issued in 1286,[204] but arranges them more usefully: specifically, he puts the entries on comedy and tragedy back in their proper alphabetical order, as in Papias. He also adds some definitions from other sources – with quite interesting results. He first gives Huguccio's explanation of comedy as *villanus cantus*, and so on, but refers to the entry on tragedy for the ways in which comedy differs from tragedy. He then adds, by way of contrast, what Papias says about comedy ("Papias autem sic dicit..."). Therefore, in addition to what further points could be found by looking up tragedy, namely, that comedy deals with private persons in a humble style, there is also Papias's doctrine that comedy uses a middle style and, though it includes the affairs of private and humble persons, it also deals with historical truth and grave persons.[205]

Balbus has several other entries of words related to comedy, including *comicus*, where he gives a modified version of Isidore's doctrine: there are two kinds of comics, that is, writers of comedy: namely, the old, who were *joculatores*, like Terence, and the new, also called satirics, like Persius and Juvenal. The latter attack vice generally, and are painted naked, because they denude vice.[206] The idea of the new comics being illustrated naked goes back to Isidore, but the notion of the old comics as *joculatores* is new to us, though we have seen the term used in connection with comedy and tragedy before. It is hard to translate, as some of its vernacular forms show: the French *jougleur* and the corresponding English "juggler," and the later form *jongleur* (resulting from a scribal confusion between *u* and *n*) and the English "*jangler*."

Under the entry *dragma*, Balbus cites both Huguccio and Papias by name: Huguccio gives Terence as an example of the dramatic genre, where only introduced persons speak. Balbus refers us to the entry *hermeneuticus*, where he illustrates another kind of dialogue, namely, the didascalic, in which master and student speak. He gives Donatus as an example (referring to the *Ars minor*), and a theological work of his own in which *Anima* as disciple

---

[203] Accursius, *Glossa ordinaria in Corpus juris civilis: Digestum* 3.2.2: "Obumbratio cortinarum sive pannorum que posita sunt in publico vel in privato loco; et dicitur scena a *schenon*, quod est 'chorda,' quia joculatores faciunt ire caballos per chordam, et similia." I use the edition of Lyons 1550, 5 vols., 1:252. The passage is cited (in defective form) and explicated in Bigongiari, "Were There Theaters," p. 208. Accursius's *Glossa ordinaria* was compiled around 1230, but individual glosses may be much older.

[204] The edition of Mainz 1460 has been reprinted (Farnborough, Hants. 1971).

[205] Balbus, *Catholicon*, under *comedia*.

[206] *Ibid.*, under *comicus*: "Duo sunt genera comicorum, scilicet comediam scribentium, scilicet veteres qui joculatores exstiterunt, ut Terentius; novi, qui et satirici, quibus generaliter vitia carpuntur, ut Persius et Juvenalis. Et nudi pinguntur, quia vitia denudent."

questions *Spiritus* as doctor.

In his entry on *histrio*, which he defines as a gesticulator or joculator who knows how to represent the various gestures and "habits" of men, he notes that histrions were representers of comedies who used masks in their recitation.[207] His definition of *persona*, in so far as it touches on our subjects, is similarly restricted to comedy: a person is a histrion, a representer of comedies, because he (im)personates various persons in various ways by representing them. He has no theatrical explanation for *larva* or *ludo* or *orchestra*, and no entry for *hypocrita* or *joculator*. He repeats Huguccio on *scena*, but adds other meanings: it can sometimes mean the whole theater, or the recitation of a written work, or the work itself, and sometimes the speaking together of different persons, or a part of the writing that is recited there (in the scene), as in Terence.

There is, then, nothing that I have found, even under related entries, that would add to or qualify Huguccio's nontheatrical account of tragedy.

Another lexicographer who wrote in the time of Balbus was the long-lived William Brito. The chronicler Salimbene met him in Lyons in 1249, and he seems to have been still active as rector of the University of Paris and procurator of the Gallican Nation in 1304.[208] In his metrical dictionary on Hebrew and Greek words, he defines *tragedus* as a singer of kings' crimes or egregious events.[209] As with the Huguccian treatment, there is no relic of the theatrical in Brito's lines, and, moreover, no notion of plot movement or style.

In contrast, Brito's two lines on *scena* manage to include most of Balbus's meanings (shade, shadow, recitation, recited poem, part of the theater, or the theater itself) and another besides (lodge, or *loggia*).[210]

---

[207] *Ibid.*, under *histrio*: "quasi histrio, id est gesticulator, joculator, qui diversos gestus et habitus hominum scit representare. Unde histriones dicebantur representatores comediarum, qui in recitatione larvas sue faciei apponentes representabant habitus et gestus diversorum."

[208] See Brito's verse dictionary, *Brito metricus*, ed. Daly, p. xi. The metrical dictionary was finished in its final form after his prose dictionary (see next note) and his *Expositiones* on Jerome's biblical prefaces, both of which were already well known in 1272, according to Roger Bacon.

[209] *Brito metricus*, p. 108:

> Hircanus *tragicus* tibi sit, fertur *tragos* hircus;
> Est *ode* cantus, *tragos* adde, sit inde *tragedus*,
> Qui regum scelera canit aut enormia gesta.　　　　　(2162–64)

In the next line he defines *tragenia* (a misreading of *tragema*, no doubt) as "vilia vel prava ... dona." He has no entry for comedy. None of these entries is in his larger prose work, *Summa Britonis, sive Guillelmi Britonis Expositiones vocabulorum Biblie.*

[210] *Brito metricus*, p. 89:

> *Scena* sit umbraculum, recitatio, vel recitatum
> Carmen; sit logium, theatri pars, umbra, theatrum.　　　　(1796–97)

See the long entries on *scenofactoria* and *scenophegia* in the *Summa Britonis*, 2:690–92.

In the various uses or discussions of tragedy and comedy that we have seen in this chapter, the most noteworthy feature, perhaps, is the newly discovered or invented principle that "the end justifies the names." In the most important formulations, those of William of Conches and Huguccio, tragedy ends in adversity and sadness respectively, and the subject matter is specified as large-scale crimes. But the form is vague. Conches speaks of a *scriptum*, which could mean any kind of writing, including prose, of fact or fiction. Huguccio is led by his understanding of the word to think of poetry, some kind of song of praise (the Greek *oda* means *cantus* or *laus*), written in high style. In both cases there is a narrative aspect, detailing the beginning in prosperity and joy, and the end in adversity and sadness.

I presume that both Conches and Huguccio thought of tragedy as dealing with the story of the deserved downfall of a great criminal, who, therefore, was not praiseworthy. This was not the usual view of those who, rather than defining tragedy, identified instances of tragedy or the substance of tragedy. For example, when Otto of Freising likens real-life events to tragedy, he is thinking mainly of undeserved suffering. If great iniquities are committed, they are committed not by the person who comes to grief, but by his persecutors. The same is true of Aelred of Rievaulx and Peter of Blois when they identify contemporary literary works, like Arthurian romances, as tragedies. John of Salisbury is an exception in seeming to emphasize falls caused by the folly or sins of the main "actors" of the tragedy of the world.

The practice of characterizing contemporary poems as tragedies was abortive, as was the deliberate composition of new tragedies. But the series of errors in the *Accessus ad Lucanum* by which Lucan rather than Nero or Seneca was labeled a tragedian or author of tragedy was prophetic of a new development: the identification of classical epics as tragedies. However, in the absence of tragic dramas, epics would indeed be the only representatives of tragedy, even in the theory of Aristotle and his successors. For Aristotle, we remember, analyzes epics in much the same way as he does tragedies, except for the acted and "spectacular" dimensions.

5

The high Middle Ages: discoveries and oblivions

The thirteenth century has been termed the greatest of centuries by an admirer of the philosophical and theological achievements of the period,[1] but it was a low point on some literary fronts. At the beginning of the century, there was the last flowering of the Arthurian movement, in French prose and German verse, but apart from these works – and splendid lyric poetry – very little influential vernacular literature was written at this time, except for the two parts of the *Roman de la Rose*. Moreover, many of the scholarly gains of the twelfth century and earlier were lost, and France and England were, in general, slower than Italy to set out on the road to recovery and discovery.

The tragedies of Seneca were discovered and studied in Italy at the end of the thirteenth century, and though an English scholar in the second decade of the fourteenth century wrote a commentary on the plays at the request of an Italian cardinal in Avignon, it is only in Italy that we see the commentary being used and find Senecan influence upon ideas of tragedy or hear discussions of the dramatic nature of ancient tragedy. A parallel discovery of Seneca's tragedies a century earlier in northern France seems to have resulted only in the preparation of a large-scale florilegium of notable sentiments.

ARISTOTLE: A LOST OPPORTUNITY

The great new figure of Antiquity in the twelfth and thirteenth centuries was Aristotle. His works were being introduced into the Latin world both directly from the Greek and through Arabic intermediaries.

Occasional mentions of tragedy were to be found in Aristotle's scientific works. For instance, he says in the *Metaphysics* that nature does not consist of episodes of phenomena, like a badly written tragedy (*mochthēra*

---

[1] James Joseph Walsh, *The Thirteenth, Greatest of Centuries*.

tragōidia).² One of the Latin versions renders this as "lugubrious tragedy,"³ which shows a certain traditional notion of the nature of tragedy.

In the *Nicomachean Ethics*, Aristotle says that it makes a great difference whether those who are connected with a given occurrence are alive or dead, much more than it matters in tragedies whether lawlessness and fearful events are simply referred to as having happened beforehand, or whether they actually occur (that is, on the stage).⁴ Robert Grosseteste gives a fairly straightforward translation of the passage,⁵ but makes it look as if the horrors of tragedy are contrasted with those of real life. This is the way Thomas Aquinas understands the passage in his commentary. The dead have the same relationship to the living in real life, he says, as recited past events – like the Trojan wars – have to events that are now occurring. He doubtless has the story of Troy still in mind when he illustrates "injustices" by naming homicide and rapine (including rape, as in the rape of Helen?), and explains "evils" as "any kind of misfortune." By preexistence in tragedies, Aristotle means "recited by poets as at one time existing." It is clear, Thomas says, that even though recited evils of the past somehow pertain to the listener, who is affected by them in a certain way, they do not change his condition. Much less do events change the condition of a dead man.⁶

No doubt Thomas chose the Trojan wars as an example of the subject matter of tragedy because, as he shows in his commentary on Aristotle's *De generatione*, he understood tragedy to mean *sermo de rebus bellicis*, "speech about war," in contrast to comedy, which is *sermo de rebus urbanis*, "speech about urban, or urbane, affairs."⁷ Perhaps he was influenced by the old

---

² Aristotle, *Metaphysics* 14.3 (Bekker 1090b19–20).
³ Aristotle, *Metaphysica, Translatio Anonyma sive Media*, book 13, pp. 265–66: "Non videtur natura accidentalis ens ex parentibus [or: ponentibus], tanquam lugubris tragedia."
⁴ Aristotle, *Ethica nicomachaea* 1.11.4 (1101a31 ff.).
⁵ *Ibid.*, Robert Grosseteste's *Recensio pura* 1.15: "Differe autem passionum unamquamque circa viventes vel mortuos contingit multo magis quam injusta et mala preexistere in tragediis vel fieri" (ed. René Antoine Gautier, 3:158). Cf. the *Translatio Antiquior:* "magis quam injusta et odibilia presistere in tragediis vel operari" (ed. Gautier, 2:89).
⁶ Thomas Aquinas, *Commentarium in Ethica (Sententia libri Ethicorum)* 1.17, *Opera omnia* (Parma 1852–73) 21:37: "Et ideo hoc modo se habent mortui ad viventes secundum considerationem hujus vite sicut se habent ea que nunc actu contingunt ad ea que olim fuerunt et nunc recitantur, puta bella trojana vel aliquid hujusmodi. Dicit ergo quod hoc quod quecumque passionum (id est, accidentium fortuitorum) contingant circa vivos vel circa mortuos multo magis differt quam quod aliqua injusta (puta homicidia vel rapine) et mala (id est, infortunia quecumque) preexistant in tragediis (id est, a poetis recitentur ut olim existentia) vel quod nunc fiant... Manifestum est enim quod preterita mala recitata, etsi quodam modo pertineant ad audientem, qui aliquo modo ad ea afficitur, non tamen ita quod immutent conditionem ipsius. Unde multo minus fortuna immutant conditionem mortui." This passage can be found in the *Supplementum* to the *Index thomisticus (ITS)*, 4:153, nos. 5–6.
⁷ Aquinas, commenting on Aristotle's observation in *De generatione et corruptione* that tragedy and comedy are created from the same letters of the alphabet, says: "ex eisdem autem litteris, transmutatis secundum ordinem aut positionem, fiunt diversi sermones, puta comedia, que est sermo de rebus urbanis, et tragedia, que est sermo de rebus bellicis" (*In libros de generatione* 1.3.4, *ITS* 4:50). Cf. *In*

glossarial definition of *tragoedica* as *bellica cantica vel fabulatio vel hircania*.[8] He enlarges upon his definitions in his commentary on Aristotle's *Politics*, where Aristotle observes that even when a comic chorus is made up of the same men as a tragic chorus, we say it is different. Thomas understands *chorus*, which was the same word as that used for the chanting of the Divine Office, as referring in Aristotle's context to those who spoke *cantiones in choreis*. By *cantio* he may have had in mind the sort of chanson performed by the minstrels of his day in Paris, where he composed this commentary during his second appointment there (around 1270). *Chorea*, which ordinarily means "dance," or "place of dancing," may be a deliberately vague word that simply means the place or occasion of the chorus's performances. Thomas's point is that when a chorus is comic, that is, speaking comedial chansons about the doings of the lowest sort of persons, it is not the same as when it is tragic, that is, speaking tragic chansons about the wars of princes.[9]

Thomas may have been inspired to associate tragedy specifically with Troy by Augustine's examples of tragic roles. He cites Augustine several times on the point of a true tragedian being a false Hector: a tragedian who represents other persons in the theaters would not be an imitation Hector unless he were really a tragedian.[10] But whereas in his commentaries on Aristotle he is thinking, apparently, of poets reciting narrative poems, he clearly realizes that Augustine in the *Soliloquies* is speaking of a stage impersonation, as when he gives the example of Roscius in *scena* as a false Hecuba and as "assimilating" Priam.[11] Thomas interprets this to mean *in theatris*; and when commenting on St. Jerome's objection to singing *in tragediarum modum* and using *theatrales moduli* in church, he speaks of singing *more theatrico*.[12] Thomas also repeatedly cites Boethius's explanation of "person" as coming from the masks that represented famous men in comedies and tragedies, so that the term came to be attributed to men of

---

Meta., 1.7.6: "ex eisdem literis diversimode se habentibus fit tragedia et comedia" (*ITS* 4:397).

[8] See chap. 3 above, n. 55

[9] Aquinas, *Sententia libri Politicorum* 3.2.8: "Sicut videmus in illis qui dicunt cantiones in choreis, quod non est idem chorus si quandoque sit comicus, id est, dicens cantiones comediales de factis infimarum personarum, quandoque autem tragicus, id est dicens tragicas cantiones de bellis principum" (*ITS* 4:270–71); see the Leonine edition, pp. A 190–91, which also gives Aristotle's text, in William of Moerbeke's translation: "Sicut et chorum quandoque quidem komicum, quandoque autem tragicum, alterum esse dicimus, eisdem sepe hominibus existentibus" (p. A 189).

[10] Aquinas, *De veritate* 1.10, ad 5: "Unde dicit Augustinus in libro *Soliloquiorum* quod tragedus qui representat alienas personas in theatris non esset falsus [Hector] nisi esset verus tragedus" (*ITS* 3:7); *Summa theologie* 1.17.1 corpus: "Et sicut dicit Augustinus in libro *Solil.*, quod tragedus est falsus Hector" (*ITS* 2:213); *ibid.* 1.17.4, ob. 2: "quia, sicut dicit Aug. in libro *Solil.*, tragedus non esset falsus Hector, si non esset verus tragedus" (*ITS* 2:214). He is citing Augustine, *Soliloquia* 2.10.18 (PL 32:893).

[11] Augustine, *Soliloquia*. Other roles mentioned are those of Andromache and Hercules.

[12] Aquinas, *Summa theologie* 2–2.91.2, ob. 2 and ad 2 (*ITS* 2:645).

dignity. But in his earliest discussion, in his commentary on Lombard's *Sentences*, he makes it clear he has a chanted narrative recitation rather than an exchange of dialogue in mind.[13] Elsewhere, he defines the old and new comedies that Aristotle refers to as representations, and characterizes them as narrations containing the conversation of men speaking to each other.[14] Thomas seems also to have known of another use of the word *tragedia*, to signify bombastic style or loudness of speech. When one speaks "with a certain tragedy," one intends to excite wonder by the magnification of words.[15]

What is not clear from the above-cited passages is whether or not Thomas knew anything about the kinds of stories traditionally ascribed to tragedy, apart from the fact that they dealt with important persons and could include various evils and misfortunes, including wars. We cannot assume that he considered such evils to be peculiarly characteristic of tragedy, any more than, say, of the works of historiographers or elegists.

A study of the explanations of Aristotle's mentions of tragedy by other commentators would undoubtedly yield an interesting variety of ideas. I shall be content here with citing only the works of Albert the Great, one of Thomas's professors. In his treatise *De generatione*, when taking up the example of comedies and tragedies as being composed of the same letters of the alphabet, he defines comedies as songs of praise sung by comics, that is, imitations of the laudable deeds of the ancients sung to an audience of villagers, as the Greek etymology indicates. Tragedies on the other hand are songs of vituperation, in which vituperations of the ancients are sung in a simple fashion among villagers or rustics. The name comes from the Greek word for goat, indicating that those who sang of filthy deeds received a filthy animal as a reward.[16]

---

[13] Aquinas, *In Sententias* 1.23.1.1 corpus, in fine (*ITS* 1:63): "In tragediis et comediis recitatores sibi ponebant quamdam larvam ad representandum illum cujus gesta narrabant decantando." See also *Summa theologie* 1.29.3, ob. 2 and ad 2 (*ITS* 2:230–31), cited by Marshall, "Boethius' Definition," p. 478; and *De potentia* 9.3, ob. 1 (*ITS* 3:253). Thomas cites Boethius's *Contra Eutychen* as *De duabus naturis*.

[14] Aquinas, *Sententia libri Ethicorum* 4.16.10: "Et dicit quod hoc maxime apparet considerando tam in veteribus quam in novis comediis, id est, representationibus collocutionum hominum ad invicem: quia si alicubi in talibus narrationibus occurreret aliquod turpiloquium," and so on (*ITS* 4:182).

[15] Aquinas, *In octo libros Physicorum* 6.11.6: "quod dictum est cum [or: in] quadam tragedia, id est, cum [or: in] quadam magnificatione verborum, ad admirationem movendam; sed non facit aliquid ad virtutem rationis" (*ITS* 4:116). See the Marietti edition, p. 434. He is commenting on Aristotle's words, "quod cum tragedia dictum est" (*ibid*, p. 432).

[16] Albert the Great, *De generatione et corruptione* 1.1.8, *Opera omnia*, 4:352: "Et hujus exemplum esse dicebant in litteris que diverso ordine posite componunt dictiones et orationes, et una littera dempta vel apposita vel aliter sita judicium et sensus orationis variatur, sicut apparet in comediis et tragediis. Sunt enim comedie carmina laudis que cantant comici, hoc est, imitationes gestorum laudabilium Antiquorum. *Comes* enim grece sonat latine villa, quia villanorum congregatione talia cantantur. Tragedie autem carmina sunt vituperationis quibus Antiquorum vituperia simpliciter inter villanos

Albert was probably influenced by the etymological explanation of the common element in *comedia* and *tragedia*, which we have seen in Huguccio, was *oda*, meaning both praise and song, so that comedy would be "farmerish praise," and tragedy "goatish praise." If so, he took the praise element of tragedy to be ironic.

In his commentary on the *Politics*, at a point where the old translation rendered Aristotle as saying that young persons should not be spectators of *iambi* and *comedia*, Albert read *lambi* and added *tragedia*. He invents an explanation for *lambi*: they are those who lap up the flavors of food and drink, whom we call *lecatores* and *histriones*. Comedians are those who sing the deeds and praises of heroes in villages and make representations of persons like Priam and Hector. He draws on Boethius's explanation of *persona* as a mask used by the histrion, and then goes on to explain that tragedians are those who recite the deeds of foul persons, like Sardanapalus.[17] He misinterprets Aristotle as opposing the opinion of Theodorus, a *gesticulator tragedie*, that very young children need not be kept away from such performances in the theaters (defined as *atria* where spectacles are held), because Aristotle believes (according to Albert) that all children should be guarded against the infection and adhesion of turpitude.[18] Turpitude, of course, is the subject matter of tragedy.

Albert manifests similar views in his commentary on the passage in the *Ethics* dealt with above, in which deeds contained in tragedies are compared to the deeds of dead men. Once again, he treats of both tragedies and comedies, this time adding comedies to the tragedies mentioned in the text. He says that the good deeds of a man who once existed, when recited by comedians to an audience, stimulate praise and glory for him. Comedians versified the sublime deeds of illustrious persons, men resplendent in the glory of complete uprightness, and recited them in theaters and other meeting places, whereas tragedians recited the foul deeds

---

cantantur, dicta a *tragos* quod est hircus: quia feda cantantes fetidum animal hircum in remuneratione accipiebant. Hec ergo carmina laudis et vituperii ex eisdem aliter ordinatis sunt litteris."

[17] Albert, *Commentarium in Politica* 7.15, § k (*Opera omnia*, 8:748–49): "Adjungit autem quod non expedit juniores spectatores fieri lamborum neque comedie neque tragedie. Lambi autem sunt lambentes sapores escarum et potuum, quos nos lecatores vocamus et histriones. Comedi autem sunt qui facta heroum canunt in villis, et representationes faciunt personarum, sicut Priami et Hectoris et hujusmodi. Propter quod etiam [in] 'persona' media producitur, ut dicit Boetius in libro *De Trinitate* [he goes on to explain that the middle vowel in *persona* is long because of the effect of the mask]... Comedia dicitur a *comos*, quod est villa, et comedi sunt qui in villis et congregationibus edunt carmina de laudibus heroum. Tragedi autem sunt qui turpium personarum facta recitant, sicut Sardanapali. Unde etiam post recitationem, hircum, quasi fetidum animal, acceperunt; et ideo dicuntur tragedi a *tragos*, quod est hircus, quem in remunerationem accipiebant." See p. 743 for the *Antiqua translatio*, and see also Albert's textual explication at the end of § k (p. 749). (I transliterate the Greek in this edition into the Latin forms that Albert presumably used.)

[18] *Ibid.*, § m (pp. 749–50).

of degenerate men, for which they received a fetid goat. The comedians for their part were rewarded by the openhandedness (*libertas*) of the audience.[19] When he goes on to characterize the effect of tragedies, he speaks of joy and sadness: "However, the foul deeds thus recited do not transform the foul person who committed them to a state of joy or sadness, because he is not present; but they do increase the gloom of his unhappiness, so that he who is unhappy in himself is darkened in the opinion of men and thus becomes more unhappy, being rendered abominable to everyone. For the *politicus* ordains comedians and tragedians for this purpose, that the virtue of men of old might be made vivid to contemporary men through the poetry of the comedian, and that the life of foul men might be made abominable to everyone through the reprehension of the tragedian."[20]

Albert's undertstanding of tragedy could be seen as the result of taking seriously the definitions of Isidore, Conches, and Huguccio stressing the fetid and criminal subject matter, therefore excluding honorable protagonists like Priam and Hector; but in assigning such characters to comedy, he goes against the definitions of these and other authorities that limited the subject matter of comedy to base persons and events. He seems to imply a different idea of comedy later in his commentary on the *Ethics*, when speaking of the extravagant person who puts out the red (or rather purple) carpet for comedians, comedians being those "who sing and recite the deeds of men in gatherings of rustics, and who are of little worth."[21] He does the same later still when speaking of the different effects of the foul speech of comedies upon the listeners: to some it was a joke, but to others it was cause for grief and a suspicion that the speakers' morals matched their speech.[22] He goes on to say that the vices of persons are recited and

[19] Albert, *Commentarium in Ethica* 1.7.17 (*Opera omnia*, 7:131): "Facta enim hominum bona a comedis et comediis recitata et in effectum non existentia, quamvis preextiterint in preterito, quando recitantur a comedis, nihil immutationis afferunt circa hominem qui facit ea, eo quod presens non est; sed apud presentes et audientes comedum excitant laudem et gloriam homin[is], qui[a] splendor fame magis clarum facit hominem qui facta illa peregit. Comedus enim dicitur a *come*, quod est villa. Et comedi sunt qui in communitatibus villarum et theatrorum et palestrarum dictato carmine recitabant sublimia facta virorum illustrium, in gloria omnis honestatis splendentium. Tragedi autem dicunt a *tragos*, quod est hircus; et tragedus qui est in palestris et theatris et conventibus hominum turpia facta degenerantium virorum dictato carmine recitabat, propter quod fetidum animal hircum in remunerationem accipit. Comedus autem libertate audientium remunerabatur."

[20] *Ibid.* (p. 132). "Turpia autem facta sic recitata turpem qui talia peregit non immutat in gaudium vel tristitiam, quia presens non est; sed tenebras sue infelicitatis augent, ut qui in se infelix fuit, obscuratus in notitia hominum infelicior fiat, et omnibus reddatur abominabilis. Idcirco enim politicus ordinat comedos et tragedos, ut ex carmine comedi presentibus impigra fiat virtus antiquorum hominum, etiam ex vituperio tragedi omnibus vita turpium fiat abominabilis."

[21] *Ibid.*, 4.1.13 (p. 293): "Comedis, qui in congregationibus rusticorum cantant et recitant facta hominum, et parvo digni sunt, multa tribuet, et in transitu communi purpuram inferens ad vie decorem, que in transitibus regum inferri consuevit."

[22] *Ibid.*, 4.3.4 (p. 324): "Hoc autem probatur ex comediis veterum et modernorum: in his enim apud quosdam erat turpiloquium, derisio enim apud quosdam erat suspicio; unde derisionem

represented in both comedies and tragedies, which were designed for recreation and for distracting the mind from its own concerns.[23] When he comes to the passage on comic and tragic choruses in the *Politics*, he gives "tragic" a positive sense: a chorus, he explains, is a musical dance ensemble (*symphonia*) that sometimes differs in form, but not in matter; a comic chorus is one that rustics dance to, whereas a tragic chorus is a chorus of nobles, to which nobles and city-dwellers dance.[24]

Aristotle's treatise that deals centrally with tragedy, the *Poetics*, was not translated from the Greek until shortly after Thomas's death. The translation was the work of William of Moerbeke, and it was done in 1278, when he seems to have been staying at the papal court in Viterbo. Only two manuscripts of it survive, both of them apparently copied in Italy. Aristotle's remarks on the iamb in chapter 4 drew the attention of a glossator, who added what Isidore had to say on the subject.[25] Perhaps the glossator was Albertino Mussato of Padua, the only known user of Moerbeke's translation in the Middle Ages. In his *Evidentia tragediarum Senece*, Mussato draws on the same chapter of the *Poetics*, but only for the point that the inventor of the iamb was unknown. In his *Vita Senece (Lucii Annei Senece cordubensis vita et mores)*, he quotes from the last chapter of Moerbeke's *Poetics*, for Aristotle's remarks about the sort of acting (*hypocrisis*) that should be objected to, namely, that which imitates "nonliberal women."[26] But Aristotle's work had no effect whatsoever upon Mussato's ideas of tragedy, which, as we shall see, were based on traditional concepts and on the newly discovered Senecan plays.

I recently concluded that Petrarch must have been using chapter 4 of

turpiloquium reputantes, turpiloquium ludum reputabant; hi autem qui reputabant suspicionem in turpiloquio, contristabantur, suspicantes quod tales in habitu essent turpiloqui quales ostendebant se esse in sermone vel facto." His point is made in a much clearer and fuller way in his earlier *Lectura in Ethica*; see the excerpt given in the Leonine edition of Aquinas's *Sententia libri Ethicorum* 4.16, p. 257, which reads in part: "Probat hanc differentiam ludorum ex comediis – que sunt de recitationibus gestorum que sunt in villis (dicitur enim a *comos*, quod est villa) – tam in antiquis quam in modernis; quia turpiloquia et ludicra verba quibusdam recitantur fuisse tantum ad derisionem, id est ad risum, que scilicet non habent inhonestatem, et quibusdam erat suspicio de vitiis dicentis; qui enim delectatur in turpibus verbis dat de se presumptionem quod sit vitiosus. Sed hi ludi multum differunt ad honestatem." Thomas explains comedies here as "representationes collocutionum hominum ad invicem," that is, simulated conversations.

[23] Albert, *Commentarium in Ethica* 4.3.4 (p. 325): "sicut in ludis comediarum et tragediarum, in quibus vitia personarum recitantur et representantur. Comedie autem et tragedie ad requiem invente sunt, ut in eis spiritus a studii vehementia remittatur; et ideo in genere ludi continentur."

[24] Albert, *Commentarium in Politica* 3.1, §n (p. 213): "Et dat simile, ibi, *Sicut et chorum*, id est, symphoniam que dicitur chorus, *quandoque comicum, quandoque autem tragicum, alterum esse dicimus, eisdem sepe hominibus existentibus*: tunc enim formaliter differt, licet sit in eadem materia successive. Est enim comicus chorus dictus a *comos*, quod est villa, et est chorus rusticorum, scilicet ad quem rustici choreas ducunt. Tragicus autem est chorus nobilium, ad quem nobiles et civiles chorizant."

[25] Aristotle, *De arte poetica*, tr. William of Moerbeke, p. xv.

[26] Kelly, "Aristotle," p. 188.

Moerbeke's translation in his *Invective contra medicum*, when he taunts his adversary for not knowing what it means to have moved from tetrameters to iambics, and for not knowing what tragedy is.[27] But I now think it much more likely that he was drawing rather on Aristotle's *Rhetoric*, where he says that those who make tragedies moved from tetrameters to the iambic.[28] I have not seen any indication that he ever explained his understanding of Aristotle's view on tragedy, or showed any sign of drawing on Moerbeke's translation of the *Poetics* in any other context. He may, however, have been drawing on Herman Alemannus's translation of Averroes's commentary on the *Poetics* for his low opinion of Arabic poets.[29]

As I have noted, Aquinas died before Moerbeke made his literal translation of the *Poetics* from the Greek, but he did know and use Alemannus's work, which was finished in the year 1256. The work survives in twenty-four manuscripts and was printed in 1481, which attests to a certain popularity.[30] But for a number of reasons, it had almost no influence on how *tragedia* was understood in the Latin West. As we shall see, the principal reason is that most of its users did not read, or were not able to read, far enough into the work to see that tragedy was being spoken of.

Alemannus had intended to translate the whole of the *Poetics* from the Arabic, but abandoned the idea because of its difficulty. He had trouble

[27] Petrarch, *Invective contra medicum*, book 3, ed. Pier Giorgio Ricci, in *Prose*, p. 656: "nescire te quid sit tragedia, aut quid de tetrametris in iambicos transisse." See Kelly, *Tragedy and Comedy*, p. 9 n. 38.

[28] Aristotle, *Rhetoric* 3.1.3. For two medieval translations, see *Rhetorica: Translatio Anonyma sive Vetus et Translatio Guillelmi de Moerbeka*. Aristotle's point is that the diction of poetry is different from that of prose: this can be seen with the authors of tragedies, who have stopped using tetrameters in favor of the iamb, which is closer to common speech, and who avoid the poetic diction used by earlier poets and still used by those who write hexameters. Moerbeke's translation reads: "Manifestat autem quod accidit; neque enim qui tragedias faciunt adhuc utuntur eodem modo, sed quemadmodum ex tetrametris in iambicum transierunt quia orationi hoc metrorum simillimum est aliorum, sic et nominum dimiserunt quecumque penes ydioma sunt, quibus autem priores ornabant, et adhuc nunc qui exametra faciunt, dimiserunt" (p. 283). Cf. the Anonymous translation: "Manifestat autem quod contingit; neque enim qui tragedias facientes amplius utuntur secundum hunc modum, sed quemadmodum et ex tetrametris ad iambicum transtulerunt se pro eo quod est in sermone hoc imitabilissimum aliorum metrorum, sic et nominum dimiserunt quecumque circa dialeticam est, quibus autem qui primo in mundo erant, et amplius nunc qui exametra facientes, dimiserunt" (p. 124). I should point out, in conjunction with Mussato's understanding of *hypocrisis* to mean a speaker's delivery, that Aristotle himself gives a similar meaning to the word a bit earlier in the *Rhetoric*, namely, 3.1.3, where he says that hypocrisy is the most important aspect of diction (style), but it has not yet been treated by anyone, for it came late to tragedy and rhapsody since the poets at first "hypocrisized" their tragedies for themselves. Moerbeke's rendition is: "Tertium autem horum, quod virtutem habet maximam, nondum autem expositum, est que circa ypocrisim. Etenim in tragicam et rapsodiam tarde devenit; ypocrisabant enim ipsis tragedias poete primum" (p. 281; cf. the Anonymous translation, p. 122).

[29] Petrarch, *Epistole seniles* 12.2, *Opera*, 2:1009. See Kelly, "Aristotle," pp. 205–06.

[30] I use the editions of Boggess and Minio-Paluello. For a table of correspondences between the chapters of the Greek *Poetics* and the Averroes–Alemannus text, see Kelly, "Aristotle," p. 164 n. 10. For Aquinas's uses of Alemannus (which do not concern tragedy), see below, p. 124.

finding anyone to aid him in interpreting either the *Poetics* or the *Rhetoric*, but while he did translate the latter in its entirety, he decided to rest content with Averroes's "middle-sized" commentary on the *Poetics*. Averroes included excerpts from the *Poetics* in his commentary, but though the excerpts seem to be influenced by the extant Arabic translation of Abu Bishr Matta, they are either taken from another translation, or are his own reinterpretations or paraphrases.[31] One of the ways in which he agrees with Abu Bishr is in translating rather than transliterating the terms "tragedy" and "comedy"; the translation for tragedy is "praise," and for comedy is "vituperation." Thus the two words are given meanings precisely opposite to those assigned them by Albert the Great.

I noted above that Albert was probably drawing on the idea that both words were compounds of *oda*, "praise." But the Arabic commentators take the whole word "tragedy" to mean a poem of praise, or the art of praise-poetry, while "comedy" is taken as dispraise. Moreover, Averroes understands tragedy as the praise of virtue, and comedy as dispraise of vice. The basis for this seemingly strange notion is what Aristotle says at the beginning of chapter 2: tragedy deals with the spudean, comedy with the phaulic.[32]

One of the most important instances in which Averroes departs from Abu Bishr's interpretation of Aristotle's text occurs at the very beginning of chapter 1, where Aristotle gives a list of poetic forms, beginning, "Epic poetry, the poetry of tragedy, also comedy," and so on. Abu Bishr takes this to mean, "Throughout all poetry and every poetic hymn we follow [or, require] either encomium or diatribe or poetic dithyramb," and so on. Averroes, however, understands Aristotle to mean that "every poem and poetic statement is either satire or eulogy." Alemannus translates it, "Omne itaque poema et omnis oratio poetica aut est vituperatio aut est laudatio." As for the other arts in Aristotle's list, Averroes takes them to refer to imitations of poetry.[33]

[31] See Charles E. Butterworth's English translation of Averroes's Arabic text: *Averroes' Middle Commentary on Aristotle's Poetics*. Unfortunately, Butterworth completely neglects Alemannus's Latin text and the modern scholars who have established it, such as Gabrieli, Tkatsch, Boggess, and Minio-Paluello (see Kelly, "Aristotle," pp. 161–63); he cites only O. B. Hardison's English translation in *Classical and Medieval Literary Criticism*, pp. 341–38. Thus he does not consider the evidence of variant readings, text divisions, and direct Aristotelian citations that the Latin tradition indicates. In his translation, Butterworth provides marginal notes of Bekker numbers for what he takes to be the corresponding portions of the Greek *Poetics*, but he does not note the chapter divisions of the Greek, and makes no attempt to sort out Averroes's commentary from Aristotle's text. A new partial translation of Alemannus's text is given by A. J. Minnis and A. B. Scott, *Medieval Literary Theory and Criticism, c. 100–c. 1375: The Commentary Tradition*, pp. 289–307.
[32] See chap. 1 above, pp. 1–2; Kelly, "Aristotle," pp. 163–64.
[33] Abu Bishr, *Poetics*, chap. 1 (Tkatsch, 1:221); Averroes on *Poetics* 1 (Butterworth, *Averroes' Middle Commentary*, 1.3, pp. 59–60); Averroes–Alemannus on *Poetics* 1 (Boggess, *Commentarium medium*, p.

Aristotle's celebrated definition of tragedy in chapter 6 becomes a statement of the essential aim of the art of praise, which is to represent an action that is willed, virtuous, and complete, which "affects souls moderately by engendering compassion and fear in them"; or, as Alemannus puts it, "the representation generates certain passions in souls that moderate themselves, to pitying or fearing" ("representatio, inquam, que generat in animabus passiones quasdam temperativas ipsarum, ad miserendum aut timendum"). Alemannus adds: "or to other similar passions" ("aut ad ceteras consimiles passiones"), indicating perhaps that he knows a better translation of the *Poetics* than Abu Bishr's, at least of the famous *katharsis* passage.[34]

Shortly after reaching this point in his translation, Alemannus must have realized that Averroes's word for praise corresponded to tragedy. He could have found this out by consulting Avicenna's *Poetics* commentary or the writings of al-Farabi, if not another translation of the *Poetics*. He begins to substitute "tragedy" for "praise" on occasion, and four times he gives an explicit gloss of *ars laudandi* as *tragedia*.[35] He does not, however, identify *ars vituperandi* with *comedia*, but rather, at two points, he associates it with *satira*.[36]

Averroes shows no sign of knowing anything about the dramatic nature of tragedy and comedy, that is, the fact that they were plays consisting of dialogue to be acted out on the stage.[37] He takes Aristotle's references to stage business to refer simply to the mannerisms of a speaker's delivery, as when discussing Aristotle's fifth or sixth element of tragedy, *opsis*, that is, visual appearance or spectacle. Averroes interprets it to mean "speculation," which Alemannus translates as *consideratio*, defined as the establishment of the correctness of belief or action, not by persuasive means, but by the speech of representation; "for the art of poetry, and especially tragedy, does not consist in argumentation or probative speculation; therefore a poem of praise does not use the art of gesticulation or changes of countenance, as does rhetoric."[38] In any case, he likens the Greek genres to

3; Minio-Paluello, *De arte poetica*, p. 41); Kelly, "Aristotle," pp. 164, 173–74.

[34] Averroes on *Poetics* 6 (Butterworth 4.20, p. 73); Averroes–Alemannus on chap. 6 (Boggess, p. 16; Minio-Paluello, p. 47); Kelly, "Aristotle," p. 165 and n. 12.

[35] Kelly, "Aristotle," pp. 166–7. The four glosses occur further on in the commentary on chapter 6; in the commentary on chapter 9; at the end of chapter 12; and at the end of chapter 25 (Boggess, pp. 18–19, 30, 38, 86; Minio-Paluello, pp. 47–48, 52, 55, 74).

[36] Alemannus, in the commentary on *Poetics* 13 and 16 (Boggess, pp. 41, 56; Minio-Paluello, pp. 56, 62); Kelly, "Aristotle," pp. 169, 184.

[37] Butterworth, p. 20, seems to assume such knowledge in Averroes, but he does not discuss the matter.

[38] Averroes–Alemannus on *Poetics* 6 (Boggess, p. 23; Minio-Paluello, p. 49): "Et pars sexta est consideratio, scilicet argumentatio seu probatio rectitudinis credulitatis aut operationis, non per sermonem persuasivum (hoc enim non pertinet huic arti neque est conveniens ei), sed per sermonem representativum; ars nempe poetrie non est consistens in argumentationibus neque in speculatione

Arabic lyric and narrative poems. His accent is on narrative when he takes up the matter of Aristotle's thirteenth and fourteenth chapters. The poem of praise (now identified by Alemannus as tragedy) should ideally treat of persons of great virtue, and of disasters that befall such persons undeservedly.[39]

Specifically, Aristotle says (and here I follow only the Alemannus translation):

It is necessary that odes, that is, poems of praises that are intended to be an instigation to virtues, should be composed of representations of virtues and of representations of things inducing fear and sadness, from which perturbation follows, as, for example, misfortunes occurring to good persons beyond their deserts. For this strongly incites the soul to receive virtues. Now when a poet changes from representing virtue to representing non-virtue, or from representing the virtuous to representing the non-virtuous, this change does nothing to incite or stimulate a person, through terror, as it were, to virtuous actions; it does not induce intense love for such actions, or fear; and it is necessary that these two things be found in laudatory poems. And this happens when the change is from the representation of virtues to the representation of misfortunes and the evil of outcomes affecting good and well-deserving persons, or when there is a change from such [misfortunes] to a representation of those who abound in virtues. For such representations stir up souls and render them eager to take on virtues.[40]

There is in this adaptation of Aristotle no longer any question of a sequence of dramatic or narrative events occurring to a protagonist, but only, in inept tragedies, a sequence from virtues or virtuous persons to their opposites, or, in effective tragedies, from virtues to misfortunes occurring to virtuous persons. Or the effective sequence can be reversed: first the

considerativa, et proprie tragedia; ideoque non utitur carmen laudativum arte gesticulationis neque vultuum acceptione, sicut utitur hiis rhetorica." See Kelly, "Aristotle," pp. 166–7. Butterworth translates Averroes as saying, in the last part of this statement: "Indeed, the art of poetry, and especially the art of eulogy, is not based on proving and disputing. That is why eulogy does not use the art of dissimulation and delivery the way rhetoric does" (p. 79).

[39] Averroes on *Poetics* 13–14 (Butterworth 6.50–59, pp. 91–95); Averroes–Alemannus on *Poetics* 13–14 (Boggess, pp. 38–45; Minio-Paluello, pp. 55–57); Kelly, "Aristotle," pp. 168–70.

[40] Averroes–Alemannus on *Poetics* 13 (Boggess, pp. 38–39; Minio-Paluello, p. 55): "Oportet enim ut ode, id est, carmina laudum per que intenditur instigatio ad virtutes, composite sint ex representationibus virtutum et ex representationibus rerum incutientium pavorem et contristantium, ex quibus sequitur perturbatio, ut sunt infortunia incidentia bonis preter merita ipsorum. Per hec enim vehemens fit incitatio anime ad receptionem virtutum; nam permutatio poete a representatione virtutis ad representationem non virtutis aut a representatione virtuosi ad representationem non virtuosi non agit aliquid per quod incitetur homo aut stimuletur quasi terrefactus ad virtutum actiones, cum talis permutatio non inducat amorem ad eas intensum neque pavorem. Et in carminibus laudativis inveniri oportet has duas res; et istud contingit quando permutatio fit a representatione virtutum ad representationem infortuniorum et maliciam successuum incidentium bonis et emeritis, aut quando fit permutatio ab istis ad representationem eorum qui virtutibus habundant. He nempe representationes exacuunt animas et festinas reddunt eas ad receptionem virtutum."

misfortunes can be presented, and then an account of virtues, or, rather, of virtuous persons (presumably in the abstract). There is no indication that the misfortunes are to be told at any length (in fact, the indication is to the contrary, since the ode is the specified form), and no indication whether or not the misfortunes are necessarily fatal or insuperable.

Averroes's comment on this passage is given by Alemannus as follows:

> And you will find many representations of the sort that he refers to among those contained in the discourses of the Law, for such things are discourses of praise urging the doing of praiseworthy deeds, as, for example, what is told of the history of Joseph and his brothers. Other similar things are in the narratives of past deeds that are called exhortative exempla.[41]

We note that in Averroes's specific example from the Scriptures, that of Joseph and his brothers, the events turn out fortunately for the characters. The same is true of the other scriptural example he gives, to illustrate Aristotle's discussion in chapter 14 of the best kinds of events for tragedy, that is, grave deeds inflicted by friends on friends, like the killing of parents. "Therefore," he says, "what is narrated of Abraham, that he was commanded to sacrifice his beloved son, contains great misery and is intended as it were for the evoking of sorrow and compassion and fear."[42] Averroes was probably referring primarily to the Koran for both examples,[43] but readers of Alemannus's translation would undoubtedly think that the reference was to the Old Testament.

In another, more general, example, Averroes reveals that the martial virtues, including wrath ("a certain sadness and perturbation with vehement desire for revenge"), are among the allowable subjects of this genre. A tragedy on this theme is composed first by praising the virtues, and then by telling of instances in which strong and virtuous men have experienced the murder of their parents or suffered other such disasters, in order to stimulate in the audience "a vehement desire for good and a love of virtue and fear lest they be deprived of any virtuous good."[44] Here it seems

[41] *Ibid.*: "Et tu reperies plures representationum incidentium in sermonibus legalibus secundum hunc modum cujus fecit mentionem, cum talia sint sermones laudativi instigantes ad opera laudabilia, ut quod inducitur de historia Joseph et fratrum suorum, et alia consimilia de narrationibus gestorum preteritorum que nominantur exempla exortativa."

[42] Averroes–Alemannus on *Poetics* 14 (Boggess, p. 44; Minio-Paluello, p. 57; cf. Kelly, "Aristotle," p. 170): "Ideoque quod narratur de Abraham, quod mandatum fuit ei de immolatione filii sui dilectissimi, valde miserabile existit, et quasi in fine commotionis ad dolorem et compassionem et pavorem."

[43] See sura 12 for Joseph, and sura 37.100–13 for a brief account of Abraham.

[44] Averroes–Alemannus on *Poetics* 13, part of Aristotle's defense of Euripides (Kelly, "Aristotle," p. 169; cf. Boggess, pp. 40–41; Minio-Paluello, p. 56): "In artem laudandi res bellicas intromittuntur ea que motiva sunt et intentiva iracundie (ira nempe tristitia quedam est et turbatio cum vehementi appetitu vindicte); et cum sic se habeat, ergo rememoratio interfectionis parentum et occasionum consimilium incidentium viris strenuis et virtuosis movet et excitat in eis vehementem appetitum

evident that the writer of a tragedy is expected to give multiple examples of "grace under pressure," so to speak, and not an account of a single suffering protagonist.

Such a view of tragedy, as dealing with the misfortunes of the virtuous and deserving, would have been far more amenable to the context of Boethius's *Consolation of Philosophy* than is William of Conches's stress on the disgusting vices that are described in tragedy. Of course, Philosophy's point, and Fortune's, too, is that misfortunes unexpectedly befall both the well-deserving and the undeserving, but Boethius's main concern is with the former.

Averroes–Alemannus allows vice a certain place in tragedy, but only in connection with the enemies of the virtuous people who suffer misfortune: "The reprehension and vituperation of faults pertain more to satire than to tragedy, and therefore they should not be detailed in tragedies as the principal intention, but by way of *circulatio* [a distortion of Aristotle's "reversal"]: and when there is mention of faults in the laudatory poem, it is only excusable when they are the faults of the enemies and of those who are hated."[45] Conches, on the contrary, implies that tragedy deals with figures who pass from prosperity to adversity through their own iniquities; and since he specifies great iniquities, he is doubtless implying what Huguccio makes clearer: that tragedy deals with the downfall of criminals of high standing. Alemannus, on the other hand, interpreting Averroes, insists that the "protagonists" of tragedy should be great in virtue and not in vice, without consideration of noble stature or greatness of worldly position.

The Averroistic understanding of tragedy as the praise of suffering virtue would undoubtedly have had a significant effect on the Latin Middle Ages if only Alemannus had not neglected to go back to the beginning of his translation and gloss "praise" as "tragedy" when he first started to deal with the subject. Since he did not do so, the fact that Aristotle's *Poetics* dealt with tragedy appears to have escaped almost every user of Averroes's Latinized commentary. The work was seemingly of such impenetrable difficulty that most readers were satisfied to pounce upon and repeat with approval the dictum moralizing all poetry as either praise or blame. And it was not lost upon some that the terms used, praise and vituperation, were

boni et amorem virtutis et timorem ne in aliquo priventur bono virtutis."
[45] Averroes–Alemannus on *Poetics* 13, rendering Aristotle's discussion of the double-structured plot, as in the *Odyssey* (Boggess, p. 41; Minio-Paluello, p. 56; Kelly, "Aristotle," p. 169): "Reprehensio et vituperatio defectuum magis pertinet satire quam pertineat tragedie. Ideoque non oportet ut ipsorum imaginatio sit in tragediis secundum principalem intentionem sed per modum circulationis. Et quando in carmine laudativo habita fuerit mentio defectuum, tunc non est excusatio quin fiat mentio in ipso inimicorum et eorum qui odio habentur."

those of epidictic or demonstrative rhetoric, as explained by Aristotle and reported by Cicero.[46]

A genius like Thomas Aquinas, who cites Alemannus's translation of Averroes on the origin of fables and poetry, corresponding to Aristotle's chapters 2 and 4,[47] would clearly have been capable of reading the whole work and making a good deal of sense out of it; but we do not know whether he did so, since he never had occasion to deal directly with the subject of tragedy and the related topics covered by the work.

One scholar who clearly studied the work thoroughly was Bartholomew of Bruges, who composed an *accessus* and *divisio textus* for it in 1307. But he only belatedly identifies laudatory poetry with tragedy, and seems totally unfamiliar with the term.[48] A florilegist named John of Fayt, in his list of dicta taken from the work, expanded one of Alemannus's glosses to produce a sentence: "Tragedia est ars laudandi";[49] but we do not know if he, or any of the scribes or rubricists of the manuscripts, who could not have avoided realizing that Aristotle's work dealt with tragedy, did anything with the knowledge.

Apart from Herman Alemannus himself (who at the beginning of his rendition recommends using Horace's *Poetria* in interpreting the work), the only person who definitely correlated the Latinized Averroes's doctrine on tragedy with traditional concepts was Matthias of Linköping. This Swedish scholar studied arts at Paris and wrote a *Poetria*, or treatise on poetics, around the third decade of the fourteenth century.[50] Matthias does not seem to have understood or accepted the complete identification of praise-poetry with tragedy postulated by the Alemannus translation. He mentions tragedy only in connection with Horace's remarks on using suitable language, but he combines Horace with Averroes–Alemannus: "These things are said about the exaltation of great things in tragedy, according to the grave style. There is, however, another genre of poem which we call satire, to which the reprehension of vices specifically belongs. It should not be included in tragedy except by way of *circulatio*: that is, despicable vices are to be shown in order to make the exaltation of virtues all the more evident."[51]

---

[46] Kelly, "Aristotle," p. 198.
[47] Aquinas, *Expositio in 1 Tim.* cap. 4 lectio 2 (*ITS* 7:495); *Summa theologiae* 1–2.32.8 (*ITS* 2:399); 2–2.94.4 (*ITS* 2:648); 2–2.167.2 obj. 2 (*ITS* 2:778); texts in Kelly, "Aristotle," p. 174.
[48] Kelly, "Aristotle," pp. 175, 178–81. For a partial edition of Bartholomew's text, see Gilbert Dahan, "Notes et textes sur la poétique au moyen âge," pp. 223–39.
[49] Kelly, "Aristotle," pp. 177–78.
[50] *Ibid.*, p. 181. Matthias's *Poetria* has been edited, with many errors, by Stanislaw Sawicki, "*Poetria* och *Testa nucis* av magister Matthias Lincopensis," pp. 128–43. In my article I was able to quote the unpublished corrected text of Birger Bergh.
[51] Matthias of Linköping, *Poetria* (Kelly, "Aristotle," 184; Sawicki, *Poetria*, p. 135).

Matthias follows Alemannus again later in contrasting tragedy with satire rather than with comedy, when speaking of Horatian distinctions: "Sometimes, as Horace says, it happens that there is talk of light things in tragedy and of grave things in satire." But in spite of this implicit acknowledgment that the proper subject of satire is *levia*, Matthias places satire on an intermediate level between tragedy and comedy: "There are three manners of poetry among Latins, which use these three styles: for tragedy speaks of great things and uses the grave style, whereas satire deals with the correction of morals and uses the middle style, while comedy treats of everyday things and admits nothing but the humble style – whence its color is to make use of no color."[52] His last phrase, "color ejus est nullo colore uti," is a reference to Geoffrey of Vinsauf's dictum, "Est quandoque color vitare colorem,"[53] in his discussion of the humorous anecdote; and Vinsauf in turn is drawing on Horace's "tragico differre colori,"[54] where he makes the point that the language of the Satyr-play should not be so far from tragedy as to be that of comedy.

It is probable that a doctrine of the three styles of poetry as applied to tragedy, satire, and comedy developed out of commentaries on the *Poetria nova*, where Vinsauf contrasts the *levia* of the *res comica* with *seria* and *matura*.[55] Guizzardo of Bologna, writing in Padua about the same time Matthias was in Paris, explains Geoffrey as saying that the matter of comedy does not wish to be colored, and then, after providing an example, he compares comedy, satire, and tragedy with each other. Satire and tragedy, he says, are higher styles, and need to be colored according to their own mode.[56] Benvenuto da Imola, as we shall see below, expands upon a similar schema in his commentary on Dante's *Comedy*. But though both Guizzardo and Benvenuto used the Averroes–Alemannus commentary, they did not realize that it dealt with tragedy.[57]

NICHOLAS TREVET ON BOETHIUS AND SENECA

Another potential source of new information on tragedy that came to light in the thirteenth century was Seneca's *Book of Tragedies*. At first, the

---

[52] *Ibid.* (Kelly, "Aristotle," p. 184; Sawicki, *Poetria*, pp. 140–41).
[53] Geoffrey of Vinsauf, *Poetria nova*, p. 255.
[54] Horace, *Ars poetica* 236.
[55] Geoffrey of Vinsauf, *Poetria nova* 1910–19. Pier Vincenzo Mengaldo, "Stili, dottrina degli," p. 436, cites a scholion to the *Rhetorica ad Herennium* that gives this paradigm: "Secundum intentionem dicimus tragedum uti alto, satirum mediocri, comedum humili genere." But he does not gives details of the source.
[56] Guizzardo of Bologna, *Recollecte super Poetria magistri Gualfredi*, fol. 15v, cited in Kelly, "Aristotle," p. 195 n. 155.
[57] See Kelly, "Aristotle," pp. 193–95 for Guizzardo, and pp. 200–04 for Benvenuto.

tragedies were simply mined for apophthegms, with the effect that Seneca Tragicus was absorbed by Seneca Moralis.[58] The Dominican encyclopedist Vincent of Beauvais (d. before 1264) does put the playwright somewhat into focus by saying in his *Speculum historiale* that Seneca composed ten tragedies (he then proceeds to give excerpts from each);[59] but he does not say what a tragedy is, and when he tells of Seneca's death under Nero, he does not mention the tragedies.[60] He does, however, give an account of Nero's own theatrical career, derived from Suetonius. He tells of Nero singing an *acroama* in the theater at Naples, and carrying on through an earthquake; and he tells how "he did not hesitate to join the *scenici* in private spectacles, and he sang tragedies while wearing a mask [*personatus*]."[61] I should note that Vincent does define tragedy elsewhere, in the *Speculum doctrinale*, as "poetry from a joyful beginning concluding in a sad end"; and in other places in the same work he gives Isidore's doctrines.[62]

Manlio Pastore-Stocchi sees another Dominican, Nicholas Trevet of Oxford, as one who brought the French moralistic interest in Seneca Tragicus to its culmination.[63] Trevet was among the most learned men in Christendom, and was recognized as such in his own day. This is illustrated by the fact that, while a professor at Oxford, he was commissioned by a cardinal at the papal court at Avignon to write an explication of the Senecan tragedies. He had sojourned in Italy earlier on, and had also spent some time at the University of Paris. He wrote original histories, and compiled commentaries on biblical, classical, and patristic works, including Augustine's *City of God*, Seneca the Elder's *Controversies*, and Livy, and, most important for our present concerns, Boethius's *Consolation of Philosophy*. The Boethius commentary is thought to be his earliest work. It was certainly composed before 1304, when he refers to it in his second Oxford quodlibet. Ruth Dean suggests that he composed it at Florence,[64]

---

[58] Smits, "Helinand of Froidmont"; Zwierlein, *Prolegomena* (see chap. 4 above); Manlio Pastore-Stocchi, "Un chapitre d'histoire littéraire aux XIVᵉ et XVᵉ siècles: *Seneca poeta tragicus*," pp. 15–16.

[59] Vincent of Beauvais, *Speculum historiale* 8.102–04, 113–14, pp. 309, 312–13. Vincent also cites texts identifying Aeschylus and Sophocles as writers of tragedies (*ibid.* 3.33, p. 98; 3.40, 42. p. 100); but the three texts in which Euripides figures (including Boethius, *De consolatione*, book 3, prose 7) do not associate him with tragedies (*Speculum historiale* 3.40, p. 100).

[60] *Ibid.* 9.9, p. 325.

[61] *Ibid.* 9.6, p. 324. For the term *acroama*, see chap. 2 above, p. 19 n. 16.

[62] Vincent of Beauvais, *Speculum doctrinale*, 3.109, col. 287: "Est autem comedia poesis, exordium triste leto fine commutans. Tragedia vero est poesis a leto principio in tristem finem desinens." In 3.110, col. 288, he gives the neutral subjects of Isidore's book 8 (republics, histories of kings, and mournful things), while in his dictionary in 1.64, col. 76, he gives the criminous subject matter of book 18.

[63] Pastore-Stocchi, "Un chapitre," pp. 17–18.

[64] Ruth J. Dean, "The Dedication of Nicholas Trevet's Commentary on Boethius," pp. 598–99. See also her account of Trevet's other works, especially his historical ventures: "Nicholas Trevet, Historian," pp. 328–30. Trevet was born between 1258 and 1268, and died in 1328.

but B. S. Donaghey argues that it must have occupied him for several years while at Oxford in the 1290s, perhaps interrupted by the Italian trip in 1298 or so. In Books 4 and 5 of the *Consolation* he develops philosophical ideas connected with current debates at Oxford at the end of the thirteenth century.[65] But the first three books are of more interest to us, for his research on them provided him with a knowledge of tragedy from nonclassical traditions which he was to bring to his analysis of Seneca's plays.

Trevet first introduces the subject of the tragic when commenting on the *scenice meretricule* of Boethius's first book:

Vocat autem eas scenicas eo quod carmina poetica consueverunt in scenis recitari. Scena enim secundum Ysydorum, *Ethimologiarum* libro 18, capitulo *De ludo scenico*, erat locus intra theatrum in modum domus insculptus [*lege* instructus] cum pulpito. Dicitur a *scena* greco vocabulo, "umbra"; unde dicebatur scena quasi obumbratio, quia ibi abscondebantur persone cantantes carmina tragica et comica.[66]

(She calls the Muses "scenic" because poetic pieces used to be recited in the scenes. For according to book 18 of Isidore's *Etymologies*, in the chapter *On the Scenic Play*, the scene was a place within the theater set up after the fashion of a house, with a pulpit. Scene is the Greek word for shade; hence it meant a shadowing, because in it were hidden persons who sang tragic and comic poems.)

In composing his commentary, Trevet constantly kept an eye on what William of Conches had said before him, and did not hesitate to borrow from him when he saw fit, but he also modified his ideas from what he considered more authoritative sources. Here, the phrase "abscondebantur persone" comes straight from the short version of Conches's commentary, whereas the long version reads "ascendebant persone." It is the long version that associates the persons with the reciting of poetry, but Trevet could have drawn this notion from some other Remigian commentary, or from Remigius himself.

Unlike Huguccio (one of Trevet's favorite authorities), who has the hiding persons come out and make gestures to the words of a reciter, Trevet identifies the hiding persons with Isidore's singers of tragedy and comedy. And since Isidore clearly identifies these with the poets themselves, perhaps this is Trevet's understanding as well.

Trevet's comment on Fortune's allusion to tragedies is as follows:

---

[65] B. S. Donaghey, "Nicholas Trevet's Use of King Alfred's Translation of Boethius, and the Dating of His Commentary," pp. 9–10, who notes that he was already a person of some importance at Oxford in 1297.

[66] Nicholas Trevet, *Expositio super librum Boecii de consolatione*, book 1, prose 1, fol. 4. Cf. the uncompleted edition by Edmund Silk, *Exposicio fratris Nicolai Trevethi anglici ordinis predicatorum super Boecio de consolacione*.

Cum dicit *Quid tragediarum*, probat mutabilitatem Fortune divulgari quotidianis clamoribus, quia clamores poetarum quotidie in theatro recitantium tragedias nihil aliud continebant quam mutabilitatem Fortune. Et nota quod tragedi dicuntur, secundum Ysydorum, *Ethimologiarum* libro 18, *De ludo scenico*, illi qui antiqua gesta atque facinora sceleratorum regum luctuoso carmine spectante populo concinebant. Unde tragedia est carmen de magnis criminibus vel iniquitatibus a prosperitate incipiens et in adversitatem terminans. Et dicitur tragedia a *tragos*, quod est hircus, *et oda*, cantus, quia hujusmodi cantus yrco remunerabatur. Dicit ergo, "Quid aliud deflet clamor tragediarum nisi Fortunam vertentem regna felicia ictu indiscreto," id est, eventu incerto: quasi diceret, "Nichil."[67]

(When she says, "What does the clamoring of tragedies," she demonstrates that the mutability of Fortune is made common knowledge in daily clamorings; for the clamorings of poets reciting their tragedies every day in the theater contained nothing other than the mutability of Fortune. And note that according to Isidore, in book 18 of his *Etymologies*, in the chapter *On the Scenic Play*, tragedians are said to be those who sang of the old deeds and crimes of wicked kings in a doleful poem while the people looked on. Hence tragedy is a poem about great crimes or iniquities beginning in prosperity and ending in adversity. And the word tragedy comes from *tragos*, meaning goat, and *oda*, song, because this sort of song was remunerated with a goat. Fortune says, therefore, "What else does the clamoring of tragedies bewail, except Fortune overturning happy kingdoms with an unforeseen blow," that is, with an uncertain outcome, as if to say, [in answer to her rhetorical question,] "Nothing.")

Trevet has taken over from Conches the definition of tragedy as dealing with great iniquities and moving from prosperity to adversity. He found confirmation of the iniquitous subject matter from Isidore. But he also found in Isidore, as we have already seen, that a tragedy was not simply a writing, as Conches had it, but a poem, and a poem that was sung in the theater. Trevet also adopted Conches's term "remunerated," but omitted his explanation of the goat as symbolic of the fetor of vice, and also omitted Conches's contrast of the movement of tragedy with that of comedy.

When Trevet comes to Philosophy's citation of Euripides under the term *tragicus*, he simply explains it as a reference to a certain Greek poet who wrote tragedies, and refers his reader to his earlier discussion of tragedy.[68] Where Philosophy cites "my Euripides," Trevet reads it, through his own or another's emendation, to refer to Eutropius, author of the *Historia Romanorum*.[69]

An English contemporary of Trevet's, William Wheatley,[70] who also wrote a commentary on Boethius, simply repeats Trevet, for the most part.

---

[67] Trevet, *Expositio*, book 2, prose 2, fol. 29. Cf. Silk, *Exposicio*, p. 200: the eight MSS he uses omit *criminibus vel*. Silk also reads *continebant* rather than the Isidorian *concinebant*.
[68] Trevet, *Expositio*, on book 3, prose 6, fol. 58v.   [69] *Ibid.*, on book 3, prose 7, fol. 60v.
[70] See Astrik L. Gabriel, "The Source of the Anecdote of the Inconstant Scholar," pp. 153–54 n. 8.

But he has an interesting variation on the *meretricule scenice* of book 1: he reads the adjective as *cenica* rather than *scenica*, and says that the passage refers to the poetical Muses that were customarily recited in *cenis*.[71] This should mean "in dinners," or "at dinner," rather than "in scenes." His concept of Muses being recited is not altogether clear, but his general idea seems straightforward.

Let us look briefly at another commentary on Boethius compiled later in the fourteenth century, or even in the fifteenth, which also draws on Trevet's work, and which has been confused with Wheatley's because of its identical incipit.[72] Earlier on it was wrongly attributed to Thomas Aquinas, and its author accordingly goes by the name of Pseudo-Aquinas. He follows Trevet in his explanation of the *scenice meretricule*, except that he has the hidden persons pronouncing, rather than singing or reciting, tragic and comic poems. He then adds William of Conches's alternative explanation of scenic as obfuscating.[73] His definition of tragedy is the result of combining Trevet and Conches: "Tragedy is a poem that reprehends vices, which begins in prosperity and ends in adversity." He gives the etymology from Trevet, as well as Trevet's citation from Isidore, to which he adds a gloss.[74]

It seems quite clear that when Trevet composed his commentary on Boethius he did not yet know of Seneca's tragedies. His commentary on the plays was written between 1314 and 1317 at the request of a fellow Dominican, Nicholas Albertini of Prato, cardinal bishop of Ostia and a member of the papal curia at Avignon.[75] Trevet was traveling in Italy while

---

[71] William Wheatley, *Exposicio libri Boecii de consolacione Philosophie*, book 1, prose 1, fol. 73v: "*Quis, scilicet permisit, has meretriculas,* i.e. has musas poeticas, *cenicas,* i.e. que in cenis consueverunt recitari, *accedere,*" and so on. MS New College 264 in the same library, fol. 19v, has a similar reading.

[72] It is thus confused in the *Index thomisticus*, from which I cite the text. See Gabriel, "The Source of the Anecdote," pp. 153–54 n. 8 and pp. 173–75 n. 57. Courcelle, *La Consolation,* pp. 322–23, 415, also mistakenly takes Wheatley's Oxford MSS to be copies of the Pseudo-Aquinas commentary.

[73] Pseudo-Aquinas, *Commentum super libris Boethii,* book 1, prose 1: "Appellat autem Philosophia Musas meretriculas scenicas quia carmina poetica in scena consueverunt pronuntiari. Ubi nota quod scena dicebatur locus umbrosus in theatro ubi abscondebantur persone pronuntientes carmina tragica vel comica; unde scena interpretatur umbratio vel umbra. Vel ideo Muse poetice dicuntur scenice, id est, umbratiles, quia sunt umbra scientie, non vera scientia, cum obumbrent mentes hominum" (*ITS* 7:124, line 255).

[74] *Ibid.,* book 2, prose 2: "Nota quod tragedia est carmen reprehensivum vitiorum incipiens a prosperitate, desinens in adversitate. Et dicitur a *tragos* grece, quod est hircus latine, et *odos,* cantus, quia cantus hujusmodi carminis hirco remunerabatur. Inde dicuntur tragedi poete qui antiqua gesta et facinora sceleratorum regum luctuoso carmine populo spectante (id est, respiciente) concinebant, sicut dicit Isidorus libro *Etymologiarum*" (*ITS* 7:135, line 190).

[75] The cardinal's letter of request and Trevet's response upon completing the commentary, along with his introductory comments and the commentary on *Thyestes,* is given by Ezio Franceschini, *Il commento di Nicola Trevet al Tieste di Seneca.* For the commentary on *Hercules furens,* see below. Piero Meloni has edited the commentaries on *Agamemnon* and *Hercules oetaeus,* and Marco Palma that on *Troades.* The cardinal's interest in Seneca was sparked by Albertino Mussato, according to Giuseppe Billanovich, "Il Livio di Pomposa e i primi umanisti Padovani," pp. 131–32.

working on his Boethius commentary, but if he consulted a Continental manuscript of Seneca he must have seen it later, during another trip to France or Italy.[76] Alternatively he may have relied entirely upon an Oxford manuscript of the play.[77]

Once Trevet found out for himself what a classical tragedy looked like, he revised his notions of the contents of tragedy and of how it was performed in the theater. But he did so mainly by studying Isidore more carefully. He was also able to quote Varro on poets in general, as cited by Augustine in the *City of God*. According to Varro, there are three kinds of theology: the fabulous, the natural, and the civil. The first, which Trevet is concerned with, is used by poets and is accommodated to, and exercised in, the theater.[78] Trevet concludes that this poetic theology consists of two parts, one of which can be called tragic and the other comic. He then cites the first section of Isidore's treatment of *tragici seu tragedi* in book 8 of the *Etymologies*, namely, the Horatian idea that a goat was their remuneration (Conches's word again), and that later on they received much honor for their fables composed "ad varietatis ymaginem."[79] Trevet omits what Isidore goes on to say in book 8 about comic poets and the differences between comic and tragic subject matter, where tragedy is described innocuously as dealing with public affairs, the histories of kings, and mournful matters. Instead, he gives the dour Lactantian characterizations of *tragedi* and *comedi* from book 18, where the subjects of tragedy are the old deeds and crimes of wicked kings.[80] But then he reverts to book 8 for Isidore's doctrine on the three modes of poetry,[81] adding, however, a completely new distinction of his own between tragic matter and the tragic mode:

Scripserunt autem poete triplici charactere, quia vel modo narrativo, in quo solus poeta loquitur, ut in *Georgicis*, vel dragmatico, ubi nusquam poeta loquitur sed

---

[76] Dean, "Dedication," p. 600, thinks he may have had sojourns on the Continent between 1304 and 1315, perhaps at Padua in 1308, and at Avignon sometime between 1308 and 1312.

[77] Richard Rouse, "New Light on the Circulation of the A Text of Seneca's Tragedies," has found indications that Oxford possessed a copy of Seneca that would explain the E readings in Trevet's C text (and thereby obviate the hypothesis that he used a Continental manuscript).

[78] Trevet, *Expositio super tragedias Senece*, Franceschini, *Il commento*, pp. 5–6, drawing on Augustine, *De civitate Dei* 6.5–7.

[79] Franceschini, *Il commento*, p. 6. This last phrase would mean something like "in a great variety of images," I suppose. It is a mistake for "ad veritatis imaginem," "in the image of truth," in Isidore, *Etymologiae* 8.7.5; one of the MSS that Franceschini uses restores the reading *veritatis*.

[80] Franceschini, *Il commento*. "Tragedi sunt qui antiqua gesta atque facinora sceleratorum regum luctuoso carmine, spectante populo, concinebant" (*Etymologiae* 18.45). As noted above, pp. 46, 49, another tradition of Isidore's text reads *luctuosa* rather than *luctuoso*, therefore, "sad crimes" rather than "sad verse."

[81] Isidore, *Etymologiae* 8.7.11. Trevet seems to have used a text that read *tragedis et comedis* (tragedians and comedians) rather than *tragedijs et comedijs* (tragedies and comedies).

tantum persone introducte, et iste modus convenit proprie tragedis et comedis; tercius modus mixtus ex duobus est, ubi et quandoque poeta loquitur et quandoque persone introducte, sicut Vergilius in [libro] *Eneidos*, cujus materia licet sit tragica tamen liber ipse more tragico non scribitur, propter hoc quod poeta ibi aliquando loquitur cum personis introductis. Vergilius ergo in *Eneidos*, Lucanus, et Ovidius, *De transformatis*, poete tragici dici possunt, quia de materia tragica, scilicet de casu regum et magnorum virorum et de rebus publicis scripserunt, sed tamen minus proprie. Seneca autem in libro qui pre manibus habetur non solum de materia tragica sed etiam scripsit more tragico; et ideo merito liber iste *Liber tragediarum* dicitur; continent enim luctuosa carmina de casibus magnorum, in quibus nusquam poeta loquitur, sed tantum persone introducte.[82]

(Poets wrote in three ways: either in the narrative mode, in which only the poet speaks, as in the *Georgics*; or in the dramatic mode, where the poet never speaks, but only introduced persons – and this mode is strictly appropriate to tragedians and comedians; the third mode is a mixture of the other two, in which sometimes the poet speaks and sometimes introduced persons, as with Vergil in the *Aeneid*. And though the matter of the *Aeneid* is tragic, the book is not written in the tragic manner, because the poet sometimes speaks as well as introduced persons. Therefore, Vergil in the *Aeneid*, Lucan, and Ovid in the *Metamorphoses* can be called tragic poets, because they wrote of tragic matter, that is, the fall of kings and great men, and public affairs; but the name is less proper to them. Seneca, however, in the book before us, wrote not only of tragic matter, but also in the tragic mode. For this reason this book is deservedly called *The Book of Tragedies*; for it contains mournful poems about the falls of great men, in which the poet never speaks, but only introduced persons.)

In his characterization of tragic matter, Trevet takes only the idea of *luctuosa carmina* from book 18, taking the *reges*, with no allegation of wickedness attached, and *res publice* from book 8. His *reges et magni viri* may have been suggested by the *reges et magnates* in Huguccio and Balbus, but Trevet shows no sign of being influenced by any other Huguccian term or idea.

One might think that Trevet not only plays down Isidore's emphasis on crime, and therefore William of Conches's emphasis on great iniquities, but also abandons Conches's requirement of movement from a beginning in prosperity to an end in adversity. True, he introduces the idea of *casus regum* (a phrase that may come directly or indirectly from Placidus), but his example of the *Aeneid* shows that one can treat of the fall of kings without leaving the matter there. However, Trevet does not go so far as to call the *Aeneid* a tragedy. When he speaks of tragedies, rather than writers of tragic matter, he adds the requirement of mournfulness, which the *Aeneid* does not, as a whole, fulfill. It may be, then, that the phrase *casus regum* is meant after all to summarize the movement from prosperity to adversity in *bona*

---

[82] Trevet, *Expositio Senece*, Franceschini, *Il commento*, pp. 6–7.

fide tragedies. But this movement is hardly characteristic of the ten Senecan tragedies, as I have already noted above in chapter 1. All of them perhaps can be said to end in adversity, except for the coda of *Hercules oetaeus*, where the hero is apotheosized, and *Medea*, where the protagonist flies off after exacting her horrible revenge; but both of these characters do leave an abundance of adversity behind them. However, the prosperous beginning is noticeably lacking in most of the plays. Only Hercules in the *Hercules oetaeus* and Hippolytus in his play begin in contentment, but in each case the contentment is remarkably short-lived. Agamemnon makes a late triumphal entry into his play, but is soon brought low, and everything before his entry reeks of adversity. Thyestes begins in adversity and is rightly suspicious of the prosperity bestowed upon him by Atreus, for it is quickly reversed.

One might suppose that the Senecan plays would confirm the notion that tragedy deals with great crimes, and no doubt Trevet accepted it as a fact. But he saw that there were good things in the plays as well. His attitude is illustrated by his causal analysis of *Hercules furens*:

Ex dictis autem patent quattuor cause hujus tragedie: quia causa efficiens fuit Seneca; causa materialis est furia Herculis in qua interfecit filios et uxorem; causa formalis consistit in modo scribendi, qui est dragmaticus, ut dictum est, et ordine partium, qui patebit in expositione; causa finalis est delectatio populi audientis, vel, in quantum hic narrantur quedam laude digna, quedam vituperio, potest aliquo modo liber hic supponi ethice, et tunc finis ejus est correctio morum per exempla hic posita.[83]

(From what has been said the four causes of this tragedy are clear. The efficient cause was Seneca. The material cause is the madness of Hercules, in which state he killed his children and his wife. The formal cause consists in the mode of writing, which is dramatic, as noted above, and in the order of the parts, which will be set out in my exposition. The final cause is the pleasure of the listeners. Or, insofar as some praiseworthy things are herein narrated, and also other things that are deserving of vituperation, this book can in some way be classified under ethics, and then its end is the correction of morals by the examples that are here presented.)

It has been suggested that the combination of *laus* and *vituperium* shows the influence of the *Commentary on the Poetics* of Averroes–Alemannus. However, the same terms are found in Aristotelian and Ciceronian rhetoric, as we have seen above, and also, more pertinently, in Aristotelian and Thomistic ethics.[84]

---

[83] Trevet, *Expositio Senece*, Franceschini, *Il commento*, p. 8. For *dragmaticus* one manuscript reads *tragicus*.
[84] See Aquinas's *Commentary on the Nichomachean Ethics* 3.1, *Opera omnia* (Parma) 21:71 (see p. 70 for two medieval Latin translations of Aristotle). See Kelly, "Aristotle," pp. 199–200.

In his prefatory letter to Cardinal Albertini, Trevet speculates in similar terms about Seneca's motives in composing the tragedies:

Cujus doctam maturitatem in arduo virtutum culmine obversantem ad scribendas tragedias reor inclinatum, ut, more prudentium medicorum qui amara antidota melleo involuta dulcore gustu inoffenso ad humorum purgamentum et sanitatis fomentum transmittunt, ethica documenta fabularum oblectamentis immersa cum jocunditate mentibus infirmis ingereret, per que, eruderatis vitiis, uberem virtutum segetem injectis seminibus procrearet.[85]

(I believe that his schooled maturity, hovering at the arduous peak of virtue, was inclined to write tragedies so that, like prudent physicians who cover bitter antidotes with honeyed sweetness and administer them for the purging of humors and the fostering of health with no offensive taste, he could enjoin ethical teachings on infirm minds in a delightful manner, by cloaking them in the appealing guise of fables, in order that by teaching the nature of vice and sowing the seeds of virtue, he might produce a fruitful harvest.)

Trevet's point is that Seneca had resorted to various other ways of imparting moral instruction before this time, and now he used the literary approach. Such a benign view of the tragedies is largely caused, no doubt, by his admiration for the high ethical standard of Seneca's other writings.

After taking a closer look at Isidore, Trevet elaborates his earlier notions of how tragedies were performed:

Et nota quod tragedie et comedie solebant in theatro hoc modo recitari: theatrum erat area semicircularis, in cujus medio erat parva domuncula, que "scena" dicebatur, in qua erat pulpitum super quod poeta carmina pronuntiabat; extra vero erant mimi, qui carminum pronuntiationem gestu corporis effigiabant per adaptationem ad quemlibet ex cujus persona loquebatur. Unde cum hoc primum carmen legebatur, mimus effigiabat Junonem conquerentem et invitantem Furias infernales ad infestandum Herculem.[86]

(Note that tragedies and comedies used to be recited in the theater in the following manner. The theater was a semicircular area in the middle of which was a small little house called the scene. In [or "on"] the scene was a pulpit, upon which the poet pronounced his poems. Outside the scene, however, were mimes who imitated the poet's speech by their bodily motions, adapting them to each character in whose person the poet was speaking. Hence, when the first poem [of *Hercules furens*] was being read, the mime would portray Juno complaining and calling upon the infernal Furies to set themselves upon Hercules.)

Trevet chose not to repeat the statement of Isidore that he had used earlier, that the tragedians sang their poems. He must have taken the singing to be a flowery word for reciting, an interpretation that could be verified by

---

[85] Trevet, *Expositio Senece*, Franceschini, *Il commento*, p. 3.
[86] Trevet, *Expositio Herculis furentis*, ed. Vincenzo Ussani jr, pp. 5–6.

Isidore's chapter on mimes: the author *pronounced* the fable before the mimes acted their imitation.

An interesting attempt to visualize Trevet's explanation can be seen in the splendid illustration of the performance of *Hercules furens* that serves as a frontispiece to the fourteenth-century Urbino codex of the commentary (I use a black-and-white copy for my own frontispiece).[87] The poet, crowned like Juno and King Lycus, stands inside a small covered structure, the "scene," which has no pulpit, but rather a simple lectern holding the book from which he is reading. The characters of the play, in appropriate costumes, are placed on the semicircular stage, while members of the audience are seated beyond.

SENECA AT PADUA

We have seen various out-of-context uses made of Seneca's tragedies throughout the Middle Ages, but the plays were probably known mainly from collections of excerpts rather than from complete texts. There is one curious misattribution that needs to be noticed. An exemplum used by James of Vitry (d. 1240) is said to come from "a certain tragedy of Seneca"; a visionary sees Nero in hell tormented in a bath of hot gold, and he invites a band of lawyers to join him, for he has reserved a place for them.[88] The reference to a tragedy of Seneca is retained in William Peraldus's *Summa de vitiis*, and in English collections;[89] but in a commentary on the Apocalypse once dubiously attributed to Thomas Aquinas and now uncertainly assigned to his fellow Dominican Hugh of St. Cher (d. 1263), it is said to come from "a certain book of Seneca's tragedies which is titled *The Book of Old Men's Trifles*."[90] The association of Seneca's tragedies with such a story

[87] Vatican Urb. lat. MS 355, fol. 1v. The illustration is reproduced in color by Ussani, facing p. 1, and in black and white by Franceschini, *Il commento*, p. xiii. I shall discuss this illustration further in my treatment of Boccaccio's ideas of ancient tragedy in my projected book, *Chaucerian Tragedy*.

[88] James of Vitry, *Exempla*, ed. Thomas Frederick Crane, no. 36, p. 14: "Legitur autem in tragedia quadam Senece quod visum est cuidam quod videret Neronem apud inferos balneantem ministrosque circa eum aurum fervens infundere, dicentemque cum videret chorum advocatorum ad se venientem: 'Huc,' inquit, 'venale genus hominum, advocati, amici mei, accedite, ut mecum in hoc vase balneetis, adhuc enim superest locus in eo quem vobis reservavi.' Caveant igitur advocati ne animas suas diabolo vendant." See p. 148 for a paraphrase and references to other occurrences. In the Spanish *Libro de los enxemplos*, it is said, "Leyesse en unos cantares que fizo Seneca." In the *Dialogus creaturarum*, it is attributed to "a certain philosopher."

[89] James of Vitry, *Exempla*, p. 148; *Liber exemplorum ad usum praedicantium saeculo XIII compositus a quodam fratre minore anglico de provincia Hiberniae*, ed. A. G. Little, no. 71, pp. 43, 139.

[90] Hugh of St. Cher (?), *Super Apocalypsim* 7, Parma edition of Aquinas, 23:385; *ITS* 7:242 line 642: "Item in quodam libro tragediarum Senece qui intitulatur *Liber de nugis senum*, dicitur, cum quidam inspiceret infernum, videns Neronem balneantem se, et multos circumstantes qui fundebant aurum calidum in balneum ipsius, Nero videns turbam advocatorum ad se venientem, ait, 'Venite huc, venale genus hominum, O advocati, amici mei, accedite huc, ut mecum in hoc vase vos balneetis.

reveals a curious idea of the meaning of tragedy, and also reveals that Seneca's genuine book of tragedies was not readily available until later on.

Padua became the chief center of full-context Senecan influence in the Middle Ages. Of course, Paduan "prehumanism" was a wide-ranging phenomenon, covering many aspects of the world of learning, especially in relation to classical Antiquity, and Seneca's dramatic works were only one focus of interest, not necessarily the most "visible" to the outside world.[91] It is noteworthy that Dante was in correspondence with one of the prominent scholars of Padua, Giovanni del Vergilio, but, as we shall see, he seems not to have known, or even known about, the Senecan tragedies.

The study of Seneca's dramas at Padua began with Lovato Lovati in the latter part of the thirteenth century. Lovati discovered the eleventh-century Etruscus codex of the tragedies at the abbey of Pomposa. Prefixed to the plays were two excerpts from Isidore, first the statement from book 18 that tragedians sang of the crimes of wicked kings before the watching people, and second the account from book 8 that tragicians originally were given a goat, but eventually received great honor for their skill in arguments of fables.[92]

Lovati's interest in the plays was chiefly metrical. He did not advance any opinion on larger issues, at least in writing. The Paduans did not know of Nicholas Trevet's commentary, and none of them matched his achievement of a full-scale exposition of the plays. But Lovati's disciple Albertino Mussato wrote a good deal on them, and furthermore composed his own Senecan tragedy, *Ecerinis*, or *The Ecerinid*, around 1314–15.[93]

In a verse epistle written a year or so after he composed his *Ecerinis*,[94] Mussato runs through most of the subjects of the Senecan plays, including

---

Adhuc enim superest locus in eo, quem vobis reservavi.'"

[91] For a survey of the Paduan proto-Renaissance, see Guido Billanovich, "Il preumanesimo padovano" and "Il tragico di Pomposa e i primi umanisti padovani."

[92] Given by Guido Billanovich, "Preumanesimo," p. 61, and by Umberto Moricca in his edition of Seneca's *Thyestes* and *Phaedra* and *Octavia*, p. x (the reading of "luctuoso carmine" is followed for book 18). On the subsequent circulation of this version of Seneca's text, see Alexander MacGregor, "L'Abbazia di Pomposa, centro originario della tradizione 'E' delle tragedie di Seneca," pp. 171–85.

[93] Albertino Mussato, *Ecerinis*, ed. Luigi Padrin. Padrin's text has been reprinted and accompanied with an English translation by Joseph R. Berrigan, *Mussato's Ecerinis and Loschi's Achilles*. An annotated Latin text and German translation is given by Hubert Müller, *Früher Humanismus in Oberitalien: Albertino Mussato: Ecerinis*, p. 92–176 (text, commentary, and notes) and 177–97 (translation). He deals with Mussato's understanding of tragedy on pp. 42–47, but does not take the *Vita Senece* into consideration, and overlooks completely the idea of heroic tragedy. For an analysis of *Ecerinis* and Mussato's other works, see Cloetta, *Die Anfänge der Renaissancetragödie*, pp. 11–76. See also Ettore Paratore, "L'influsso dei classici, e particolarmente di Seneca, sul teatro tragico latino del Tre e Quattrocento," pp. 23–33; Girolamo Arnaldi, "Il mito di Ezzelino da Rolandino a Mussato."

[94] Mussato, Epistle 1, to be found on pp. 39–42 of his poetical works, hereafter *Opera poetica*. The cited line numbers are based on my own count.

"Phaedra's dire love" and Thyestes's banquet. He sums up the matter of tragedy thus:

> Facta ducum memorat, generosa nomina regum,
> Cum terit eversas alta ruina domos. (87–88)

(It memorializes the deeds of dukes and the pedigrees of kings,
as it crushes overturned houses in deep ruin.)

After emphasizing the point that the noble iambic poetry of tragedy deals only with the nobility,[95] he formulates this purpose for the genre:

> Vox tragici mentes ad contingentia fortes
> Efficit, ignavus diluiturque metus. (93–94)

(The voice of the tragic poet makes minds strong in vicissitude,
and [in consequence] cowardly fear evaporates.)

Like Trevet, then, Mussato comes to a rather more sanguine idea about the effect of tragedy than could readily be hoped for from its unpromising subject matter.

In another summation in the same epistle, however, in which he purports to show how tragedy is a useful and profitable kind of poetry, he stresses negative rather than positive lessons: it shows that only mutability is constant, that the glory of great leaders is false, that the image of death is omnipresent; and it sets forth the struggles of uncertain life which contain every kind of cruelty ("que species omnis crudelitatis habent").[96]

It is the latter sort of moral that his *Ecerinis* calls to mind. It presents the rise and fall of the "Tyrant of Padua," Ecerinus, that is, Ezzelino da Romano, and seems to have been written, to some extent, at least, as a warning against a current threat to Padua from another tyrant, Cangrande della Scala.[97] Far from being high born, Ecerinus was begotten by the devil. Courage in the face of adversity is indeed treated in the work, but not as a lesson proposed to the listeners; rather it is a boast made by the villainous protagonist:

> Adversa vires fortibus prebet viris
> Fortuna, viles opprimit. (459–60)

(Contrary Fortune bestows strength on strong men,
while she crushes the worthless.)

Seneca's Medea says almost the same thing: "Fortune fears the strong,

---

[95] Mussato, Epistle 1, lines 89–92, quoted in Kelly, "Aristotle," p. 189.
[96] Mussato, Epistle 1, lines 105–18.
[97] See Winfried Trillitzsch, "Die lateinische Tragödie bei den Prähumanisten von Padua," pp. 451–453; Joseph R. Berrigan, "Early Neo-Latin Tragedy in Italy," pp. 87–89.

crushes the cowardly."[98] But while the evil Medea ends in vengeful triumph, the evil Ezzelino is destroyed. The work has been analyzed as having a happy end, from this point of view.[99] However, the point of view from which happiness and unhappiness is predicated is invariably taken to be that of the protagonist. We should note, furthermore, that, whereas Medea killed her own innocent children to spite Jason, Ezzelino's guiltless nieces and nephews are killed in hideous fashion after the tyrant's death. The perpetrators of this atrocity can only with difficulty be thought of as the forces of good. At the end we are assured that God treats all according to their merits,[100] which can be readily accepted, at least eschatologically. But it is not a lesson given prominence in many Senecan dramas.

Mussato's tragedy might seem to fit perfectly the definition of tragedy set forth by William of Conches: a writing of great iniquities beginning in prosperity and ending in adversity. We have seen that Seneca's plays in general do not follow this pattern, and furthermore their action is restricted to a short period of time, whereas the *Ecerinis* covers the protagonist's entire lifetime. However, Mussato shows no sign of knowing about Conches's plot formula, or the similar formulas of Huguccio and Balbus. But he is aware of the Boethian passage that is the object of Conches's gloss, and he appeals to it more than once, even though it is hardly compatible with the Senecan plays and his own imitation.

Mussato sets forth some of his notions in his *Evidentia tragediarum Senece*.[101] This work is in the form of dialogue between himself and Lovati, who died in 1309; but, like the verse epistle cited above, it was written in 1315 or 1316, after the *Ecerinis*, to which it refers. It was composed at the request of Marsiglio of Padua, who wished to know something about tragedies. Marsiglio may have been puzzled about the Averroes–Alemannus discussion of tragedy, since he seems to have been the compiler of the *Parvi flores*, perhaps during his time as rector of the University of Paris in 1312–13. This anthology of philosophical sayings draws on the *Commentary on the Poetics*, but without including any mention of tragedy.[102]

Mussato has Lovati characterize tragedy thus: it is "the description, in the form of lamentation, of an overthrown kingdom."[103] When Mussato

---

[98] Seneca, *Medea* 159: "Fortuna fortes metuit, ignauos premit."

[99] Daria Perocco, "Albertino Mussato e l'*Ecerinis*," p. 347.

[100] Mussato, *Ecerinis*, ed. Padrin, lines 622–24:

> Stat judicii conscius equi
> Judex rigidus, judex placidus;
> Donat justos, damnat iniquos.

[101] Mussato, *Evidentia tragediarum Senece*, ed. Anastasiós Megas, pp. 123–27.

[102] Kelly, "Aristotle," pp. 187–88.

[103] Mussato, *Evidentia*, p. 124: "Tragedie cujusque subjectum est eversi regni cujusque sub

asks him the authority for this definition, Lovati cites Fortune's question in Boethius: "What else does the clamor of tragedies bewail but Fortune's overthrow of felicitous kingdoms by an unforeseen blow?" But what felicitous kingdoms, we may ask, are bewailed in Seneca's tragedies, not to mention the *Ecerinis*? Is unworried happiness, or the shock of its unexpected dissolution, really the central issue in the Senecan world?

Mussato has a fuller discussion of the nature of tragedy in his *Vita Senece*.[104] After he quotes from the last chapter of Moerbeke's translation of Aristotle's *Poetics* on the defense of poetry,[105] he speaks of Seneca as an author of tragedies: "He took up the tragic stylus, the supreme and grandiloquent apex of the poetic art, fitting to the eminence, as well as to the downfall and death, of kings and leaders, in accordance with what Boethius says in the *Consolation*."[106] Here he cites Fortune's rhetorical question again. He goes on to quote Ovid and Horace on the preeminence of the style, and observes: "It is more fitting that the highest sadnesses, joys, and other passions of the soul be expressed and represented through tragedic poems than through other kinds of meters."[107] It turns out that tragedy, which is defined as "the style of high matter," has traditionally taken two metrical forms, depending on a further distinction within the high subject matter. If the tragedic poets deal with the ruin and fall of great kings and princes, and in particular describe their disasters, battles, slaughters, seditions, and sad actions, they use the iambic meter, as Sophocles did in the *Trachine* (that is, *Trachiniae*, or *Maidens of Trachis*) and as Seneca does in his ten tragedies. But if the poets treat of open wars in the field waged by sublime kings and dukes, and their triumphant victories, then they use the heroic meter, as did Ennius, Lucan, Vergil, and Statius.[108] Horace spoke of all of these poets when he said (*Ars poetica* 73–74): "Res geste regumque ducumque et tristia bella, / Quo scribi possent numero monstravit Homerus" ("Homer demonstrated the meter in which the

deploratione descriptio." He makes the same point in other words, thus: "Et harum aliarumque tragediarum materia principalior est de infortuniis conquestio" (*ibid.*).

[104] Mussato, *Vita Senece (Lucii Annei Senece cordubensis vita et mores)*, ed. Megas, pp. 154–61.

[105] See above, p. 117.

[106] Mussato, *Vita Senece (Lucii Annei Senece)*, p. 159: "Sumpsit itaque tragedum stilum, poetice artis supremum apicem et grandiloquum, regum ducumque eminentiis atque ruinis et exitiis congruentem, juxta illud *De consolatione* Boetii."

[107] *Ibid.*, pp. 159–60: "Proprius enim per trageda carmina exprimuntur et representantur summe tristitie, gaudia, et alie passiones anime quam per alia genera metrorum."

[108] *Ibid.*, p. 160: "Dicitur itaque tragedia alte materie stilus, quo dupliciter tragedi utuntur: aut enim de ruinis et casibus magnorum regum et principum, quorum maxime exitia, clades, cedes, seditiones, et tristes actus describunt – et tunc utuntur hoc genere iambicorum, ut olim Sophocles in *Trachinis* et hic Seneca in his decem tragediis – aut regum et ducum sublimium aperta et campestria bella et triumphales victorias – et tunc metro heroyco ea componunt, ut Ennius, Lucanus, Virgilius, ac Statius."

deeds of kings and dukes and sorrowful wars could be written"). He concludes by giving the etymology of tragedy, but even though he cites Horace's line about the vile goat, he gives an ingenious new interpretation: the poets who thus describe noble and sublime things are honored above all others, and a goat used to be sacrificed for them.[109]

It is noteworthy in all of this that Mussato is not speaking of style in our sense of the word, that is, relating to forms of expression. He does touch briefly on this kind of idea in another work, the introduction to his *De obsidione Patavii*, where he contrasts *eloquium altum et tragedum* with a manner of writing more readily intelligible to the people at large.[110] But in the *Vita Senece* the term *stilus* seems to refer mainly to subject matter and meter, though there may be a reference to stylistic writing in the term *apex grandiloquus*.

In summary, Mussato believes that tragedy was a genre of elevated subject matter. When the events were mainly disastrous, the iambic meter was more appropriate. But when the glories and triumphs of wars were to be described, the dactylic hexameter was used.

By substituting triumph for sadness in Horace's statement of the subject of heroic verse, Mussato implies that these poems usually end happily. He has therefore come, by a highly circuitous route, to parallel the ancient Greek understanding of tragedy, which admitted all kinds of outcomes, as long as the subject matter and characters were noble. He could have come to this conclusion at first hand, perhaps, from a careful study of Aristotle's *Poetics*, for, as I noted earlier in this chapter, Mussato seems to have been unique among the men of letters in the Middle Ages in having access to the original text of the *Poetics* as translated into Latin by William of Moerbeke. He could also have arrived at the conclusion that epics can have the same characteristics: but it would have been very difficult to achieve such understandings of Aristotle's text, given that neither Homer's epics nor any of the Greek plays or other works that Aristotle alludes to were known to him, and given Moerbeke's literal and unglossed renderings. Consider, for instance, the following excerpts from chapter 2, in which we saw (in chapter 1 above) that both tragedy and epic deal with the spudean. First, a modern translation:

Since mimetic artists portray people in action, and since these people must be either good [*spoudaioi*] or bad [*phauloi*] (for men's characters practically always conform to these categories alone), they can portray people better than ourselves, worse than ourselves, or on the same level ... For instance, Homer, represented superior men,

---

[109] *Ibid.*: "Prehonorantur enim poete sic nobilia et sublimia describentes, quibus imolabatur hircus."

[110] Kelly, "Aristotle," p. 193, n. 149. Mussato's introduction is edited by Cloetta, *Anfänge*, pp. 70–72, and Megas, p. 19.

Cleophon men like us, Hegemon of Thasos (the first writer of parodies) and Nicochares (author of the *Deiliad*) inferior men ... This very distinction also separates tragedy from comedy: the latter tends to represent men worse than present humanity, the former better.[111]

Here is Moerbeke's version:

Quoniam autem imitantes imitantur agentes, necesse autem hos aut studiosos aut pravos esse (mores enim fere semper hiis assecuntur solis, malitia enim et virtute secundum mores differunt omnes), aut meliores quam secundum nos aut pejores aut et tales ... Puta Homerus quidem meliores, Cleofon autem similes, Igimon autem Thasius (parodias poetizans primus) et Nicokhares (qui *Diliadem*) pejores ... In ipsa autem differentia et tragodia ad komodiam distat: hec quidem enim pejores, hec autem meliores imitari vult nunc.[112]

I translate:

Since, however, those who imitate imitate those who act, it is moreover necessary that these be either zealous or vicious (for morals almost always fall into these categories alone, for all persons differ in morals by reason of evil or virtue), either better than according to ourselves or worse or such [as we are] ... For instance, Homer [imitates] better persons, Cleofon similar persons, and Igimon the Thasian, first to poetize parodies, and Nikokhares, who [wrote] the *Deliad*, worse persons ... Moreover, in this very difference tragedy also is distinguished from comedy: for this one now wishes to imitate worse men, but this one better.

What Mussato made of this passage, we do not know, but there is no indication that he tried to cope with it or similar passages.

The idea that Homer dealt with tragic matter in epics was not only Aristotelian, but also Horatian, and it must surely be Horace who inspired Mussato. Mussato went a step further in his *Ecerinis*, and gave it some of the qualities of an epic. Though he noted the variety of the lyric meters and the speech of the *persone introducte* of the Senecan tragedies,[113] and imitated them in his own tragedy, he did not believe that the nonintervention of the author's voice was essential to tragedy. He inserted a brief narrative stretch (lines 86–90), which reads something like a modern stage direction, but which was meant to be spoken by the reciter. His tragedy was not to be acted out, but was rather to be recited in the same way that Statius recited the *Thebaid*. Mussato makes this comparison himself, and gives his work an epic-style title: not *Ecerinus*, but *Ecerinis*.[114]

In an early epistle, Mussato rejected, in Augustinian terms, all acting out

[111] Aristotle, *Poetics* 2, tr. Halliwell, pp. 32–33.

[112] *Ibid.*, tr. Moerbeke, pp. 4–5.

[113] Mussato, *Evidentia tragediarum*, pp. 124–26; see the excerpts given by Pastore-Stocchi, "Un chapitre," 29.

[114] Mussato, Epistle 4, lines 25–28, *Opera poetica*, p. 48, drawing on Juvenal 7.82–86. See Kelly, "Aristotle," p. 191.

of poetry.[115] But in the *Vita Senece*, his reading of the end of Aristotle's *Poetics* has convinced him that some acting is acceptable,[116] but it is unlikely that he thought of any acting of tragedy other than the gesticulations of the poet while reciting, or of a reciter who substituted for the poet. In spite of the fact that in his *Cento from Ovid's Tristia*, written during his own exile in 1318,[117] he adapts the verses about the dancing of Ovid's poems to apply to tragedy,[118] he does not seem to have had the Isidorian notion of silent actors matching movements to the poet's words.

When Mussato cited Horace directly in the *Vita Senece*, he simply ignored the "vileness" of the tragic goat. But in the *Cento*, as also in his first epistle, he could write away any unacceptable characterizations of his ideal genre that he found in his authorities. For instance, when Ovid says that even in tragedy, which is the gravest kind of writing, there is always to be found the matter of love, Mussato in his epistle modifies the lines to suggest that tragedy is the gravest kind of poetry because it expresses the virtues of the dominant mind; and in the *Cento* he implies that because tragedy is the most serious form of poetry, it always has Mussato's own love. Similarly, when Ovid says that tragedy sometimes indulges in obscene laughter and shamelessness, he changes the assertions to a denial, both in the first epistle and in the *Cento*.[119]

Mussato's *Ecerinis* caused an immediate sensation in Padua. He was crowned with the poetic laurel because of it, in December 1315, and there began the custom, enforced by statute, of reciting the tragedy every year during the Christmas season. The readings took place in the Palazzo Comunale of Padua, in the presence of the poet. On 17 December 1317, Mussato's friend, Guizzardo da Bologna, finished a complete commentary on the work.[120] We have seen that Guizzardo in his commentary on Geoffrey of Vinsauf's *Poetria nova* considered tragedy to be a style: satire and tragedy are higher styles than comedy. But he does not use the term style in his discussion of the form – that is, the *tragicus modus agendi* – of the *Ecerinis*. Tragedy, he says, is an iambic poem appropriate to its matter. A tragic *tractatus* deals with the high matter of the miseries and ruin of

---

[115] Mussato, Epistle 7, lines 75–76, *Opera poetica*, p. 55; written before March, 1309.
[116] Kelly, "Aristotle," pp. 188, 191.
[117] Guido Billanovich, "Preumanesimo," p. 80.
[118] Mussato, *Cento ex Ovidii Tristibus*, lines 139–44, *Opera poetica*, p. 93; Kelly, "Aristotle," p. 191. For Ovid, see chap. 2 above, p. 30.
[119] Mussato, Epistle 1, lines 73–76, *Opera poetica*, p. 40; *Cento*, lines 135–38, *Opera poetica*, p. 93; texts in Kelly, "Aristotle," p. 192.
[120] Guizzardo's *Commentum* is edited by Padrin following his text of the play, on pp. 67–267. The commentary is usually attributed as well to a co-author, Castellano da Bassano, but I take him to be a later editor. See Kelly, "Aristotle," p. 193 n. 150.

outstanding and excellent men, as Horace says: "Res geste regumque ducumque et tristia bella." Guizzardo differs from Mussato, then, in taking a pessimistic rather than an optimistic view of the content of Horace's line. He also differs from Mussato in his understanding of the relationship between iambic and heroic poetry. He says that the same subject matter can be treated in heroic verse, as Horace goes on to point out. But Horace also shows that the writers of Greek tragedies used iambic verse – "The socks and grand buskins took this foot" (he explains these terms as the footwear of comic and tragic poets) – and Seneca, too, in his Latin tragedies; whence Boethius said, "What else does the clamor of tragedies bewail but Fortune overturning happy kingdoms with an undiscerned stroke?"[121] From its placement, one would think that the citation of Boethius is meant to say something about the meter of tragedy. But unless the *iambus* is being called an *ictus indiscretus*, Guizzardo must mean the words to refer to what he said above about the *miserie et ruine insignium et excellentium*.

If Guizzardo's characterization of tragedy is more in keeping with Boethius than are Mussato's various explanations, it is not in keeping with Guizzardo's own statement of the final cause of the *Ecerinis* as *tyrannorum vituperatio et detestatio*.[122]

Another Paduan admirer of the *Ecerinis* was Pace of Ferrara, who, like Guizzardo, wrote a commentary on the *Poetria nova*.[123] In his accessus to Vinsauf's work, he draws extensively on the commentary of Averroes–Alemannus, and though he credits Aristotle's *Poetria* and Horace's *Poetria* with giving the "parts" of poetry as elegy, comedy, tragedy, and satire, his true source is undoubtedly Matthew of Vendôme's *Ars versificatoria*, which he goes on to cite in a different connection.[124] We recall that when Matthew introduced his four poetic ministers of Philosophy, he spoke mainly in terms of style. Tragedy appeared as a figure of ferocious tumidity, described in Horatian and Ovidian terms.[125]

Sometime after Guizzardo finished his commentary on the *Ecerinis*, Pace wrote a short exposition of the same work, called *Evidentia Ecerinidis*.[126] He names some of the Greek tragedies said to have been written by Sophocles, namely, the *Odyssey*, the *Iliad*, the *Oedipod*, and *Hercules furens*. The inclusion of Homer's works is a clear indication that Pace was simply drawing on

---

[121] Guizzardo, *Commentum*, pp. 80–81; text in Kelly, "Aristotle," p. 194.

[122] Guizzardo, *Commentum*, pp. 79–80; text in Kelly, "Aristotle," pp. 193–94.

[123] Pace's commentary is not published; see Kelly, "Aristotle," p. 195 n. 158 for details. See also Philip A. Stadter, "Planudes, Plutarch, and Pace of Ferrara," pp. 140–52.

[124] See Kelly, "Aristotle," pp. 197–98, where I do not recognize Matthew as Pace's source for the parts of poetry, and suggest Isidore, *Etymologiae* 8.7.4–8, as a possible influence (see p. 83 above).

[125] See chap. 4 above, p. 93.

[126] Pace of Ferrara, *Evidentia Ecerinidis*, pp. 203–05.

some list of Greek works, perhaps from a commentary on the *Ars poetica*. No doubt Mussato found a reference to the *Trachiniae* in a similar source. We saw that Guizzardo explicitly derived his knowledge of Greek tragedies from Horace. Pace goes on to name the ten Senecan plays, and then says:

> Tragedy is high matter, comedy vile; whence Horace says, "A comic affair does not desire to be expounded in tragic verses." Now the style of tragedies properly suits the declines of falling kingdoms and of kings and dukes. Whence Boethius says, "What else does the clamor of tragedies bewail but Fortune overturning happy kingdoms with an unforeseen blow?"[127]

He says that the word tragedy comes from the Greek for goat, which was the kind of footwear (that is, made of goatskin?) used by tragedians in the recitations of their scenes. The iambic foot is proper to the matter of tragedy, since it is attuned to exclamations, and laments. Unlike Guizzardo, he states the object of the *Ecerinis* in positive terms: the increase of virtue, particularly prudence.[128]

In general, Mussato, Guizzardo, and Pace rely on the same sources for their notions of tragedy, though they do not draw the same conclusions from them. Apart from the actual tragedies of Seneca, their chief authority is Horace in the *Ars poetica*. But they also put great stock on Fortune's mocking question from the *Consolation of Philosophy*. Like Mussato, Guizzardo and Pace seem to have used an unglossed text of Boethius. None of the three show the slightest hint of knowing what any of the commentators say on tragedy – for instance, William of Conches's idea of writing that begins in prosperity and ends in adversity. They get the etymology of tragedy from a definite source or sources, perhaps including book 8 of Isidore's *Etymologies* or a Horatian commentary. But they appear to have no inkling of the acted dimension of tragedy, whether from Horace's precepts or from the chapters of Isidore's book 18.

As for Mussato's idea of writing an original tragedy in the Senecan vein, it was only much later in the century that anyone seems to have thought of imitating him, as we shall see in the next chapter. When all is said and done, the impact of the rediscovery of Seneca's tragedies was less than could have been expected in Italy, and was virtually nonexistent elsewhere.[129]

---

[127] *Ibid.*, p. 203: "Tragedia alta materia est, sicut comedia vilis; unde Oracius: 'Versibus exponi tragicis res comica non vult.' Proprie autem tragediarum stillus corruentum regnorum et regum et ducum declinationibus congruit; unde Boetius: 'Quid aliud tragediarum clamor defflet nisi indiscreto ictu Fortunam fecilia [*sic*] regna vertentem?"

[128] *Ibid.*, pp. 203–04.

[129] I shall speak more about the effects of Seneca's plays on ideas of tragedy in the chapter on Boccaccio in my book on Chaucerian tragedy.

DANTE AND HIS COMMENTATORS

The ferment over Seneca in Padua seems not to have attracted the attention of Italy's greatest poet, who was working on his masterpiece at the time that Mussato produced most of the works we have been discussing. In fact, Dante seems not to have been familiar even with the more available comedies of Terence.[130]

Twice in the *Inferno*, Dante as narrator refers to his poem as a comedy, "this comedy," and "my comedy."[131] The second reference comes shortly after his guide, Vergil, refers to his own poem about Aeneas as "my high tragedy."[132] It has never been thought, to my knowledge, that Dante meant the latter designation to indicate that the title, or a title, of Vergil's work was *Tragedy*. It would seem no more likely that he intended to call his poem about hell, with or without the next two installments on purgatory and heaven, *Comedy*. However, the reference to *Paradiso* in the *Monarchia*, "sicut in paradiso comedie jam dixi," if it is authentic, must probably be understood as authenticating the title as well, thus: "as I have already said in *Paradise* of *The Comedy*."[133] At any rate, the assumption that this was the poem's title, or at least part of the poem's title, was made early on and won the day, and every commentator felt obliged to give an explanation of what it meant, usually contrasting comedy as a generic term with tragedy and other genres.

Many Dante scholars believe that Dante himself confirmed that *Comedy* was the title of his work, and that he explained what it meant in a letter that he wrote to Cangrande della Scala. But I support the view that the *Epistle to Cangrande*, at least beyond the first three paragraphs, is not by Dante. The body of the letter is, however, of great interest as a commentary, and I shall take it up as such in due course.[134]

When Dante takes up the subject of tragedy and comedy in his early *De vulgari eloquentia*, he gives no indication that there is any dramatic or dialogic aspect to the genres. They are simply two of three kinds of poetry that he deals with, the other being elegy. These forms are differentiated on the basis of subject matter, style, and meter. His notion of tragedy is summed up in a single sentence:

---

[130] See Giorgio Brugnoli's notes to his edition of the *Epistle to Cangrande, Opere minori*, pp. 617–19; Kelly, *Tragedy and Comedy*, pp. 1–2.

[131] Dante, *Inferno* 16.128; 21.2.

[132] *Ibid.* 20.113.

[133] Dante, *Monarchia* 1.12.6. See the edition of Pio Gaia in *Opere minori di Dante Alighieri*, p. 582, and his introduction, pp. 494–97; he agrees with Pier Giorgio Ricci in his edition, pp. 158–59, that the interjection is authentic, but notes many others who have denied it.

[134] See Kelly, *Tragedy and Comedy*, pp. 11–18 and 61–111, for details of my analysis of *Cangrande*.

Stilo equidem tragico tunc uti videmur quando cum gravitate sententie tam superbia carminum quam constructionis elatio et excellentia vocabulorum concordat.[135]

(We are seen to be using tragic style when the most noble verse forms, elevated construction, and excellent vocabulary are matched with profundity of substance.) He specifies the matter of tragedy as restricted to the highest subjects, namely, self-defense, love, and virtue (*salus, amor,* and *virtus*).[136] He arrived at these subjects by considering what is worthiest in the three main areas of human endeavor: in the area of usefulness, safety is clearly the main concern, and this involves prowess in arms; in the area of what is most pleasurable, it is the fire of love, the most precious object of desire; and in the area of what is honest or right, it is clearly virtue, that is, uprightness of will.[137] In vernacular poetry, the hendecasyllabic line is the best for tragedy; the stanzas should be of equal size, without responsory (repetition of the opening, as in a balade), and all on the same subject; he cites his *Donne ch'avete intelletto d'amore* from the *Vita nova* as a good example.[138] I give here the first of the five stanzas of this poem, which has the distinction of being the first work in any European vernacular language in the Middle Ages to be designated by its author as a tragedy, or as meeting the requirements of tragedy:

> Donne ch'avete intelletto d'amore,
> I' vo' con voi de la mia donna dire,
> Non perch'io creda sua laude finire,
> Ma ragionar per isfogar la mente.
> Io dico che pensando il suo valore,
> Amor sì dolce mi si fa sentire,
> Che s'io allora non perdessi ardire,
> Farei parlando innamorar la gente.
> E io non vo' parlar sì altamente,
> Ch'io divenisse per temenza vile;
> Ma tratterò del suo stato gentile
> A respetto di lei leggeramente,
> Donne e donzelle amorose, con vui,
> Ché non è cosa da parlarne altrui.[139]

(Ladies who have perfect understanding of love,
I would speak with you of my own lady;
not that I think to exhaust her praises,
but by talking of her to uncloud my mind.
I declare that when I think of her worth,
Love is so sweetly felt in me

---

[135] Dante, *De vulgari eloquentia* 2.4.7.
[136] *Ibid.* 2.4.8.   [137] *Ibid.* 2.2.6–7.   [138] *Ibid.* 2.8.8; 2.12.3.   [139] Dante, *Vita nova* 19.

that if I did not fail in boldness,
I would make others fall in love by my speech.
And I do not wish to speak so grandly
that fear would make me become worthless;
but I will treat of her noble nature
lightly – lightly in comparison to her –
telling you, amorous ladies and damsels,
what is not to be spoken to others.)

We note that in the *De vulgari eloquentia* Dante judges this poem to fulfill the criterion of the most superlative speech, even though in the poem itself he says that he will eschew such speech. In the final stanza, he addresses his poem as if it were a young and plain daughter of Love adorned with the praise of his lady.

It is doubtful that when he composed this lyric he considered it to be a tragedy, or in the tragic style, since in his long commentary in the *Vita nova* he makes no reference to this sort of generic category. I take it, then, that it was only when he was working on the *De vulgari eloquentia* after the turn of the fourteenth century that he hit on the generic paradigm of tragedy, comedy, and elegy, and classified the most expert lyric poems by himself and others under the category of tragedy. That is, he categorizes the poets and poems that he singles out for praise throughout this chapter, notably those named as examples of treating the worthiest subjects, namely, Bertran de Born on arms, Arnaut Daniel on love, Giraut de Bornelh on rectitude, and Cino da Pistoia on the love that is friend to rectitude,[140] as tragic poets, and their poems as tragedies. In contrast, he labels the *Inferno* a comedy within the *Inferno* itself; he had the generic requirements of comedy in mind as he composed it.

So far as I know, other readers of the *De vulgari eloquentia* have not so much as entertained this conclusion, that Dante considered lyric poems that met the requirements of tragedy to be tragedies. This holds true even of those who do not believe that Dante himself formulated the different analysis of tragedy that appears in the *Epistle to Cangrande*, for they, along with the believers in its authenticity, are under the impression that there was a unitary understanding of tragedy in the Middle Ages that included a narrative component and a disaster factor. It is one of the main purposes of the present study to show that there was no such uniform view of tragedy. The lyric poems that Dante names pass the "duck test" for tragedy: anything that looks, walks, and quacks like a duck is a duck; anything that has the subject, form, and language of tragedy is a tragedy.

Whether Dante's notions of comedy and tragedy were originally wide

---

[140] *De vulgari eloquentia* 2.8.8

enough to include long narrative poems like the *Inferno* and the *Aeneid* is not clear. The *Aeneid* does not fulfill the requirement of having even stanzas, since it has no stanzas at all; but then this and the other characteristics that Dante named for tragedy in the *De vulgari eloquentia* were specifically limited to vernacular poetry. The *Aeneid* was presumably counted by him among those ancient tragedies and comedies whose writing could not change, alluded to in the *Convivio*.[141] For Latin tragedies, the dactylic hexameter would clearly be the best, since that is what the *Aeneid* used.

Dante's stipulation of the long hendecasyllabic line for vernacular tragedy is not absolute; for he says that heptasyllabic lines can also be used, as long as the hendecasyllabics predominate. Specifically, a hendecasyllabic should open each stanza. When stanzas open with heptasyllabics, the tragedy tends to take on a shadow of elegy.[142] This insistence on suitable meters might make us think of Averroes's attribution to Aristotle of the notion that "the goodness of the art of praise consists in a long meter rather than a short."[143] Alemannus's first use of "tragedy" as a substitute for "art of praising" comes only well after this passage, and his first explicit identification of the art of praising as tragedy still later.[144] But the metrical emphasis, together with the Averroes–Alemannus restriction of tragedy to the praise of virtue, is enough to counsel an open mind on the possibility of Averroist influence. However, Alemannus never uses the term comedy, and, though he renders Averroes as giving a low ranking to elegy, as used for incitement to lust,[145] Dante's characterization of elegy as the style of the miserable and as using humble speech would seem to indicate a quite different kind of lowness, perhaps like that of Ovid's frivolous love-elegies, which Ovid contrasts with the sublime poems of tragedy.[146] Nevertheless, there is a suggestive linking of tragedy and elegy in Averroes–Alemannus: the *carmen laudativum*, known as *consecutivum*, is one in which an elegiac part precedes a "tragediac" poem as a kind of prologue, containing other matter, to make the praise seem more attractive.[147]

[141] Dante, *Convivio* 1.5.8; Kelly, *Tragedy and Comedy*, p. 1.

[142] Dante, *De vulgari eloquentia* 2.12.5–6.

[143] Averroes–Alemannus on *Poetics* 5 (Boggess, *Commentarium medium*, p. 16; Minio-Paluello, *De arte poetica*, p. 46): "Dixit: Et bonitas artis laudandi consistit in metro prolixo, non in curto." Cf. Butterworth, *Middle Commentary* 4.20, p. 73: "He said: The art of eulogy is brought into being when recourse is had to long poetic meters rather than short ones."

[144] Averroes–Alemannus on *Poetics* 6 (Boggess, *Commentarium medium*, pp. 18 and 19; Minio-Paluello, *De arte poetica*, pp. 47 and 48); see above, p. 120.

[145] Averroes–Alemannus on *Poetics* 3 (Boggess, *Commentarium medium*, p. 10; Minio-Paluello, *De arte poetica*, p. 44); Kelly, "Aristotle," pp. 186 and 206.

[146] See chaps. 1 and 2 above.

[147] Averroes–Alemannus on *Poetics* 18 (Boggess, *Commentarium medium*, p. 58; Minio-Paluello, *De arte poetica*, pp. 62–63): "Est carmen quod apud nos nominatur consecutivum; et est carmen in quo

The only other instance of a threefold paradigm of tragedy, comedy, and elegy that has been found so far is that of John de Herent, in a gloss written in 1349. According to him, elegy deals with miseries and is written in pentameters and hexameters (that is, the elegiac couplet, a hexameter followed by a pentameter); the subject of comedy is banquets; and tragedy treats of the deeds of kings, like Alexander.[148] Dante's specification that comedy can use either the middle or the humble vernacular may reflect Papias's doctrine: comedy deals with private and humble persons in a middle and sweet style rather than the high style of tragedy, but it can also deal with persons of great importance and historical events. But Papias's treatment of tragedy, which repeats Isidore's subject matter of the crimes of wicked kings, bears no resemblance to Dante's presentation. Balbus in his *Catholicon* repeated Papias on comedy and referred the reader to the entry on tragedy for the differences between comedy and tragedy; there Dante could have seen that tragedy used high style and comedy low, but the added notes of crime, movement from joy to sorrow, and even great characters are foreign to Dante's account.[149]

Dante resembles the Paduans in not adopting a Conchian or Huguccian plot movement for tragedy, and there is no reason to think that he did it for comedy. We can conclude, both from his analysis of the worthiest subjects in the *De vulgari eloquentia* and from his classification of the *Aeneid* as a tragedy, that he did not connect sadness or lamentation with tragedy. For though the *Aeneid* deals with disasters, the overall emphasis is on triumphs, as Mussato noted concerning tragedies written in dactylic hexameters.

That Dante persisted in dissociating tragedy from negative subjects and lamentation is indicated by his confession, towards the end of *Paradiso*, that in his attempt to describe and praise the beauty of Beatrice he was defeated more than any *comico* or *tragedo* in dealing with his theme.[150] This passage reveals also that one of Dante's sources identified the *tragedus* with the poet who wrote tragedies. It also indicates that he believed that the style of comedy was appropriate not only for his treatment of hell, but also for detailing the most sublime aspects of heaven.

There was, then, no time for Dante to have changed his mind on the subject of genres. Of course, there is no reason to think that he could not have changed his mind at all; he did change his mind earlier on the question of tragedy, since when he wrote the *Vita nova* he did not have the category

colligatur pars elegiaca carmini tragediaco; et est, ut multipliciter [or: universaliter] dicatur, premissio quasi prologi alicujus alterius materie carminum [or: carmini] laudativo, quatinus laus speciosior videatur."
[148] In Faral, *Les arts*, p. 337; Kelly, *Tragedy and Comedy*, p. 2.
[149] See chaps. 3 and 4 above; Kelly, *Tragedy and Comedy*, pp. 6–9.
[150] Dante, *Paradiso* 30.22–24.

of tragedy in mind at all and therefore did not consider the lyrics to be tragedies, but only later reanalyzed them as such. But the sort of change that proponents of the Dantean authorship of *Cangrande* must postulate, even if Dante had had time to make it, would be extremely radical. For, according to *Cangrande*, the matter of tragedy proceeds from what is admirable and quiet to what is filthy and horrible. This is hardly consistent with the noble subjects of love, virtue, and self-defence that Dante named in the *De vulgari eloquentia*. At most, such a tragedy would deal with noble subjects that are destroyed, degraded, or defiled. Furthermore, since there is no way in which one could say that *Donne ch'avete intelletto d'amore* is admirable and quiet in the beginning and filthy and horrible in the end, he would have had to de-classify it as a tragedy. The same is true of any other poetic work treating of Beatrice, and true also of Virgil's *Aeneid*.

Dante's unusual views of the genres of poetry, as set forth in the *De vulgari eloquentia*, were not available to his admirers later in the century – except, perhaps, to Boccaccio, but only fleetingly, and not when he came to expound upon the *Comedy*. One of the earliest commentators, Graziolo de' Bambaglioli, avoided commenting on the terms comedy and tragedy altogether.[151] But perhaps the very earliest comment we have on Dante's work is Guido da Pisa's two-line epitaph, which calls Dante *poeta comicus, necnon et satirus et liricus atque tragedus*.[152] Presumably he was saying that Dante employed aspects of four genres in his *Comedy*, even though he named it after only one. He says in his commentary that Dante is a tragedic poet here because he tells of the great deeds of sublime persons.

Guido's understanding of tragedy involves a good-to-bad sequence, in contrast to the opposite movement in comedy, in combination with what Isidore says in book 8 of the *Etymologies*:

Certain poets are called tragedic, and their science is called tragedy. Now tragedy is a kind of poetic narration which in the beginning is admirable and pleasing, but in the end or outcome is fetid and horrible; and because of this it is named from *tragos*, goat, and *oda*, song; hence tragedy is a "goatish song," that is, fetid like a goat, as appears in Seneca's tragedies. Or, as St. Isidore says in the eighth book of his *Etymologies*, "Tragedies are so called because at the beginning the prize for the

---

[151] Graziolo de' Bambaglioli, *Il commento dantesco*.

[152] Guido da Pisa, *Expositiones et glose super Comediam Dantis*, ed. Vincenzo Cioffari, p. 6; see Antonio Canal, *Il mondo morale di Guido da Pisa*, p. 62. In *Tragedy and Comedy*, p. 19, I report Canal's theory that the Laurentian MS Plut. 40.2 preserves elements of an earlier commentary by Guido on the whole *Comedy*; but Cioffari in two articles published only in 1989 – "Did Guido da Pisa Write a Commentary on the *Purgatorio* and the *Paradiso*? (Pluteo 40.2 and Its Relation to the Guido da Pisa Commentary)," and "The *Anonimo Latino*: One of the Earliest Commentaries on Dante's *Commedia*" – maintains instead that another early Latin commentary underlies the text; he has compiled and edited it as *Anonymous Latin Commentary on Dante's Commedia: Reconstructed Text*. It contains no discussion of tragedy or comedy.

singers was a goat. Whence too Horace: 'Who competed for a vile goat with a tragic poem.'" Certain other poets are called comic, and their science is comedy. Now comedy is a kind of poetic narration that has the harshness of some misery in the beginning, but its matter is prosperously terminated, as is apparent in the comedies of Terence.[153]

Guido notes that Dante's poem fits the sequence of comedy. This, I believe, is the earliest explanation of Dante's designation of his work as a comedy, and of his imputed title of *Comedy*, and it was to be the most popular.

Guido alludes to the comedies of Terence and the tragedies of Seneca. He never quotes Terence, and, though he does cite passages from all ten of the Senecan plays, he may have been drawing on a collection of excerpts, since he does not seem to be aware of their dialogue format; and, as I have noted above, they do not have the stipulated favorable-to-unfavorable movement. It is also doubtful that he knew Horace at first hand.[154]

Guido identifies the best comic poets as Plautus and Terence, but instead of ranking Seneca among the best in tragedy, he names only Homer and Vergil. He would have known Homer only by report, of course, and his naming of Vergil was confirmed by Vergil's own characterization of the *Aeneid* as a high tragedy in the *Inferno*. Guido has no gloss on this passage. The *Aeneid* is clearly just as lacking in the fetid and horrible ending of tragedy as is Dante's poem. Jacopo della Lana, who seems to draw on Guido to some extent,[155] does offer a gloss on Vergil's remark. He says that comedy deals with the "news" (*novelle*) of those who start out in life small and feeble and of small fortune and go on to be great, strong, and well favored in the end. Tragedy, on the other hand, treats of the news of those who are grand and splendid in the beginning, but are reduced in the end to low estate and no esteem. This is the very pattern that we see in Vergil's account of Troy, and that is why he calls it a tragedy. He calls it high, because of its high style and diction.[156] In other words, Lana is saying,

[153] Guido da Pisa, *Expositiones*, pp. 5–6: "Quidam dicuntur tragedi, et eorum scientia dicitur tragedia. Est autem tragedia quedam poetica narratio que in principio est admirabilis et grata, in fine vero sive exitu est fetida et horribilis; et propter hoc dicitur a *tragos*, quod est hircus, et *oda*, quod est cantus; inde tragedia quasi 'cantus hircinus,' idest fetidus ad modum hirci, ut patet per Senecam in suis tragediis. Vel, ut dicit beatus Ysidorus octavo libro *Ethymologiarum*: 'Tragedi dicuntur eo quod initi[o] canentibus premium erat hircus, quem Greci *tragos* vocant. Unde et Oratius: "Carmine qui tragico vilem certavit ob hircum."' Quidam vero dicuntur comici, et eorum scientia comedia. Est autem comedia quedam narratio poetica que in principio habet asperitatem alicujus miserie; sed ejus materia prospere terminatur, ut patet per Terrentium in suis comediis."

[154] See Kelly, *Tragedy and Comedy*, pp. 20–21.

[155] See Luis Jenaro-MacLennan, *The Trecento Commentaries on the Divina commedia and the Epistle to Cangrande*, pp. 22–58.

[156] Jacopo della Lana, *Commento alla Commedia di Dante*, ed. Luciano Scarabelli, 1:350: "Tragedia è una poetria opposita alla comedia, imperocchè la comedia tratta novelle di quelli che nel principio sono stati piccoli e fievoli e da poca fortuna, e nella fine grandi, forti, e graziosi; la tragedia è l'opposito, chè tratta novelle di quelle di quelli che nel principio sono stati grandi ed eccellenti, nel fine piccioli e

Vergil did not mean to call the whole *Aeneid* a tragedy, but only the part about Troy. From the viewpoint of Aeneas himself, presumably, the *Aeneid* should be called a comedy.

Dante's son Jacopo was also influenced by Guido's commentary, but not in the matter of poetic genres. Instead of following Guido's tragedy–comedy–satire–lyric stylistic paradigm, he introduces the four styles of tragedy, comedy, satire, and elegy, the same four that are treated in different sequences by Geoffrey of Vinsauf and Pace of Ferrara. Except for the addition of satire, which he says uses the mode of reprehension, Jacopo's list matches Dante's own in the *De vulgari eloquentia*, and his explanation somewhat resembles Dante's specification of subject matter for tragedy and elegy, and also in not connecting tragedy and comedy with joy and sorrow. For Jacopo says only that tragedy, as shown by Lucan and by Vergil in the *Aeneid*, treats of "architectonic magnificences." Elegy treats of various forms of misery, and Boethius is noted as an example. For comedy, which he characterizes as dealing with every subject, he gives no example, but simply says that the title of Dante's work proceeds from this fact.[157] I speculated above that Dante was drawing on Papias's doctrine of comedy as dealing with both humble and great persons and historical events. Perhaps this was to be Dante's doctrine in his projected fourth book of the *De vulgari eloquentia*, and perhaps Jacopo was privy to it, interpreting it to mean that comedy could include every subject.

Filippo Villani, in his *Life and Character of Dante the Celebrated Comic Poet*, claims personal knowledge of what Dante intended in his poem. He says that Dante told his uncle, Giovanni Villani, the reasons why he wrote it in Italian.[158] As for why Dante was a comic poet, that is, why he called his work a comedy, Villani did not have to resort to family report, since he was able, he thought, to quote Dante directly on this point. Villani was the first person to have access to the letter of explanation that Dante purportedly wrote to Cangrande della Scala. He was also the last person to quote the letter in the Middle Ages.

di nessuno valore. Or trattando di Troia Virgilio, che fu grande, vittoriosa, ed eccelsa, e poi fu condotta a destruzione, fu necessario che tal trattato fosse tragedia, e perchè nelli affari di Troia fu necessario nomar Euripilo, sì come auguro de' Greci, però dice che così lo chiama l'alta sua tragedia; e nota che dice 'alta,' cioè che è d'alto stile e dittato."

[157] Jacopo Alighieri, *Chiose alla cantica dell'Inferno*, ed. Jarro, pp. 43–44: "Il cui ordine brievemente così comincio che, secondo quello che ciertemente appare, in quattro stili ogni autentico parlare si conchiude, de' quali il primo tragedia è chiamato, sotto 'l quale, particularmente d'architettoniche magnificenze si tratta, si come Lucano, e Vergilio nell'*Eneidos*; il secondo, commedia, sotto il quale generalmente e universalmente si tratta di tutte le cose, e quindi il titol del presente volume procede; il terzo, satira, sotto il quale si tratta in modo di ripensione, siccome Orazio; il quarto el ultimo, elegia, sotto il quale d'alcuna miseria si tratta, si come Boezio."

[158] Filippo Villani, *De vita et moribus Dantis poete comici insignis*, ed. Angelo Solerti, p. 88; Kelly, *Tragedy and Comedy*, p. 71.

What about Dante's other commentator son, Pietro? Does he show any sign of direct knowledge of his father's intentions concerning the generic designation of his tripartite poem? In the first version of his commentary, he simply explains what he takes to have been the ancient practice of comedy, which turns out to be a very Isidorian notion, probably derived from Trevet's Seneca commentary. Poets recited their poems in the scene of the theater while mimes acted it out; he gives an example from the beginning of Seneca's *Hercules furens*, though without naming it. If the poem was performed in rustic fashion, it was called a comedy. Its style consisted of matter beginning with a sad recitation and ending with a joyful one. This was the reason why Dante wished his poem to be named a comedy. Another reason was that the poet of comedy was supposed to speak "remissly" and not "highly," and Dante therefore used the vernacular, as rustics do, since as a comic he had to be humble and remiss, according to Horace and Isidore.[159] Pietro's logic is not quite clear here. First of all, he seems to say that another reason for calling his poem a comedy is that it was written in the vernacular; but then he implies that, *since* the poem was a comedy (because of the movement from sadness to joy), he had to use a remiss style. Whatever Pietro's precise meaning, it is clear that he is very far from the substance and spirit of the *De vulgari eloquentia* in assuming that the vernacular was always remiss and humble.

In his discussion of tragedy, as in his analysis of comedy, Pietro is clearly drawing on Huguccio, both for the movement (joy to sorrow), and for the tragic–comic salutation, and on Isidore of Seville, specifically, book 8 for the etymology of tragedy, and book 18 for the subject matter and tone, namely, the old deeds and crimes of kings in mournful song. He adds the note that tragedy was delivered in a loud and clamorous voice, as indicated by Boethius's reference to the clamor of tragedies; and for these reasons, he says, Seneca titled certain of his poems tragedies.[160] Pietro's conclusion about Seneca is more acceptable than Guido's, who made everything ride on the turn of subject matter from favorable to unfavorable.

When Pietro calls tragedy a style and refers to other poetic genres, he may be echoing his brother's commentary, or the so-called second or third

---

[159] *Petri Allegherii super Dantis ipsius genitoris Comediam commentarium*, ed. Vincenzo Nannucci, pp. 9–10. The *inferno* section of Nannucci's edition has been reprinted in *Il "Commentarium" di Pietro Alighieri nelle redazioni ashburnhamiana e ottoboniana*, intro. Egidio Guidubaldi, but with gross errors of omission and distortion.

[160] *Ibid.*, ed. Nannucci, p. 10: "Tragedia vero est alius poeticus stylus et cantus, et oppositus comedie; nam incipit a letis et finit in tristibus. Et dicitur a *tragos*, quod est hirquus, et *oda*, cantus, quasi 'hirquinus cantus,' quod talia canentibus, antiqua gesta videlicet et facinora regum luctuoso cantu, dabatur hirquus in premium, secundum Isidorum. Unde Horatius: 'Carmine qui tragico vilem certavit ob hirquum.' Et loquitur elate et clamose; unde Boetius in libro *De consolatione*: 'Quid aliud tragediarum deflet clamor,' etc. Et ex his Seneca certa sua poemata tragedias titulavit."

versions of the *Ottimo commento*. The author of at least the original forms of the *Ottimo* is now taken to be Andrea Lancia. He does not deal with the subjects of comedy and tragedy in his "first version," or in a still earlier version,[161] but in the "second version" he treats of the same four genres listed by Jacopo Alighieri, namely, tragedy, comedy, satire, and elegy. Like Mussato, he sees tragedy as dealing with two different subjects: magnificent things, or matter beginning in felicity and ending in misery. For the first category, he gives the examples of Lucan and Vergil's *Aeneid*, which he may have taken from Guido da Pisa (he knew his commentary at least in an Italian epitome). There are also two general subject heads for comedy: it deals with things low, middling, and high (Jacopo's "all things"?), or it begins in misery and ends in felicity. Examples are Ovid's *Metamorphoses* and Dante's *Comedy*.[162] Ovid fits only the first group, but Dante presumably fits both the first and the second.

In the "third version" of the *Ottimo*, which is really a fourth recension, produced some time after the death of the painter Giotto in 1337, perhaps by a reviser other than Lancia, the discussion of genres begins with comedy and substitutes an account based on Papias: comedy uses a middle style and deals with humble persons, but sometimes treats authoritative persons as well, and history. As for tragedy, the earlier version's first kind is retained: it is a poetic style that deals with magnificent things, as in Lucan and Vergil; but then Papias's Isidorian account is added: the ancient works and felonies of scelerate kings are written in this style with tearful verses – which the reviser illustrates by citing the beginning lines of the *Pharsalia*, *Thebaid*, and *Aeneid*.[163]

In a second version of his commentary, Pietro Alighieri also adopts Papias's view of comedy, and cites him explicitly: it deals with the deeds of private and humble persons in a middle and sweet style, but it also sometimes uses a high style, as Horace notes. Then he sums up Huguccio's doctrine of the opposite plot movements of comedy and tragedy, with the reference to the salutation of tragic beginning and comic end.[164] He omits his earlier theatrical account of tragedy and comedy.

[161] See Saverio Bellomo, "Primi appunti sull'*Ottimo commento* dantesco."

[162] Andrea Lancia, "second version"' of the *Ottimo commento*, Proemio, ed. Luciano Scarabelli, 1:95–98, p. 97: "Il titolo del libro è questo: *Comedia di Dante Alighieri*; or bene è consequente il nome a la cosa. A la esposizione del qual vocabolo è da sapere che quattro sono li stili del poetico parlare, cioè tragedia, comedia, satira, e elegia. Tragedia si è lo stile nel quale si tratta magnifiche cose, siccome è Lucano, Virgilio nell'*Eneida*, o vero tragedia è lo stilo che comincia da felicitade e finisce in miseria. Comedia è uno stile che tratta comunemente di cose basse, mezzane, e alte, o vero che comincia in miseria e termina a la felicitade, come Ovidio nel *Metamorphoseos*, e qui l'autore."

[163] "Third version" of the *Ottimo commento*, proem given by Giuseppe Vandelli in the course of his study, "Una nuova redazione dell'*Ottimo*," see specifically p. 144; the text is also given in Kelly, *Tragedy and Comedy*, p. 26 nn. 10–11.

[164] The Ashburnham–Barberini variant of Pietro's commentary; text in Kelly, *Tragedy and Comedy*, pp. 30–31.

In yet another version of his commentary, Pietro starts out by citing Isidore as saying that comedy was a poetic song dealing with the deeds of private and humble persons in a modest style, whereas tragedy used a high style and dealt with the sad deeds of kings (Isidore, of course, does not mention style). He then gives Horace's doctrine on using the supreme style for comedy on occasion; finally, he adds Huguccio's points, as before.[165] In both of his later commentaries, Pietro notes that each of the three parts of Dante's poem has a comic ending, in referring to the heavens. The conclusion that it actually consists of three comedies is reflected in a copy of the poem made in 1354, which by the 1420s had made its way to Spain, and this was also the assumption of one of Benvenuto da Imola's auditors, Giovanni da Serravalle.[166]

Some time after Pietro Alighieri produced the first version of his commentary, and some time before Boccaccio wrote the first version of his *Trattatello in laude di Dante*, therefore, around 1350 according to my deductions, an unknown reader of Dante produced an accessus to the *Comedy* that drew upon the commentaries of Guido da Pisa and Pietro. We do not possess this accessus in its original form, but only as it was adapted by the compiler of the *Epistle to Cangrande* to serve as part of an introduction to *Paradiso*.[167] The original author, whom I call the Accessor, took over from Guido the characterization of comedy and tragedy as differing because of their opposite movements, and also his citations of Seneca and Terence. He took over from Pietro the reference to the Huguccian tragic–comic salutation, and his notion of speaking remissly in comedy, which entails using the vernacular.[168]

Other commentators of this time or a little later, specifically, Alberigo da Rosciate, Guglielmo Maramauro, and Giovanni Boccaccio, do not expound upon tragedy when discussing why Dante called his work *Comedy* (in Maramauro's case, his account of tragedy has probably been lost).[169] The next commentator to deal with tragedy was Benvenuto da Imola, who,

---

[165] The Ottoboni variant of Pietro's commentary; text in Kelly, *Tragedy and Comedy*, pp. 31–32.

[166] See chap. 6 below, p. 207.

[167] Kelly, *Tragedy and Comedy*, pp. 11–18; for the text of the original accessus as conjecturally distinguished from the interpolations of the compiler, see pp. 104–06.

[168] *Epistle to Cangrande* 10.29, ed. Brugnoli, pp. 614–18: "Differt ergo a tragedia in materia per hoc, quod tragedia in principio est admirabilis et quieta, in fine seu exitu est fetida et horribilis; et dicitur propter hoc a *tragos*, quod est hircus, et *oda*, quasi 'cantus hircinus,' id est fetidus ad modum hirci, ut patet per Senecam in suis tragediis. Comedia vero inchoat asperitatem alicujus rei, sed ejus materia prospere terminatur, ut patet per Terentium in suis comediis. Et hinc consueverunt dictatores quidam in suis saltutationibus dicere loco salutis: 'tragicum principium et comicum finem.' Similiter differunt in modo loquendi: elate et sublime tragedia, comedia vero remisse et humiliter." See Kelly, *Tragedy and Comedy*, pp. 35–38.

[169] *Ibid.*, pp. 32–33, 43–48. I shall deal with what can be deduced about Boccaccio's ideas of tragedies from his other writings as a prologue to my study of Chaucerian tragedy, in preparation.

like Pietro, left three versions of his commentary.[170] I shall report mainly on his final version, which became available shortly after his death in 1386 or 1387.

Benvenuto distinguishes three styles of poetry: tragedy, satire, and comedy. Of the first, he says:

Tragedy is a high and proud style; for it deals with memorable and horrifying deeds, like changes of kingdoms, the uprooting of cities, conflicts in war, deaths of kings, the destruction and slaughter of men, and other great disasters; and those who describe such things are called *tragedi* or *tragici*, like Homer, Vergil, Euripides, Statius, Simonides, Ennius, and many others.[171]

Like Guido da Pisa he does not include Seneca in his list of tragic poets, even though he quotes his tragedies extensively throughout his commentary; but Guido at least mentions him in his discussion of tragedy, which Benvenuto does not.

Benvenuto characterizes satire as a middle and tempered style, like that of Horace, Juvenal, and Persius, whereas comedy is a low and humble style dealing with the common and vile deeds of rustics, as in Plautus, Terence, and Ovid. Dante's poem is all three styles, so that it could have been titled *Tragedy* or *Satire* rather than *Comedy*; in fact, Benvenuto says, *Satire* would have been the most appropriate, because it wonderfully and audaciously reprehends vices of every kind and spares the dignity, power, and nobility of no one. Dante's poem is a comedy, not because it fits the characterization of comedy that he has just given, but rather because comedy begins in sad matter and is terminated in joyful matter, as Isidore says in his *Etymologies*, and also because it is in a low style, linguistically speaking: that is, it is in the vernacular rather than in Latin.[172]

Isidore, of course, says nothing about the sequence of subject matter in comedy. Rather, the movement from *tristia* to *leta* was first stipulated by Osbern of Gloucester and passed on by Huguccio, Balbus, and others. If Benvenuto knew that the opposite movement was associated with tragedy by the same authorities, he does not mention it. We saw that he did say that it dealt with disasters, but this need not mean that a tragic work had to move from joy to sadness; for instance, in the *Aeneid* of Vergil, one of the authors he names as having used the genre, Aeneas's disasters occur mainly

---

[170] See Carlo Paolazzi, "Le letture dantesche di Benvenuto da Imola a Bologna e a Ferrara e le redazioni del suo *Comentum*," now incorporated into his book, *Dante e la "Comedia" nel Trecento*, pp. 223–76.

[171] Benvenuto da Imola, *Comentum super Dantis Aldigherij Comoediam*, ed. Locaita, 1:18: "Tragedia est stylus altus et superbus; tractat enim de memorabilibus et horrendis gestis, qualia sunt mutationes regnorum, eversiones urbium, conflictus bellorum, interitus regum, strages et cedes virorum, et alie maxime clades; et talia describentes vocati sunt tragedi, sive tragici, sicut Homerus, Virgilius, Euripides, Statius, Simonides, Ennius, et alii plures."

[172] Benvenuto, *Comentum*, 1:19; Kelly, *Tragedy and Comedy*, pp. 49–50.

at the beginning, and he ends in joy. Benvenuto does not actually say that tragedy deals not only with great evils but also with great persons, but this is what he means; for he says that Dante's work is a tragedy because it describes the deeds of popes, barons, and other magnates and noblemen.[173] Benvenuto says that Dante has Vergil call the *Aeneid* a "high tragedy" because it is a high style and deals with high things.[174] Francesco da Buti, who finished his commentary in 1395, says that Vergil's poem is called "high" because it is in high style, and it is called a "tragedy" because it deals with the deeds of princes and begins with joyful things and ends in sadness and adversity. But he goes on to say that tragedy by its very definition is in high style, and therefore the noblest of poems; and it is also the noblest because it treats of the highest possible matter, namely, gods, kings, and princes; and it begins in felicity and ends in misery. It is not clear that this last feature is part of the reason for the nobility of tragedy; nor is it clear how such descriptions fit the *Aeneid*. Buti then gives a very inventive etymology of tragedy: it means "goat song," and was so named because a goat has a prince-like look in the front, because of its horns and beard, but a rear end that is filthy and naked.[175] As we shall see in the next chapter, Giovanni da Serravalle will improve upon this explanation.

Buti characterizes comedy as dealing with middling persons in a middle style, and as beginning in adversity and ending in felicity, like the fables of Terence and Plautus.[176] This corresponds with his treatment of the three styles of tragedy, comedy, and satire in his accessus to Terence: tragedy requires a sublime style, which deals with the greatest things and persons and uses high rather than common speech; comedy uses a middle style and deals with middling persons and things; and satire uses low style and has a corresponding subject matter.[177]

Finally, Filippo Villani draws on the etymology of tragedy and comedy and the plot structure of tragedy set forth by the Accessor, as incorporated

---

[173] Benvenuto, *Comentum*, 1:19: "Tragedia quidem, quia describit gesta pontificum, principum, regum baronum, et aliorum magnatum et nobilium, sicut patet in toto libro."

[174] *Ibid.*, 2:88; Kelly, *Tragedy and Comedy*, p. 56.

[175] Francesco da Buti, *Commento sopra la Divina comedia*, ed. Crescentino Giannini, 1:531–32: "Dice Virgilio che la sua *Eneide* è alta tragedia; questo finge Dante per dimostrare che in alto stile è fatta e che si dee chiamare tragedia con ciò sia cosa che tratti de' fatti de' principi, e comincia dalle cose liete e finisce nelle triste et avverse. Tragedia è poema più nobile che tutti li altri, però che in alto stilo, e tratta della più alta materia che si possa trattare, cioè delli idii e de' re e delli principi, et incomincia da felicità e termina in miseria. Et interpetrase tragedi canto di becco, chè come il becco à dinanzi aspetto di principe per le corna e per la barba, e dietro è sozzo, mostrando le natiche nude, e non avendo con che coprirle. Così la tragedia incomincia dal principio con felicità e poi termina in miseria." Buti's characterization is repeated in the *Commento alla Divina commedia d'Anonimo Fiorentino del secolo* xiv, ed. Pietro Fanfani, 1:451–52; see Kelly, *Tragedy and Comedy*, p. 58.

[176] Buti, *Commento*, 1:543.

[177] Buti, *Accessus in Terentium*, ed. Gian Carlo Alessio, "Hec Franciscus de Buiti," pp. 109–16, §§ 22, 31; Kelly, *Tragedy and Comedy*, p. 59.

into the *Epistle to Cangrande*, and then introduces Buti's idea that tragedy was named after the front and rear ends of a goat. He alleges that all of Seneca's plays follow this pattern, and that it is confirmed by Boethius. He concludes with other comments taken from *Cangrande*.[178]

This unprecedented interest in tragedy and comedy, understood not in the usual way as ancient and obsolete genres, but as current and available forms because of Dante's palpably contemporary comedy, seems not to have generated any new comedies or tragedies, with the possible exception of Boccaccio's *Comedia delle ninfe fiorentine*. Dante's view of tragedy, as requiring high style and high subjects and nothing else – no consideration of, or necessary connection with, specific persons, emotions, sequence of events, sins or crimes, misfortunes, or lessons – was a very peculiar understanding of the term, and no one seems to have come close to his conception, except perhaps his son Jacopo. In saying that tragedy treats of *architettoniche magnificenze*, Jacopo may have meant to say that it has a high subject matter presented in a stylistically appropriate way. He cites the *Pharsalia* and the *Aeneid* as examples. All the commentators had to face the fact that the *Aeneid* was called a tragedy within Dante's own comedy, and for most of them this was an important ingredient in their analysis of tragedy, but the result was not always satisfactory. Buti simply imposed the felicity-to-misery sequence on it, in spite of its manifestly happy ending, but Lana more sensibly limited this tragic sequence of events to Vergil's account of the fall of Troy, thereby indicating that the *Aeneid* contained a tragedy, but was not itself a tragedy. However, none of them, it seems, came close to concluding that Dante's love poems, like *Donne ch'avete*, could be considered tragedies. The subject matter would hardly have struck them as of comparable importance to the classical epics that they took to be the prime exemplars of the genre.

BOETHIUS IN FRENCH

After noting the considerable attention paid to tragedy in fourteenth-century Italy, we turn to the rest of Europe and find mainly lack of awareness or puzzlement concerning the term *tragedia*. I have not found any uses of the term in German sources after the twelfth century; and Spain is not heard from until the fifteenth century, except as the site of Alemannus's translation of Averroes's *Poetics* commentary in the thirteenth. Nicholas Trevet, who traveled in Italy and France and taught in Oxford, wrote in French as well as in Latin, and commented on Seneca's tragedies at the

---

[178] Filippo Villani, *Il commento al primo canto dell'Inferno*, ed. Giuseppe Cugnoni, pp. 34–35; new edition by Saverio Bellomo, *Expositio seu Comentum super Comedia Dantis Allegherii*, pp. 43–44.

request of a cardinal in Avignon, might be expected to have had some influence later on in all three countries. We have seen some sign of his Seneca commentary being used in Italy, but in France and England there is no recorded knowledge of Seneca's tragedies, not to mention the commentary on them, until the fifteenth century (in England). Some small use was to be made of Trevet's Boethius commentary in France, and it was to be decisive in the Chaucerian breakthrough. Chaucer, however, is unique, as we shall see in the next chapter. In the remainder of this chapter, I wish to concentrate on the references to tragedy that surfaced in France in works translated from the Latin.

We shall begin by looking at the ways in which Boethius's allusions to tragedy were interpreted. Since there are more than three hundred extant manuscripts of the *Consolation of Philosophy* dating from the eleventh through the fifteenth century,[179] it would seem not unreasonable to suppose that a Boethian understanding of tragedy would be widespread. We have already seen, however, that some of the commentators on the work put forth explanations of tragedy that were at variance with the context – notably the stipulation or implication that tragedy dealt with misfortunes that criminals brought upon themselves. But at least most of these commentators were on the right track, which cannot be said of many of the translations of the *Consolation* into French.[180]

The oldest of the translations was made early in the thirteenth century by an anonymous Burgundian.[181] *Tragediarum clamor* is translated as "li criz des tragedies," and tragedy is explained as a book composed of the evils, felonies, and misfortunes of kings, counts, and rich men.[182] The explanation seems to be largely derived, doubtless indirectly, from Isidore. According to Keith Atkinson, the translator drew on William of Conches for his glosses (but, as we have seen in the previous chapter, Conches did not transmit the Isidorian passage which criminalizes tragedy), and he used

---

[179] Barnet Kottler, "The Vulgate Tradition of the *Consolatio Philosophiae* in the Fourteenth Century."

[180] I wish to express my gratitude for assistance rendered to me on this subject by Dr. J. Keith. Atkinson of the University of Queensland, Professor Glynnis M. Cropp of Massey University in New Zealand, and Professor Richard A. Dwyer of Florida International University.

[181] See Richard A. Dwyer, *Boethian Fictions: Narratives in the Medieval French Versions of the Consolatio Philosophiae*, pp. 129–31: "List of All Manuscripts of the *Consolatio* in Medieval French." I shall give Dwyer's numbering of the versions, as well as that of Antoine Thomas and Mario Roques, *Histoire littéraire de la France*, p. 545, keyed to Dwyer's system in the review of Dwyer by J. K. Atkinson, where D = Dwyer and HLF = Thomas. In the case of the first translation mentioned here, D 1 = HLF 1. It has been edited by Margaret Bolton-Hall, *A Critical Edition of the Medieval French Prose Translation and Commentary of De consolatione Philosophiae of Boethius contained in MS 2642 of the National Library of Austria, Vienna*. See her Introduction, 1: 74–78, for date and provenance.

[82] French Boethius D 1 (HLF 1), ed. Bolton-Hall, 2:35–36, on *De consolatione*, book 2, prose 2: "Tragedie est livres faiz des malvaistiez et des felonies e des mesadventures des reis e des contes e des riches homes." This passage is given by Glynnis M. Cropp, "Fortune and the Poet in Ballades of Eustache Deschamps, Charles d'Orléans, and François Villon," p. 129.

as well the commentary of Adalbold of Utrecht and the Vatican Mythographers.[183]

The translator renders Boethius's *tragicus*, which refers to Euripides, as "the master tragedian."[184] Like the commentators we have looked at, he does not know about Euripides as a writer of tragedy,[185] and the same will be true of the other translators. This translator renders *scena vite* accurately enough as "the obscurity of this age,"[186] but translates *scenice meretricule* as "common bordello-women."[187]

The second translation, also in prose, was done in the region of Hainault at the end of the thirteenth century.[188] When the translator comes to Fortune's rhetorical question, he takes it to refer to the laments of poets in their *tregeces*.[189] Whether or not the word *tragediarum* was corrupted as *trageciarum* in his Latin text of the *Consolation*, he seems unfamiliar with tragedy, for he renders *tragicus* simply as "the poets."[190] He seems to take "scenic" to mean sordid,[191] though he interprets "scene" as shade.[192]

Another prose translation from the turn of the fourteenth century, by Bonaventura da Damena, seems not to have rendered either of the two references to tragedy. The scenic prostitutes are translated as "vile women,"[193] and the scene of life seems to be "the miserable port [or "gate"] of this world."[194] Peter of Paris's translation of the same time renders the clamor of tragedies as "le cri des cragedies."[195] The form of the word could be a mistake by the scribe rather than the translator, but the translator is clearly unfamiliar with tragedy, because he interprets *tragicus* as "a wise man named Tragicus," who, whenever he saw anyone glorifying himself would cry out in a loud voice a proverb in Greek,

---

[183] Atikinson, review of Dwyer, p. 142. Adalbold's commentary, which I have not examined, dates from the beginning of the eleventh century. See Courcelle, *La Consolation*, pp. 297–99.

[184] French Boethius D 1, ed. Bolton-Hall, 2:82, on book 3, prose 6: "li maistres tragediens."

[185] *Ibid.*, 2:86, on book 3, prose 7: "la sentence d'Euripedis, mon deciple."

[186] *Ibid.*, 2:39, on book 2, prose 3: 'l'oscurité de cest siecle."

[187] *Ibid.*, 2:5, on book 1, prose 1: "ces comunes bordelieres." In a longish gloss on the Muses (2:6), *meretricule* is rendered by itself as "putains."

[188] French Boethius D 2 (HLF 2), ed. J. K. Atkinson, *A Critical Edition of the Medieval French Prose Translation of the De consolatione Philosophiae of Boethius Contained in MS 898 of the Bibliothèque Municipale, Troyes.*

[189] *Ibid.*, 2:37, on *De consolatione*, book 2, prose 2: "Autres choses ne plaingnet li poete en leur tregeces fors ce que Fortune tourne si soubitement li roiaumes boins euireus."

[190] *Ibid.*, 2:82, on book 3, prose 6: "li poete crioient."

[191] *Ibid.*, 2:7, on book 1, prose 1: "cestes laides puterieles."

[192] *Ibid.*, 2:40, on book 2, prose 3: "en l'ombre de ceste vie."

[193] Bonaventura da Damena, Franco-Italian Boethius D 3 (HLF 8), Paris, Bibliothèque Nationale MS fr. 821 (via Atkinson), fol. 27c, *De consolatione*, book 1, prose 1: "ces vils femes."

[194] *Ibid.*, fol. 30a, on book 2, prose 3: "Tu ne panse qe tu arivas au miser port de cist monde."

[195] Peter of Paris, French Boethius D 4 (HLF 4), Vatican MS lat. 4788 (via Atkinson), fol. 26b. The manuscript is dated 1309, and was probably written in Cyprus; the translation itself was probably made within the previous few years.

"Doxa, doxa," and so on.[196] He interprets the scenic prostitutes as being *vielles*, "old," perhaps from seeing it rendered as *viles*; but he means old, since he explains that the Muses are so called because versified science is the earliest science that one is exposed to as a child.[197] *Hec vite scena* becomes "the world of this life."[198]

Each of the translations mentioned so far survives in a single manuscript, but that made by Jean de Meun exists in fifteen or more copies. He translates *tragediarum clamor* simply as "the cry of tragedies," though one manuscript puts "the tragedian" for "tragedies," and another substitutes "strange gods."[199] *Tragicus* is "uns poetez tragiciens."[200] Jean takes scenic to mean "abandoned to the people," which may mean "exposed to public shame";[201] but he interprets scene as "the curtain and the shade."[202]

A translation from around the second or third decade of the fourteenth century, which renders prose with prose and verse with verse, exists in four copies.[203] The translator understands tragedies to mean *chansons de geste*.[204] Scenic means "filthy," and scene is "ditch."[205] A revised version of this translation, dating from the middle of the fourteenth century, to which Jean de Meun's prologue came to be attached, exists in sixty-four known copies, forty-eight of them with a set of glosses added during the second half of the century, perhaps before 1383.[206] For Fortune's question, "What does the clamor of tragedies bewail," the unglossed text puts, "Of what are the chansons of jougleurs?"[207] We might suspect that *tragediarum*

---

[196] *Ibid.*, fl. 51b. [197] *Ibid.*, fol. 6b–c. [198] *Ibid.*, fol. 28a.

[199] Jean de Meun, French Boethius D 5 (HLF 3), ed. V. L. Dedeck-Héry, "Boethius' *De consolatione* by Jean de Meun," p. 189: "li cries de tragedies" (MS B: *des tragediens*; MS R: *destraunge dieus*).

[200] *Ibid.*, p. 214; one MS reads *traicien*.

[201] *Ibid.*, p. 173: "ces comunes putereles abandonnees au peuple."

[202] *Ibid.*, p. 191: "en la cortine et en l'ombre de ceste vie."

[203] French Boethius D 6 (HLF 5), now being edited by Atkinson from the base text of Paris, Bibliothèque Nationale MS fr. 1096, with variants from Amiens, Bibliothèque Municipale MS 412, Bern, Burgerbibliothek MS 365, and Montpellier, Ecole de Médicine MS 43. See Atkinson and Cropp, "Trois traductions de la *Consolatio Philosophiae* de Boèce," which also deals with D 7 (HLF 6) and D 9 (HLF 9).

[204] French Boethius D 7, Paris MS fol. 15r–v: "que chantent autre chose les chançons de geste fors que les faiz de Fortune qui, a coup desproveu, bestorne les royaumes de grant noblece?" *Tragicus* is "the poet" (*li poetes*), fol. 35.

[205] *Ibid.*, fol. 2v: "ces ordes puterelles"; fol. 16v: "en la fosse de ceste mortel vie."

[206] French Boethius D 7 (HLF 6), now being edited by Glynnis M. Cropp; see her studies, "Les manuscrits du *Livre de Boece de Consolacion*," "*Le livre de Boece de Consolacion*: From Translation to Glossed Text," and "Les gloses du *Livre de Boece de Consolacion*," and her earlier essay, "Two Historical Glosses in *Le Livre de Boece de la Consolacion*." Dijon MS 525, dated 1362, is the oldest known copy, and lacks the Jean de Meun prologue. For the composite nature of this prologue, see Cropp, "Le prologue de Jean de Meun et *Le livre de Boece de Consolacion*."

[207] French Boethius D 7, Sydney University MS Nicholson 7 (fifteenth century), fol. 17: "de quoy sont les chancons des Juglers." Dr. Cropp informs me that the oldest MSS have the same reading.

was interpreted as referring to tregetours or "tregetries," taken to mean the poems of tregetours. Tregetour was a synonym of juggler/jongleur or minstrel.[208] But the term *tragicus* is interpreted as a "saturian" or "satirian" poet.[209] The glossed text of the first-cited passage retains the word "tragedies," but with an explanation: "Of what are the chansons of tragedies, that is, the gests that the jougleurs chant"; but in twenty-five or so of the manuscripts, *tragedies* has been corrupted to *nugedres* (or *nugedies* or *migedres*), which would indicate an unfamiliarity with tragedy on the part of the scribe first responsible for the mistake.[210] The glossator himself was drawing upon and abbreviating the long version of Conches's commentary, but he chose not to pass on Conches's definition of tragedy,[211] giving rather one of his own which did not limit it to any specific content. However, he did give the long Conches gloss on the overthrow of happy kingdoms: "that is to say, of kings and powerful men who at various times were overthrown and confounded by an unforeseen chance of Fortune, for one does not know the day nor the hour of misadventures to come."[212] The translator of this version rendered *scenice meretricule* as "ces vilz ribaudes," and *scena* as "vilté."[213] We have seen similar translations earlier, and it may be that the words were interpreted as connected with *obscena*, "the obscene."

A rendering of the *Consolation* entirely into verse, which comes from the earlier part of the fourteenth century, interprets *scenice* as *estonans*, "astonishing" (that is, I take it, "stupefying"). "This scene of life" is translated as meaning only "this world."[214] *Tragediarum clamor* becomes "the cry of tragedies in writings":

---

[208] See F. Godefroy, *Dictionnaire de l'ancienne langue française*, 8:50 under *tre(s)geteor*; one of the recorded forms is *tragitaour*. See also the *Oxford English Dictionary* under "tregetour," "tregetry." Cropp notes this suggestion in "Les gloses," p. 374 n. 20.

[209] D 7, Sydney MS, fol. 37: "dont un Poetes saturien s'escrie." Cropp, "Boèce et Christine de Pizan," gives "satiriens," drawing on several MSS (p. 406).

[210] An example of the latter kind of glossed D 7 MS is Auckland Public Library, Grey MS 119, fol. 32: "De quoy sont les chançons de nugedres, c'est a dire des gestes que chantent les jougleurs." See Cropp, "Les gloses," p. 374, who suggests that perhaps some derivative of the Latin *nuge* (i.e., *nugae*), "trifles," was intended.

[211] *Ibid.*, p. 375.

[212] D 7, Auckland MS (given in Cropp, "Fortune and the Poet," p. 130): "C'est a dire des roys et des puissans qui sont aucunes foiz foulez et confonduz par cas de Fortune despouveuz, car l'en ne scet le jour ne l'eure des mesavantures qui adviennent."

[213] D 7, Sydney MS, fols. 4v, 19.

[214] French Boethius D 8 (HLF 7), currently being edited by Atkinson from Paris, Bibliothèque Nationale MS fr. 576 and the incomplete MS fr. 1543. These passages occur in MS 576 on fols. 6a and 22c. In his review of Dwyer, Atkinson indicates that this translation would be better called the Picard verse version than the version of the Anonymous of Meun. He dates it *c.* 1315–34. See his analysis, "A Fourteenth-Century Picard Translation-Commentary of the *Consolatio Philosophiae*," where he says that it comes from east Picardy or possibly Hainault (p. 32).

Que ploere aultre cose li cris
Des tragedies ens escrips
Fors que Fortune despourveue
Les grans regnes jus en bas rue.[215]

This suggests that the translator used the commentary of William of
Conches, who defined tragedy as a *scriptum*, whereas Nicholas Trevet
considered it a *carmen*.[216] Like Conches, therefore, he removes tragedy from
the theater, and even from the minstrel's stage. This is confirmed by his
rendering of *tragicus exclamat* as "of which one reads [in?] a tragedy" ("dont
on list une tragedie").[217]

Another verse version, written in the Burgundian dialect in 1336 by a
Dominican friar named Renaut de Louhans, exists in thirty or so copies. He
does not render *scenice* or *scena* or *tragicus*, but he has a most interesting
interpretation of Fortune's rhetorical question:

Que veulx tu plus que je te die?
Regarde bien la tragedie:
Quant l'on fait une bonne feste
Que menestriers chantent de geste,
Soit de Rolent et d'Olivier,
Soit de Charlon ou soit d'Ogier,
Soit de celui que tu vouldras,
Tousjours en la fin trouveras
Que celui que met en hault ma roe
En la fin le gette en la boe.[218]

I render freely as:

What more do you want me to say to you?
Take a good look at tragedy:
when one makes a great feast,
where minstrels sing of adventure,
whether of Roland and Oliver,
or Charlemagne or Ogier,
or of anyone you wish,
you will always find at the end
that whomever I set high on my wheel
at the end I throw into the mud.

[215] French Boethius D 8, MS 576,fol. 20d, book 2, prose 2, lines 359–62.
[216] Atkinson thinks that the translator used Trevet's commentary (review of Dwyer). He says that he
also used Fulgentius, and Vincent of Beauvais's *Speculum historiale*.
[217] French Boethius D 8, MS 576, fol. 35b, book 3, prose 6, line 5.
[218] Renaut de Louhans, French Boethius D 9 (HLF 9), Paris Bibliothèque Nationale MS fr. 578, fol.
15a–b; text supplied by Béatrice Atherton from the edition that she is preparing as a dissertation at
the University of Queensland. For a study of the MSS of Renaut, see Atherton and Atkinson, "Les
manuscrits du *Roman de Fortune et de Félicité*."

Although this interpretation does not convey the literal meaning, the overthrow of happy kingdoms, it is faithful to the general context of the Boethian passage. But it is done at the expense, perhaps, of accurate reporting; for it seems very far from the truth, to judge from the surviving *chansons de geste*, that all or even most of the principal characters in them ended in misfortune. Even Roland and Oliver usually end happily, except, of course, in the *Chanson de Roland*. However, the fact that Fortune rarely plays an explicit role in the chansons[219] is neither here nor there, since Fortune was just a literary conceit, the embodiment of chance or the force of circumstances, and could be extrapolated into any situation. I should note that in the story of Croesus, which Fortune introduces in Boethius not as an example of sudden disaster, but as an example of unexpected good fortune, the king's *curriculum vitae* is continued in this translation to his eventual downfall. The popular glossed translation also attaches Conches's account of Croesus's ultimate fate.[220]

A revision of Renaut's text, done later in the fourteenth century by an anonymous Benedictine monk, survives in over thirty manuscript copies, and in print.[221] It follows Renaut's treatment of Fortune's question fairly closely, except that it omits the lines of proper names of the subjects of the chansons de geste – perhaps because the reviser realized that it was anachronistic to have Fortune refer to persons like Charlemagne who lived after the time of Boethius.[222] But he translates *tragicus exclamat* as: "of which a Greek clerk cries out in one of his tragedies" ("Dont un clerc grec ainsi s'escrie / En un siene tragedie").[223] He renders Philosophy's question, "An tu in hanc vite scenam nunc primum subitus hospesque venisti?" in this way: "Es tu ores venus muable / En ce transitoire habitacle?"[224] The interpretation of scene as "dwelling place" would fit Isidore's explanations in the *Etymologies*.

We see, then, that though the translators of Boethius were not entirely benighted on the subjects of tragedy and the theater, many of them were, unless they made use of a commentary or glossed text.[225] But in none of the

---

[219] Pointed out by Cropp, "Fortune and the Poet," p. 132 n. 20.

[220] French Boethius D 7; see Dwyer, *Boethian Fictions*, pp. 41–44.

[221] French Boethius D 10 (HLF 10), dated by Dwyer *c.* 1380. I draw on excerpts supplied by Dwyer from the print of Geneva, Jean Croquet, before 1481, and by Atkinson from Brussells, Bibliothèque Royale MS 11244.

[222] *Ibid.*, Geneva print, p. 39; Brussells MS, fol. 15a.

[223] *Ibid.*, Brussells MS, fol. 35d (cf. Geneva text, p. 82).

[224] *Ibid.*, Brussells MS fol. 16c; Geneva print, p. 43.

[225] I omit from consideration D 11 (HLF 11), a verse abbreviation of Renaut (fourteenth century); D 12, a later mixed version, Aberystwyth, National Library MS 5038 (early fifteenth century?); and D 13, the mixed version printed by Colard Mansion, Bruges, 1477, and reprinted by Antoine Verard, Paris, 1494.

versions is there a clear notion either that tragedies were a special genre of literature in Boethius's day, or that they are a surviving special genre still practiced by minstrels. The most common view seems to be that tragedy is an obsolete synonym for chanson de geste, and that chansons de geste in Boethius's day, at least according to Fortune, constantly bewailed her overthrow of happy kingdoms. Renaut de Louhans's version, we saw, had Fortune make the same point about the familiar chansons of later times, which dealt with characters who were in fact generally victorious rather than unfortunate. In the most popular of translations, sometimes called the vulgate version (D 7), tragedy first disappeared altogether, being understood as a "chanted poem," and Fortune was made to refer to the chansons of jougleurs, while the tragic author became a "saturian" poet. When the translation received a set of glosses later on, "the chansons of jougleurs" was replaced with "tragedies," but tragedy was explained in the gloss as referring to the deeds or events that jougleurs recounted. Then, in the great majority of glossed manuscripts, "tragedies" disappeared again, this time being replaced with a nonsense word, "nugedres" or the like.

Doubtless the chief interest in Boethius at this time was as a philosopher rather than a poet. Though not all classical poets had disappeared from view (some works of Ovid and Vergil were still popular), Horace was one of the victims of the scholastic neglect of literature. However, some interest in the principles of writing poetry survived into later times. One example is to be seen in a fourteenth-century treatise on metrics, *Regule de arte versificandi*.[226] The author recognizes four kinds of poetry, namely, comedy, tragedy, satire, and elegy – the four species named by Matthew of Vendôme, in a different order.[227] Comedy deals with the *mores* of five kinds of persons, namely, old men, youths, servants, matrons, and handmaidens, as in the comedies of Terence; tragedy deals with the infelicity of sublime persons, as in Lucan and Statius; satire, as demonstrated by Horace, Persius, and Juvenal, has various vices and sins as its subject; and elegy treats of the affections of lovers, as in Ovid.[228] The definition of tragedy would suit Seneca's plays perfectly, since they deal exclusively with the unhappiness of noble persons from beginning to end. It might even fit Vergil's *Aeneid*, even though Aeneas ends happily. The definition says nothing about a need to end in unhappiness; and it is obvious that Aeneas

---

[226] *Regule de arte versificandi*, excerpted by Thurot, from Sorbonne MS 1782 in Paris, Bibliothèque Nationale.

[227] See above for other variations in Pace of Ferrara and Jacopo Alighieri.

[228] *Regule de arte*, p. 418: "Comedia agit de moribus quinque personarum, scilicet senum, et juvenum, servorum, matronarum, et ancillarum, ut comedie Terentii; tragedya, de infelicitate sublimium personarum, ut facit Lucanus et Statius; satira, de variis viciis et peccatis, ut facit Oratius, Persius, Juvenalis; elegia, de affectionibus amantium, ut Ovidius."

and most of the other characters experience much unhappiness during the course of the poem.

If the *Ars poetica* was no longer generally available, and if the *Poetics* was yet to be discovered, there was some vernacularizing of ideas of tragedy from at least one other of Aristotle's works. Nicholas Oresme completed his translation of the *Nicomachean Ethics* for Charles V in 1370. He understands the passage in which Aristotle refers to tragedy in the same way as did Thomas Aquinas, and in fact Oresme used Aquinas's commentary, among others.[229] The translation itself is somewhat obscure,[230] but his explanations are clear. Oresme is original (with respect to Aquinas) in giving romances as examples of tragedies. He says that tragedies are compositions (*ditiés*), like romances, that deal with various great and notable deeds.[231] Even more than Aquinas's comment on this passage, Oresme's gloss makes us wonder whether he considers misfortunes to be characteristic of, or predominant in, tragedies. He goes on to say that the narrations of such romances or compositions do not affect the happiness of the living persons who listen to them; still less do events of the present time affect the dead (he adds that Aristotle is talking only of the happiness of this life).[232]

In light of Oresme's narrative view of tragedy, it is surprising that he has a dramatic understanding of comedy. What is more, he does not have some sort of Isidorian dumbshow in mind, but rather the theatrical plays of his own time, in which one actor takes the part and speaks the words of St. Paul, say, while another represents Judas, and a third a hermit.[233] Perhaps he was inspired to make the equation between ancient comedies and modern plays by St. Thomas's comment about old and new comedies as representations and narrations containing dialogue, in which, of course,

[229] Nicholas Oresme, *Le livre de ethiques d'Aristote.* In addition to Thomas's commentary, he used those of Albert the Great and Walter Burley (p. 40).
[230] *Ibid.* 1.17, pp. 137–38: "Mais il a difference entre les fortunes qui adviennent as amis des vis et celles qui adviennent as amis des mors, et est moult plus grand que n'est la difference des mauvaistiez et injustices que l'en raconte es tragedies jadiz estre faictes ou resgart des vis ou des mors, et par ceste difference povons nous arguer a cest propos."
[231] *Ibid.*, comment 5: "Sont ditiez, comme rommans, qui parlent et traictent de aucuns grans faiz notables."
[232] *Ibid.*, comment 6: "Car les narracions que l'en fait en telz rommans ou ditiez ne muent en rien la felicité de ceulz qui vivent et les escoutent, et les faiz qui aviennent presentement redondent encore moins a ceuls qui sont mors, qui rien n'en sentent ne riens n'en scevent ne rien n'en oyrent dire. Et est assavoir que Aristote ne parle fors de la felicité de ceste vie; et les mors ne sont en ceste vie, fors tant seulement ou memoire des vis."
[233] *Ibid.* 4.25, p. 271, comment 7 (where Aristotle contrasts the morals of old comedies with those of the present): "Il entent ici par comedies aucuns gieux, comme sont ceulz ou un homme represente saint Pol, l'autre Judas, l'autre un hermite, et dit chason son personnage et en ont aucuns roulles et rimes. Et aucunes fois en telz giex l'en dit de laides paroles, ordes, injurieuses, et deshonestes."

Thomas was referring to old and new from Aristotle's point of view.

Oresme's editor says that his use of the word "tragedie" was apparently unprecedented in the French tongue.[234] Our survey of the Boethian translations shows that this is not true, but it is the case that he introduced the word independently of that tradition, and was quickly followed by others using other sources. Evrard de Conty, in translating the pseudo-Aristotelian *Problemata* for Charles V (therefore, before the king's death in 1380),[235] glosses *tragedie* or *tragedique* as a manner of speaking.[236] Another translation made for Charles V, of Augustine's *City of God*, by Raoul de Praelles, completed in 1375, provides an Isidorian explanation of both tragedy and comedy.[237] Praelles's commentary is based entirely on book 18 of the *Etymologies* with its stress on the evils treated in tragedy[238] and on its theatrical context. But the latter subject has been updated, partially in accord with Nicholas Trevet's later views in his Seneca commentary (which Trevet may have anticipated in his own commentary on Augustine's *City of God*),[239] and partially by reference to contemporary plays. The scene,[240] he says, was a small house in the middle of the theater, in which there was a lectern (*letrin*), where the tragedies and comedies of the poets were read, and there were people in disguise,[241] who imitated the appearances of those about whom one sang and about whom the plays were made, just as can be seen nowadays in dramatic plays (*jeux de personnaiges*) and charivaris. There were players of various instruments, and others who disguised themselves and counterfeited the persons about whom the tragedy or comedy spoke.[242] Unlike Oresme, Praelles seems to have remained faithful to Isidore's idea of silent actors, even in the face of the contrary modern precedent.

[234] Oresme, *Ethiques d'Aristote*, pp. 137–38 n. 1.

[235] *Dictionnaire de biographie française*, 13:307.

[236] Godefroy, *Dictionnaire*, 7:784.

[237] I use the excerpts given by Meiss, *French Painting: The Limbourgs*, p. 442 n. 204, presumably from Paris Bibliothèque Nationale MS fr. 25 (see p. 342). Godefroy, under "scène," uses the printed text of 1486.

[238] Raoul de Praelles, *Cité de Dieu* 1.31: "Tragedie est faicte de faiz enormes des grans roys et des grans princes et de leurs cruaulties et mauvaistiez."

[239] I have not had the opportunity to examine Trevet's Augustine commentary.

[240] The mistaken form *asena* appears in Meiss's text, but the correct *scene* is reported by Godefroy.

[241] "Et y avoit gens desguisez . . ." I disagree with Meiss's translation, *French Painting*, p. 52: "and there people in disguises . . ." as if "there" referred to the scene. There is no suggestion in the text that the scene is thought of as a changing-room or hiding-room for the actors. I also question Meiss's assumption that Praelles means that masks were used in the disguisings.

[242] *Ibid.*: "[La scene] est une petite maison ou milieu du theatre en la quelle avoit ung letrin ou len lisoit les tragedies et comedies des poetes et y avoit gens desguisez qui faisoient les contenances de ceulx pour lequelz len chantoit et faisoit ses jeux, ainsi comme tu vois que len fait encores au jour duy les jeux de personnaiges et charivalis. Et y avoit joueurs de divers instrumens et autres qui se desguisoient et contrefaisoient les personnens de qui la tragedie ou comedie parloit."

Boethius in French

Other sources of knowledge or opinion about tragedy were, of course, available in late medieval France: for instance, John of Salisbury's *Policraticus*, a French translation of which was possessed by Charles V,[243] and the dictionaries of Huguccio and Balbus. But availability does not always mean use, and sometimes use means misuse. In the fullest adaptation of Balbus into French, the Latin definition of *tragedia* is stripped down and distorted: "hircina lanx vel hircinus cantus, id est fecidus," and the French definition comes out of nowhere: "c'est une maniere de tractier de hystoire ou d'acune diverse matiere." *Tragicus* and *tragedus* are defined as "escriveur de telle matiere."[244]

Other possible references would be in the various accounts of the emperor Nero. For instance, James of Varazze's *Golden Legend* notes that his dedication to singing was such that he surpassed all citharists and tragedians, an idea carried over in John of Vignay's translation of the 1330s.[245] But in giving Orosius's account of Nero singing the *Iliad* in a tragic habit as Rome was burning, James puts "a turgid habit," and transforms the work to the *Helyed*; and John changes the habit to "a habitacle" (that is, a small structure or room).[246]

I make no claim to having compiled a complete inventory of the available references to, or uses or distortions of, "tragedy" at this time. But I hope that the survey that I have given is representative both of the variety, and often of the vagueness, of the usages. In the next chapter we shall see how some French poets reacted to the word "tragedy," and we shall also begin to see, in France and elsewhere, some signs of generic inventiveness in addition to theoretical explanations. That is to say, we shall see some new tragedies as well as new ideas of tragedies. So far, self-conscious authors of tragedies have been rare: apart from William of Blois and his lost tragedy, there were only John Garland and Albertino Mussato, and, after the fact, Dante. Both Garland and Mussato believed that they were making a unique

---

[243] L. Delisle, *Recherches sur la librairie de Charles V*, 2:*85 no. 501: "Policraticon translaté en françois par frère Denis Foulechat... A mons. d'Anjou, le 7 octobre 1380."
[244] Mario Roques, *Recueil général des lexiques français du moyen âge*, 1: *Lexiques alphabétiques*, 2:421, from Paris, Bibliothèque Nationale MS lat. 13032.
[245] James of Varazze (Jacobus a Voragine), *Legenda aurea*, ed. T. Graesse, p. 377 ("De sancto Petro apostolo"): "Cantibus intendebat, ita ut omnes cytharistas et tragedos superaret"; Jehan de Vignay, *Legende doree*, fol. 129: "Il estoit si ententif a chant quil surmontoit toutes herpeurs et toutes trajedieurs."
[246] *Ibid.*: "Miratus qualis et quanta fuerit succensio Troje, Romam per septem dies et noctes succendi fecit, quod ex altissima turri prospectans letatusque flamme pulchritudine turgido habitu *Helyedam* [for *Iliadem*] decantabat"; "Apres ce il sesmerveilla et pensa quele lestinction de Troye avoit esté, et fist mettre le feu a Romme par sept jours et sept nuyts, et il regardoit dune haulte tor et avoit tresgrant joye de la beaulte de la flamme, et chantoit en ung habitacle la chancon de *Helyade*."

167

addition to an obsolete genre. Dante, on the contrary, believed that tragedy was a current genre and that he had added to it. He was before his time, but this was to be the wave of the future. However, only one section of the medieval wave, Chaucer's, was to have a significant ripple effect.

6

Final variations

I begin the end of my general survey of ancient and medieval ideas of tragedy at the end of the fourteenth century. The most important development occurred in England, with Chaucer and his fifteenth-century disciples, Lydgate and Henryson. These authors are so significant in the history of tragedy that I shall devote a separate study to them: "Chaucerian Tragedy." The reader may eventually find full details there, but I shall give a brief summary below, in order to round out our picture of ideas and forms of tragedy in the later Middle Ages. It will be followed by a look at the usages of French authors at the turn of the fifteenth century, specifically, William of Machaut, Eustace Deschamps, Christine de Pisan, and, most important, Philip of Mézières.

The other loci of tragedies or tragic theory at the end of the Middle Ages, apart from Belgium, where an odd joke-tragedy was composed by Reyner de Wael in 1447, are Italy and Spain. The Italians were inspired by Seneca, and, at least at the beginning, by Mussato's imitation of Seneca, and wrote tragedies in Latin verse on both contemporary and classical subjects. The Spaniards, centered around the marquis of Santillana, were aware of Seneca's plays, but were more influenced by the commentaries on Dante's *Comedy* in their ideas of tragedy. However, three vernacular authors of tragedies go their own way. At the end or turn of the century, the Castilian masterpiece *Celestina*, which ends disastrously for its protagonists, is first called a comedy and then a tragicomedy – both misnomers arising from a comedy of errors. At the same time, back in Italy, an oppositely misnamed Latin dramatic work was written and published: the *Tragedy of the Triumph of Louis XII*, by Giovanni Armonio. A short time earlier, the Italian Latinist tradition merged with Spanish interests in two dramas about Ferdinand of Aragon by the brothers Carlo and Marcellino Verardi: the *History of Granada*, billed as neither a tragedy nor a comedy, and the tragicomedy *Ferdinand Delivered*. As far as the plot of this latter play goes, it partakes of both comedy and tragedy in ways opposite to the *Celestina*, since, like William of Conches's definition of a comedy, it begins in adversity and ends in prosperity.

ENGLAND: CHAUCER AND THE FUTURE

Awareness of the word "tragedy" is rarer in England in the fourteenth century than it is in France and Italy. Ranulph Higden uses the term several times in his *Polychronicon*, but John Trevisa, in his translation of Higden, consistently gives it as "geste."[1] English collections of exempla speak of the story of Nero in hell inviting lawyers into his bath of molten gold as coming from a tragedy of Seneca's.[2] The surgeon John Arderne considers the Bible to be a tragedy, by which he seems to mean "book"; he recommends it and other tragedies as the source of humorous tales.[3] Other bizarre notions of tragedy can be found in the fifteenth century. Only two persons were familiar with the real tragedies of Seneca at this time, the Dominican scholar Nicholas Trevet at the beginning of the fourteenth century, whom I have treated above, and the Benedictine chronicler Thomas Walsingham at the end. Trevet explains the tragedies in the light of Isidore of Seville's definitions, while Walsingham relies on Papias.[4] Walsingham uses tragedy figuratively when he writes about "a more than tragic matter" – a killing in Westminster Abbey – and refers to his accounts of the Peasants' Revolt as tragedies.[5] Lydgate in the next century knew about Seneca's plays, but only pretends to have read them, as is obvious when he says that they tell of Jason's eventual restoration to Medea.[6]

On the Continent, the late-medieval flow of cultural interests created a hiatus between "science" and literature. For the most part the professional scholars, the cognoscenti, were attracted to philosophy and theology; they left letters to dilettanti, who lost sight of many classical poets along the way. Even in Italy, where Horace was still read and where Seneca was taken up and appreciated as literature, there was much that was not understood, including Aristotle's *Poetics*, which was available, but read only by Mussato, and that glancingly. Not even Giovanni Boccaccio, one of the most learned of the Italian men of letters, understood the evidence of how ancient tragedy and comedy were performed; but he did know what they

[1] Ranulf Higden and John Trevisa, *Polychronicon*, ed. Churchill Babington and Joseph Rawson Lumby, 4.9, 11 (4:394–95, 458–59), 7.16 (7:460–61).
[2] See chap. 5 above, p. 134.
[3] John Arderne, *Practica*, fol. 65v (= 25v); Latin text in Kelly, "The Non-Tragedy of Arthur," p. 93 n. 17.
[4] *Prohemia poetarum Fratris Thome de Walsingham*, fol. 178.
[5] Walsingham, *Chronicon Angliae*, pp. 206, 301, 312; *Ypodigma Neustriae*, p. 335. Texts in Kelly, "Non-Tragedy," pp. 94–95 nn. 21–24.   [6] John Lydgate, *Fall of Princes* 1.2384–87.

looked like on parchment or paper from seeing the actual plays of Seneca, Plautus, and Terence. Boccaccio's *De casibus virorum illustrium* had nothing to do with his notions of tragedy, which he understood to be a kind of staged production practiced by the ancients. But Chaucer, because of his very ignorance of the distorted dramatic traditions that Boccaccio was drawing on, was able to apply an idea of tragedy to the Italian author's collection of historical accounts of great men coming to grief.

Chaucer learned of tragedy primarily from Fortune's remark in the *Consolation of Philosophy*, that the clamor of tragedies bewails the unexpected overthrow of happy kingdoms. We have seen that William of Conches's gloss on this passage explains tragedy as a writing about great iniquities that begins in prosperity and ends in adversity, and that this definition was taken over by Nicholas Trevet and combined with Isidore of Seville's specification of subject matter: the crimes of wicked kings. The result, limiting tragedy to notorious criminals who deserved their misfortune, contradicted Boethius's point that misfortunes come unexpectedly, even upon the innocent. Fortunately, Chaucer inherited a gloss that Boethianized Trevet's definition by leaving out all reference to crimes and iniquities. Tragedy was characterized in his copy of the *Consolation* only as a poem beginning in prosperity and ending in adversity.[7]

Chaucer composed a set of tragedies of his own in the series that later became the *Monk's Tale*, in which form it preserved as a subtitle what was perhaps its original title: *De casibus virorum illustrium*. This shows that Chaucer had concluded that Boccaccio's work consisted of tragedies. He drew on its episodes only very sparingly, however, and gave a completely different purpose for recounting stories of falls.

Boccaccio intended his accounts to serve as exempla demonstrating that sinners in high places inevitably came to grief.[8] Such a proposition is palpably false as a universal statement, and dubious as a generality; and its implied corollary, that well-behaved illustrious men can be guaranteed good treatment by Fortune (meaning, in real terms, God), is even more frequently contradicted by experience. He could, of course, have made his proposition seem true by limiting his examples to cases of deserved comeuppance, but in fact a good half or more of his histories show virtuous or harmless protagonists falling for no good reason at all. Whether or not

---

[7] The original Latin form of this gloss is to be seen in Cambridge University Library MS Ii 3.21, fol. 37 (ed. Silk, p. 142): "Tragedia dicitur carmen de prosperitate incipiens et in adversitate terminans." Chaucer's translation in his *Boece* is: "Tragedye is to seyn a dite of a prosperite for a tyme, that endeth in wrecchidnesse" (*The Riverside Chaucer*, pp. 409–10). See Kelly, "Non-Tragedy," pp. 95–96. and "Chaucer and Shakespeare on Tragedy," pp. 193–94.

[8] Bergen in his edition of Lydgate's *Fall of Princes* gives both the original and the revised versions of Boccaccio's Preface, 1:xlvii–xlviii.

Chaucer was aware of the contradictions inherent in Boccaccio's rationale for his series, he produced, at the beginning of his own series, a pair of completely valid lessons, after first specifying the overall Boethian purpose of tragedy as lamentation over misfortunes. He does all this in his opening stanza, a masterpiece of concision:

> I wol biwaille, in manere of tragedie,
> The harm of hem that stoode in heigh degree,
> And fillen so that ther nas no remedie
> To brynge hem out of her adversitee.
> For certein, whan that Fortune list to flee,
> Ther may no man the cours of hire withholde.
> Lat no man truste on blynd Prosperitee;
> Be war by thise ensamples trewe and olde.
>
> (*Monk's Tale*, 1991–98)

The two truths stated in the last four lines are these: first, that when good fortune turns bad, that is, when external circumstances are such that no course of action can prevent disaster, one can only accept the inevitable; and second, that sometimes disasters are caused by a complacence in one's good fortune. The warning at the end – "Beware!" – refers mainly to the second lesson, and can be translated as follows: "Take all possible precautions to prevent falls." But it can also be seen to encompass an instruction concerning the first lesson: "Be resigned to what follows if the precautions are insufficient."

Proper precautions against falls must naturally include virtuous living, since several of the following tragedies show divinely initiated retribution against sinners: Lucifer, Adam, Nabuchodonosor, Balthasar, and Antiochus IV Epiphanes. It is true that the account of Nabuchodonosor violates the definition of tragedy by ending happily, for God arbitrarily brings an end to his punishment and restores him to his former position, for which the king is suitably grateful. However, the "tragic segment" of his life was meant to serve as an exemplum to his son Balthasar, which he is blamed for not heeding, and he is not given a second chance. Neither is Antiochus, even though, unlike Nabuchodonosor, he actively repents after his downfall; his punishment is carried out to its horrible end.

Other sinners fall without any specified intervention from God, namely, Nero and Holofernes; the one is brought down by a rebellion of his own people, and the other, who promotes the cult of Nabuchodonosor as a god, by a mere woman, Judith. Two other tragic protagonists come to disaster because of women, Samson and Hercules, both of whom could have been portrayed as deserving their fate because of sins: Samson for his weakness for Philistine prostitutes, and Hercules for his adulterous liaisons; and both for committing suicide. But their suicides are not counted as faults, and the co-respondent women are ignored or neutralized: Hercules's abandonment of Deianira for Iole and Omphale is not mentioned, nor is Samson's interlude with the prostitute of Gaza, and Dalila is elevated as his second wife. The cause of Samson's fall is specified as his foolish trust in his wives, while Hercules's fall is faultless, except for not foreseeing the unexpected, unless we are to take the adage, "Ful wys is he that kan hymselven knowe" (*Monk's Tale*, 2140), as somehow indicting him for a lack of self-knowledge. It is instructive to compare Chaucer's *Tragedy of Hercules* with the second Senecan play on the same hero, *Hercules oetaeus*, which, as noted in the last chapter, ends "happily" – at least as happily as a saint's martyrdom. Even though his relationship with Iole is fully exposed, Hercules is able to claim from heaven that his *virtus* has joined him to the supernal beings.[9]

The fall of the protagonist of Chaucer's concluding tragedy, *Cresus*, is blamed upon his pride, which has been analyzed by some readers as a sin; but it is more justly seen to be a species of folly akin to Samson's. It is a brash overconfidence in his own good fortune, a foolish trusting, as it were, in blind Prosperity. Alexander the Great is said to have been a sinner of sorts, since his weakness for wine and women is mentioned; but these faults are not noted as causal factors in the domestic betrayal that cost him his life. Likewise, in the two remaining small-scale tragedies in Chaucer's original series, those of Zenobia and Julius Caesar, only external circumstances, and not any moral or intellectual failing, are blamed for the final adversity.

As for the protagonist of his large-scale tragedy, *Troilus and Criseyde*, I am prepared to argue that Troilus is best seen (that is, in Chaucer's intention) as being similarly inculpable, morally and even intellectually (including his exercise of prudence and discretion), for the hard fate he eventually suffers. But it should be obvious from the above that any sort of faulty protagonist can be readily accommodated to Chaucer's theory of tragedy, and those readers who find Troilus to be endowed with some sort of "tragic flaw" can find a parallel in the *Monk's Tale*.

It seems that after Chaucer finished *Troilus* he added four more tragedies to his original series, all of them dealing with no-fault falls: these are the "modern instances" of King Peter of Spain, King Peter Lusignan of Cyprus (I shall give his complete tragedy in the next section), Barnabo Visconti, and Hugelino of Pisa; the account of Visconti, at least, must be late, for he died only in December 1385. When Chaucer later assigned the expanded set to the Monk in his *Canterbury Tales*, he gave him a fresh explanation of tragedy in his prologue. He originally concluded the

---

[9] Seneca, *Hercules oetaeus* 1942–43: "Iam virtus mihi / In astra et ipsos fecit ad superos iter."

Monk's turn by having the Host "interrupt" him, since he had threatened to tell a hundred tragedies, by complaining that they were boring; but in his final version he has the Knight call a halt to the Monk's recitation on the grounds that he has found the tragedies too depressing. The Host then expresses his agreement, but for his original reason: the tragedies recounted thus far were not "reported" sufficiently well to command his attention.

Perhaps Chaucer felt free to agree with his Host on the inadequacy of his early tragedies after having produced another tragedy of significantly better reportage. *Troilus and Criseyde* vies with Milton's *Paradise Lost*, written three centuries later, for the honor of the greatest narrative poem in the English language. It has no near rival for being the best tragedy of the Middle Ages. When Chaucer states his purpose in the first line, "the double sorwe of Troilus to tellen," it should not be taken to be a variant in his understanding of tragedy as proceeding from prosperity to adversity, for Troilus's first sorrow is not treated as real adversity. It is rather treated, in a half-sympathetic, half-exasperated way, as a function of his initial prosperity. Chaucer enlarges this phase of the story a great deal from the corresponding sections of his main source, Boccaccio's *Filostrato*, for the purpose, I would argue, of lulling his audience into sharing Troilus's sense of well-being, in spite of his warning at the outset of the second sorrow to come. At least, this seems to be the effect that his work has had on many readers.

Later in his prologue to book 1, Chaucer restates the idea of double sorrows in such a way that it might be taken to refer to the final sorrows of Troilus and Criseyde at the end:

> Now herkneth with a good entencioun,
> For now wil I gon streght to my matere,
> In which ye may the double sorwes here
> Of Troilus in lovynge of Criseyde,
> And how that she forsook hym er she deyde.   (1.52–56)

This passage may have inspired Robert Henryson a century or so later to write another tragedy detailing the miserable end of Criseyde.[10] For in spite of what he says here, Chaucer does not have Criseyde die before Troilus, but rather gives the impression that she lives on after Troilus's death in her new commitment to Diomede, not at all happy, but ashamed and guilt-ridden at her betrayal of Troilus.

Henryson in his *Testament of Cresseid* is able to rely on Chaucer's poem to conjure up his protagonist's original prosperity, so that he can begin his

---

[10] Robert Henryson, *The Testament of Cresseid*. He calls it a tragedy in the opening stanza.

story with her final set of adversities. Diomede gives her a "libel of repudie" (that is, he divorces her), and she goes in secret shame to her father's house. She contracts leprosy, which is first seen as a punishment of the gods for blasphemy, but then as a purely natural affliction. In the leprosarium, she recalls her previous happiness in Troy, with no thought of Troilus or her treatment of him. But when Troilus passes by and gives her gold, not recognizing her, but being reminded of her, she admits her own faults for the first time, and dies in great remorse. Henryson's final lesson is less severe than Chaucer's, who advised both men and women to avoid human love altogether. Henryson instead addresses worthy women and urges them to learn by Cresseid's lamentable example not to mingle deceit with their love.

Henryson's version of the Troilus and Criseyde tragedy was passed on to the sixteenth century along with Chaucer's, but John Lydgate was more influential in continuing Chaucer's understanding and practice of tragedy. Lydgate had an Isidorian notion of ancient tragedy as an acted form which much resembles Boccaccio's ideas, and he explains it at great length in the *Troy Book*.[11] But he followed Chaucer's lead in regarding the currently practiced genre of tragedy as a purely narrative form. In translating Laurence of Premierfait's expanded version of the *De casibus* into English verse as the *Fall of Princes*, he combined Boccaccio's stress on retribution with Premierfait's stress on Fortune to match Chaucer's emphases both on lack of caution and on the unexpectedness of misfortune, and he reinforced Chaucer's generic classification with envoys pointing up lessons of tragedy. The Chaucer–Lydgate tradition of tragedy was handed on in William Baldwin's *A Mirror for Magistrates*, which was designed as a sequel to the *Fall of Princes*, and from there it was bequeathed to Shakespeare. The Chaucerian nature of Shakespeare's understanding of tragedy can best be seen not in the titles of his plays, which may not be his, but in his characters' uses of the term: it refers to disasters that come without warning to persons of all sorts, but usually to the innocent.[12]

LAMENTS IN FRANCE

In the last chapter, we saw how the various translators of Boethius floundered in dealing with the terms "tragedy" and "tragic," even when drawing on learned commentators, and we saw a similarly confusing variety of meanings in the translations of other works. The poets, in general, were not more enlightened. Guillaume de Machaut had somehow heard of tragedy, or the

---

[11] Lydgate, *Troy Book* 2.842–926 (ed. Berger, 1:168–71).
[12] Kelly, "Chaucer and Shakespeare on Tragedy," pp. 198–200.

authors or performers of tragedy, but he or his source completely missed the mark in guessing what it was all about. In his *Prise d'Alexandrie*, written some time after the assassination of Peter of Lusignan, king of Cyprus, in 1369, he has a mythological prologue on the birth of the king. A parliament of gods and goddesses was held, and also present were lesser figures: nymphs, satyrs, fairies, and tragediennes. It was the function of the tragediennes to make sacrifices to the gods and perform the divine office.[13]

Eustace Deschamps seems to have thought that "les Tragèdes" was a name for the Trojans: they perished because of too great estate, while the Greeks fell through pride, and the Sodomites through sins of the flesh.[14] There may be some notion here that the Trojans were tragic people par excellence, since elsewhere Deschamps appears to think that tragedians are poets who specialize in lamentations. The countries of the West should employ tragedians and Arethusa (who turned to water for weeping) to bewail the death of Bertran du Guesclin (d. 1380).[15] He asks the "targedian" in another poem not to forget the sorrow caused by slander against true love.[16] I should note that Deschamps apparently has nothing to

---

[13] Guillaume de Machaut, *La prise d'Alexandrie; ou, Chronique du roi Pierre Ier de Lusignan*, pp. 1–2:

> La ot maint Dieu de grant puissance
> Et digne de grant reverence,
> Et maintes deesses aussi,
> Que je ne nommeray pas ci,
> Car trop longue chose seroit
> Qui tous et toutes nommeroit:
> Nymphes de bois et de rivieres,
> Satireaus de toutes manieres.
> Les tragedianes y vindrent
> Qui mult humblement se contiendrent
> (Tragedianes sacrefice
> Font aux diex, et divin office;
> Et nymphes en poeterie,
> Ce sont fees, je n'en doubt mie).   (lines 11–25)

Vesta is said to be the sovereign mistress of nymphs and tragediennes and their temples (lines 91–95).

[14] Eustace Deschamps, *Oeuvres complètes*, no. 940 (Autre balade), 5:153–55:

> Par orgueil finerent Gregois,
> Par trop grans estas li Tragede,
> Par pechié de char Sodomois.   (lines 42–44)

[15] *Ibid.*, no. 206 (2:27–28):

> Picardie, Champaigne, et Occident
> Doivent pour plourer acquerre
> Tragediens, Arethusa requerre
> (Qui en eaue fut par plour convertie),
> A fin qu'a touz de sa mort les cuers serre.   (lines 15–19)

[16] *Ibid.*, no. 503 (3:331):

> Hé, my amis, qui vous a diffamé
> Toudis soit il en la palus perie!
> A tous jours mais a mon cuer affamé;
> Targedien, ce dueil n'oubliez mie.   (lines 17–20)

say on comedy. Around 1421, he translated Vitalis of Blois's *Geta*, but if he used a copy that called it a comedy, he ignored the designation.[17] Also noteworthy is the fact that in his balade *Discussion avec la Fortune*, in which Fortune defends herself in much the same way as she does in Boethius, and which may draw on Boethius, he does not have her speak of tragedies.[18] We may, nevertheless, be able to deduce with some assurance from his earlier balades that he knew of the word tragedy and understood it to be a poetic lamentation, but perhaps lyric rather than narrative in form.

We can draw a similar conclusion, of tragedy understood as a formal lament, about Philippe de Mézières in a work of Latin prose written in 1389–90, namely, *A Tragedic or Declamatory Prayer on the Passion of Our Lord*.[19] One might think from this title and the pairing of *tragedicus* and *declamatorius* by *seu* in the prologue and later that he is explaining the two words as somewhat equivalent. But more probably the *seu* should be taken as additive rather than alternative: the prayer is both tragedic and declamatory, with tragedic meaning "lamentable." This is how Mézières refers to the work at the beginning of the first part, after the preliminary material: *Oracio declamatoria et tragedica*.[20] He usually calls it just *oracio tragedica*, but sometimes *oracio seu declamacio tragedica*,[21] *tragedica declamacio*,[22] a *dictamen*,[23] a *tractatus*,[24] and, simply, a *tragedia*.[25] He means by the title and its variants a heartfelt lamentation and petition, in which he describes the Passion of Christ and the lack of devotion it has received, and prays that the Passion and all its accoutrements be placed in the scales with his soul and the souls of all faithful Christians when they die, so that their sins will be outweighed by Christ's merits. He does not connect the term "tragedy" with poetic form or high style; his own work is in prose and he humbly disparages its style.[26] A tragedy is necessarily inspired by sad events, but it can have a favorable outcome:

Cum enim in ponderacione animarum nostrarum ... Deum Patrem post Filium stilo simplici et minus devote invocaverimus, per necessarium etiam judicatur ut

---

[17] *Ibid.*, no. 1494 (8:211–46): *Le traicté de Getta et d'Amphitrion mis du latin en françois*, edited earlier with an introduction by Queux de Saint Hilaire (Paris 1872).

[18] *Ibid.*, no. 1134 (6:56–58); the title is supplied by the editor. See Cropp, "Fortune and the Poet."

[19] The work begins with the words, "Prologus in oracione tragedica seu declamatoria Passionis domini nostri Jhesu Xpisti." I am grateful to Susan Dickman for drawing my attention to Mézières's interesting work. See N. Jorga, *Philippe de Mézières, 1327–1405, et la croisade au XIV⁴ siècle*, pp. 471–76, for the date and a partial summary.

[20] Mézières, *Oracio tragedica* 1.0, fol. 141.

[21] *Ibid.*, Prologue, fol. 131.   [22] *Ibid.*, 1.9 (fol. 145v).

[23] *Ibid.*, 4.3 (fol. 192).   [24] *Ibid.*, 4.6 (fol. 197).

[25] *Ibid.*, 2.9–10 (fols. 155v, 156v, 157); 2.35 (fol. 182); 3.1–2 (fols. 183r–v, 184v); 5.11 (fol. 209 bis).

[26] *Ibid.*, 1.9 (fol. 145v): "tragedicam declamacionem passionis nostri salvatoris grosso stilo et inculto, licet lacrimabili, recensendo."

Final variations

pro dulci conclusione presentis tragedie post lacrimas invocemus etiam Spiritum Sanctum, consolatorem fidelium.[27]

(For since in the weighing of our souls . . . we invoked God the Father after the Son in our simple and undevout style, it is judged necessary also for a sweet conclusion to the present tragedy that we invoke as well the Holy Spirit, the consoler of the faithful.)

He also takes a respite from the sorrow of the Passion after reciting the Lord's death and burial by looking forward to the joy of the Resurrection.[28]

Some narration is necessary in his tragedy, and Mézières envisions a reader alleging that it is enough, without going on to add various examples and parables:

Quia oratio tua tragedica quasi narrative dictata, in fide fundata, non indiget probatione, sed devota et lacrimabili contemplatione.[29]

(Because your tragedic prayer is as it were spoken in a narrative fashion and based on our faith, it does not need proof but rather devout and tearful contemplation.)

The intellectual voice that speaks to him periodically answers this objection decisively:

Manifestum est enim in disputationibus quod in omni proponente et conclusionem suam approbare volente, tria requiruntur, scilicet audiencia, probationes et argumenta demonstrabilia et concludencia, et, tercio, conclusione autentiquare. Si vero proponens mediis penitus obmissis anteponet conclusionem, affirmando ipsam esse veram, utique a magistro respondente talis propositio seu conclusio simpliciter et juste denegabitur.[30]

(It is manifest in disputations that everyone who proposes a point and desires to establish his conclusions needs three things, namely, an audience, proofs and arguments that are demonstrable and conclusive, and third, to authenticate it with a conclusion. If however the proposer puts forward his conclusion beforehand, omitting all of the middle elements, affirming it to be true, certainly such a proposition or conclusion will be simply and justly denied by the responding master.)

---

[27] *Ibid.*, 1.16 (fol. 148v).

[28] *Ibid.*, 1.10 (fols. 145v–146), preceded by a "Small Prologue of respite from the sorrow of the Passion of the Lord tragedically renewed, tending to joy of the Lord's Resurrection" ("Prologus parvus de respiracione doloris passionis Domini tragedice refricate, tendens ad gaudium resurrectionis Domini"). See the table of contents, fol. 134, where the chapter is summarized thus: "Hic petit orator a Domino consolari de gaudio resurrectionis Domini, ipsam gloriosam resurrectionem, occurrenciaque ad eam, et apparaciones Domini jocundas in statera apponi, Jhesum resurgentem fenici avi soli in mundo pie comparando" ("Here the orator asks from the Lord to be consoled by the Resurrection of the Lord, by placing the Resurrection itself, and the occurrences that went with it, and the delightful apparitions of the Lord in the scales, piously comparing the rising Jesus to the phoenix, the only bird of its kind in the world"). [29] *Ibid.*, 2.10 (fol. 156v). [30] *Ibid.*

However, in the fourth part of his work he inserts what he calls "a certain incident" that he recognizes as somewhat tangential to his main petition, namely, the disastrous aftermath of the capture of Alexandria. In dealing with it, he moves "from the tragedic declamation in the present volume to a bitter tragedy" ("de tragedica declamacione in presenti volumine ad tragediam amaram prosequendo").[31] But his telling of this incident becomes a twofold or threefold tragedy. In his narration of "the matter of lamentation and tragedy" that followed upon the victories of Peter of Lusignan,[32] after describing the ill-advised withdrawal of the Christian forces from Alexandria, he proceeds "from bitter declamation to tearful and most bitter tragedy" in telling of the holy death of the disappointed supporter of the campaign, Peter Thomas, patriarch of Constantinople, which, however, at least for him, had a happy ending, because "in the midst of shining miracles he happily brought his final day to an end."[33] But the sorrow, of course, remained with Mézières and the other survivors, and more sorrow awaited:

Dicunt enim philosophi et in vulgari proverbio narratur, videlicet, quod Fortuna sola dedignatur venire, Seneca atestante; utique cortina cortinam trahit, cortina videlicet meroris hujus veterani scribentis cortinam doloris trahendo et lacrimas amaras renovando nunquam affectu cessabit, declamationemque super lamentationem tragedicam multiplicando, heu heu! Unde sumam exordium lamentandi et refricandi lacrimas que nunquam deficient huic infelici veterano.[34]

(For philosophers declare, and it is stated in a common proverb, as Seneca notes, that Fortune disdains to come unattended; surely curtain drags along curtain, the curtain, that is, of the grief of this veteran writer, dragging the curtain of sorrow and renewing bitter and never-ceasing tears in his heart, and multiplying declamation upon tragedic lamentation, alas, alas! Whence I will take up the exordium of lamenting and of starting tears afresh that will never be lacking to this unhappy veteran.)

He is speaking of the assassination in 1369 of Peter of Lusignan, king of Cyprus, under whom he served as chancellor. Machaut called the king's assassination a martyrdom,[35] and Mézières undoubtedly agreed. Earlier on,

---

[31] *Ibid.*, Prologue to part 4 in the table of contents (fol. 137).
[32] *Ibid.*, 4.2 (fol. 192): "ne materia lamentationis et tragedie post tantas victorias in presenti narratione deficiat."
[33] *Ibid.*, table of contents for 4.6 (fol. 137v): "Hic orator veteranus et nomine indignus [i.e., ipse Philippus] de declamacione amara in tragediam lacrimabilem et amarissimam texendo et lacrimas provocando recitat mortem sanctissimam beati patriarche legati apostolici, qui pro dolore tante vilitatis reliquende Alexandriam, miraculis coruscantibus feliciter diem clausit extremum." At the beginning of the chapter itself, he speaks of it as "another tragedic declamation": "Nunc vero ad aliam declamationem tragedicam non sine lacrimis refricando veniamus" (fol. 196).
[34] *Ibid.*, 4.6 (fol. 196).
[35] Machaut, *Prise*, line 8759.

he called his account of Peter a *hystoria lugubris et lacrimabilis*,[36] in which "he recites declamatorily the tearful and cruel death of so great a king" ("recitat declamatorie lacrimabilem et crudelem mortem tanti regis"), concluding with an account of the vengeance of God against the perpetrators.[37] By this just vengeance, all of the guilty parties ended their cursed days with a bad death and in external misery, except for the fratricidal brother who usurped the throne of Cyprus, with no Christian prince raising an objection. There he awaits, as the common proverb has it, with Cain, the vengeance of God on body and soul, unless he should do condign penance for so great a crime. Mézières believes that there also survives, along with this fratricide, a certain baron, Remundus Babin by name, now about a hundred years old, in whose house the betrayal was fabricated.[38]

He concludes his account by saying that the above suffices for "the second tragedic declamation," for the exordium of the new militia of Christ's Passion that was not brought to pass, and for the *flores gestorum*, or outstanding deeds, of King Peter.[39] His use of *exordium* here and earlier would seem to indicate that he has subsumed it, like *declamatio* and *tragedia*, under the umbrella of lamentation. He admits that even though this *narratio* of the renowned king and his deeds, especially at Alexandria, will please some readers, it is not directly pertinent to the matter of this treatise, namely, the tragedic and declamatory petition. But nevertheless the treatise in substance aims at nothing other than an increase in devotion towards the Passion; the king's victories against the enemies of the faith are inspiring, and his betrayal should serve as a lesson in caution to future warriors in the cause. These matters for lamentation from this duplicate tragedic declamation are therefore not irrelevant to the principal objective ("Et hec de duplici declamatione tragedica non utique ab re lamentanda").[40]

Mézières's tragic account of Peter should be compared with Chaucer's brief *Tragedy of Peter, King of Cyprus*:

> O worthy Petro, kyng of Cipre, also
> That Alisandre wan by heigh maistrie,
> Ful many an hethen wroghtestow ful wo,
> Of which thyne owene liges hadde envie.
> And for no thyng but for thy chivalrie
> They in thy bed han slayn thee by the morwe.
> Thus kan Fortune hir wheel governe and gye,
> And out of joye brynge men to sorwe.[41]

---

[36] Mézières, *Oracio*, Prologue (fol. 131v). [37] *Ibid.*, table of contents (fol. 137v).
[38] *Ibid.*, 4.6 (fols. 196v–197). For Raymond Babin, see Jorga, *Philippe de Mézières*, pp. 103, 389.
[39] Mézières, *Oracio*, 4.6 (fol. 197). [40] *Ibid.* (fol. 197r–v).
[41] Geoffrey Chaucer, *Monk's Tale* 2391–98, *The Riverside Chaucer*, p. 247.

The outline of the story in Chaucer's rendition is basically the same as Mézières's, and so is the accent on lamentation. But in Mézières's case the sorrow is more personal, and this is a point of great importance in his understanding of tragedy.

Earlier on, when telling of the shameful retreat from Alexandria, Mézières drew on the words of St. Ambrose, who wrote tragedic matter about a virgin martyr of Antioch,[42] to characterize Peter Thomas's "declamatory and tragedic epistle" against those responsible for it, written during the tempestuous journey back to Cyprus, in which he anathematized them and foretold God's vengeance upon them.[43]

At one point, Mézières's intellectual voice says that his tragedy is to be humbly "sung" before the crucified Christ,[44] which may indicate that the term has a poetic connection for him, as may his remark that he summarizes his material in a tragedic *cantilena*:

I abbreviate the favorable beginnings and the beginnings of the wondrous sorrows of God that He worked in our days – resulting in the end, alas, in great detriment for our faith – in a lamentable and truly tragedic song which constantly renews my old age.[45]

Here he refers to a lyric form telling a narrative with both good and bad beginnings and a bad end. But there is no bad end and no deteriorating movement envisaged for the *Oracio tragedica* as a whole. In part 1, after various preliminaries about the nature of his petition, he recounts the history of Christ's Passion, taking note also, as we have seen, of the joy of the Resurrection, then formulating his petition in various ways, invoking the Holy Spirit as a sweet conclusion of his tragedy, and invoking also the aid of the Blessed Virgin Mary. His tired fingers imposed an end on his work at this point, he says at the beginning of part 2, but the heavenly or intellectual voice rebukes him for presuming to present such a great petition to God without first undergoing worthy labor, and it instructs him in the proper attitudes, and also defends him against invidious complaints of prolixity in his prayer, and then, through many chapters, discusses the

[42] Mézières, *Oracio* 4.4 (fol. 193v): "Utar etenim verbis beati Ambrosii quamdam materiam tragedicam virginem antiocenam gloriosam martirem tangentem describentis."
[43] *Ibid.*, 4.5 (fol. 195): "In qua quidem fortuna buliente, beatus patriarcha, tactus corde dolore intrinsecus, quamdam epistolam declamatoriam et tragedicam contra milites et falsos capitaneos qui falsum [et] mal[i]gnum consilium regi dederant, ipsos anathematisando ac de vindicta Dei in ipsos prophetisando, manu propria, lacrimando, cum difficultate propter commotionem fluctuum, scripsit."
[44] *Ibid.*, 2.9 (fol. 155v): "Si vero hanc tragediam coram crucifixo humiliter et fiducialiter, non cursorie, decantaveris."
[45] *Ibid.*, 4.1 (fols. 190v–191): "Abreviando namque inicia pulcra iniciaque dolorum et mirabilium Dei que operatus est in diebus nostris, heu heu in fine versa in confusionem fidei, in cantilenam lamentabilem et vere tragedicam que in dolore intimo renovare consuevit senectutem meam."

great treasure trove of the Passion in terms of gold and silver and various precious stones, and through other comparisons and considerations.[46]

In part 3, the unnamed old veteran who is making this prayer (which, as we have seen, is how Mézières refers to himself) at first rejoices and glorifies God's works, admiring the voice's teaching on the treasure of the Passion, and feeling refreshed and consoled. But he goes on to accuse himself of torpor, and in the third chapter "he weaves a prolix tearful and tragedic declamation, speaking to God of his own ingratitude."[47] Eventually, a spiritual apothecary teaches him to make a medicine out of the elements of the Passion. Then comes part 4: after his account of King Peter, he goes on to tell of his retirement to a life of contemplation, in which, however, he is constantly tempted to try to raise another army. Mézières concludes his account of the tangential "incident" of part 4 by having the voice tell him that many good and great enterprises in this world end in the bitterness of tears, and that he should now dismiss the "incidents" and return to obtaining from God the conclusion of the present tragedic oration.[48] In part 5, he prays to become suitable to obtain his petition, and inserts a dialogue between himself and God as physician, following the lead of William of Paris (that is, William of Auvergne). He concludes by saying that his sufficiently prolix presentation should suffice for the obtaining of tears, "so that, my soul, enticed by this multifariously ventilated tragedy to compunction and tears, in my often repeated prayer, you may be moved more devoutly through grace, so that sweet Jesus, who makes the mournful happy, as is clear in the Gospel, may in His clemency deign to prepare for us this table of tears and finally, in affirming my declamatory little petition, mercifully grant it".[49] He intended to write a sixth part, but never finished it, leaving only an outline in the table of contents. He wished to treat of the virtue of charity as it concerned the Passion, and to give examples and parables illustrating the contents of its treasury, so that at last his petition could be seen to be granted and his languishing soul transformed. He notes that it is not the work of a day or a year, but that it often happens, at the divine lover's discretion, in a moment or in the blink of an eye.[50]

---

[46] *Ibid.*, 2.1–35 (fols. 150v–183).

[47] *Ibid.*, table of contents for 3.3 (fol. 136v): "Hic orator texit prolixam declamacionem et tragedicam, Deo loquendo de ingratitudine sua."

[48] *Ibid.*, table of contents for 3.9 (fol. 138).

[49] *Ibid.*, 5.11 (fol. 209 bis): "ut, videlicet, anima mea, alecta hac tragedia multipharie ventillata ad compunctionem et lacrimas in oratione mea sepe replicata, devocius per gratiam movearis, ut, videlicet, dulcis Jhesus, qui lugentes beatificat, ut patet in evangelio, hanc mensam lacrimarum clementer nobis preparare dignetur et finaliter peticiunculam meam declamatoriam affirmando misericorditer concedat."

[50] *Ibid.*, table of contents for part 6 (fol. 138v).

We have in Mézières's conclusion to part 5 and his outline of part 6 final assurances that the whole purpose and import of his tragedy is not sorrow for its own sake, not a helpless mourning over what cannot be restored or recovered, but rather sorrow as a means to ultimate happiness.

In a long work written around the same time as the *Oracio tragedica*, namely, *Le songe du vieil pelerin*, which is peopled with various personifications and figurative usages, he says in an explanatory key that the term "tragedy" is used figuratively for a piteous lamentation or declamation.[51] This would indicate that its proper, as opposed to figurative, meaning is something else. In the work itself, "tragedy" seems to function simply as a synonym for a "complaint." We hear of Amoureuse concluding her piteous tragedy near the end of the second book, and are told that Ardant Desir and her sister Bonne Esperance begin the third book with a piteous tragedy and very bitter lamentation.[52] He does not refer to tragedy in his *Epistre au roi Richart*, which he wrote in 1395 with the intention of fostering peace between England and France and encouraging a new crusade.[53] However, in his *Epistre lamentable et consolatoire*, his last known work, written in 1397 and addressed to the duke of Burgundy, he seems at one point to call the Christian defeat at Nicopolis in 1396 at the hands of the Turks a "piteuse tragedie" – which would be a rare metaphorical usage. But it may be that he is rather calling his own account of the disaster a tragedy.[54] He characterizes a parable dealing with the same event as "une piteuse tragedie remplie de grant lamentation."[55]

The terms "tragedy" and "tragedic" may have been new to him in 1389.

---

[51] Mézières, *Le songe du vieil pelerin*, 1:114: "Tragedie est prinse en figure pour une piteuse lamentacion ou declamation." This passage is noted by Renate Haas, "Chaucer's *Monk's Tale*: An Ingenious Criticism of Early Humanist Conceptions of Tragedy," p. 51; she notes that a similar explanation is given in his *Livre de la vertu du sacrament de mariage et du reconfort des dames mariées*, fol. 136. This work is preserved only in the 189 folios of Paris Bibliothèque Nationale MS fr. 1175; Mézières's French prose rendition of Petrarch's Griselda story makes up chapters 4–7 of book 3, and is on fols. 165v–175v. See Elie Golenistcheff-Koutouzoff, *L'histoire de Griseldis en France au XIVᵉ et au XVᵉ siècle*, p. 34 (the Griselda story is edited on pp. 151–82). On Mézières's dramatization and versification of the story, *Estoire de Griseldis*, see Laura Hibbard Loomis, "Secular Dramatics in the Royal Palace, Paris, 1378, 1389, and Chaucer's 'Tregetoures,'" pp. 252–53, and cf. pp. 247–48.

[52] Mézières, *Songe* 2.171 (1:629): "Quant l'Amoreuse ot finee sa piteuse tragedie"; 3.178 (2:115): "Et premierement par le premier chappitre d'une piteuse tragedie et lamentacion tresamere que fait Ardant Desir et sa suer Bonne Esperance en parlant a la royne de la determinacion faicte du doleureux departement de la royne et des dames de la nef francoise."

[53] Mézières, *Epistre au roi Richart*.

[54] Mézières, *Epistre lamentable et consolatoire sur le fait de la desconfiture lacrimable du noble et vaillant roy de Honguerie par les Turcs devant la ville de Nicopoli en l'empire de Boulguerie*, 16:458; he is addressing the king of France: "Rafreschi et renouvelle en Dieu la douleur en ton cuer de la piteuse tragedie de la vergoingne et de la perte cy-dessus repetee" ("Refresh and renew in God the sorrow in your heart from the piteous tragedy of the shame and of the loss hereabove repeated").

[55] *Ibid.*, p. 516.

He did not employ them when he covered similar material earlier, at least in the *Vita Petri Thome*, written in 1366,[56] and the words do not appear in his most frequently cited source in the *Oracio*, namely, the *Rhetorica divina* of William of Auvergne.[57] Mézières would seem to be in the same tradition as the author of the *Tragedia super captione regis Francie Johannis*, which is only known through the report of Victor Le Clerc, who says it is a *complainte* in prose over the disaster of Poitiers and the capture of the French king in 1356.[58]

Finally, let me note the understanding of tragedy shown by Christine de Pisan in her *Livre du corps de policie* (*c.* 1405), drawing on Valerius Maximus. She cites the response made by "Eripides," a great poet, on being asked to delete a sentiment from a tragedy that he had made. She interrupts to give Valerius's alleged explanation of tragedy as a kind of composition that reproves things badly done in government and community or by princes. The poet answered that he did not create his works in order to blame anyone or to be blamed, but to inspire good living.[59] Since Valerius does not in fact define tragedy when telling this story, nor does he make Euripides so humble,[60] Christine was doubtless drawing on the French paraphrase of Simon de Hesdin and Nicholas de Gonesse, in which Valerius's statements are "at times scarcely distinguishable from the translators' commentary."[61] This concept of tragedy coincides with Isidore's designated subject matter of tragedy (the bad deeds of kings), but not his purpose. For rather than stressing the mournfulness of such deeds, as in Isidore's explanation, the tragic poet of Christine's definition was to

[56] See Jorga, *Philippe de Mézières*, p. vii; published by the Bollandist Godefried Henschen, *Acta sanctorum*, vol. 3 of January, under 29 January (pp. 611–38 of the nineteenth-century reprint).

[57] William of Auvergne, *Rhetorica divina, sive Ars oratoria eloquentie divine*, in *Opera omnia*, 1:336–406. The form *tragedicus* does occur in an insular document of 1252, according to R. E. Latham, *Revised Medieval Word-List from British and Irish Sources*, p. 489.

[58] Victor Le Clerc, *Histoire littéraire de la France*, 24:436.

[59] Christine de Pisan, *Le livre du corps de policie*, chap. 11, pp. 33–34: "Je leur puis dire sans arrogance quele chose respondit Eripides, qui fut ung grant poete, a ceulx d'Athenes qui lui prierent qu'il rostast [or: ostast] une sentence de une tragedie qu'il avoit faicte. Tragedie, dit Valere, est une maniere de dictier qui represent choses mal faictes en ordre de policie et de communité, ou de princes. Il dit qu'il ne faisoit pas ses dittiés pour estre reprins ne pour reprendre, mais a fin qu'il introduisit a bien vivre." For an English translation, contained in a MS of about the third quarter of the fifteenth century, see the edition of Diane Bornstein, *The Middle English Translation of Christine de Pisan's Livre du corps de policie*, p. 64. The definition is rendered thus: "Tragedie, Valere seithe, it is a maner of a ditee that blameth thyngis that be evyll done in order of policie of the comonte or of prynces."

[60] Valerius Maximus, *Memorabilia* 3.7, external example 1: "Ne Euripides quidem Athenis arrogans uisus est, cum, postulante populo ut ex tragoedia quandam sententiam tolleret, progressus in scaenam, dixit se ut eum doceret, non ut ab eo disceret, fabulas componere solere" ("Not even Euripides was considered arrogant by the Athenians when, on being asked by the people to remove a certain sentiment from a tragedy, he went onto the stage and declared that he was accustomed to compose his plays for their instruction, not to be instructed by them").

[61] Robert H. Lucas, "Mediaeval French Translations of the Latin Classics to 1500," pp. 225, 247–48.

point out their wickedness, or, in Euripides's more positive point of view, to urge persons to avoid doing similar evil and to do the right thing. (We note that she does not go so far as to conclude that she herself is writing tragedy.) Christine used a version of the vulgate French Boethius,[62] and perhaps its rendition of *tragicus* as a "satirian poet," if she was aware of it, reinforced her idea of tragedy as a critique of morals.

We can conclude that there was, among the French authors, some awareness of tragedy either as an old or as a current genre, but there was little motivation to revive it or contribute to it. Even Mézières, though seemingly conscious of adopting a new word, appears to be indulging in a figure of speech rather than writing in a separate genre. That is, he is noting some likeness between the complaint, in its various familiar forms, and tragedy, which he may have understood to be a classical form of literature or even drama. The same may also be true of Deschamps and the author of the fugitive tragedy on the capture of King John, and true as well of Christine de Pisan – though in her case tragedy would be a synonym for satire rather than complaint. But in Italy, we find several examples of authors who deliberately take a neoclassicist attitude towards tragedy.

ITALIAN LATINISTS

The latter-day imitation of Mussato's imitation of Seneca was apparently the result of Coluccio Salutati's championing of both Seneca and Mussato.[63] The earliest attempt at continuing Mussato's enterprise was made by a scholarly soldier named Giovanni Manzini della Motta, who started a tragedy on the capture of Verona and the fall of Antonio della Scala in 1387; he himself was in the army of the besieger, Giangaleazzo Visconti. This choice of subject jibes more with Mussato's example than with Seneca's, except, of course, for the *Octavia*, which was accepted as Seneca's. In a letter written to a friend in 1388,[64] Manzini says that he began the tragedy while on the campaign, but still had not finished it. He included with the letter a Chorus from the completed portion of the play, for the friend's inspection and comment.[65]

The Chorus is in fact all that survives of the text of the tragedy, and even

---

[62] Cropp, "Boèce et Christine de Pizan" (see chap. 5 above pp. 160–61).
[63] Cloetta, *Anfänge*, pp. 82, 90.
[64] There is a collection of thirty-three of his letters contained in a MS of the fourteenth century, some of which were edited by Pietro Lazeri, *Miscellanea ex manuscriptis libris Bibliothecae Collegii Romani Societatis Jesu*; cited by Cloetta, *Anfänge*, p. 77 n. 2.
[65] Lazeri, *Miscellanea*, p. 224 (Cloetta, *Anfänge*, p. 79 n. 2).

that has not been published in full.[66] It is in a Boethian rather than a Senecan meter, and bids us observe the various movements of Fortune ("Fortune varios cernite motus"). It comes at the point, Manzini tells his correspondent, when Verona was captured and Vicenza surrendered on its own, and the tyrant Scaliger fled to Venice, and it expresses the joy of the people.[67] Manzini left the army at this point, and we can only conjecture whether he followed up della Scala's misfortunes further in tragic verse, or came to any clear notion of the final form of his tragedy and of the requirements and attributes of tragedy in general. It seems from what he did write, however, that joy was to be more prominent at the end of his tragedy than sorrow, joy, that is, at the overthrow of a tyrant, with no tears lost for how and when the tyrant went wrong. In this, as with his original choice of subject matter, he was a worthy. student of Mussato.

Shortly after Manzini embarked on his unfinished venture, an associate of his named Antonio Loschi wrote a complete new Senecan tragedy, *Achilles*, in 1390 or a bit earlier.[68] Loschi was born in the 1360s and died only in 1441. He was an official in the service of Antonio della Scala in Verona until its capture in 1387, and then he went to Florence, where Salutati befriended him. By 1388 or so, he was with Manzini in Pavia.[69] Unlike Mussato and Manzini, and like the genuine Seneca, Loschi went to a traditional Greek topic for his tragedy and composed the sort of work that Ovid spoke of in his *Tristia*, dealing with "Achilles turned tender for love."[70]

The *Achilles* is divided into five acts, each consisting of a scene of dialogue and a Chorus. In the first act, Paris goes against his better judgment, of wanting to end the war by a marriage alliance, and agrees to trick Achilles into an ambush by using his sister Polyxena as bait. The second act introduces Achilles himself, who muses that Cupid is a stronger god than Jupiter, for he has brought an end to the war. As Paris's emissary leads him off, he reflects on how favorable Fortune has been to him:

[66] Cloetta, *Anfänge*, p. 80, gives all that Lazeri printed, namely, eleven lines.
[67] *Ibid.*, pp. 79–80 n. 3: "Capta civitate Verone et dedita sponte Vicentia, Scaligero tyranno ad Illyricos sinus Venetamque urbem profuge profecto, gaudio populus pariter admirando, ut subinterea fluctuabat, talium verborum congratulans fusione."
[68] Antonio Loschi, *Achilles*. The edition by Giovanni da Schio has been reprinted along with Padrin's edition of Mussato's *Ecerinis*, with facing English translations by Joseph R. Berrigan. For analyses of the play, see Cloetta, *Anfänge*, pp. 91–147; Berrigan, "Early Neo-Latin Tragedy," pp. 89–92; Paratore, "L'influsso," pp. 36–40; Guido Paduano, "La prototragedia e le categorie del discorso drammatico."
[69] Cloetta, *Anfänge*, pp. 83–84, 93–95.
[70] As Cloetta, *Anfänge*, p. 108, points out, Loschi drew specifically on chapters 34 and 35 of Dares Phrygius's account.

O quam libens Fortuna seu Celi favor
Parem superno vexit Eacidem Jovi!   (360–61)

(Oh, how willingly Fortune or the favor of Heaven
elevated Achilles to be the equal of supernal Jupiter!)

Achilles is not indulging in Luciferian or Adamic ambition here; there is no prideful rebellion or ungrateful disobedience in his thoughts, and he nowhere admits to wrongdoing on any front. He does not even seem to suggest that he somehow has earned or deserved such good treatment from the divine powers. He simply believes that it is coming to him and he gladly accepts it.

In Act 3, Hecuba reveals Achilles's assassination to Priam who, in the midst of incoherent but foreboding ravings by Cassandra, orders a celebration. Acts 4 and 5 show the Greek reactions to the ambush. In Act 4, a messenger gives the details to a Chorus of Greeks: he takes a cosmic view, indicating that Achilles was mistaken to think that he had ascended above the power of the stars; he was under their ultimate control, and he willingly – because unknowingly – went to meet his destiny. He died without self-pity or lamentation, but only with defiance and denunciation of Trojan treachery. The Greek Chorus reflects on the inevitable passing of joy and prosperity. In Act 5, Menelaus assures Agamemnon that the gods will avenge the crime. They consult Calchas, and he tells them that Achilles's son Pyrrhus will conquer Troy. The final Chorus of Greeks, however, is gloomy and fatalistic.

From the viewpoint of the titular protagonist, or nonprotagonist,[71] this drama follows a movement from prosperity to adversity better than any tragedy of Seneca's. To a certain extent, there is the opposite movement for the antagonists, namely, Hecuba and the other Trojans, but there are sufficiently clear reminders of Troy's coming destruction. The end product must be considered tragic by almost any definition.

The next Latin tragedy to be composed in Italy, *Progne*, was written forty years later by the eighteen-year-old Gregorio Correr, or Corraro, in 1428–29.[72] Like Loschi, he modeled his work on Seneca and chose a classical subject, this time the story of Tereus, king of Thrace, his wife

[71] Paduano, "Prototragedia," p. 107, judges that *Achilles* lacks a protagonist, since Achilles makes only one appearance on the stage. But, of course, no one really appeared on the stage in this closet-drama, which is in fact entirely centered upon Achilles.

[72] Gregorio Correr, *Progne*, ed Laura Casarsa. Cloetta, *Anfänge*, pp. 147–221, gives an exhaustive analysis. See also P. Bahlmann, *Die Erneuerer des antiken Dramas und ihre ersten dramatischen Versuche, 1314–1478* pp. 30–32; Berrigan, "Latin Tragedy of the Quattrocento"; Berrigan, "Gregorii Corrarii Veneti *Liber satyrarum*"; Paratore, "L'influsso," pp. 40–44; Casarsa, "La *Progne* di Gregorio Correr"; Paolo Preti, "Correr, Gregorio."

Procne, their son Itys, and Procne's sister Philomena, from Ovid's *Metamorphoses*.[73] He says at the beginning that he is imitating Seneca's *Thyestes* in having a shade from the underworld introduce the action: Tantalus sets the scene in Seneca's play, and Diomedes of Thrace in his. But he does not follow Seneca in naming his play after the recipient of the act of revenge, Thyestes; if he had done so, he would have called it *Tereus*. Rather, he follows Seneca's *Medea* in designating the worker of revenge as his protagonist.

The story of Procne is perhaps the most revolting in Ovid's whole unsavory collection of monstrous tales, and Correr takes full advantage of its horror. It begins with the appearance of Diomedes, a predecessor of Tereus as king of Thrace, who used to feed his horses on human flesh. He has been forced to come out of hell, where he suffers punishment for his crimes, which he freely confesses, to tell of even more horrendous crimes that are about to happen. A Chorus then speaks a welcoming ode for Tereus's return. Act 2 begins with Tereus admitting his guilt in a soliloquy, and then telling Progne a long story about Philomena and her attendants having been lost at sea. The Chorus speaks an ode about the dangers of sea voyages. In the long third act, Correr replaces Ovid's device, of having Philomena weave her story into a cloth that is taken to Procne by an old woman, with an escaped survivor, old Pistus, who arrives and informs Progne and her nurse of what really happened: Tereus raped Philomena, cut her tongue out, and killed all of her attendants, except for Pistus. Progne begins to plot revenge, but first goes to rescue her sister. We are informed in the opening argument that all this happened at the time of the triennial orgy of Bacchus, and Progne takes the Bacchantes to where Philomena is being held and has them kill the guards. In the play itself, a Chorus of Bacchantes utters a long speech calling for a sacrifice to Bacchus, followed by Progne's command to execute the guards. Thereupon she leads her sister forth, and then works out the details of her revenge over the protests of the nurse – who, however, finally agrees to go along with the plan. After an intervening Chorus, musing on rather irrelevant themes, the fourth act introduces a messenger who tells the Chorus how he saw Progne kill her son Itys and, with Philomena's help, cut him up and prepare a meal of him for Tereus. The Chorus responds briefly that Progne has surpassed Medea in cruelty.

The fifth act begins with Tereus again soliloquizing. Everything is in a favorable condition, and he cannot understand why he has a sense of malaise:

[73] Ovid, *Metamorphoses* 6.424–674.

Festum diem celebrare quid vetat mihi,
Animumque turbat mobilem incerto metu?
Quid heret animus? Prospero regnum in statu est.
Ego quid tremiscam nescio, timeo tamen.   (956-59)

(What prevents me from celebrating this festive day
and disturbs my restless mind with vague fear?
Why is my mind perplexed? The kingdom is prosperous.
Why I tremble I know not, but I fear nevertheless.)

He goes on to recall strange omens, but he is aware of no reason for them. We are to assume, apparently, that he is not disturbed by any guilt over what he has done to Philomena. Progne then utters an aside of her own, noting that Tereus thinks himself immune to any evil. She mentally urges him to satisfy his hunger on consecrated food and drive away thirst with the blood of his son. We are to assume that he proceeds to eat the prepared remains of Itys. Tereus then tells Progne that only the sight of his son can restore his usual tranquillity, she reveals to him what has happened, and has Philomena bring in his son's head. Tereus is horrified. He tells his murdered son that he himself deserved this death, and he cries out against Progne's ghastly crime. Progne, however, shows no remorse. She has achieved her greatest wish: Tereus's sorrow. The play ends with the following dialogue:

Pro.   Perjure Tereu, virgines stupro opprimis.
Ter.   Tu, seva, natum.
Pro.   Fateor, et juvat tuum.
Ter.   Quid meruit infans?
Pro.   Gnatus emeruit mori
         Tuapte culpa.
Ter.   Vindices testor deos.
Pro.   Pocius pudoris numen intacti voca.
Ter.   Te te sequentur Furie.
Pro.   Itys solus patrem.

                                                    (1055-60)

(*Progne*:   Perjured Tereus, you oppress virgins with defilement.
Tereus: You, savage woman, your own son.
Progne: I admit it, and it delights me that he is yours.
Tereus: What did the child deserve?
Progne: Your son deserved to die because of your own guilt.
Tereus: I call on the gods to avenge it.
Progne: Rather, invoke the god of undefiled decency.
Tereus: Furies will pursue you!
Progne: Itys alone will go with his father!)

In the argument, Correr notes the poetical tradition that Progne was turned into a swallow, Philomena into the bird of her own name (that is, the nightingale), and Tereus into a hoopoe, but he does not incorporate any such transformation into his play, nor does he mention in the argument or dramatize in the play Ovid's detail that Tereus drew his sword and attempted to kill the two sisters (it was at this point that the metamorphoses took place).

When Chaucer selected Philomena to join Medea, Cleopatra, and other "martyrs of love" for treatment in his *Legend of Good Women*, he ended the action with the doleful reunion of the two sisters at the point where Philomena is rescued, giving no hint of any thought of revenge. He simply leaves them to dwell in sorrow. The only slip from decorousness noted on the part of either woman is the mention that Progne, on reading the woven message that her sister had sent her, could not speak "for sorwe and ek for rage."[74]

According to Ovid, Tereus raped Philomena again, and repeatedly, immediately after tearing her tongue out (lines 561–62). Chaucer suggests instead that he often returned to her place of imprisonment to satisfy his lust: he "kepte hire to his usage and his store" (2337). Correr, in contrast, eliminates all subsequent sexual crimes from his account of Tereus, and increases rather the bloodiness of Progne, by introducing her killing of the guards. At the end of the story, Ovid, though he first speaks of Procne's "crudelia gaudia" (653), concentrates on Philomena's joy as she hurls the head of Itys into Tereus's face. Correr, of course, cannot provide for a tongueless character in his play, and he accordingly keeps Progne's ferocious and unrepentant delight to the fore, and gives her the last word.

His tragedy well illustrates the sort of crime that Huguccio spoke of as the subject of tragedy, and it also fits Isidore's second characterization of tragedy, as dealing with the old crimes of wicked kings. Correr learned his Seneca well. It can hardly fit Huguccio's characterization of beginning in joy, given the introductory monologue by Diomedes. It is followed by real joy on the part of the Chorus, it is true, and this in turn is followed by Tereus's internal monologue of hope that he will be able to conceal his crime; but this is not the sort of joy that Huguccio intended when contrasting the sequence of events in tragedy to those of comedy.

Correr's play was staged for Queen Elizabeth at Oxford in 1566,[75] and

---

[74] Chaucer, *Legend of Good Women* 2374. See Kelly, *Love and Marriage in the Age of Chaucer*, pp. 102–03.

[75] Frederick S. Boas, *University Drama in the Tudor Age*, pp. 104–05. *Progne* was printed at Venice in 1558, and the Oxford production seems to have been adapted to some extent by one of the canons of Christ Church, James Calfhill. See the abstract of a paper by Leicester Bradner, "From Petrarch to Shakespeare," p. 33: "One may compare Corrado's [sic] finely wrought, if imitative, tragedy of *Progne*, which the dons of Christ Church had the good taste to produce for Queen Elizabeth's visit in 1566, with the incredibly primitive and vulgarized tragedy of *Orestes* written in England during the same decade."

therefore he can be said to have played a role in encouraging later English tragedians to go to Ovid for their Senecan plays; but they did not follow him in Senecanizing Ovid by reducing the qualms of conscience in his characters. As G. K. Hunter says, speaking of Thomas Kyd and Shakespeare, "Tenderness in the midst of horror is a characteristic of both *Spanish Tragedy* and *Titus*; it is a characteristic of Ovid; it is not a characteristic of Seneca."[76]

Another Senecan drama was written by Leonardo Dati in 1441 or 1442, namely, *Hiensal, Tragedy* (or, *The Tragedy of Hiensal*).[77] Dati was a native of Florence and an official of the curia of Eugenius IV, which at that period was centered in Florence. His play takes its subject not from Greek mythology but from Roman history, namely, Sallust's *Jugurthine War*. It was designed for a proposed literary competition organized by Leon Battista Alberti, which was to take *invidia*, that is, envy or jealousy, as its theme.[78] The titular character, Hiensal, is one of the two sons of Micipsa, king of Numidia. When Micipsa dies, he leaves the realm not only to Hiensal and his brother Adherbal, but also, much to Hiensal's resentment, to their bastard cousin Jugurtha. Hiensal is jealous of his own rights, and, it is implied (though he himself never admits it), envious of Jugurtha's military successes. He insults him, and Jugurtha takes vengeance by having him assassinated.

This slender plot is fleshed out by some allegorical scenes. In the first act, two personifications, Ambition and Modesty, discuss Envy, and then two real persons, Asper and Polimites, do the same, and so does the Chorus. In Act 2, Polimites appears with the aggrieved Hiensal, and tries in vain to assuage his passion against Jugurtha. Then Polimites, alone with the Chorus, says that Hiensal's fates are hurling him to an end that he willingly accepts: "Quo eum volentem fata precipitant sua" (221), a line reminiscent of what the messenger says of Achilles, in a much different context, in Loschi's play.[79] He goes on to say, "No one will ever be happy if he does not wish it" ("Hominum nemo felix umquam erit / Invitus," 225–26). This

[76] Hunter, "Seneca and the Elizabethans," pp. 165–66. In referring to *Titus Andronicus*, he agrees with Howard Baker in saying that "only a determination to find Seneca in every woodpile could have suppressed the Philomela story in order to reveal *Thyestes* as the source (p. 165).

[77] Leonardo Dati, *Hiensal*, ed. Berrigan. In the preface to Cardinal Prospero Colonna, the name of the protagonist is given in apposition to *tragedia*: "in Hiensalem, tragediam, prefatio" (p. 94); but in one version of Dati's letter to the reader, Hiensal is in the genitive: "Quo facilius meam hanc Hiensalis tragediam habeas" (p. 92).

[78] *Ibid.*, pp. 84–87; see also Berrigan, "Latin Tragedy," pp. 7–9; Francesco Flamini, "Leonardo di Piero Dati, poeta latino del secolo XV," 16: 34–48, and 22: 415–17; R. Ristori, "Dati, Leonardo." Dati was born in 1408 and eventually became bishop of Massa and served as secretary to the popes from Callixtus III to Sixtus IV. He died in 1475.

[79] Loschi, *Achilles* 644: "In fata properat quilibet libens sua" ("Each person hastens willingly to his own fates").

sums up the truculent protagonist very well. As the Chorus says, "Every envious man is miserable" ("Miser est quilibet invidus," 240).

The third act opens with an obscure discussion between Hiensal and his more moderate brother, in which it is difficult to tell whether the planned insults to Jugurtha have already been executed or soon will be. Dati's introductory remarks to the reader are somewhat clearer on the nature of the insults, which involve Hiensal's failing to give Jugurtha a seat of honor and his suggesting that Micipsa was not in his right mind when he made him heir. The point of the act, Dati says, is to show how the envious behave towards those whom they resent; and the fourth act shows how the latter respond. Accordingly, in Act 4, Jugurtha monologues his resentment, and justifies himself in retaliating. Act 5 introduces two new personifications, Discord and Perfidy, to report that Jugurtha's servants broke into Hiensal's house by night and slaughtered him and all his retinue. In a final scene, Hiensal's mother Phenissa and other matrons are about to celebrate the feast of Bacchus when a messenger comes to say that Hiensal's house has been invaded, but that Hiensal has escaped. A second messenger quickly follows, with the report that Jugurtha has slain Hiensal. Phenissa faints, and the matrons turn the palace into a house of mourning, while noting the evil that Envy can produce.

We cannot safely distill any general notion of tragedy from this work, except that tragedy focuses on disasters. Dati's introductory material does not explain the genre, but only outlines the events and notes how envy functions in each of the five acts.

The final work of this genre to be considered here is the *De captivitate ducis Jacobi tragoedia*, composed by Laudivio Zacchia da Vezzano around 1465.[80] It is a Senecan play in five acts that deals not with classical stories or events, but with very recent history, like Manzini's projected tragedy. It is dedicated to Borso d'Este, duke of Ferrara, and treats of Borso's close friend, the condottiere Jacopo Piccinino. However, the work is given a classical setting, and it is filled with references to the Roman gods.

In the first act, Borso himself appears as King Borsius, who praises the bravery of Jacobus, through whom the current peace has been achieved. A priest of Apollo then tells of wonders predicting Jacobus's death, and a Chorus worries over his fate. In Act 2, an augur shares the priest's fears, the Chorus praises Jacobus, and a messenger announces Jacobus's marriage to

[80] Laudivio Zacchia da Vezzano, *De captivitate ducis Jacobi tragoedia*, ed. Carlo Braggio; see Bahlmann, *Die Erneuerer des antiken Dramas*, pp. 51–52; Wilhelm Creizenach, *Geschichte des neueren Dramas*, 1:527–29; 2:345 n. 1. For the surname Zacchia, see Antonio Stäuble, "L'idea della tragedia nell'Umanesimo," pp. 55 and 65, citing F. Babinger, "Laudivius Zacchia, Erdichter der *Epistolae magni Turci*." Earlier scholars assigned him to the de' Nobili family (see *De captivitate*, ed. Braggio, p. 58 n. 2).

Drusiana (the natural daughter of Francesco Sforza of Milan). In Act 3, set in Naples, a messenger from Jacobus tells King Ferantus (Ferdinand or Ferrante I of Naples) of his master's imminent arrival, and the Chorus sings the praises of Drusiana. Act 4 continues with Ferantus, who is convinced by an advisor that Jacobus is a dangerous enemy who should be put to death. Then Jacobus, now in prison, appears as a speaker for the first time, awaiting his fate with resignation. The advisor announces to him the king's decision and carries out the execution, but then expresses admiration for the constant manner with which Jacobus accepted his death. Finally, the Chorus condoles with Drusiana, not, surprisingly, over her husband's death, but over his captivity. Correspondingly, in the final act, a messenger informs Borsius that Jacobus has been arrested but not yet condemned to death. Borsius, however, seems to assume that he is dead; he contemplates revenge and sets about marshalling his forces. The piece ends with the Chorus lamenting the instability of Fortune.

Piccinino was taken into custody on 24 June 1465, and put to death within a month, on 12 July. Perhaps Zacchia first composed his tragedy when news of the imprisonment reached Ferrara, and then imperfectly modified it on hearing of his death. He portrays his hero as entirely faultless and virtuous, the victim of the perjured king and his unscrupulous henchman. Although it is certain that Sforza, his father-in-law, connived at his death, there is no hint of any such accusation in the tragedy.

All of these Seneca-inspired works are commonly assigned to the Renaissance rather than to the Middle Ages, and the paltriness of the collection is reflected in the words of Joseph Berrigan: "For some mysterious reason men of the Italian Renaissance did not find tragedy congenial."[81] He is speaking of the kind of tragedy that Seneca wrote, but the same holds true of any other definition of tragedy that might have been current. He notes that these fourteenth- and fifteenth-century tragedies were not intended for real performance.[82] We can say that they are medieval, in that sense at least: they seem designed only for recitation, not acting; or if there was any intention of having them acted, it would undoubtedly have been in Isidorian fashion, with a single reciter and multiple mummers. This idea of how comedies and tragedies were performed in the ancient world appears to have prevailed and persisted until the last part of the fifteenth century, when, we are told, the actors in productions of Plautus and Terence began speaking their own lines, and classical theater finally joined the medieval stage in becoming truly

---

[81] Berrigan, "Early Neo-Latin Tragedy," p. 92.
[82] *Ibid.*, and see Cloetta, *Anfänge*, p. 221.

dramatic. But how, when, and where it happened is not documented.[83]

Another work that could be mentioned under the rubric of Italian Latinists is a prose dialogue dealing with the sack of Cesena in 1377. It is called both a tragedy and a comedy by its copyists, though not by its author. It will serve me in the next section as an introduction to my treatment of *Celestina*, called by its author both a comedy and a tragicomedy, as an example of generic misnomers. I shall also treat there Marcellino Verardi's tragicomedy about Ferdinand of Aragon, and Giovanni Armonio's triumphal tragedy of Louis XII's conquest of northern Italy.

THEORY AND PRACTICE IN SPAIN

Throughout the course of this survey we have seen many examples of generic awareness and generic ignorance existing side by side in the same region. One writer will be acquainted with the tragedies of Seneca, while a compatriot will come across the word "tragedy" without having heard anything about its meaning, and others will know scraps of definitions or explanations from various sources. We can find this situation strikingly illustrated in fifteenth-century Spain, not only in talk about tragedy, but also in works that are called tragedies. But before proceeding to Spain, let me give two other examples of generic miscasting, from Italy and the Low Countries, respectively.

The Italian example is the above-mentioned Latin prose dialogue on Cesena, which has been given the title of *De casu Cesene*. It was written, we can be assured, by Lodovico da Fabriano of Perugia, in the same year and month as the disaster, namely, February 1377 (the city fell on 1 February).[84] In one manuscript, dating from the end of the fourteenth or beginning of the fifteenth century, it is called a tragedy and attributed to Coluccio Salutati: *A Certain Tragedy on the Fall of Cesena Composed by Coluccio de' Salutati da Stignano, Chancellor of Florence*.[85] Another copy of the fifteenth century calls it a comedy and attributes it to Petrarch: *A Comedy Composed by*

---

[83] See Stäuble, *La commedia umanistica del Quattrocento*, pp. 188–91.

[84] Francesco Novati, "Un umanista fabrianese del secolo XIV, Giovanni Tinti," appendix 1: "Sull'autore del *De casu Caesenae*," pp. 135–46, citing the colophon of a copy made shortly after 1470, namely (Vatican) MS Chigiano H.IV.3: "Hoc fecit Sr. Ludovichus de Fabriano anno Domini M.CCC.LXX.VII in civitate Perusii, et isto anno et tempore fuit quod supra narratum est; mense autem prout in opere supra concluditur" (p. 141). See the edition by Giancarlo Schizzerotto, *De casu Cesene*.

[85] Novati, "Un umanista," p. 138, citing (Rome) Biblioteca Corsiniana MS 33.E.23: *Tragedia quedam de casu Cesene edita per Colutium de Salutatis de Stignano cancellarium florentinum*. Schizzerotto notes another MS that calls the work a tragedy (*De casu Cesene*, p. 26). See Stäuble, "L'idea," p. 58.

Mr. Francis Petrarch, Laureate, on the Destruction of the City of Cesena.[86]
Of the various tests of comedy listed by Boccaccio when puzzling over the question of why Dante called his poem a comedy,[87] the *Fall of Cesena* pretty much fails them all but one (of course, the same was true of Dante's work!). The one characteristic that *Cesena* almost meets is that of being entirely in dialogue. But the dialogue is in prose, whereas presumably Boccaccio assumed that comic dialogue would be in verse, as in the plays of Plautus and Terence. Modern scholars who have commented on it might also allege that it fulfills the criterion of humble and remiss style, since they note that it falls far below Salutati's style (Petrarch's authorship is out of the question, of course, since he was dead by the time of the event). But Boccaccio further specified that comic language is that of *feminette*, "little women," who, though they would have spoken Latin in classical times, since that was their vernacular, would hardly be speaking even a crude form of it in modern times.

As for the copyists who called the dialogue a tragedy, we may observe, on the one hand, that we have not seen the word applied to anything like it during the course of our long survey. But, on the other hand, we can note that it fits very well some of the prominent characterizations of tragedy that we have seen, notably those of Boethius and Isidore of Seville, when these characterizations are read on their own, without benefit of learned explications. Fortune's question in Boethius, demythologized and reconstructed, yields this definition of tragedy: "a clamorous lamentation over the unexpected destruction of a felicitous realm." Book 8 of Isidore's *Etymologies* can give us this: "a dialogue of sorrowful things concerning a republic or the history of a king." Book 18 might seem less relevant, even if one leaves aside the theatrical mode (one reciter, accompanied by silent actors) and formulates a definition based on tone, form, and subject: "a doleful verse account of the ancient deeds and crimes of wicked kings." The *Fall of Cesena* is not about the remote past, but about the present, it is in prose, not in verse, and it concerns the horrible atrocities not of a king, but of a cardinal – namely, the papal legate Robert of Geneva.[88] Nevertheless, one can easily agree that it accords with the essence or spirit of Isidore's characterization.

---

[86] *De casu Cesene*, ed. G. Gori, "*De eccidio urbis Caesenae anonimi auctoris coaevi comoedia*: L'eccidio di Cesena del 1377, atto recitabili di anonimo scrittore coetaneo"; Gori edits the work from Florence, Biblioteca Laurenziana Plut. 90 inf. 13, on pp. 17–30. The title occurs only in the colophon: *Comedia edita a laureato viro domino F. Petrarca super destructione civitatis Cesene explicit*. See Cloetta, *Komödie*, p. 55 n. 1, who notes that the work appears on fols. 29–32 of the MS, and that earlier, on fols. 22v–25v, the prose romance of *Medea* is given, also attributed to Petrarch, but called *Opus nobilissimum* rather than *comedia*. Cf. Gori, "*De eccedio*," p. 4.

[87] See Kelly, *Tragedy and Comedy*, pp. 45–47.

[88] Robert of Geneva was the future Clement VII: in September 1378 he was elected by the French cardinals as the first pope of the Avignon schism (he ruled until his death in 1394).

De casu Cesene can be analyzed as a one-act play in which the horrible details of the sack of the city are progressively revealed in four scenes.[89] The first scene is a discussion between two characters: John tells Conrad that he has heard a terrible rumor, which, as the dialogue proceeds, turns out to be a report of the capture of the illustrious city of Cesena and the massacre of its inhabitants. In the second scene, the two speakers encounter a resident of Cesena who escaped after witnessing the initial horror. After giving terrifying details, he leaves them to go back for news of what happened to the city after he fled. In a brief third scene, John and Conrad see the departing Cesenan encounter a messenger, and in the final scene the messenger describes the further atrocities that occurred. The piece ends with the Cesenan determined to go and give aid to the survivors, and with John and Conrad bidding him and the messenger farewell. All in all, it is a very effective and moving presentation, which makes its later designation as a comedy seem all the more inappropriate.

The next example, a tale by Reyner de Wael of Brussels, dated 1447, told in Latin distichs, reveals an opposite kind of inappropriateness.[90] The author says that the story is both true and ridiculous. It deals with two men and a wolf who fall into a wolf trap. It ends badly for the wolf, but the men are rescued; and though they have to pay for their rescue, the ending could hardly be called tragic except in some bizarre understanding of the term. Therefore, when Reyner or a scribe calls the piece a *tragedia* at the end, he does not seem to know what a tragedy is supposed to be in any of the traditional senses. It has been suggested that the term was being used ironically;[91] but ironical usage presupposes well-established straightforward usage, and we have no reason to assume such a presupposition in this case.

My final example of seeming unfamiliarity with traditional meanings of tragedy and comedy, and consequent incongruity in their application, brings us to Spain, as promised: it concerns the play, or series of dramatic dialogues, usually called *Celestina*.[92]

Celestina has a complicated printing history, and there are many areas of dispute over the author and evolution of the piece. I offer the following simplified hypothetical account. Fernando de Rojas, a student of law at the University of Salamanca in the 1490s, found an unfinished dialogue about a young man, Calisto, who falls in love with Melibea, and seeks the aid of the old bawd Celestina. The original author, he tells us, called the work a

---

[89] I follow the scene divisions given by Gori. For discussions of the content, see Cloetta, *Komödie*, pp. 54–67; Paratore, "L'influsso," pp. 33–36.

[90] Cloetta, *Komödie*, pp. 123–26.

[91] *Ibid.*, p. 126.

[92] For cited editions see the Bibliography, under Rojas. The critical edition of Miguel Marciales (1985) was seen through the press by Brian Dutton and Joseph T. Snow after Marciales's death.

comedia, and I presume that he intended to tell a story on the lines of the *Pamphilus*, much as the archpriest of Hita did in the *Libro de buen amor*: after the lover seduces the girl, he marries her. Rojas, I posit, not knowing the meaning of *comedia*, nevertheless retained the word in his characterization of the piece, but brought the story to a completely different conclusion: after Calisto has his way with Melibea, he slips off a ladder and is killed, and Melibea commits suicide. In the earliest extant edition of the work, printed around 1499, there is no title except what can be gathered from the opening rubric: *Argumento del primer auto desta Comedia*.[93] In another edition, printed in 1500, Rojas gives an elaborate title: *Comedia de Calisto y Melibea: La qual contiene de más de su agradable y dulce estilo muchas sentencias filosofales e avisos muy necessarios para mancebos, mostrándoles los engaños que están encerrados en sirvientes y alcahuetas*.[94] We can assume from this description that he considers a pleasant style, philosophical ideas, and moral admonitions (specifically, in this case, warnings to young people of the deceptions of servants and bawds) suitable to comedy. In a set of acrostic verses in which he gives his name, he seems to say of the original author's piece that he had never seen, except for Terence's, a work of such high and fine style; he notes also that it was in the Castilian vernacular:

Jamás no vi sino terenciana,
Depués que me acuerdo, ni nadie la vido,
Obra de estilo tan alto y sobido,
En lengua común vulgar castellana.[95]

In an expanded version, perhaps first printed in 1500 but surviving only in later editions,[96] Rojas omits the reference to Terence[97] (one wonders if he

[93] Rojas, *Comedia*, *c.* 1499: *Celestina*, ed. Marciales, 2:17; facsimile, ed. Archer M. Huntington, sig. a 1. See Clara Louisa Penney, *The Book Called Celestina in the Library of the Hispanic Society of America*, p. 28.
[94] Rojas, *Comedia*, Toledo 1500: Marciales, 2:1; facsimile, ed. Daniel Poyán Días, sig. [a i]. Marciales puts *alcauetas* for *alcahuetas*.
[95] *Ibid.*, sig. a iii. Another edition (Seville? 1501?) has, for the first line: "Jamás yo no vi Terenciana." See the reproduction in Penney, *The Book Called Celestina*, p. 3. The lines now mean: "I have never seen a Terentian work in such high style in Castilian." Marciales, *Celestina*, 1:7, thinks that this is in fact the author's original meaning; he takes *sino* as a misreading of an abbreviation for *huna* (meaning *una*), with the next editor omitting *sino* because it did not make sense.
[96] See Humberto López Morales, ed., *La Celestina* (Madrid 1976), Introducción, p. xx. See also Peter N. Dunn, *Fernando de Rojas*, pp. 35–36. The earliest extant Spanish edition of this version is that of Saragossa 1507, but an Italian translation by Alfonso Ordóñez was published in Rome in 1506 by Eucharius Silber. See Kathleen V. Kish, *An Edition of the First Translation of the Celestina*. I use the facsimile edition of Seville, *c.* 1518–20, *Libro de Calisto y Melibea y de la puta vieja Celestina*, ed. Antonio Pérez y Gómez (Valencia 1958), Marciales's text L, 1:7 (see López Morales, pp. xiii–xiv).
[97] The lines now read (*Libro*, sig. [a ii verso]; Marciales, 2:7):

Jamás yo no vide en lengua romana
Despúes que me acuerdo, ni nadie la vido,
Obra de estilo tan alto, subido
En tosca ni griega ni castellana.

had any firsthand knowledge of Terence's plays). He also states that the title of his work has been criticized by some readers who say that it should not be called a comedy, since it ends in sadness, but should rather be called a tragedy. Rojas appeals to the original author, who wished to call it a comedy because of the beginning, which is pleasant. He, however, will compromise and call it a tragicomedy.[98] It seems quite likely that, though his readers may have known the tradition that tragedy begins in joy and ends in sadness, and may even have told it to Rojas, he did not get the point, but rather came away with the idea that tragedy was about sadness and comedy about joy, and therefore he could solve everything by designating his work as a mixture of tragedy and comedy. But Rojas was not resigned to relinquishing the straightforward category of comedy altogether. In his original introduction to the Argument, he stated: "There follows the Comedy of Calisto and Melibea, written in reproach of those mad lovers who, conquered in their disordered appetite, call and proclaim their mistresses to be their god; composed also as a warning against the wiles of bawds and wicked and lying servants." In the revised edition, he changed it to: "There follows the Comedy or Tragicomedy of Calisto and Melibea" and so on, thereby allowing his readers to choose between genres.[99]

No doubt the word *tragicomedia* was suggested to Rojas by a more learned reader acquainted with Plautus's characterization of *Amphitruo* as a *tragicocomedia*. The term was first applied to modern works by Tito Livio Frulovisi in the 1430s, and then by Marcellino Verardi in 1493 in his *Fernandus servatus*.[100] Verardi's brother Carlo says in a preface to the play that, like the *Amphitruo*, it should be called a tragico-comedy, because the persons and the action (that is, the violation of royal majesty) pertain to

---

[98] *Ibid.*, sig. a iii (Marciales, 2:12–13): "Otros han litigado sobre el nombre, diziendo que no se avía de llamar Comedia, pues acabava en tristeza, sino que se llamasse Tragedia. El primer auctor quiso dar denominacion del principio que fue plazer, y llamola Comedia. Yo viendo estas discordias entre estos extremos partí agora por medio la porfia, y llamela tragicomedia." Keith Whinnom, "Interpreting *La Celestina*: The Motives and the Personality of Fernando de Rojas," pp. 63 and 67, assumes, as I do, that the original author intended his work to be a comedy from beginning to end, and that Rojas betrayed his intention in giving it a disastrous end, but he admits to no ignorance of tragedy and comedy on Rojas's part; rather, he thinks that Rojas did not consider the deaths of Calisto and Melibea as tragic and failed to realize that others might consider them so, and he covered up his error with a joke, by coining the spurious term *tragicomedia*.

[99] Marciales, *Celestina* 2:15. The original form of the statement appears in the edition of 1500, cited above, and also in a manuscript of the first part of Act I recently discovered by Charles Faulhaber, which may be in Rojas's hand and may antedate the earliest editions; see Faulhaber's "*Celestina* de Palacio: Madrid, Biblioteca de Palacio, MS 1520" and "*Celestina* de Palacio: Rojas's Holograph Manuscript?" I quote the text from his edition in the latter, p. 29: "Siguese la Comedia de Calisto y Melibea, conpuesta en reprehension delos locos enamorados que, vencidos en su deshordenado apetito, a sus amigas llaman y dizen ser su dios. Asi mesmo fecha en aviso delos engaños delas alcauetes y malos y lisongeros servientes."

[100] María Rosa Lida de Malkiel, *La originalidad artística de La Celestina*, p. 51.

tragedy, while the happy end pertains to comedy.[101] The Fernandus of the title is Ferdinand of Aragon, and the play dramatizes his successful escape from an attempt on his life in 1492.

It is interesting that earlier in 1492 Carlo Verardi himself had written and published a play in which Ferdinand was the protagonist, this time dramatizing his conquest of Granada. In his preface to this work, Verardi characterized it as neither a tragedy nor a comedy, and therefore not subject to the rules of either genre. But his own rules of classification differ from those that he would apply to his brother's play. For one thing, the fact that it deals with a real event removes it from the realm of both comedy and tragedy, which take fables as their subjects. His idea of the contents of tragedies and comedies can be seen from this statement:

> Praesertim cum ulla hic tyrannorum scelera
> Non sitis audituri, aut fastus regios,
> Intolerandam vel bonis superbiam,
> Quae saepe describi solent tragoediis,
> Neque audientur lenonum hic perjuria,
> Servorum technae, aut meretricum blanditiae;
> Avara non usquam lena hic inducitur,
> Milesve gloriosus, aut sycophanta impudens,
> Edaxve parasitus, vel matrona impudens,
> Paterve durus, aut amator cupidus,
> Et reliqua quae in Grajis nostrisque comicis
> Spectata praebent voluptatem plurimam;
> Verum pudica honestaque hic sunt omnia
> Summoque cuncta perfecta consilio,
> Virtute semper duce, Fortuna comite;
> Fides bonique mores et probitas vigent;
> Nullus superbiae, nullus avaritiae est
> Locus relictus, aut foedis amoribus.[102]

(Especially since here you are not about to hear
any crimes of tyrants or arrogance of kings
or pride that is intolerable to good people,
which things are often written of in tragedies;
nor will there be heard here the perjury of pimps,
the wiles of servants, or the blandishments of whores;

---

[101] Marcellino Verardi, *Fernandus servatus*, ed. H. Thomas, esp. p. 437, Carlo Verardi's preface addressed to Cardinal Mendoza, archbishop of Toledo: "Potest enim hec nostra, ut *Amphitruonem* suum Plautus appellat, tragicocomedia nuncupari, quod personarum dignitas et regie majestatis impia illa violatio ad tragediam, jucundus vero exitus rerum ad comediam pertinere videantur." See Marvin T. Herrick, *Tragicomedy: Its Origin and Development in Italy, France, and England*, pp. 4–6.

[102] Carlo Verardi, *Historia baetica*, ed. Roberto Bravo Villarroel, Prologue, pp. 68–70. I leave the classical spellings of *ae* and *oe* in the text, since the Italian humanists at this time had begun to observe them, especially in printed texts.

no avaricious procuress is brought on anywhere here,
or braggart soldier, or impudent sycophant,
or voracious parasite, or impudent matron,
or harsh father, or greedy lover,
or all the other things that give the most delight
in the Greek comics and our own;
but rather all things here are modest and honest,
and everything is brought about with the highest counsel,
with virtue always in the lead and with Fortune as companion;
fidelity and good morals and probity flourish;
no place is left for pride, and none for avarice,
or for filthy loves.)

In this view of tragedy, there is no place for a virtuous hero like Ferdinand, or even, it would seem, for Fortune as an adverse figure.

Fernandus servatus is dedicated to the archbishop of Toledo, and it would surely have had some early circulation in Castile. It may have provided the indirect inspiration for Fernando de Rojas's title. We should note that the printer of the 1493 edition, Eucharius Silber, was also the printer of the earliest extant version of Rojas's *Tragicomedia*, namely, the Italian translation of 1506. In both cases, the Plautine form *tragicocomedia* is used.[103]

A play with a happy ending that was designated a tragedy by its author was written in Venice around 1500 or a bit later, namely, the *Tragedy Concerning Italian Matters and the Triumph of Louis, the Most Christian King of France and Unvanquished Duke of Milan*, by Giovanni Armonio Marso, dealing with the invasion of northern Italy by Louis XII, then duke of Orleans, in 1494–95, and his defeat of the forces of Ludovico Sforza.[104] It begins in misery and ends in peace and joy, as can be gathered from the rubric of the first act:

Primus actus tragedie, in quo Italia primum loquitur, conquerens de humana infelicitate qua affecta redacta sit in miseriam, cum olim omnium provinciarum esset regina, nunc volvente tempore esset miserrima. Sic indignabunda sororem Romam convenit ab eaque petens auxilium, accepit consilium ut Ludovico regi Francie adhereret christianissimo, qui pacem libertatemque dabit.[105]

(The first act of the tragedy, in which Italy speaks first, complaining about the human infelicity that has afflicted her and reduced her to misery; she who once was

[103] See Verardi, *Fernandus*, ed. Thomas, p. 433, and Kish, *First Translation of the Celestina*, pp. 25, 31, 42, 43, 47.
[104] *Iohannis Harmonii Marsi de rebus italicis deque triumpho Ludovico XII regis Francorum tragoedia*, ed. Gilbert Tournoy. The version of the title given above is that of the rubric to the fifth act, p. 64: "Quintus actus tragedie de rebus italicis deque triumpho Ludovici christianissimi regis Francie Mediolanique invictissimi ducis." The play exists only in a single manuscript, Paris, Bibliothèque Nationale lat. 16706, a presentation copy for Louis XII. Note that the spellings *ae* and *oe* are not used here, but they are in the first printed edition of Armonio's comedy *Stephanium*, cited below, which must date from the same time as his tragedy. [105] *Iohannis Harmonii Marsi de rebus*, p. 26.

queen of all provinces has now become in the course of time the most miserable. Thus indignant she meets with her sister Rome to ask her aid, and she accepts her counsel to join with Louis, most Christian king of France, who will give her peace and freedom.)

The Chorus's final speech is a song of joy, beginning, "Gaudeat dies clarior astro" ("Let this day rejoice, brighter than a star").[106]

In this case we can be assured that the name of tragedy was not applied to the work out of ignorance of traditional associations of the word. Armonio does not discuss the title or form of his work at all, except to say, in the Preface addressed to Louis, after recalling his victory and the beneficial results that it brought about: "I have therefore put together this little tragedy out of these events, and divided it into five acts" ("His igitur tragediolam hanc contexui, in quinque divisam actus").[107] His comedy, *Stephanium*, thought to have been composed slightly before his tragedy, but, unlike it, publicly recited and printed immediately,[108] also contains five acts. However, it is entirely in iambic verse (or Armonio's attempt at iambic verse), whereas *De rebus italicis* also contains choral lyrics in various meters, like Seneca's tragedies.[109]

In his prologue to *Stephanium*, Armonio shows that he is well acquainted with Donatus's introduction to his commentary on Terence, including both the Evanthian and Ciceronian sections. It is quite clear that, if Armonio had to choose between calling his play about Louis a comedy or a tragedy, there were more reasons for choosing tragedy than comedy, given Evanthius's distinctions between the two genres. *De rebus italicis* has the imposing characters, great dangers, and historical basis of tragedy, rather than the lower characters, trivial problems, and fictional events of comedy; it shares with comedy only the happy ending. Aristotle would have agreed that *De rebus italicis* is a tragedy, on the basis of the corpus of Greek tragedies, as we have seen in the first chapter. It would have been possible for Armonio to have read Aristotle in Giorgio Valla's Latin translation of the *Poetics*, which he published in Venice in 1498.[110] Alemannus's translation of Averroes's *Commentary on Aristotle's Poetics*, which first appeared in print in Venice in 1481,[111] is also potentially relevant, for in it

---

[106] *Ibid.*, p. 71.   [107] *Ibid.*, p. 25.

[108] *Ioannis Harmonii Marsi comoedia Stephanium*, ed. Walther Ludwig, with a German translation. The Latin text is also given by Graziella Gentilini, *Il teatro umanistico veneto: La commedia*, along with an Italian translation. Gentilini also gives bibliographical details of the early editions (pp. 73–74). The title of the first, thought to be before 1502, is: IOANNIS HARMONII MARSI COMOEDIA STEPHANIVM VRBIS VENETAE GENIO PVBLICE RECITATA.

[109] The echoes of Seneca in Armonio's play are not many, but there are some clear examples of his influence. They are noted by Tournoy in his edition.

[110] See Ludwig, *Ioannis Harmonii Marsi comoedia*, p. 16.

[111] *Ibid.*

Final variations

tragedy is characterized as dealing with the praises of virtuous men. But since Armonio's dramas show no clear influence of the *Poetics* in any form, it is more likely that he arrived at his inclusive concept of tragedy on his own.

In a recent study arguing that Fernando Rojas shows himself to be an *aficionado* of the moral works of Seneca in the *Celestina*, it is assumed that he would also have been familiar with Seneca's tragedies; and it is suggested that he may have adopted the term *tragicomedia* because of a comment that Seneca makes in one of his epistles: namely, that Roman plays (*fabulae togatae*), because they contain some elements of seriousness, are midway between comedies and tragedies.[112] But this picture of Rojas is at variance with his admitted ignorance of accepted meanings of tragedy and comedy.

In comparison with his Italian contemporaries and his Spanish critics, then, Rojas was quite limited in his knowledge of literary traditions, and this uninformed tradition won out in Spanish, at least as far as the word *comedia* is concerned: it came to be used regularly to designate any dramatic work, whether humorous or serious – or, in our modern parlance, "comic" or "tragic." However, it may be that this use of the word was informed by an older tradition, that of Papias, who mixed properties of tragedy with comedy. I have hypothesized that this mix was behind Dante's use of the word.[113] It came into prominence again in Spain with the publication in Seville in 1490 of the *Universal vocabulario* of Alfonso de Palencia (1423–92). His definition runs: "Comedy is that which deals with deeds of low persons; and it is not in such grand style as tragedy, but is rather in a middle and sweet style; and much of the time it treats of historical truth and grave persons."[114] Tragedy, on the other hand, was "whatever the ancients pronounced in tearful verses."[115]

Alfonso de Palencia, then, like Fernando Rojas, manifests no knowledge of Seneca or more recent learned medieval ideas about tragedy; but there

---

[112] Louise Fothergill-Payne, *Seneca and Celestina*, pp. 127–28, citing Seneca, *Epistulae* 8.8: "Habent enim hae [togatae nostrae] quoque aliquid severitatis, et sunt inter comoedias ac tragoedias mediae" (for a fuller citation, see p. 9 above). She maintains that in the expanded *Tragicomedia*, Rojas "mocks the dramatic pathos of the Senecan tragedy" (p. 133).

[113] Kelly, *Tragedy and Comedy*, pp. 8–9. See p. 148 above.

[114] Alfonso de Palencia, *Universal vocabulario*, ed. John M. Hill, p. 38 (fol. 86b): "Comedia es la que comprehende fechos de personas baxas y no es de tan grande estilo como la tragedia mas es de mediano y suave; y muchas vezes de fe historial y tratta de personas graves." Under *comici*, p. 39 (fol. 86d), he also gives Papias's doctrine about comedy dealing with joyful things, tragedy tearful, and the two kinds of comics: the old, like Terence, wrote of amusing things, while the new, like Persius and Juvenal, reprehended vices. See Kelly, *Tragedy and Comedy*, p. 8 n. 31. Under *fabula* (fol. 151b, given here under *argumento*, p. 13), he says that the authors of comedy always write of possible things, whereas authors of tragedies mixed in impossible things.

[115] *Ibid.*, p. 187 (fol. 506b): "Tragedia ... qualquier cosa que los antiguos pronunciavan en versos llorosos."

was far less excuse for ignorance in the case of Palencia, for some of his older humanist contemporaries in Spain were very well informed. The most important was Iñigo López de Mendoza (1398–1458), lord of Hita, who became marquis of Santillana in 1445, one of the greatest men of letters in Castile in the earlier fifteenth century. He presents an interesting parallel to Chaucer in that, on the basis of a definition of tragedy, he concluded that the accounts of Boccaccio's *De casibus* were tragedies, and he set about writing a similar narrative of disaster in imitation of the form. Like Lydgate, who in England at this time was composing tragedies for the *Fall of Princes*, he portrayed his aggrieved suppliants as appearing to Boccaccio himself as a character. But, since he put a happy end to the narrative, he called it a comedy, and gave it the title of *Comedieta de Ponça* (*The Comedyette of Ponza*).[116]

The disaster in question, which Santillana began to write his tragedy about, was the naval battle of Gaeta, near the island of Ponza, in 1435, in which King Alfonso V of Aragon ("the Magnaminous") and his three brothers were taken captive. Santillana has a vision in which the mother of the captives, and three of their wives, speak to Boccaccio, who has been summoned from heaven by their lament. Boccaccio, speaking Italian, agrees to listen to, and to tell, their story, and the queen mother proceeds to recount it. But when she gets to the point of giving the text of the letter telling of the capture, she dies, and Boccaccio disappears from the vision without a word from the poet. Instead, he turns to "comedying" ("comediando," line 666), calling on Calliope, Melpomene, Clio, and the other Muses for help. The goddess Fortune appears to the three surviving ladies and promises the release of the captives. Santillana then sees the released prisoners before him, "de quien mi comedia e proçesso canta" ("of which my comedy and process sings," 950). In a final stanza, dawn comes, Fortune and her company disappear, and the poet is left greatly consoled.

Santillana finished his *Comedieta* early in 1436, and it was only some years later, in a letter written to Violante de Prades in 1443, that he explains the work and its title. Poets, he says, use three kinds of name for their compositions: tragedy, satire, and comedy. Tragedy is that which contains the falls of great kings and princes, like Hercules, Priam, and others, whose lives begin happily and continue so for a long time and then end sadly. Seneca the Younger wrote of them in his tragedies, and so did John Boccaccio in his *De casibus virorum illustrium*. Satire is the sort of composition employed by the poet Satirus, which reprehends vices and praises virtues; Horace used it later, as Dante notes (citing *Inferno* 4.89).

[116] Iñigo López de Mendoza, marqués de Santillana, *Comedieta de Ponça*, ed. Maxim P.A. Kerkhof. See Miguel A. Pérez Priego, "De Dante a Juan de Mena: Sobre el género literario de 'comedia.'"

Final variations

Comedy has troublesome and sad beginnings, but the middle and end of its days are happy, joyful, and fortunate. Terence used it, and so did Dante in his poem, where he first says he saw infernal sorrows and torments, then purgatory, and then, happily and fortunately, paradise.[117] Santillana was familiar not only with the plays of Seneca, which he arranged to be translated into Castilian for the first time,[118] but also with Dante's *Comedy*, or rather his "three comedies" of *Inferno, Purgatorio*, and *Paradiso* – which is how he speaks of Dante's book in his *Proemio*.[119] This concept, that each of the three *cantiche* of Dante's poem was a comedy, is reflected in a copy that Santillana possessed, dated 1354, and may derive from the analysis of Pietro Alighieri. He had versions of the commentaries not only of Pietro, but also of Jacopo della Lana and Benvenuto da Imola.[120] As we shall see below, the

---

[117] The letter is edited by Kerkhof, *Comedieta*, pp. 269–77, the pertinent part on pp. 271–74: "Yo començé una obra a la qual llamé *Comedieta de Ponça*. E tituléla d'este nonbre por quanto los poetas fallaron tres maneras de nonbres a aquellas cosas de que fablaron, es a saber tragedia, sátira, e comedia. Tragedia es aquella que contiene en sý caýdas de grandes rreyes e príncipes, asý commo de Ércoles, Príamo [e] Agamenón, e otros tales, cuyos nasçimientos e vidas alegremente se començaron e grande tienpo se continuaron e después tristemente cayeron. E de fablar d'éstos usó Séneca el mançebo, sobrino del otro Séneca, en las sus tragedias, e Johan Bocaçio en el libro *De casibus virorum yllustrium*. Sátira es aquella manera de fablar que tovo un poeta que se llamó Sátiro, el qual rreprehendió muy mucho los viçios e loó las vyrtudes; e d'ésta después d'él usó Oraçio, e aun por esto dixo Dante: 'El altro e Oraçio satiro qui vene,' etc. Comedia es dicha aquella cuyos comienços son trabajosos e tristes, e después el medio e fin de sus días alegre, gozoso, e bienventurado; e d'ésta usó Terençio Peno, e Dante en el su libro, donde primeramente dize aver visto las dolores e penas ynfernales, e después el purgatorio, e alegre e bienaventuradamente después el paraýso." The text reads "a Agamenón," but I have emended the *a* to *e*, which is the reading of the text given by Angel Gómez Moreno and Kerkhof, *Obras completas* pp. 435–37.

[118] Santillana says this in a letter datable between 1445 and 1452; see Nicholas G. Round, "Las traducciones medievales, catalanas y castellanas, de las tragedias de Séneca," p. 190. He had an Italian translation of Seneca's tragedies in his library: Mario Schiff, *La bibliothèque du Marquis de Santillane*, pp. 111–12. The Catalan translation of Antón Vilaragut, a form of which was influential on Castilian versions, gives an Isidorian definition of tragedy: Seneca's pieces are called tragedies because they contain dolorous accounts of the cruelties of kings and great princes ("Són dites tregèdies per ço com contenem dictats plorosos de crueltats de reys he de grans prínceps," Round, "La traducciones," p. 192). Round says that all of the Spanish versions of the tragedies manifest "a predominant interest in the examples and the moral precepts to be drawn from the text. They show very little understanding of the plays as dramas, and little humanistic scholarship" (p. 816).

[119] Santillana, *Proemio*, in *Obras completas*, pp. 444–45: "Después de Guido [Guinicelli] e Arnaldo Daniel, Dante escrivió en terçio rimo elegantemente las sus tres comedias: *Infierno, Purgatorio*, e *Paraýso*." He is making the point that Latin and Greek metrical works are in the sublime style, while metrical works in the vernacular, like Guinicelli's, Daniel's, and Dante's, are in the middle style, as are the Latin proses of Boethius's *Consolation*. The *Proemio* is a letter accompanying a collection of Santillana's poems that he sent to Pedro de Portugal shortly after becoming marquis.

[120] Santillana had two copies of the *Comedy* in his library (Schiff, *La bibliothèque*, pp. 271–72, 275–303), the second of which has the Castilian translation of Enrique de Villena in the margins. The Italian text itself in this second manuscript, Madrid, Biblioteca National MS Ii-110 (now 10186), is dated 1354; the Latin rubrics for the *Inferno* refer to the "first *cantica*" of the "comedy" of Dante, but the rubrics for *Purgatorio* and *Paradiso* speak of the "second book" and the "third book" of the "comedies" of Dante (*ibid.*, pp. 275–76). MS Ii-122 (now 10207), noted by Schiff, *La bibliothèque*, pp. 303–04, is a translation of Florence, Biblioteca Laurenziana Ms. Ash. Dant. 2 cc. 1–10, which begins with Jacopo della Lana's proem and carries on with the first version of Pietro Alighieri's

translation and commentary of Giovanni da Serravalle also considered Dante's work to consist of three comedies.

Enrique de Villena (1384–1434), who translated Dante's *Comedy* for Santillana on the margins of the above-noted copy, also translated Vergil's *Aeneid* at the same time, in 1427–28.[121] In his introduction to the latter, he distinguishes four kinds of ancient poets, namely, tragic, satiric, comedic, and lyric.[122] The tragic deal with the deeds of princes and battles and those who have a happy beginning and a sad end. The name comes from the Greek for goat, because the goat climbs the highest rocks, and just so tragic poets speak of high things with high words. Vergil, of course, was one of them, and for this reason the *Aeneid* is treated tragically.[123] Dante, we remember, has Vergil call his work an *alta tragedia*, and perhaps Villena was swayed by this designation in coming up with his ingenious explanation. He may mean to say that tragedies can deal either with deeds of princes, like Aeneas, and battles, on the one hand, or, on the other hand, with those who, unlike Aeneas, come to a sad end. If so, he resembles Albertino Mussato with his two kinds of tragedies, the one dealing with disasters in iambic verse, as in the tragedies of Seneca, and the other treating of triumphs in heroic verse, like the *Aeneid*. Villena was acquainted with at least some of Seneca's plays: he quotes from the *Troades* and the *Thyestes* several times in his *Treatise of Consolation*, written in 1423 or 1424,[124] and in

commentary; see Margherita Morreale, "Apuntes bibliográficos para el estudio del tema 'Dante en España hasta el s. XVII,'" pp. 102–03. In his second and third commentaries, Pietro noted that each of the parts of Dante's work had a comic ending, which could have led to the conclusion that it consisted of three comedies; see Kelly, *Tragedy and Comedy*, pp. 31–32, and see above, p. 154. Madrid Biblioteca National MS Ii-123 (now 10208) is the first part of Benvenuto's third commentary on the *Inferno*. Kerkhof, *Comedieta*, pp. 271–72, n. 21, gives the portion of its text dealing with the three styles of tragedy, satire, and comedy; for the original Latin, see Kelly, *Comedy and Tragedy*, pp. 48–50.

[121] Schiff, *La bibliothèque*, pp. 89–90, 309–10.
[122] As we have seen, these are the four categories named by Isidore of Seville and Guido da Pisa.
[123] Enrique de Villena, *La Eneyda*, text supplied to me by Julian Weiss, while awaiting the edition of Pedro M. Cátedra, from Madrid, Biblioteca Nacional MS 17945, fol. 20: "Es de notar que quatro fueron las maneras de los poethas. Los unos se dizían trárgicos [sic], que tractavan los fechos de los príncipes e de las batallas e los que avién elegre prinçipio e triste fyn. E deziése de *tragos* que es cabrón en griego, que ansí como el cabrón sube ha las más altas peñas, ansí los trágicos dizién altas cosas por altas palabras. [Explanations of the *satíricos*, *comédicos*, and *líricos* follow: the satiric poets reprehended vice, the comedic dealt with events in villas, and the lyric sang of ancient deeds.to the lyre.] E Virgilio fue de los trágicos e por eso esta *Eneyda* trágicamente es tractada." See the discussion by Julian Weiss, "Juan de Mena's *Coronación*: Satire or *Sátira*?," p. 122. I am grateful to Professor Weiss for many helpful references.
[124] Villena, *Tratado de la consolación*, ed. Derek C. Carr, pp. 27, 65, 78, 120, 129. He is not simply drawing on a *florilegium*; he knows about the dialogic nature of the plays, since in the first of these references he cites Seneca "en la ficta locuçión de Ulixes," quoting *Troades* 765. He also draws heavily on Boethius's *Consolation*, especially book 2, and he alludes to Nicholas Trevet's gloss on book 1, prose 1, ad v. *scenicas meretriculas* (p. 30; Carr quotes the gloss in the fifteenth-century Castilian translation of Trevet's commentary). He also refers to "the sea of histories" and to Boccaccio's *De casibus* for the many accounts of death therein (p. 60).

the still earlier *Twelve Labors of Hercules* (1417) he draws on *Hercules furens* and *Hercules oetaeus*.[125] He characterizes the matter of this last-named work as more satiric than tragic, even though tragic poets have told the story of Hercules.[126]

Diego de Valera (1412?–1488) names tragic, comic, lyric, and satiric not as ancient genres, but as the four current modes of speaking, in a note to his prose *Treatise in Defense of Virtuous Women* (written in 1445 or earlier). The only characteristic he gives for the tragic and the comic is the order of events: the tragic deals with things that begin in happiness and have a sad and dolorous end, whereas the comic is about things with a sad beginning and a prosperous and happy end.[127] Like Santillana, he must see Dante as the author of three comedies, since he refers to the *Inferno* as his first comedy.[128]

The most important author of the time was Juan de Mena, whose understanding of tragedy was also influenced by Dante scholarship. In the second preamble to his *Coronación*, composed in 1438, he gives the doctrine of Benvenuto's second or Ferrarese commentary on the styles of tragedy, satire, and comedy. Tragedy is a composition about high deeds in a valiant, proud, and high style; it was used by Homer, Vergil, Lucan, and Statius. He then adds a point that is not in Benvenuto: tragedy commences in high beginnings, but falls to sad and disastrous ends.[129] Benvenuto wrongly attributed to Isidore the opposite characterization for comedy, which Mena gives (from sad beginnings to happy ends),[130] and one might suppose that Mena simply applied the reverse movement to tragedy.

[125] Villena, *Los doze trabajos de Hércules*, ed. Margherita Morreale, pp. 9, 133, 136.

[126] *Ibid.*, p. 7: the work encourages good morals and discourages bad, "en tanto que la materia presente mas es satira que tragica, ya sea tragicos la ayan deduzida."

[127] Diego de Valera, *Tratado en defensa de virtuosas mugeres*, ed. Mario Penna, p. 63 note 2: "La presente materia es sátira, para lo qual bien entender es de saber que todos los que escrivieron tomaron uno de quatro modos de fablar, los quales son: trágico, cómico, lírico, ssátiro. Trágico, es fablar de cosas que ayan començado en alegría, e ayan avido fin triste e doloroso. Cómico, es de cosas que ayan avido començamiento triste, e fin próspero e alegre." The lyric mode reprehends and praises in meter, and satire praises virtues and reprehends vices. For the date of the work, see Penna's introduction, p. cxx.

[128] *Ibid.*, p. 73 note 49: "Segunt el Dante en la primera Comedia suya, Fortuna es un ministro enbiado por la divinal Providencia," and so on, referring to *Inferno* 7.65–96.

[129] Juan de Mena, *Coronación*, ed. Feliciano Delgado León, p. 54: "Tragédico es dicha el escritura que fabla de altos fechos y por bravo y sobervio y alto stilo. La qual manera siguieron Omero, Virgilio, Lucan, y Stacio. Por la escritura tragédica, puesto que comiença en altos principios, su manera es acabar en tristes y desatrados fines." For Benvenuto's Ferrara commentary, see Michele Barbi, "La lettura di Benvenuto da Imola e i suoi rapporti con altri commenti," parts 1 and 2, and cf. Carlo Paolazzi, "Le letture dantesche di Benvenuto da Imola a Bologna e a Ferrara e le redazioni del suo *Comentum*." See Kelly, *Tragedy and Comedy*, pp. 48–56, esp. pp. 49–50, for the pertinent passages.

[130] Mena, *Coronación*, p. 54: "El tercero stilo es comedia, la qual tracta de cosas baxas y pequeñas y por baxo y humilde stilo; y comiença en tristes principios y fenesce en alegres fines, del qual usó Terencio."

However, Mena is not drawing directly on Benvenuto, but on the commentary of Giovanni da Serravalle, who had been one of Benvenuto's auditors.[131] His Latin translation of the *Comedy* and accompanying commentary were done at the request of an Italian cardinal and two English bishops at the Council of Constance (1414–17), and a copy came to be possessed by the hold-out Spanish pope, Benedict XIII (Pedro de Luna).[132] In addition to giving Benvenuto's doctrine about the style and subjects of tragedy,[133] he also draws on Franceso da Buti for the tragic plot, which as we have seen, Buti derives from the front and rear appearances of a goat. But Serravalle takes this ingenious comparison a step (or rather several steps) further, by imagining the goat in motion: "And tragedy is so called from the Greek *trahos*, which in Latin means goat; for a goat has a beautiful aspect; but when it passes it gives off a mighty stink from its tailquarters. Tragedy has a similar effect: it begins with joyful and exalted and great estates but eventually finishes in extremely sad conditions."[134]

Serravalle follows his mentors in considering classical epics to be tragedies, including Vergil's *Aeneid*, even though it does not end sadly, and even though he was acquainted with Seneca's tragedies.[135] He was similarly acquainted with Terence's comedies,[136] but he accepted Dante's work not only as a comedy, but as three comedies, even though he explicates a title that should indicate only one comedy: *Incipit prima cantica comedie Dantis*

---

[131] Giovanni da Serravalle, *Translatio et comentum totius libri Dantis Aldigherii*, ed. Marcellino da Civezza and Teofilo Domenichelli, pp. 570, 741 (commenting on *Purgatorio* 13 and 27, respectively). The editors' question as to whether Serravalle heard Benvenuto in Bologna or Ferrara (p. xvi) can be definitely answered in favor of the latter.

[132] Da Civezza and Domenichelli, *Translatio et comentum*, pp. xix–xxi; Louis M. La Favia, "Il primo commento alla *Divina commedia* in Spagna," p. 2. Benedict XIII was deposed by the Council in 1417, but he died unsubmissive around 1423. The cardinal who commissioned the work was Amadeo da Saluzzo, and the bishops were Robert Hallum, bishop of Salisbury from 1407 until his death in 1417, and his predecessor at Salisbury, Nicholas Bubwith, who served as bishop of Bath and Wells from 1407 to 1424. Hallum (or Hallam) was chancellor of Oxford from 1403 to 1405. Serravalle notes that he had visited England (*Translatio et comentum*, p. 259, commenting on *Inferno* 20), probably around 1398 (see p. xvii), which, of course, would have been before Chaucer's death.

[133] Serravalle, *Translatio*, Preambula, p. 12: "Tragedia est que tractat de rebus altis et magnis cum superbo, idest alto, stilo, sicut sunt subversiones regnorum et provintiarum, diluvia, strages; quo stilo tragedico usi sunt Homerus, Virgilius, Lucanus, et Statius."

[134] *Ibid.*: "Et dicitur tragedia a *trahos* [see p. xxxii] grece, quo latine sonat sicut yrcus; nam yrcus habet faciem et partes anteriores pulchras, habet aspectum ab ante letum et pulchrum; sed cum petransit, post se dimittit fetorem magnum ex parte caude. Similiter facit tragedia, que incipit a letis et excelsis et magnis statibus, tandem finit in tristibus valde magnis."

[135] *Ibid.*, p. 233 (commenting on *Inferno* 18): "Tunc fuit ibi rex Cholchis, qui habebat filiam pulcherrimam, nomine Medeam, que erat litterata, prudens, incantatrix demonum, magica; noverat omnes virtutes erbarum, ut habetur in alia Tragedia Senece." His reference to "another tragedy" of Seneca's doubtless indicates that he has earlier referred to a tragedy other than *Medea*, but I have not searched the preceding commentary for such a reference.

[136] *Ibid.*, p. 236: "Terentius vero, in *Eunucho*, idest in secundo suo libro, qui vocatus *Eunuchus*, dicit quod hec Thays, meretrix thebana, habebat duos amasios," and so on.

Aldigherii, poete florentini, in qua tractatur de Inferno. He says: "When it is said that in the first there is a treatment of hell, it follows that in the other comedies, that is, the second and third, other things will be treated."[137] The sentiment that he gives from Aristotle's *Poetica* on this page (that is, from Alemannus's translation of Averroes's commentary), probably comes from Benvenuto, like another reference further on.[138]

We have seen that the marquis of Santillana almost wrote a tragedy of the Chaucerian sort, but was foiled when his subject matter turned into the stuff of comedy. But there were three works called tragedies that were composed in the Iberian Peninsula at this time, all of them perhaps around the year of the marquis's death, 1458. First, there was that of Pedro, constable of Portugal (1429–66), who was the addressee of Santillana's *Proemio* (written at some point between 1446 and 1449). Pedro deals specifically with one category of genre in his *Satire of Happy and Unhappy Life*, written originally in Portuguese sometime before 1449, and translated by himself into Castilian sometime before the middle of 1453. In the dedicatory letter to the Castilian version, which is all that we possess, he tells his sister Isabel, queen of Portugal, that he calls his work a satire because the word means reprehension, and also because it comes from *satura*, which means eulogy.[139] In it he quotes knowledgeably from Seneca's "first tragedy," *Hercules furens*, and his "fourth tragedy," *Phaedra*, or, as he says it is called, *Ypolito Carmine*.[140] His next work, *Stanzas on Scorn and Contempt for the Beautiful Things of the World*, written between 1451 and 1453, obviously belongs to the *De contemptu mundi* genre. It is of interest for our topic because, in addition to showing familiarity with Boccaccio's *De casibus*[141]

---

[137] *Ibid.*, Preambula, p. 22: "Dum dicitur quod in prima tractatur de Inferno, restat quod in aliis comediis, scilicet secunda et tertia, tractabitur de aliis." The rubric to *Purgatorio* reads: "Secunda Comedia, sive Purgatorium Dantis" (p. xxviii).

[138] *Ibid.*: "Vult etenim Aristotiles in *Poetica* quod nobiles invenerunt poesim, quando fecerunt versus ad exaltandum magna gesta et vituperandum turpia; dicit enim Aristotiles, quod omnis oratio poetica nihil aliud est nisi laudatio vel vituperatio." The corresponding passage in Benvenuto is found only in his finished, or third, version of his commentary (Kelly, "Aristotle," p. 201). But Serravalle's use of it doubtless indicates that it was originally in the Ferrarese lectures; and the same must be true of the reference on p. 426 (Preambula to the "Secunda comedia"): "De materia Inferni dicit Aristotiles in *Poesi* sua, quod inferius est locus inconsolabilis," which is to be found in Benvenuto's first and third versions (Kelly, "Aristotle," p. 203 and note 202).

[139] Pedro de Portugal, *Sátira de felice e infelice vida*, ed. Luís Adão da Fonseca, *Obras completas do condestável dom Pedro de Portugal*, p. 5. Cf. Elena Gascón Vera, *Don Pedro, Condestable de Portugal*, pp. 77–78, who compares Pedro's definition with Santillana's. She mistakenly characterizes the latter's 1443 letter explaining the *Comedieta* as the preface to the work, and thinks that Pedro would therefore have seen and been influenced not only by Santillana account of satire, but also his characterization of tragedy (p. 144).

[140] Pedro, *Sátira*, pp. 23, 86, 88.

[141] Pedro, *Coplas del menesprecio e contempto de las cosas fermosas del mundo*, *Obras completas*, pp. 179–80 (citing Boccaccio's dedicatory letter to Mainardo Cavalcanti, written for the revised version of the *De casibus*), p. 246 (referring to his account of the fall of Samson).

Theory and practice in Spain

and citing Seneca's *Medea*,[142] Pedro recounts the episode of Croesus's unexpected deliverance from Boethius's *Consolation*, just before tragedies are characterized as bewailing Fortune's sudden overthrow of happy kingdoms.[143] However, Pedro's tragedy does not fit the Senecan mold, on the one hand, or, on the other hand, the form that William of Conches derived from the Boethian passage. But it may very well be that he did get his notion of tragedy from his own reading of Boethius, unencumbered by the sort of Conchesque gloss that influenced Chaucer's narrative idea of the genre.

Pedro's tragedy concerns his reaction to the death in 1455 of his sister, Queen Isabel.[144] In the colophon he, or the scribe, calls it *The Tragedy of the Celebrated Queen Lady Isabel*,[145] but in the first meter Pedro refers to it more accurately as his own tragedy:

> O vos ojos mios, dexad el llorar,
> E tu, mano triste, la pluma açierta.
> O tu, rude lengua, dexa de gridar,
> Pues sabes que es çierto no ser cosa çierta.
> La ciega Fortuna no quieras blasmar,
> Tus plantos dexados, la fabla despierta
> Por que mi tragedia puedas explicar
> E la clara Fama no se quede muerta,
> Mas dure por siempre pues deve durar.

> (O my eyes, stop weeping,
> and you, sad hand, take up the pen.
> O you, rude tongue, stop complaining,
> for you know it is certain that nothing is certain.
> Do not seek to blame blind Fortune.
> Put your laments aside and begin to speak,
> so that you can expound my tragedy,
> and bright Fame will not remain lifeless
> but live forever, as she deserves.)

[142] *Ibid.*, pp. 198–99, referring to Ovid's and Seneca's accounts of Medea's invocation to Hecate; see Seneca, *Medea* 833–42.

[143] Pedro, *Coplas del menesprecio*, p. 189, referring to Boethius, *De Consolatione*, book 2, prose 2: "Were you unaware that Croesus, king of the Lydians, being formidable to Cyrus a short time before and soon thereafter miserably consigned to the flames of the pyre, was defended by rain sent from heaven?" Pedro attributes only his troubles to Fortune and his deliverance to a singular miracle of God, his life being extended because of his virtues and noble qualities, as Boethius notes ("por singular milagro de Dios fue de la muerte librado, e con lluvia manante del çielo otra segunda ves por sus virtudes e noblesas fue alongada la su fin, segund Boeçio tañe").

[144] Pedro, *Tragedia de la insigne reina dona Isabel*, ed. Adão. I also refer to the edition of Carolina Michaëlis de Vasconcelos. Isabel died on 2 December 1455, and the work seems to have been finished by May 1457, except for the Prologue, which is dated 1459 (pp. 29–30). See the abstract of a paper by Charity Cannon Willard, "El Condestable Don Pedro and the *Tragedia de la insigne Reyna Isabel.*"

[145] Pedro, *Tragedia*, ed. Adão, p. 348: "Loado Dios ffenesçe bienaventuradamente la tragedia de la insigne reyna doña Ysabel."

Final variations

He goes on to ask winged Fame to tell her news, while weeping, and to make his great misfortune ("mi mal grande") known to all.[146] His tragedy, then, is not primarily about a misfortune that has happened to someone else, but about a sorrow that he himself has experienced. For Chaucer, "myn tragedye" means "my tragedy about Troilus"; but for Pedro, "mi tragedia" means "my tragedy about myself."

Pedro then tells of a dream in which his sister appeared to him, with sad eyes and troubled visage, but speechless, and then he recounts the ominous signs that occurred the next day (meter 1). He next tells of returning from the green fields, where he was trying to assuage his sorrow, and encountering a man who told him to prepare for bad news. Ravenous Fortune, the man says, is not satisfied with having killed Pedro's father. He is to remember what the blind lady has done to others from the beginning of the world, starting from Adam, whom she drove from the paradise of life to the land of misery; then there were Nimrod, Cadmus, Thyestes, Jocasta and Oedipus, Theseus, and Agamemnon; there was Solomon, transformed from the peak of wisdom to folly and idolatry; the chaste queen Dido, who killed herself; the noble and virtuous King Croesus; Xerxes, Alcibiades, Hamilcar, Hannibal, Pompey, and Caesar; Arthur, king of the English, and Alfonso the Learned, both brought low from their previous great power. On the other hand, others were raised from low to high estate, like Marcus Varro, a butcher who became dictator; Gaius Marius, who from very low lineage became a famous emperor; and Octavian, who from being a poor man was elevated to be emperor of the world for many years (prose 1). He then tells Pedro that the princess his sister has died, and this is confirmed by a second messenger (proses 2 and 3). After uttering expressions of great sorrow and wild recriminations, Pedro sees an old man standing before him, holding three apples in his right hand, to indicate "three times" (presumably, past, present, and future – thereby identifying him as Time himself).[147] He listens to Pedro's complaints for a long time, and then begins to speak (meter 3). There follows a Boethian dialogue in which the grieving narrator is finally brought to his senses (prose 4 to prose 8, with intervening meters).

Pedro's brief survey of fallen men may have been indebted to Boccaccio, but if so, he did not conclude that Boccaccio's histories were tragedies, as did Santillana. He refers to Boethius by name, and both the content and the prosimetrical form of his *Tragedy* are clearly indebted to the *Consolation*. As I indicated above, he may have taken the meaning of tragedy from Fortune's question and concluded that it referred to a lamentation over a disaster

[146] *Ibid.*, p. 309.
[147] So Michaëlis, *Tragedia*, p. 24.

suddenly inflicted by Fortune. The closest that we have seen to this conception of the term is among the French, where it was used to indicate a lyric or prose complaint. Chaucer considered lamentation to be one of the purposes of tragedy, but rather than lamenting over his own loss, the author of tragedy was to grieve over the wretchedness into which some outstanding figure of history (or pseudo-history) had consciously fallen, whether deservedly or not. Pedro does not show Queen Isabel to have *suffered* a fall into misfortune. He does show her as grieving when she appears in his dream, but she seems to be grieving not over her own early death, but rather over the effect it will have on her brother. However, to judge from the evidence before our eyes, Pedro seems also to have attached the notion of a Boethian consolation to his idea of tragedy.[148]

The next work to be considered is also a self-tragedy, namely, that of the Valencian author Johan Roiç de Corella, knight and professor of theology (*c.* 1440–97). The bare bones of the story he tells is remarkably like that of Chaucer's *Troilus and Criseyde*, concerning a lover who finds that his lady is unfaithful to him. But unlike Chaucer's tale, and like the stories of Corella's Castilian namesake, Johan Rois, archpriest of Hita, in the *Libro de buen amor*, he tells the love story in the first person. The work exists in two manuscripts: one, the Mayans codex, devoted entirely to the works of Corella, was copied sometime before 1496; the other, a general anthology called *Jardinet de Orats* (*Garden of Madmen*), is dated 1486. In the former, the work is called *TRAGEDY: Explaining an Unfortunate Event That Happened to Him at the Hands of a Lady*; in the table of contents, it is listed simply as *The Tragedy*.[149] In the *Jardinet*, it is called *Tragedy of Caldesa Made by Mossèn Corella*,[150] identifying the lady of the tragedy with the woman addressed in two lyric works of Corella, *To Caldesa*, in the Mayans manuscript, and *Debate with Caldesa* in *Jardinet*.[151] I have not seen this identification with Caldesa questioned by any modern writer, but I think that it should be

---

[148] Gascón Vera argues for a Senecan influence as well on the consolatory aspect of Pedro's work. She notes that while the sense of serenity and acceptance at the end of the *Tragedia* fits the definition of comedy rather than tragedy, there is a similar relatively happy end, of Stoic resignation, in Seneca's tragedies (*Don Pedro*, p. 146).

[149] See the edition of Roiç de Corella by Josep Almiñana Vallés, *Obres de Joan Roiç de Corella*, vol. 1, [fol. o]: *La Tragedia*; and [fol. 37v]: *TRAGADIA* [sic] *rahonant un cas afortunat que ab una dama li s'esdevench*; the work is transcribed in 2:683–86. The *Obres* of Almiñana's title refers only to the works found in the Mayans MS, but sometimes, as with the Caldesa exchange mentioned below, he reproduces other works in his commentary. See also R. Miquel y Planas, ed., *Obres de J. Roiç de Corella*; Eliseu Climent, ed., *Obra profana*.

[150] Almiñana Vallés, ed., *Obres de Joan Roiç de Corella*, 1:14: *Tregedia* [sic] *de Caldesa feta per mossèn Corella*. See the reproduction of the first page of the text in Martín de Riquer, *Història de la literatura catalana*, *Part antiga*, 3:291. For the title "mossèn," see the discussion of Mossèn Gras below.

[151] Corella, *De mossèn Corella, per Caldesa* (Almiñana, *Obres*, 1: [fol. 135v] and 2:823); *Cobles de mossèn Corella a Caldesa; Resposta de Caldesa a mossèn Corella*; and *Replica mossèn Corella a Caldesa* (ibid., 2:592–95).

treated with caution, if only because of the differences in tone that are noticeable: he is quite cruel with Caldesa, whereas with the lady of the tragedy he is – even though devastated – ultimately compassionate. The nearly unanimous conclusion of scholars that the poems deal with events in his own life is also questionable.

Corella's tragedy is a short prose account, which he claims to be writing in great distress, of the discovery he has just made that his beloved has been unfaithful to him. In his extreme sorrow, he wonders if paper will let such a great crime be written on it, and he envisions the world destroying itself in apocalyptic upheavals. But finally, in a calmer mood, he starts to tell the story. It happened in Valencia, after Joan II succeeded to the throne in 1458 upon the death of his brother Alfonso the Magnanimous – who, in addition to being king of Aragon, was also Alfonso III of Valencia (these kings, of course, were two of the captives dealt with by Santillana in his *Comedieta*). Martín de Riquer argues that the event in question occurred in the second half of 1458 itself, and assumes that the tragedy was written immediately afterwards.[152] This would make it the work of a very young man – for it is certain that he could have been only eighteen or nineteen years old at that time, since his mother was still acting as his guardian *ex causa minoris etatis* in August of 1453.[153] Such wardship came to an end, for boys, at the age of fourteen, according to the rules of Roman civil procedure that had long been in force in Spain.[154]

Corella continues: a wonderful damsel of incomparable beauty finally accepted him after long service, and it would be a long history, he says, to recount the amorous talk that they had together. After some time in this blessed state, he came to her house one day, and she, after admitting him, told him that she was expecting another person, and that she would return shortly after finishing her business. She left him in a locked room, but failed to return in good time. As the greater part of this unlucky day

---

[152] Riquer, *Història*, 3:298, 316.

[153] *Ibid.*, p. 255. The document is quoted as reading ungrammatically, "ex causa minoris etate."

[154] See William Durant, *Speculum judiciale*, 1:251: book 1, title *De tutore*, section *Generaliter*, no. 14: The cure of a curator and the tutelage of a tutor end in the same way, if an orphan or a subadolescent has a curator as well as a tutor, and at the same time, namely, at the end of the twelfth year in a woman and at the end of the fourteenth year in a male ("Eisdem quoque modis cura finitur quibus tutela, si pupillus seu impubes habet curatorem, et eodem tempore, scilicet in duodecimo anno in muliere et in quatuordecimo anno in masculo"); see also 1:193, 290, 576, 677. Guardians were also assigned in certain cases to "adults" as well, ending when they reached twenty-five, or the end of adulthood, that is, adolescence (*ibid.*, 1:251–52, 255; 2:247), but not "because of minor age." Riquer, *Historia*, 3:256, speculates that such minority could extend to the age of twenty, and Almiñana, *Obres*, 2:396, to the age of twenty-five. I should note that the discussion of the ages of man cited by Almiñana as being in the decretals of Boniface VIII is actually from the ordinary gloss of John Andrew to Boniface's *Liber sextus*, Proem, ad v. *perfectus* (col. 6 of the Lyons 1606 edition of *Corpus juris canonici*). For the Archpriest of Hita's use of Durant's *Speculum* in the *Libro de buen amor*, see Kelly, *Canon Law and the Archpriest of Hita*.

("aquest egipçiach dia," line 47) passed, sad thoughts began to disturb him. He finally found a little window that looked out onto the patio of the house, and saw a man enter with an air of being expected. After waiting in agony while the rest of the day went by, he at last saw the man and his lady emerge together, she showing signs of great amorousness, and he bidding goodbye to her in a vulgar way, saying "Adeu sies, manyeta," giving the last syllable a lewd stress (70). She finally came to the room where he had been kept waiting, seeming greatly apologetic for the delay. She had tried to remove the color and heat of the battle of Venus from herself with cold water, and she feigned joy to see him. But she looked soiled, as if a person with dirty hands had handled red roses and white lilies, "for the person of the gallant who had reposed with her was far different from the delicate nature of so tender a damsel" (86–88). As she made her excuses, he spoke, in extreme sorrow, with eyes on the ground, and told her that the world would convulse and the moon turn to blood if he ever served her again, and he would be torn limb from limb if God ever permitted his eyes to see her again (his direct speech is in blank verse, lines 97–124).

The "inclita senyora" realized at once from the doleful style of his words that he knew the truth, and she immediately began to weep and admit her great guilt, telling him (also in blank verse) that there was no punishment in hell severe enough for it. Death would be sweet if she could only die in his arms, and, if she lived, she would wash his feet with tears like Magdalen (129–42). The author says: "If it be folly to begin what is impossible to finish, it would be madness to try to write down the different emotions that warred in my dolorous thoughts after hearing her reply with such humble words!" (143–45). He wished that he could drink of the river of Lethe and forget the past. Filled with such "impossible sentiments," he left the room, or rather the tomb, where he had suffered such pain. "Taking up the pen, which often dispels grief, I write this present account, which is stained with my own blood, for the color of the ink matches the color of the sorrow that speaks" (154–56). Thus ends the tragedy.

This very moving work is not matched or approximated by any of Corella's other works. Since he does not actually use the word "tragedy" in it, we are left to decide its precise meaning for ourselves. It is quite clear that the term connotes sorrow, but does it signify primarily a narrative mode of the Chaucerian kind, or a French-like lyric mode, as with Pedro of Portugal? Corella composed a number of narratives of classical disasters, mainly derived from Ovid, which one might expect to be associated with tragedy: there is the *Dolorous Complaint of Queen Hecuba*, which contains a denunciation of Fortune and her restless wheel;[155] *The History of Leander and Hero*;[156] *The Garden of Love*, set in Pluto's kingdom, where Corella hears devotees of Venus recount their misfortunes, beginning with Myrrha: the *Lamentation of Myrrha*, also called a "complaint" ("plant"), and followed by the self-accounts of Narcissus and Thisbe;[157] a similar *Lamentation of Byblis*;[158] a letter written by Medea to ladies about the ingratitude of Jason, to give them an example of honest living: which ends not with any summing up of wisdom for her designated addressees, but rather with her vicious malediction of Jason after she cuts off her children's heads and throws them at him;[159] the record of a gathering held in the house of Berenguer Mercades, where Corella serves as the scribe for the "historial poesies" in prose told by some noble men of Valencia: namely, the sad Ovidian stories of Cephalus and Procris, Orpheus, Scylla (daughter of Nisus), Pasiphaë, and Procne and Philomela;[160] and the *Feigned Letter that Achilles Wrote to Polyxena in the Siege of Troy after the Death of Hector* and Polyxena's letter of response, in which she sees the gods as envious of Troy's prosperity and as bringing adverse fortune upon it at the hands of Achilles and the other Greeks.[161] But he uses the word tragedy only in *The Judgment of Paris*, which consists of, first, a letter to him by Johan Escriva telling the classical story and asking Corella for an allegorical interpretation; and second, Corella's response.[162] Corella agrees to explain the allegory, or more properly the tropology or moral significance, of this poetic fiction in his humble style, noting that most of his time is spent in the study of sacred theology and the writing of sermons (lines 284–89).[163] In choosing Venus, Paris in effect chose carnal delight, with dreadful results. He took the beautiful Helen with him to Troy, "and, as a result, even to the present day among all the living, all nations speak in sorrow, with tragedy sad beyond all things, of the misery and cruel destruction of Troy" ("per la

---

[155] Corella, *Plant doloros de la reyna Ecuba*; Almiñana, *Obres*, 2:630–37; for the reference to Fortune, see lines 248–54. It has been suggested that he was drawing not only on *Metamorphoses* 13 for this piece, but also on the Catalan translation of Guido's *Historia destructionis Troje* (see Almiñana, *Obres*, 2:439). Joan Ruiz i Calonja, *Història de la literatura catalana*, p. 198, states that the piece is based on Seneca's *Troades*, but he does not support the claim.

[156] Corella, *La istoria de Leander y Hero*, *Obres*, 2:668–81.

[157] Corella, *Lo Jardi de Amor*, *Obres*, 2:703–15; *Lamentacio de Mirra*, p. 703; "lo plant de Mirra," p. 708.

[158] Corella, *Lamentacio de Biblis*, *Obres*, 2:716–19.

[159] Corella, *Escriu Medea a les dones la ingratitut e desconeixença de Jeson, per dar-los exemple de honestament viure*, *Obres*, 2:720–35.

[160] Corella, *Parlament ho collacio que s'esdevench en casa de Berenguer Mercader*, *Obres*, 2:736–59.

[161] Corella, *Letra fengida que Achilles escriu a Policena, in lo setge de Troya, apres mort Hector*, *Obres*, 2:760–62.

[162] Corella, *Lo johi de Paris*, *Obres*, 2:763–74.

[163] Corella is mentioned as a master in theology as early as 1469 (Almiñana, *Obres*, 2:398). Corella explains here that the allegorical sense deals with natural philosophy, the tropological with moral philosophy, and the anagogical with theology (lines 291–95).

qual, encara de present, entre tots los vivents, per tragedia sobre totes trista, de la miseria e cruel destrucçio de Troya totes les nacions ab dolor parlen," lines 413–14). From the context, "tragedy" here would seem to signify not a history of disaster, but rather a style of lamenting over disaster – therefore, to answer our question posed above, a lyric rather than a narrative genre. Presumably, however, Corella would know at least about Dante's use of comedy as a narrative genre, for just before making the above comment he refers to the last canto of the *Inferno*, noting that "lo poeta florenti" put Brutus and Judas in the center of hell (lines 378–80). We can only surmise what he made of Vergil's reference to his own high tragedy in canto 20.

The third tragedy to be considered, is, like the other two, *sui generis*. Like Corella's, it was written in Catalan, namely, the *Tragedy Composed by Mossèn Gras, Which is Part of the Great Work of the Deeds of the Famous Knight Lancelot del Lac, in Which is Clearly Shown How Much Harm Jealousies Cause in Affairs of Love, and How Nothing Can Deter Those Who Truly Love*. It was published in Barcelona in 1496, but only nine folios near the beginning survive.[164] It was dedicated to the count of Ischia (the island near Naples), and since it deals with a theme popular towards the end of the reign of Alfonso the Magnanimous, it may come from around the last years of that monarch's life. Nothing is known about Gras. The title *mossèn*, the Catalan equivalent of *monsieur* or *monsignor*, as used at this time, indicates that he was a knight; he may have been Lluís Gras, whose works are mentioned alongside a work of Corella's in an inventory of 1485, who in turn may have been the ambassador of that name sent to Tunis in 1444 and 1445.[165] The work begins with the episode at the start of the French prose *Mort Artu*, in which Lancelot appears in the tourney at Winchester wearing the sleeve of the maid of Escalot, and Queen Guenevere, on hearing about it from Gawain, furiously banishes Lancelot from her. The grieving author delivers an exclamation about the harms, perils, and anguish that love causes by reason of such scornful acts and mistreatment of lovers.[166] The story proceeds with the incident of the poisoned apple, in which the queen is falsely accused of murder, when it breaks off. The *Mort Artu*, of course, goes on to

---

[164] *Tragèdia ordenade per mossèn Gras, la qual és part de la gran obra dels actes del famós cavaller Lançalot del Lac, en la qual se mostra clarament quant les solàsias* [sic, for *gelòsias*?] *in les coses de amor danyen, e com als qui vertaderament amen ninguna cosa los desobliga*, ed. Martín de Riquer, text on pp. 131–39. The recto sides of fol. 1 (the first of three marked a iij) and fol. 7 (marked b j), designated as pp. 1 and 13 by Riquer, are reproduced by Francisco Vindel, *El arte tipográfico en España durante el siglo XV*, pp. 195–96.

[165] Jorge Rubió Balaguer, "Lituratura catalana," p. 851; Riquer, "La *Tragèdia*," p. 117.

[166] Gras, *Tragèdia*, chap. 9, rubric: "Exclamació que fa lo actor dolent-se dels dans, perills, e congoxes que amor se procura per causa de aquests desdenys, e mal tractes que als enamo[rats] ..." A folio is missing at this point, taking with it the rest of the rubric and Gras's entire outburst. The tragedy resumes on p. 13, sig. b j, noted above.

show that the love of Lancelot and Guenevere was a major factor in the destruction of the Arthurian realm, but Gras cannot have continued his tragedy to that point, since his purpose was not to condemn their love, but rather to condemn the obstacles put in its way by Guenevere's unfounded suspicions.

Riquer assumes that Gras was imitating Corella in choosing *Tragedy* for his title.[167] But since the title speaks of Gras in the third person, and since the text was apparently published a generation after it was written, it is possible that the designation of tragedy was not Gras's but the printer's. However, there may be indications in the text that Gras knew of one or more definitions of narrative tragedy, namely, the prosperity-to-adversity paradigm of Conches–Trevet–Chaucer, and the joy-to-sadness variant of Osbern–Huguccio–Pietro Alighieri.[168] When Lancelot withdraws to a hermitage to try to ease the pain of his separation from Guenevere, Gras tells us: "How often did there come to his mind his past prosperity and present misery!" ("Quants voltes ach conexença de sa passada prosperitat e present misèria," chap. 11). Meanwhile, in Arthur's court, "fickle Fortune, envious of all good fortune, not content with having made the queen sad from having been joyful" ("la vària Fortuna, de tot benaventurat envejosa, no contenta de haver fet la reyna de joyosa trista"), prepared the greatest evil that she could for her (chap. 12), namely, her condemnation to death.

But Gras clearly did not end his tragedy by leaving his protagonists in their states of wretchedness, as the above-noted formulas dictated. The title itself indicates a situation in which Lancelot suffers much but remains true, with hope of future resolution. Moreover, in his dedicatory letter, Gras tells the count of Ischia, who was no doubt Johan de Torrelles, brother-in-law of King Alfonso's mistress, Lucrezia,[169] that he wanted to use Lancelot and Guenevere as examples to lovers of his own time, not only to show the harm that can come from a too-ready belief in false reports, but also to demonstrate how a faithful lover in continuing to serve a beloved who has wronged him, as Lancelot did in rescuing the queen, can expect not only reconciliation, but a "new and more fervent union than the first" ("nova e més fervent unió que la primera").

If the tragedy did in fact end with Lancelot's championing of the queen against the knight who had accused her, and the subsequent passionate reunion of the two lovers, it would be more like a Conchian comedy than a tragedy, beginning in adversity and ending in prosperity. But we can

---

[167] Riquer, *Història*, 3.295.

[168] See Kelly, *Tragedy and Comedy*, Index under "tragedy," pp. 132–33, and also the Index below, for various formulas of tragedy.

[169] Riquer, "La *Tragèdia*," pp. 115–17: there are references to him between the years 1452 and 1472.

conjecture, with Riquer, that the happy reconciliation of Lancelot and Guenevere, even though the climax and exemplary heart of the work, was followed by a summary account of later events leading up to their parting, with a brief mention of their deaths.[170] Gras summarizes such a conclusion in his letter to the count, by speaking of "the persevering charity of the two reconciled lovers, which, beyond the ultimate and forced separation of their dear persons, but not of their wills, remained and endured to the end of their lives" ("la perseverada caritat dels dos reconsiliats amats, que ultra la última e forçada separació de les cares persones, no dels volers, se estès e fins a la fi de la vida perdurà"). This is the sort of ending that Troilus would have been only too content with if he had discovered that the signs and reports of Criseyde's unfaithfulness were unfounded – as in fact is the case in Dryden's version of the tragedy – even if there was still no hope of her ever returning to him.[171]

As was to be expected, the sporadic tragedies written in Spain and elsewhere in the fourteenth and fifteenth centuries come close to matching in inventiveness the wide variety of earlier ideas about the nature and forms of tragedy.

---

[170] *Ibid.*, 125. Riquer estimates that we possess 60 percent of the work (including the missing folio), counting from the first chapter, that is, twenty pages, and that therefore another twelve pages are missing at the end.

[171] See John Dryden's revision of Shakespeare's *Troilus and Cressida*, which he subtitled *Truth Found Too Late*. Dryden, of course, as his title indicates, does not have a qualified happy ending of this sort, but has Cressida kill herself before Troilus finds out the truth of her constancy. See Sergio Rufini, " 'To Make that Maxim Good': Dryden's Shakespeare," pp. 243–80.

Conclusion

Nowadays "tragedy" is one of those words that everyone thinks everyone else knows about and has always known. That is to say, it is commonly thought that the term conjures up a fairly uniform idea, an idea that has been relatively constant throughout the ages, give or take various refinements of theory. I trust that the above history of the word has shaken this belief. We have seen that in ancient Greece tragedies could, and often did, end happily, and that this eventuality was integrally incorporated into the analysis of Aristotle, who produced the first poetics and critique of tragedy (to use Lubomír Doležel's distinction between descriptive and prescriptive accounts):[1] Euripides's fortunately resolved *Iphigenia Among the Taurians* vies with Sophocles's disaster-bound *Oedipus the King* for his choice of all-time best tragedy. The conclusion in irretrievable misfortune came to dominate and control the semantic field of tragedy in later antique times, when tragedy took various forms on and off the stage, and in applications to events or characteristics perceived as belonging to "the tragedy of life." But it could stand for bombast as well as disaster, and happy endings could still be seen in practice: Dracontius's *Tragedy of Orestes* ends with as tranquil a resolution as Aeschylus's *Oresteia*. The *exitus tristes* of Diomedes, moreover, did not have to end in total disaster for the protagonist: there could be a pyrrhic victory or even a triumph of revenge, as in Seneca's *Medea*.

In the early Middle Ages, dramatic and literary tragedy was lost to sight, and with it went the metaphor of tragedy. A great range of meanings was produced by etymological or "archeological" guesswork from the shards of tragedy that were to be found in various writings – for instance, the references to *tragediarum clamor* and *tragicus* in Boethius's *Consolation of Philosophy* – and in the remains of the Roman theaters. Isidore of Seville in his second try at defining tragedy and comedy said that tragedies were mournful poems dealing with the crimes of wicked kings – which is not a

---

[1] Lubomír Doležel, *Occidental Poetics: Tradition and Progress*, p. vii.

bad summing up of many tragedies, notably Seneca's, though Huguccio's later characterization of family crimes is even better. Isidore had the advantage of being able to see where tragedies were performed, and he concluded from what evidence he had that they were recited on the stage by the poets themselves while silent actors illustrated the words by gestures. In the twelfth century, John of Salisbury achieved a rare understanding of ancient tragedy and its figurative usage, but others for the most part produced creative mixtures of authentic classical echoes and postclassical distortions. Aristotle's *Poetics* came on the scene in the thirteenth century, but only in its Averroistic metamorphosis, according to which tragedy was assigned the praise half of the rhetorical praise–blame function. An important development came at the turn of the fourteenth century with the recovery, in some limited circles, of actual Roman tragedies, the ten Senecan plays. But even for those who read and mastered these plays, the mysteries and distortions surrounding the word "tragedy" were not completely dissolved, and, of course, for those who only encountered excerpts in florilegia or who only heard of the titles, or who did not hear of them at all, other meanings continued to hold sway and multiply. Dante and his commentators provide interesting examples. Dante himself was not acquainted with Senecan tragedy, and he accepted a stylistic idea of the term, according to which he "retrofitted" his own and others' love lyrics as tragedies, and also classified Vergil's *Aeneid* as such. Some of the commentaries on his *Comedy*, including the spurious *Epistle to Cangrande*, do refer to Seneca's tragedies, and characterize them as having not only disastrous endings (which is true of most), but also joyful or tranquil beginnings (which is not true of any of the plays). Only Pietro Alighieri shows any knowledge of an acted, or actable, dimension to the tragedies, but it is the Isidorian idea, via Nicholas Trevet, of "dumbshow with voice-over." Other commentators remained completely in the dark about the form of the tragedies as stage-plays, and the same holds for Albertino Mussato, who took the momentous step of writing an imitation of Senecan tragedy. French authors of the fourteenth century were like Dante in not knowing about Seneca, but unlike him, some of them – Mézières, at least, and the author of a tragedy on the capture of King John, and perhaps Deschamps – accepted tragedy as a mood rather than a style, and applied the term to poems or discourses of complaint.

It has been alleged by a scholar who believes that tragedy was a common genre in the Middle Ages that, since Boethius's dialogue was widely read and vastly influential, "the medieval writer and his audience understood a concept of tragedy" in a highly philosophical sense; that is, "to the right-thinking flawless hero . . . and to the right-thinking audience, tragedy cannot lie in loss of earthly goods or position or even in death."[2] This is an extreme, but nevertheless typical, example of overreading medieval texts in terms of modern generic ideas about "the tragic."

As I noted in the Preface, this study has been designed as an antidote to such overreadings by concentrating not on abstract definitions of the ideal tragedy or the tragic spirit and its manifestations in literature (whether under the name of tragedy or not), but rather by giving a history of the word "tragedy": the various ideas that the term gave rise to, and the "things" that were designated by the term. I have been less interested in the accurate recovery of ancient ideas by the Middle Ages than in the new combinations of ideas that were produced by confused traditions. As can be readily deduced from what I have just said about Seneca, it has not been my purpose to trace the recovery of his plays so much as to see how peculiarly medieval notions prevented an accurate understanding of them.

Even if Mussato had produced a work of literary merit, it would be of less interest to my enterprise (given my initial premises) than the creation or invention of a new kind of tragedy. We have found very few instances of authors who thought of themselves as writing tragedy in a way not practiced by the ancients. There were William of Blois, John of Garland, and Dante (after the fact), and we observed some signs among the French poets a little later than Chaucer. We do not know whether William of Blois considered himself unique or original in composing a tragedy, or whether others of his age produced what they called tragedies. But knowledge of the word was fairly widespread in the twelfth century, and we do know that Otto of Freising thought of himself as writing "in the manner of tragedy." Others, perhaps including Matthew of Vendôme, may have thought of themselves as writing in tragic style; and certainly some authors did think of other contemporary writers as having written tragedies – including, it seems, Arthurian stories of heroic suffering. John of Garland, however, looked upon tragedy as an empty genre: only one author, namely Ovid, had acted upon the definition and written a tragedy, and that was lost. By composing another himself, Garland brought the form up to its previous numerical strength.

At the end of the fourteenth century, a number of significant regional varieties of tragedy emerged. The most important occurred in England, because Chaucer's experiments with tragedy led directly to Shakespeare. In France, various ideas of tragedy had been introduced in translations and adaptations of Boethius and Aristotle, but the only forms of tragedy that emerged were lamentations. In Italy, a few humanist tragedies on classical

---

[2] Robert M. Lumiansky, "The Alliterative *Morte Arthure*, the Concept of Medieval Tragedy, and the Cardinal Virtue Fortitude," pp. 98–101.

themes were produced at the end of the fourteenth century and during the fifteenth, with Seneca's examples in mind. Seneca became well known in Spain in the fifteenth century, but the actual tragedies that were composed there were of quite different forms.

We must conclude that in spite of the currency of ideas of tragedy in the fourteenth and fifteenth centuries, even where Seneca's tragedies were known, there was little impulse to contribute original compositions to a genre of tragedy – the above-noted exceptions proving the rule – and little generic idea of "the tragic," in the sense of exemplifying a typical emotion or reaction of tragedy (however understood). There were recognized literary genres in the Middle Ages dealing with disaster and death, notably lives of famous men, lives of the saints, cautionary exempla, and complaints. But the first three of these genres concentrated on praising or blaming the victims or perpetrators, while the fourth normally stressed the author's own loss and eliminated any story element. There was no generic demand for the sort of empathetic sorrow for the disasters of others that both Aristotle and Chaucer required of tragedy. Such expressions of sorrow can be found, of course – though sad stories are not very abundant in the Middle Ages – but they are "tropic" rather than generic.

The widest used such expression of sorrow was the soulless trope of personified chance, the figure of Fortune. Most of the ideas and emotions that were to become connected with "tragedy" and "tragic" in the sixteenth century were to be found in varying degrees in the conceit of the "mistress" or "goddess" of good and bad luck. Nowadays most readers find references to Fortune completely lacking in inspiration and the very opposite of empathetic; and though the convention could not have been nearly so deadly in the Middle Ages, it was such an easy and overworked poetic ploy, and one so devoid of any personal considerations, that Boredom must have been Fortune's frequent companion. This was the experience of the Host of Chaucer's pilgrimage on hearing the Monk's tragedies, where Fortune is all too often the leading lady, but not the experience of the Knight, who found the accounts moving – too moving – and depressing. But neither of these characters, and not Chaucer himself, could have realized that he had hit upon a new way to reconstitute the old soporifics of lamentation over misfortunes and to put them into a new/old category that has retained its vitality to the present. Chaucer could have found his primary inspiration of a plot-based genre in the figure of Fortune's wheel, which was introduced by Boethius and had received an extensive development in medieval literature. But instead, he was inspired by Fortune's reference to the genre of tragedy and a definition that limited it to movements from prosperity to adversity. This definition was fitted to the downward arc of Fortune's wheel, and comedy to the upward arc; but the step was not taken, at least consciously, of accommodating tragedy to the entire fortunal cycle of rising from obscurity or wretchedness to prosperity, and then falling back to an unprosperous condition. The genre's victory over the trope remained secure until the genre was invincible and a permanent part of our mentality, while Fortune has disappeared below the horizon. O Fortune, where is thy sting? Sad to say, tragedy, the chronicle of ever occurring disasters, remains with us. But the best-expressed tragedies have given us much solace and comfort.

Bibliography

PRIMARY SOURCES

Abelard, *Theologia christiana*, PL 178.

Abu Bishr Matta, Arabic trans. of Aristotle's *Poetics*, ed., with Latin trans., Jaroslaw Tkatsch, rev. A. Grudeman and T. Seif, *Die arabische Übersetzung der Poetik des Aristoteles und die Grundlage der Kritik des griechischen Textes*, 2 vols. (Vienna, 1928–32).

Accessus ad auctores, ed. Huygens, *Accessus ad auctores*, pp. 9–54.

Accursius, *Glossa ordinaria in Corpus juris civilis*, 5 vols. (Lyons 1550).

Acron, Pseudo-, *Pseudacronis scholia in Horatium vetustiora*, ed. Otto Keller, 2 vols. (Leipzig, 1902–04); ed. Hauthal, see Scholia in Horatium, Gamma Scholiast.

Aelred of Rievaulx, *Speculum caritatis*, ed. A. Hoste and C. H. Talbot, *Aelredi Rievallensis opera omnia*, vol. 1: *Opera ascetica*, CCM 1 (1971).

Albert the Great, *Opera omnia*, ed. Auguste Borgnet, 38 vols. (Paris 1890–99).

Aldhelm, *De metris et enigmatibus*, MGH Auctores antiquissimi 15.

Alemannus, Herman, see Averroes.

Alighieri, Dante, see Dante.

Alighieri, Jacopo, *Chiose alla cantica dell'Inferno*, ed. Jarro (Florence 1915).

Alighieri, Pietro, *Petri Allegherii super Dantis ipsius genitoris Comediam commentarium*, ed. Vincenzo Nannucci (Florence 1845) (the reprint in *Il "Commentarium" di Pietro Alighieri nelle redazioni ashburnhamiana e ottoboniana*, intro. Egidio Guidubaldi [Florence 1978], has serious omissions and distortions, and should not be used).

Andrew, John, *Glossa ordinaria in Librum sextum Bonifacii octavi* in *Corpus juris canonici*, 3 vols. (Lyons 1606), vol. 3, part 1.

Anonymous of Florence, *Commento alla Divina commedia d'Anonimo Fiorentino del secolo XIV*, ed. Pietro Fanfani, 3 vols. (Bologna 1866–74).

Anonymous Latin Commentary on Dante's Commedia: Reconstructed Text, ed. Vincenzo Cioffari (Spoleto 1989).

Anthologia latina, vol. 1, part 1, ed. Alexander Riese (Leipzig 1894), new edition ed. D. R. Shakelton Bailey (Stuttgart 1982); part 2, ed. Riese (Leipzig 1906).

Apuleius, *Metamorphoses (The Golden Ass)*, LCL.

Aquinas, Thomas, *Opera omnia*, 24 vols. (Parma 1852–73).

   In *octo libros Physicorum Aristotelis expositio*, Marietti edition, ed. P. M. Maggiòlo (Turin 1954).

Bibliography

Opera omnia, Leonine edition (incomplete): vol. 47.2: *Sententia libri Ethicorum (Commentarium in Ethica nichomachea)* (Rome 1969); vol. 48, *Sententia libri Politicorum* (Rome 1971).

Opera omnia, ed. Roberto Busa, *Supplementum* to the *Index thomisticus (ITS)*, 7 vols. (Stuttgart 1980).

Aquinas, Pseudo-, *Commentum super librio Boethii de consolacione*, in Aquinas, *Opera omnia*, Parma, 24:1–147; *ITS* 7:121–72.

Super Apocalypsim, see Hugh of St. Cher.

Arderne, John, *Practica*, Bethesda, National Library of Medicine MS acc. no. 146304.

Aristotle, *Poetics* (Greek text), ed. D. W. Lucas (Oxford 1968); Latin translation by William of Moerbeke, ed. Lorenzo Minio-Paluello, *De arte poetica*, Aristoteles latinus 33, ed. 2 (Brussels 1968); English translation, tr. Stephen Halliwell, *The Poetics of Aristotle: Translation and Commentary* (London and Chapel Hill 1987).

Ethica nicomachea, medieval translations, ed. René Antoine Gautier, Aristoteles latinus 26.1.3, 5 vols. (Leiden 1972–74): vol. 2 *Translatio Antiguior*; vol. 3, Robert Grosseteste's *Recensio pura*.

Metaphysica, Translatio Anonyma sive Media, ed. Gudrun Vuillemin-Diem, Aristoteles latinus 25.2 (Leiden 1976).

Rhetorica, Translatio Anonyma sive Vetus et Translatio Guillelmi de Moerbeka, ed. Bernhard Schneider, Aristoteles latinus 31.1.2 (Leiden 1978).

Armonio Marso, Giovanni, *Stephanium, Ioannis Harmonii Marsi comoedia Stephanium*, ed. and tr. Walther Ludwig (Munich 1971); ed. and tr. Graziella Gentilini, *Il teatro umanistico veneto: La commedia* (Ravenna 1983).

Tragedia de rebus italicis deque triumpho Ludovici christianissimi regis, ed. Gilbert Tournoy, *Iohannis Harmonii Marsi de rebus italicis deque triumpho Ludovici XII regis Francorum tragoedia* (Louvain 1978).

Atkinson, J. K., *see* Boethius.

Augustine, *Confessions*, LCL.

De civitate Dei, LCL; French translation by Raoul de Praelles, *Cité de Dieu*, excerpts in Millard Meiss *et al.*, *French Painting in the Time of Jean de Berry*, part 2: *The Limbourgs and Their Contemporaries*, 2 vols. (New York 1974), 1:442 n. 204.

De doctrina christiana, CSEL 80.

De ordine, CSEL 63.

Soliloquia, PL 32.

Augustine, Pseudo-, *De symbolo*, see Quodvultdeus.

Sermones suppositicii, PL 39.

Averroes, *Middle Commentary on Aristotle's Poetics*, Latin translation by Herman Alemannus, critical edition, *Averrois Cordubensis Commentarium medium in Aristotelis Poetriam*, ed. William Franklin Boggess (University of North Carolina diss., 1965; available from Xerox University Microfilms, Ann Arbor, Michigan); edition from 5 MSS: ed. Minio-Paluello in Aristotle, *De arte poetica*, pp. 39–74; English translation by O. B. Hardison in *Classical and Medieval Literary Criticism*, ed. Alex Preminger *et al.* (New York 1974);

Bibliography

excerpts in English translation in A. J. Minnis and A. B. Scott, *Medieval Literary Theory and Criticism, c. 100–c. 1375: The Commentary Tradition* (Oxford 1988; rev. ed. 1991), pp. 289–307.

Middle Commentary on Aristotle's Poetics, English translation of Arabic text, tr. Charles E. Butterworth, *Averroes' Middle Commentary on Aristotle's Poetics* (Princeton 1986).

Avicenna, *Poetics Commentary*, tr. Ismail M. Dahiyat, *Avicenna's Commentary on the Poetics of Aristotle* (Leiden 1974).

Babio, ed. and tr. Andrea Dessì Fulgheri, in F. Bertini, general ed., *Commedie latine*, 2:129–301.

Balbus Januensis, John, *Catholicon* (Mainz 1460, repr. Farnborough, Hants. 1971).

Baldwin, William, *et al.*, *A Mirror for Magistrates*, ed. Lily Bess Campbell, *The Mirror for Magistrates* (Cambridge 1938); includes editions of 1549–87.

Bambaglioli, Graziolo de', *Il commento dantesco*, ed. Antonio Fiammazzo (Savona 1915).

Bartholomew of Bruges, *Brevis expositio super Poetriam Aristotelis*, Paris, Bibliothèque Nationale MS lat. 16089; excerpts in Gilbert Dahan, "Notes et textes sur la poétique au moyen âge," pp. 223–39; and H. A. Kelly, "Aristotle–Averroes–Alemannus," pp. 179–81.

Bede, *De arte metrica*, ed. H. Keil, *Grammatici latini*, vol. 7.

Benvenuto da Imola, *Comentum super Dantis Aldigherij Comoediam*, final version of his commentary, ed. James Philip Lacaita, 5 vols. (Florence 1887).

Berengar of Poitiers, *Apologia*, ed. R. M. Thomson, "The Satirical Works of Berengar of Poitiers: An Edition with Introduction," *Mediaeval Studies* 42 (1980) 89–138.

Bernard of Cluny, *De contemptu mundi*, ed. H. C. Hoskier (London 1929).

Bernard of Utrecht, *Commentum in Theodulum*, ed. Huygens, *Accessus ad auctores*, pp. 55–69.

Bertini, Ferruccio, general ed., *Commedie latine del XII e XIII secolo*, 6 vols. (Genoa 1976–).

Boccaccio, Giovanni, *Tutte le opere*, gen. ed. Vittore Branca, 12 vols. (Milan 1964–).

De casibus virorum illustrium, first version (*c.* 1356–73), facsimile of the 1520 Paris edition, ed. Lewis Brewer Hall (Gainesville 1962); second version, *c.* 1374, ed. Pier Giorgio Ricci and Vittorio Zaccaria, *Tutte le opere*, vol. 9 (1983).

Boethius, *Contra Eutychen et Nestorium (De duabus naturis, De Trinitate)*; *De consolatione Philosophiae*: *The Theological Tractates*; *The Consolation of Philosophy*, LCL.

Medieval versions of *De consolatione Philosophiae*: 1st French translation (Burgundian, early thirteenth century), ed. Margaret Bolton-Hall, *A Critical Edition of the Medieval French Prose Translation and Commentary of De consolatione Philosophiae of Boethius Contained in MS 2642 of the National Library of Austria, Vienna* (University of Queensland diss., 1990); 2nd French translation (Hainault, late thirteenth century), ed. J. K. Atkinson, *A Critical Edition of the Medieval French Prose Translation of the De consolatione Philosophiae of Boethius Contained in MS 898 of the Bibliothèque Municipale, Troyes*, 3 vols. (University of

Bibliography

Queensland diss., 1976); 5th French translation, by Jean de Meun, ed. V. L. Dedeck-Héry, "Boethius' *De consolatione* by Jean de Meun," *Mediaeval Studies* 14 (1952) 165–275; 7th French translation, Sydney, Sydney University MS Nicholson 7 (fifteenth century); for details of other French translations, see chap. 5 above; German translation by Notker Labeo, *Boethius de consolatione Philosophiae*, ed. E. H. Sehrt and Taylor Starck, *Notkers des Deutschen Werke*, vol. 1 (Halle 1933–34); new ed. by Petrus W. Tax (Tübingen 1986–90). Latin text and glosses and Chaucer's *Boece*, Cambridge, Cambridge University Library MS Ii 3.21, ed. Edmund Taite Silk, *Cambridge MS Ii.3.21 and the Relation of Chaucer's Boethius to Trivet and Jean de Meung* (Yale University diss., 1930; Ann Arbor, Xerox University Microfilms, cat. no. 70–23051–02800).

Brito, William, *Summa Britonis, sive Guillelmi Britonis Expositiones vocabulorum Biblie*, ed. Lloyd W. Daly and Bernardine H. Daly, 2 vols. (Padua 1975).

Brito metricus: A Mediaeval Verse Treatise on Greek and Hebrew Words, ed. Lloyd W. Daly (Philadelphia 1978).

Buti, Francesco da, *Commento sopra la Divina commedia*, ed. Crescentino Giannini, 3 vols. (Pisa 1858–62).

Accessus in Terentium, ed. Gian Carlo Alessio, "Hec Franciscus de Buiti," *Italia medioevale e umanistica* 24 (1984) 64–122, esp. 109–16.

Cato (Pseudo-), *Nomina Musarum* (incipit: "Clio gesta canens transactis tempora reddit"), *Minor Latin Poems*, LCL (1935), p. 634; *Anthologia latina*, part 1, 1:134 (no. 664); MGH Auctores antiquissimi, 5.2-251–52.

Chaucer, Geoffrey, *The Riverside Chaucer*, general ed. Larry D. Benson (Boston 1987); for the *Boece*, see also under Boethius.

Christine de Pisan, *Le livre du corps de policie*, ed. Robert H. Lucas (Geneva 1967); fifteenth-century English translation, ed. Diane Bornstein, *The Middle English Translation of Christine de Pisan's Livre du corps de policie* (Heidelberg 1977).

Christus patiens, PG 38:131–38.

Chrysostom, John, *Commentary on Matthew*, PG 58.

Cohen, Gustave, general ed., *La "comédie" latine en France au XII siècle*, 2 vols. (Paris 1931).

Commentum einsidlense in Donati Artem majorem, ed. Hermann Hagen, *Anecdota helvetica quae ad grammaticam latinam spectant*, a supplementary volume to Keil, *Grammatici latini*, vol. 7, pp. 202–66.

Conrad of Hirsau, *Dialogus super auctores*, ed. Huygens, *Accessus ad auctores*, pp. 71–131.

Correr, Gregorio, *Progne*, ed. Laura Casarsa, in Zaccaria and Casarsa, *Il teatro umanistico veneto*, pp. 97–174, with the Italian translation of Ludovico Domenichi (1561), pp. 183–236.

Councils and Ecclesiastical Documents Relating to Great Britain and Ireland, ed. Arthur West Haddan and William Stubbs, 3 vols. (Oxford 1869–78).

Dante, *Monarchia*, ed. Pier Giorgio Ricci (Milan 1965); ed. Pio Gaia in *Opere minori di Dante Alighieri*, vol. 2 (Turin 1986).

Le opere di Dante, testo critico della Società dantesca italiana (Florence 1921).

Dante, Pseudo-, *Epistola ad Canem Grandem*, ed. Giorgio Brugnoli in P. V. Mengaldo *et al.*, eds., Dante, *Opere minori* (Florence 1979), 2:512–21,

226

Bibliography

598–643; ed. Kelly, *Tragedy and Comedy from Dante to Pseudo-Dante*, pp. 102–11.

Dati, Leonardo, *Hiensal*, ed. J. R. Berrigan, "Leonardo Dati, *Hiensal Tragoedia*: A Critical Edition with Translation," *Humanistica lovaniensia* 25 (1976) 84–145.

Deschamps, Eustace, *Oeuvres complètes*, ed. Auguste Queux de Saint Hilaire (vols. 1–6) and Gaston Raynaud (vols. 7–11) (Paris 1878–1903).

Dio Cassius, *Roman History*, LCL.

Diomedes, *Ars grammatica*, ed. H. Keil, *Grammatici latini*, vol. 1.

Donatus, Aelius, *Aeli Donati Commentum Terenti*, ed. Paulus Wessner, 2 vols. (Leipzig 1902–05, repr. Stuttgart 1963–66).

Dracontius, Blossius Aemilius, *Opera*, ed. Friedrich Vollmer, MGH Auctores antiquissimi 14 (1905).

Orestis tragoedia, ed. Emanuele Rapisarda, *La tragedia di Oreste* (Catania 1951).

Dryden, John, *Troilus and Cressida; or, Truth Found Too Late*, ed. Maximilian E. Novak, George R. Guffey, and Alan Roper, *The Works of John Dryden*, vol. 13 (Berkeley 1984).

Durant, William, *Speculum judiciale*, 2 vols. (Basel 1574, repr. Aalen 1975).

Ekkehard of Aura, *Chronicon universale*, MGH Scriptores 6.

Ekkehard of St. Gall IV, *Casus Sancti Galli*, MGH Scriptores 2.

Ennodius, Magnus Felix, *Opera*, ed. Friedrich Vogel, MGH Auctores antiquissimi 7 (Berlin 1885).

Erfurt Anonymous (twelfth century), *In Boethii Consolationem commentarius*, ed. Edmund Taite Silk, *Saeculi noni auctoris in Boetii Consolationem Philosophiae commentarius* (Rome 1935).

Eugenius Vulgarius, *Sylloga*, ed. Paulus von Winterfeld, MGH Poetae 4 (1989).

Euripides, *Tragedies*, LCL.

Eusebius, *Historia ecclesiastica* (PG 20); ed. Theodore Mommsen, *Eusebius Werke*, vol. 2, part 1, Griechischen christlichen Schriftsteller 9.1 (Leipzig 1903).

Evanthius (Evanzio), *De fabula*, ed. Giovanni Cupaiuolo (Naples 1979).

Expositio in Terentium (Commentarius recentior), partially edited in *Scholia terentiana*, ed. Schlee, pp. 163–74.

Fabriano, Lodovico da, *De casu Cesene*, ed. G. Gori, "*De eccidio urbis Caesenae anonimi auctoris coaevi comoedia:* L'eccidio di Cesena del 1377, atto recitabili di anonimo scrittore coetaneo," *Archivio storico italiano*, ser. 2, 8.2 (1858) 3–37; ed. Giancarlo Schizzerotto, *De casu Cesene*, in *Teatro e cultura in Romagna dal Medioevo al Rinascimento* (Ravenna 1969), pp. 40–67.

Faral, Edmund, *Les arts poétiques du XIIᵉ et du XIIIᵉ siècle* (Paris 1924).

Festus, Sextus Pompeius (second century AD), *Epitome* of Marcus Verrius Flaccus's *De verborum significatu*, ed. W. M. Lindsay, in J. W. Pirie and Lindsay, *Glossaria latina*, vol. 4 (Paris 1930).

Fulgentius, *Mythologiae*, ed. Rudolf Helm, *Opera* (Leipzig 1898).

Garland, John of, *Parisiana poetria*, ed. Traugott Lawler, *The Parisiana Poetria of John of Garland* (New Haven 1974).

Geoffrey of Monmouth, *Historia regum Britannie*, ed. Neil Wright, *The Historia Regum Britannie of Geoffrey of Monmouth*, vol. 1: *Bern Burgerbibliothek, MS 568* (Cambridge 1984).

Bibliography

Geoffrey of Vinsauf, *Documentum de arte versificandi*, original version, ed. Faral, *Les arts*, pp. 265–320; expanded version, excerpts in Traugott Lawler, *The Parisiana Poetria of John of Garland* (New Haven 1974), pp. 327–32.

Poetria nova, ed. Faral, *Les arts*, pp. 197–262.

Gervase of Canterbury, *The Chronicle of the Reigns of Stephen, Henry II, and Richard I*, ed. William Stubbs, 2 vols., Rolls Series 73 (London 1879–80).

Gilbert of La Porrée, *Commentum in Boethii tractatus*, PL 64; ed. N. M. Haring, *The Commentaries on Boethius by Gilbert of Poitiers* (Toronto 1966).

Glossaria Ansileubi, ed. J. W. Pirie and W. M. Lindsay, *Glossaria latina*, vol. 4 (Paris 1930, repr. 1965).

Goetz, Georg, *Corpus glossariorum latinorum*, 7 vols. (Leipzig 1888–1923).

Gras, *Tragèdia ordenade per mossèn Gras, la qual és part de la gran obra dels actes del famós cavaller Lançalot del Lac, en la qual se mostra clarament quant les solàsias* [sic, for *gelòsias?*] *in les coses de amor danyen, e com als qui vertaderament amen ninguna cosa los desobliga*, ed. Martín de Riquer, "La *Tragèdia de Lançalot*, texto artúrico catalán del siglo XV," *Filologia romanza* 2 (1955) 113–39.

Gratian, *Decretum*, ed. Emil Friedberg, *Corpus iuris canonici*, 2 vols. (Leipzig 1879–81, repr. Graz 1959), vol. 1.

Greek Anthology, The, LCL.

Grosseteste, Robert, see Aristotle.

Guido da Pisa, *Expositiones et glose super Comediam Dantis*, ed. Vincenzo Cioffari (Albany, NY, 1974).

Guizzardo of Bologna, *Commentum super tragedia Ecerinide*, ed. Luigi Padrin, *Ecerinide: Tragedia* (Bologna 1900, repr. *c.* 1969), pp. 67–267.

Recollecte super Poetria magistri Gualfredi, Vatican MS Ottob. lat. 3291.

Haring, Nicholas M. (Nikolaus M. Häring), see Gilbert of La Porrée, Heiligenkreuz Anonymous, Hugh of Honau, Thierry of Chartres.

Heiligenkreuz Anonymous, *Commentarium in Boethii Consolationem*, MS Heiligenkreuz 130, fols. 5v–76; excerpts in Nicholas M. Haring, "Four Commentaries on the *De consolatione Philosophiae* in MS Heiligenkreuz 130," *Mediaeval Studies* 31 (1969) 287–316.

Henry IV, *Epistolae*, ed. Carl Erdmann, *Die Briefe Heinrichs IV*, Deutsches Mittelalter 1 (Leipzig 1937).

Henryson, Robert, *The Testament of Cresseid*, ed. Denton Fox (London 1968); also included in *The Works of Robert Henryson*, ed. Fox (Oxford 1981).

Higden, Ranulf, *Polychronicon*, with the translation of John Trevisa, ed. Churchill Babington and Joseph Rawson Lumby, 9 vols., Rolls Series 41.1–9 (London 1865–86).

Honorius Augustodunensis, *De anime exsilio et patria*, PL 172.

Gemma anime, PL 172.

Horace, *Satires*; *Epistles*; *Ars poetica*, LCL.

Hugh of Honau, *Liber de diversitate nature et persone proprietatumque personalium non tam latinorum quam ex grecorum auctoritatibus extractis*, ed. Nicholas M. Haring, "The *Liber de diversitate naturae et personae* by Hugh of Honau," *Archives d'histoire doctrinale et littéraire du moyen âge* 29 [year 37] (1962) 103–216.

Hugh of St. Cher (?), *Super Apocalypsim*, in vol. 23 of the Parma edition of Aquinas'

Bibliography

Opera; in vol. 7 of *ITS*.

Huguccio, *Magne derivationes*, Oxford, Bodleian MS Laud Misc. 626.

Huygens, R. B. C., *Accessus ad auctores; Bernard d'Utrecht; Conrad d'Hirsau*, ed. 2 (Leiden 1970).

Isagoge in theologiam, ed. Arthur Landgraf, *Ysagoge in theologiam*, in *Ecrits théologiques de l'Ecole d'Abélard*, Spicilegium sacrum lovaniense 14 (Louvain 1934), pp. 61–285.

Isidore of Seville, *Etymologiae, sive Origines*, ed. W. M. Lindsay, 2 vols. (Oxford 1911), to be used with the annotations of Faustino Arévalo's edition, PL 82; Lindsay's text with Spanish translation and notes José Oroz Reta and Manuel-A. Marcos Casquero, eds., intro. by Manuel C. Díaz y Díaz, *Etimologías: Edición bilingüe*, 2 vols. (Madrid 1982–83).

James of Varazze (Jacobus a Voragine), *Legenda aurea*, ed. T. Graesse (Dresden 1846, repr. Breslau 1890).

Jean de Meun, *see* Boethius.

Jehan de Vignay (John of Vignay), *Legende doree* (Paris: Verard, 1496).

Jerome, *Adversus Jovinianum*, PL 23.

  Commentum in Ephesios, PL 26 (repr. 1884).

  Epistolae, CSEL 56.

John of Salisbury, *Policraticus*, PL 199; ed. C. C. J. Webb (Oxford 1909).

Keil, Heinrich, ed., *Grammatici latini*, 7 vols. (Leipzig, 1855–70).

Lactantius, *De ira Dei*, CSEL 27.

  De mortibus persecutorum, ed. J. Moreau, Sources chrétiennes 39 (Paris 1954).

  Diuinae institutiones, CSEL 19.

Lambert of Hersfeld, *Annales*, ed. Oswald Holder-Egger, *Lamperti monachi hersfeldensis opera*, Scriptores rerum germanicarum (Hanover 1894).

Lana, Jacopo della, *Commento alla Comedia di Dante*, ed. Luciano Scarabelli, *Comedia di Dante Allagherii col commento di Jacopo della Lana*, ed. 2, 3 vols. (Bologna 1866).

Lancia, Andrea, *Ottimo commento*, Proemio, "second version," ed. Scarabelli (who attributes it to Lana), *Comedia di Dante*, 1:95–98; "third version," excerpts given by Guiseppe Vandelli in the course of his study, "Una nuova redazione dell'*Ottimo*," *Studi danteschi* 14 (1930) 93–174.

Lawler, T., *see* Garland.

Liber exemplorum ad usum praedicantium saeculo XIII compositus a quodam fratre minore anglico de provincia Hiberniae, ed. A. G. Little (Aberdeen 1908).

Livy, *Ab urbe condita*, LCL.

Loschi, Antonio, *Achilles*, ed. and tr. Vittorio Zaccaria, in Zaccaria and Casarsa, *Il teatro umanistico veneto*, pp. 7–96; the edition of Giovanni da Schio (Padua 1843) is reprinted with facing English translation by Joseph R. Berrigan (Munich 1975).

Lucian, *Works*, LCL.

Lydgate, John, *Troy Book*, ed. Henry Bergen, 4 vols., Early English Text Society, extra series 97, 103, 106, 126 (London 1906–35).

  Fall of Princes, ed. Henry Bergen, 4 vols., Early English Text Society, extra series 121–24 (London 1924–27).

Bibliography

Machaut, Guillaume de, *La prise d'Alexandrie; ou, Chronique du roi Pierre Ier de Lusignan*, ed. L. de Mas Latrie (Geneva 1877, repr. Osnabrück 1968).

Marbod of Rennes, *Liber decem capitulorum*, ed. Rosario Leotta (Rome 1984).

Matthew of Vendôme, *Ars versificatoria*, ed. Faral, *Les arts*, pp. 109-93; *Opera omnia*, 3:39-221.

Milo, ed. and tr. Paola Busdraghi, in Bertini, *Commedie latine*, 1:139-95; ed. and tr. Marcel Abraham, in Cohen, *La "comédie*," 1:153-77; *Opera omnia*, 2:57-72. *Opera omnia*, ed. Franco Munari, *Mathei Vindocinensis opera*, 3 vols. (Rome 1977-88).

Matthias of Linköping, *Poetria*, ed. Stanislaw Sawicki, "*Poetria och Testa nucis* av magister Matthias Lincopensis," *Samlaren* n.s. 17 (1936) 109-52, pp. 128-43.

Megas, Anastasios, 'Ο προουμανιστικός τῆς πάδουας *(Lovato Lovati – Albertino Mussato)* καὶ οἱ τραγῳδίες τοῦ L. A. Seneca *[The Prehumanistic Circle of Padua (Lovato Lovati–Albertino Mussato) and the Tragedies of L. A. Seneca]*, supplement *11* of 'Επιστημονικὴ 'Επετηρὶς τῆς Φιλοσοφικῆς Σχολῆς τοῦ 'Αριστοτοτελείου Πανεπιστεμίου Θεσσαλονίκης (Salonika 1967), pp. 123-27

Mena, Juan de, *Coronación*, ed. Feliciano Delgado León (Cordova 1978).

Mézières, Philippe de, *Epistre lamentable et consolatoire sur le fait de la desconfiture lacrimable du noble et vaillant roy de Honguerie par les Turcs devant la ville de Nicopoli en l'empire de Boulguerie*, ed. J. Kervyn de Lettenhove, *Oeuvres de Froissart*, 25 vols. (1867-77, repr. Osnabrück 1967) 16: 444-523.

Livre de la vertu du sacrament de mariage et du reconfort des dames mariées, excerpts in Elie Golenistcheff-Koutouzoff, *L'histoire de Griseldis en France au XIVe et au XVe siècle* (Paris 1933), pp. 151-82.

Le songe du vieil pelerin, ed. G. W. Coopland, 2 vols. (Cambridge 1969).

Epistre au roi Richart, ed. and tr. G. W. Coopland, *Letter to King Richard II: A Plea Made in 1395 for Peace Between England and France* (Liverpool 1975, New York 1976).

Oracio tragedica seu declamatoria Passionis domini nostri Jhesu Christi, Paris, Bibliothèque Mazarine MS 1651, fols. 129-209bis.

Miles gloriosus (anonymous twelfth-century "elegiac comedy"), ed. and tr. Robert Baschet, in Cohen, *La "comédie"*, 1:179-210.

Moricca, Umberto, .ed., *Seneca's* Thyestes *and* Phaedra *and the pseudo-Senecan* Octavia, ed. 2 (Turin 1947).

Mussato, Albertino, *Opera poetica*, in *Historia augusta Henrici VII caesaris et alia que extant opera* (Venice 1636).

De obsidione Patavii, Introduction, ed. Cloetta, *Anfänge*, pp. 70-72; ed. Megas, p. 19.

Ecerinis, ed. Luigi Padrin, *Ecerinide: Tragedia* (Bologna 1900, repr. *c.* 1969); repr. with English translation by Joseph R. Berrigan, *Mussato's Ecerinis and Loschi's Achilles*, Humanistische Bibliothek 2, Texte 17 (Munich 1975); annotated Latin text and German translation, ed. and tr. Hubert Müller, *Früher Humanismus in Oberitalien: Albertino Mussato: Ecerinis* (Frankfurt 1987).

Evidentia tragediarum Senece, ed. Megas, pp. 123-27.

Lucii Annei Senece cordubensis vita et mores (Vita Senece), ed. Megas, pp. 154-61.

Nicholas I, *Epistolae*, MGH Epistolae 6.

Bibliography

Notker Labeo, *Boethius de consolatione Philosophiae*, ed. E. H. Sehrt and Taylor Starck, *Notkers des Deutschen Werke*, vol. 1 (Halle 1933–34); new ed. by Petrus W. Tax (Tübingen 1986–90).

Orderic Vitalis, *Historia ecclesiastica*, ed. Marjorie Chibnall, 6 vols. (Oxford 1969–80).

Oresme, Nicholas, *Le livre de ethiques d'Aristote*, ed. Albert Douglas Menut (New York 1940).

Osbern of Gloucester, *Liber derivationum*, ed. Angelo Mai, *Thesaurus novus latinitatis, sive Lexicon vetus*, Classici auctores e vaticanis codicibus editi 8 (Rome 1936).

Otto of Freising, *Gesta Frederici*, ed. G. Waitz, *Ottonis et Rahewini Gesta Friderici I. Imperatoris*, ed. 3 (Hanover 1912); ed. Franz Josef Schmale (Berlin 1965).

Chronica, sive Historia de duabus civitatibus, ed. Walther Lammers (Berlin 1960).

Ovid, *Works*, LCL.

Pace of Ferrara, *Evidentia Ecerinidis*, ed. Megas, pp. 203–05.

Palencia, Alfonso de, *Universal vocabulario*, Seville 1490; entries edited by John M. Hill, *"Universal vocabulario" de Alfonso de Palencia: Registro de voces españolas internas* (Madrid 1957).

Pamphilus, ed. and tr. Stefano Pittaluga, in Bertini, *Commedie latine*, 3:11–137; ed. and tr. Eugène Evesque, in Cohen, *La "comédie,"* 2:167–223.

Papias, *Elementarium doctrinae rudimentum*, Vatican MS Ottob. lat. 2231; ed. Bonino Mombrizio, ed. 4 (Venice 1496, repr. Turin 1966), with a supplement for the missing section from *pecus* to *placidus* from ed. 1 (Milan 1476); letter A, ed. Violetta De Angelis, 3 vols. (Milan 1977–80).

Paschasius Radbertus, *Expositio in Matheo*, PL 120; ed. Beda Paulus, 3 vols., CCM 56–58 (1984).

Paulus Diaconus, *Homiliarius*, PL 95.

Paulus Orosius, *Historiae adversum paganos*, CSEL 5.

Pedro de Portugal, *Tragedia de la insigne reina dona Isabel*, ed. Carolina Michaëlis de Vasconcelos, ed. 2 (Coimbra 1922); also in Adão da Fonseca, ed., *Obras completas.*

Obras completas do condestável dom Pedro de Portugal, ed. Luís Adão da Fonseca (Lisbon 1975).

Peter of Blois, *Epistolae*, PL 207.

Liber de confessione sacramentali, PL 207.

Peter Cantor, *Verbum abbreviatum*, short version, PL 205; long version, excerpts in John W. Baldwin, *Masters, Princes, and Merchants: The Social Views of Peter the Chanter and His Circle*, 2 vols. (Princeton 1970).

Petrarch, *Opera* (Basel 1554, repr. Ridgewood NJ 1965).

Prose, ed. Guido Martellotti *et al.* (Milan 1955).

Petronius, *Satyricon*, LCL.

Philostratus, *The Life of Apollonius of Tyana*, LCL.

Placidus, *Glossae*, ed. J. W. Pirie and W. M. Lindsay, *Glossaria latina*, vol. 4 (Paris 1930, repr. 1965).

Plato, *Theaetetus*, LCL.

Plautus, *Comedies*, LCL.

Pliny the Younger, *Letters*, LCL.

Bibliography

Plutarch, *Moralia*, LCL.

Porphyrio, Pomponius, *Commentarius in Horatium Flaccum*, ed. Wilhelm Meyer (Leipzig 1874).

Prudentius, *Peristephanon liber*, LCL.

Querolus, sive Aulularia, ed. and tr. Willi Emrich (Berlin 1965).

Quintilian, *Institutio oratoria*, LCL.

Quintilian, Pseudo-, *Mathematicus*, ed. Lennard Håkanson, *Declamationes xix maiores Quintiliano falso ascriptae* (Stuttgart 1982), no. 4, pp. 60–84.

Quodvultdeus, *De symbolo*, CCL 60.

Regule de arte versificandi, excerpts in Thurot, *Notices et extraits*, p. 418.

Remigius of Auxerre, *In Artem Donati minorem commentum* see *Commentum einsidlense*. *In Artem Donati minorem commentum*, ed. W. Fox (Leipzig 1902).

    Commentum in Boethii opuscula, ed. Edward Kennard Rand (but attributed to Eriugena), *Johannes Scottus*, Quellen und Untersuchungen zur lateinischen Philologie des Mittelalters 1.2, ed. Ludwig Traube (Munich 1906, repr. Frankfurt 1966), pp. 30–80 (tractates nos. 1–3, 5) and 99–106 (no. 4).

    In Boethii Consolationem Philosophiae commentum, Vatican MS Pal. lat. 1581 (tenth or eleventh century), variant version; Vatican MS Regin. lat. 1433 (twelfth century), scattered glosses; Vatican MS lat. 4254 (fourteenth century), revised version; excerpts in Hans Naumann, ed., *Notkers Boethius* (Strasburg 1913); excerpts in Edmund Taite Silk, ed., *Saeculi noni auctoris in Boetii Consolationem Philosophiae commentarius*, Papers and Monographs of the American Academy in Rome 9 (Rome 1935).

    Commentum in Martianum Capellam, ed. Cora E. Lutz, 2 vols. (Leiden 1962–65).

    In Sedulii Paschale carmen, in Sedulius, *Opera omnia*, CSEL 10.

Roiç de Corella, Johan, *Obres*, ed. R. Miquel y Planas, *Obres de J. Roiç de Corella* (Barcelona 1913); ed. Eliseu Climent, *Obra profana* (Valencia 1983); ed. Josep Almiñana Vallés, *Obres de Joan Roiç de Corella*, 2 vols. (Valencia 1984–85).

Rojas, Fernando de, *Comedia de Calisto e Melibea*, manuscript, ed. Charles B. Faulhaber, "*Celestina* de Palacio: Madrid. Biblioteca de Palacio, MS 1520," *Celestinesca* 14.2 (November 1990) 3–39 (facsimile and transcription); "*Celestina* de Palacio: Rojas's Holograph Manuscript?" *Celestinesca* 15.1 (May 1991) 3–52 (critical edition). Printed versions: facsimile of *c.* 1499, ed. Archer M. Huntington (New York 1909); facsimile of Toledo 1500, ed. Daniel Poyán Días (Geneva 1961); revised *c.* 1500 as *Tragicomedia de Calisto e Melibea*, facsimile of Seville *c.* 1518–20, *Libro de Calisto y Melibea y de la puta vieja Celestina*, ed. Antonio Pérez y Gómez (Valencia 1958); Italian translation by Alfonso Ordóñez (Rome 1506), ed. Kathleen V. Kish, *An Edition of the First Translation of the Celestina* (Chapel Hill 1973); modern editions: ed. Humberto López Morales, *La Celestina* (Madrid 1976); ed. Miguel Marciales, *Celestina: Tragicomedia de Calisto y Melibea*, 2 vols. (Urbana 1985).

Rusticus, *Synodicum*, ed. Eduard Schwartz, Acta conciliorum oecumenicorum 4.1 (Berlin 1922–24).

Santillana, Iñigo López de Mendoza, marqués de, *Comedieta de Ponça*, critical edition, ed. Maxim P. A. Kerkhof (Madrid 1987).

    Obras completas, ed. Angel Gómez Moreno and Kerkhof (Barcelona 1988).

Bibliography

Scholia in Horatium.
Aleph-Beth Scholiast, *Scholia Aleph*: ed. H. J. Botschuyver, *Scholia in Horatium אב in codicibus parisinis latinis 17897 et 8223 obvia, quae ab Herico Autissiodorensi profecta esse videntur* (Amsterdam 1942).
Gamma Scholiast, *Scholia Gamma*, Paris, Bibliothèque Nationale MS lat. 7975: ed. Ferdinand Hauthal, *Acronis et Porphyrionis commentarii in Q. Horatium Flaccum*, 2 vols. (Berlin 1864–66).
Lambda-Phi-Psi Scholiast, *Scholia Lambda*: ed. H. J. Botschuyver, *Scholia in Horatium λφψ: Codicum parisinorum latinorum 7972, 7974, 7971*, (Amsterdam 1935).
Pi Scholiast: *Scholia Pi*: ed. H. J. Botschuyver, *Scholia in Horatium πurχ: Codicum parisinorum latinorum 10310 et 7973, additis nonnullis ex codicibus parisino latino 9345 et leidensi vossiano 21* (Amsterdam 1939).
Vienna Scholiast, *Scholia vindobonensia ad Horatii Artem poeticam*, ed. Joseph Zechmeister (Vienna 1877).
Scholia terentiana, ed. Friedrich Schlee (Leipzig 1893).
Seneca, *Tragedies*, LCL.
Serravalle, Giovanni da, *Translatio et comentum totius libri Dantis Aldigherii*, ed. Marcellino da Civezza and Teofilo Domenichelli (Prato 1891).
Servius, *In Vergilii carmina commentarii*, ed. Georg Thilo and Hermann Hagen (Leipzig 1878–87, repr. Hildesheim 1961); Harvard edition: ed. A. F. Stoker *et al.*, *Serviani in Vergilii carmina commentarii*, vol. 3 (Oxford 1965).
Silk, E. T., *see* Boethius, Remigius, Trevet.
Suetonius, *Works*, LCL.
Tacitus, *Dialogus*, LCL.
Teobaud, *Acta, translationes, et miracula sancti Prudentii martyris, Acta sanctorum*: October, vol. 3 (Antwerp 1770, repr. Paris 1868), pp. 348–78.
Terence, *Comedies*, LCL.
Tertullian, *De spectaculis*, CCL 1.
Theodulf of Orleans, *Carmina*, ed. Ernst Dümmler, MGH Poetae latini 1 (1881).
Thierry of Chartres, *Commentarius in Boethii librum contra Eutychen et Nestorium: Fragmentum londinense*, ed. N. M. Haring, *Commentaries on Boethius by Thierry of Chartres and His School* (Toronto 1971), pp. 231–56.
Commentarius super Rhetoricam ad Herennium, ed. Karen Margareta Fredborg, *The Latin Rhetorical Commentaries by Thierry of Chartres* (Toronto 1988).
Thurot, Charles, *Notices et extraits des divers manuscrits latins pour servir à l'histoire des doctrines grammaticales au moyen âge*, Notices et extraits des manuscrits de la Bibliothèque Impériale et autres bibliothèques 22.2 (Paris 1868).
Trevet, Nicholas, *Expositio super librum Boecii de consolatione*, Vatican MS lat. 562 (late fourteenth century); ed. Edmund Taite Silk, *Exposicio fratris Nicolai Trevethi anglici ordinis predicatorum super Boecio de consolacione* (uncompleted and unpublished; copies available from the Sterling Memorial Library, Yale University).
Expositio super tragedias Senece, partial editions: introduction and commentary on *Thyestes*, ed. Ezio Franceschini, *Il commento di Nicola Trevet al Tieste di Seneca* (Milan 1938); commentary on *Hercules furens*, ed. Vincenzo Ussani jr, *L.*

Bibliography

Annaei Senecae Hercules furens et Nicolai Treveti Expositio, vol. 2 (Rome 1959); commentary on *Agamemnon*, ed. Piero Meloni (Palermo 1961); commentary on *Hercules oetaeus*, ed. Piero Meloni (Palermo 1962); commentary on *Troades*, ed. Marco Palma (Rome 1977).

Vacca, *Vita Lucani*, ed. Karl Hosius, *Lucani Bellum civile*, ed. 3 (Leipzig 1913), pp. 334–36.

Valera, Diego de, *Tratado en defensa de virtuosas mugeres*, ed. Mario Penna, *Prosistas castellanos del siglo XV*, vol. 1, Biblioteca de autores españoles 116 (Madrid 1959), pp. 55–76.

Valerius Maximus, *Facta et dicta memorabilia*, ed Karl Kempf (Leipzig 1888, repr. Stuttgart 1966).

Vandelli, Giuseppe, *see* Lancia.

Verardi, Carlo, *Historia baetica*, ed. and tr. Roberto Bravo Villarroel, *La Historia baetica de Carlo Verardi: Drama histórico renacentista en latín sobre la conquista de Granada* (Monterrey, Mexico 1971).

Verardi, Marcellino, *Fernandus servatus*, ed. H. Thomas, *Revue hispanique* 32 (1914) 428–57.

Vergil, *Works*, LCL.

Villani, Filippo, *Il commento al primo canto dell'Inferno*, ed. Guiseppe Cugnoni (Città di Castella 1896); ed. Saverio Bellomo, *Expositio seu comentum super Comedia Dantis Alleghcrii* (Florence 1989).

De Vita et moribus Dantis poete comici insignis, ed. Angelo Solerti, *Le vite di Dante, Petrarca, e Boccaccio* (Milan 1904–05), pp. 82–90.

Villena, Enrique de, *La Eneyda*, Madrid, Biblioteca Nacional MS 17945. I have not yet seen the sequestered edition of Pedro M. Cátedra (Barcelona 1985).

Los doze trabajos de Hércules, ed. Margherita Morreale (Madrid 1958).

Tratado de la consolación, ed. Derek C. Carr, Clásicos castellanos 208 (Madrid 1976).

Vincent of Beauvais, *Speculum quadruplex: naturale, doctrinale, morale, historiale*, 4 vols. (Douai 1624, repr. Graz 1964–65).

Vitalis of Blois, *Aulularia*, ed. and tr. Ferruccio Bertini, in Bertini, *Commedie latine*, 1:17–137; ed. and tr. Marcel Girard, in Cohen, *La "comédie,"* 1:59–106.

Geta, ed. and tr. Feruccio Bertini, in Bertini, *Commedie latine*, 3:139–242; ed. and tr. Etienne Guilhou, in Cohen, *La "comédie,"* 1:1–57.

Vitry, James of, *Exempla*, ed. Thomas Frederick Crane, *The Exempla or Illustrative Stories from the Sermones vulgares of Jacques de Vitry* (1890, repr. New York 1971).

Walsingham, Thomas, *Chronicon Angliae*, ed. Edward Maunde Thompson, Rolls Series 64 (London 1874).

Prohemia poetarum Fratris Thome de Walsingham, London, British Library MS Harley 2693, fols. 131–202v.

Ypodigma Neustriae, ed. Henry Thomas Riley, Rolls Series 28.7 (London 1876).

Wheatley, William, *Exposicio libri Boecii de consolacione philosophie*, Oxford, Bodleian Library, Exeter College MS 28; *ibid.*, MS New College 264.

William of Auvergne, *Rhetorica divina, sive Ars oratoria eloquentie divine*, in *Opera omnia*, 2 vols. (Paris 1674, repr. Frankfurt 1963), 1:336–406.

Bibliography

William of Blois, *Alda*, ed. and tr. Marcel Wintzweiller, in Cohen, *La "comédie,"* I:107–51.

William of Conches, *Moralium dogma philosophorum,* ed. John Holmberg, *Das Moralium dogma philosophorum des Guillaume de Conches* (Uppsala 1929). *Glose in Juvenalem,* ed. Bradford Wilson, *Glosae in Iuvenalem* (Paris 1980). *Glose super librum Boecii de consolacione,* original short text: Vatican MS lat. 5202, fols. 1–40v (thirteenth century); Paris Bibliothèque Nationale MS lat. 14380 (fourteenth century); Vatican MS Ottoboni 1293 (sixteenth century); revised long text: London, British Library MS Royal B 3, fols. 1–143; Vatican MS Ottoboni lat. 612, fols. 6–100.

William of Malmesbury, *Gesta regum Anglorum,* ed. Thomas Duffus Hardy (London 1840, repr. Vaduz 1964).

Wipo, *Vita Conradi Salici,* PL 142.

Zaccaria, Vittorio, and Laura Casarsa, *Il teatro umanistico veneto: la tragedia: Antonio Loschi, Achilles; Gregorio Correr, Progne,* Testi e studi umanistici, 2 (Ravenna 1981).

Zacchia da Vezzano, Laudivio, *De capitivitate ducis Jacobi tragoedia,* ed. Carlo Braggio, *Giornale ligustico* 11 (1884) 50–76, 111–32.

SECONDARY SOURCES

Altaner, Bertold, *Patrology,* tr. Hilda C. Graef (New York 1961).

Amat, Roman d', ed., *Dictionnaire de biographie française,* vol. 13 (Paris 1975).

Arnaldi, Girolamo, "Il mito di Ezzelino da Rolandino a Mussato," in Doglio *et al., Rinascità della tragedia,* pp. 85–97.

Atkinson, J. Keith, Review of Dwyer, *Medium aevum* 47 (1978) 141–45.

"A Fourteenth-Century Picard Translation-Commentary of the *Consolatio Philosophiae,*" in Minnis, *The Medieval Boethius,* pp. 32–62.

and Glynnis M. Cropp, "Trois traductions de la *Consolatio Philosophiae* de Boèce," *Romania* 106 (1985) 198–232.

Atherton, Béatrice, and J. Keith Atkinson, "Les manuscrits du *Roman de Fortune de de Félicité,*", *Revue d'histoire des textes* 22 (1992) 169–251.

Babinger, F., "Laudivius Zacchia, Erdichter der *Epistolae magni Turci,*" *Sitzungsberichte der Bayerischen Akademie der Wissenschaften,* Philosophisch-historische Klasse 13 (Munich 1960), pp. 5–11.

Bahlmann, P., *Die Erneuerer des antiken Dramas und ihre ersten dramatischen Versuche, 1314–1478* (Münster 1896).

Barbi, Michele, "La lettura di Benvenuto da Imola e i suoi rapporti con altri commenti," part 1: "il ms. Ashburnhamiano 839 e il codice Caetani," *Studi danteschi* 16 (1932) 137–56; part 2: "Il ms. Ashburnhamiano 839 e il commento di fra Giovanni da Serravalle," *ibid.* 18 (1934) 79–98.

Beare, W., *The Roman Stage,* ed. 3 (London 1964).

Bellomo, Saverio, "Primi appunti sull'*Ottimo commento* dantesco," *Giornale storico della letteratura italiana* 157 (1980) 368–82, 532–40.

Berrigan, Joseph R., "Early Neo-Latin Tragedy in Italy," *Acta Conventus neo-Latini Lovaniensis* (Munich 1973), pp. 85–93.

Bibliography

"Gregorii Corrarii Veneti *Liber satyrarum*," *Humanistica lovaniensia* 22 (1973) 10–38.

"Latin Tragedy of the Quattrocento," *Humanistica lovaniensia* 22 (1973) 1–9.

Bieber, Margarete, "Maske," Pauly-Wissowa, *Realencyclopädia* 14 (1930) 2070–120. *The History of the Greek and Roman Theater*, ed. 2 (Princeton 1961).

Bigongiari, Dino, "Were There Theaters in the Twelfth and Thirteenth Centuries?" *Romantic Reviews* 37 (1946) 201–24.

Billanovich, Giuseppe, "Il Livio di Pomposa e i primi umanisti Padovani," *La bibliofilia* 85 (1983) 125–48.

Billanovich, Guido, "Il preumanesimo padovano," in Girolamo Arnaldi *et al.*, *Il trecento*, vol. 2 of *Storia della cultura veneta* (Vicenza 1976), pp. 19–110.

"Il Seneca tragico di Pomposa e i primi umanisti padovani," *La bibliofilia* 85 (1983) 149–69.

Bishop, T. A. M., "The Prototype of the *Liber glossarum*," in M. B. Parkes and Andrew G. Watson, eds., *Medieval Scribes, Manuscripts, and Libraries: Essays Presented to N. R. Ker* (London 1978), pp. 69–84.

Boas, Frederick S., *University Drama in the Tudor Age* (Oxford 1914, repr. New York 1966).

Bolton, Diane K., "Remigian Commentaries on the *Consolation of Philosophy* and Their Sources," *Traditio* 33 (1977) 381–94.

"The Study of the *Consolation of Philosophy* in Anglo-Saxon England," *Archives d'histoire doctrinale et littéraire du moyen âge* 44 (1977) 33–78.

Bradner, Leicester, "From Petrarch to Shakespeare" (abstract), *Renaissance News* 5 (1952) 32–34.

Brink, C. O., *Horace on Poetry*, 2 vols. (Cambridge 1963–71).

Brugnoli, Giorgio, "La tradizione manoscritta di Seneca tragico alla luce delle testimonianze medioevali," *Atti della Accademia Nazionale dei Lincei*, Series 8: *Memorie, Classe di scienze morali, storiche, e filologiche* 8 (1959) 201–89.

"Le tragedie di Seneca nei florilegi medioevali," *Studi medievali* 3.1 (1960) 138–52.

Canal, Antonio, *Il mondo morale di Guido da Pisa* (Bologna 1981).

Casarsa, Laura, "La *Progne* di Gregorio Correr," in Doglio *et al.*, *Rinascità della Tragedia*, pp. 119–34.

Chambers, E. K., *The Medieval Stage*, 2 vols. (London 1903).

Arthur of Britain (London 1927, repr. New York 1967).

Cioffari, Vincenzo, "Did Guido da Pisa Write a Commentary on the *Purgatorio* and the *Paradiso*? (Pluteo 40.2 and Its Relation to the Guido da Pisa Commentary)," *Studi danteschi* 57 (1985) 145–60 (published in 1989).

"The *Anonimo Latino:* One of the Earliest Commentaries on Dante's *Commedia*," *Mediaevalia* 12 (1986) 127–53 (published in 1989).

Cloetta, Wilhelm, *Beiträge zur Literaturgeschichte des Mittelalters und der Renaissance*, vol. 1: *Komödie und Tragödie im Mittelalter*; vol. 2: *Die Anfänge der Renaissance-tragödie* (Halle 1890–92).

Courcelle, Pierre, "La culture antique de Remi d'Auxerre," *Latomus* 7 (1948) 247–54.

La Consolation de Philosophie dans la tradition littéraire: Antécédents et postérité de

Bibliography

Boèce (Paris 1967).

Creizenach, Wilhelm, *Geschichte des neueren Dramas*, ed. 2, 3 vols. (Halle 1911–23).

Croppe, Glynnis M., "Boèce et Christine de Pizan," *Le moyen âge* 87 (1981) 387–417.

"Two Historical Glosses in *Le livre de Boece de la Consolacion*," *New Zealand Journal of French Studies* 2.2 (1981) 5–20.

"Le prologue de Jean de Meun et *Le livre de Boece de Consolacion*," *Romania* 103 (1982) 278–98.

"Les manuscrits du *Livre de Boece de Consolacion*," *Revue d'histoire des textes* 12–13 (1982–83) 263–352.

"Les gloses du *Livre de Boece de Consolacion*," *Le moyen âge* 42 (1986) 367–81.

"*Le livre de Boece de Consolacion*: From Translation to Glossed Text," in Minnis, ed., *The Medieval Boethius*, pp. 63–88.

"Fortune and the Poet in Ballades of Eustache Deschamps, Charles d'Orléans, and François Villon," *Medium aevum* 58 (1989) 125–32.

Cunliffe, John W., *Early English Classical Tragedies* (Oxford 1912).

Cunningham, J. V., *Woe or Wonder* (Denver 1951), reprinted in *The Collected Essays of J. V. Cunningham* (Chicago 1976).

Curtius, Ernst Robert, *European Literature and the Latin Middle Ages*, tr. Willard R. Trask (London 1953).

Dahan, Gilbert, "Notes et textes sur la poétique au moyen âge," *Archives d'histoire doctrinale et littéraire du moyen âge* 47 (1980) 171–239.

Daley, Brian E., "Boethius' Theological Tracts and Early Byzantine Scholasticism," *Medieval Studies* 46 (1984) 158–91.

Daly, Lloyd W., and B. H. Daly, "Some Techniques in Mediaeval Latin Lexicography," *Speculum* 39 (1944) 229–39.

De Angelis, Violetta, "Indagine sulle fonti dell' *Elementarium* di Papias, lettera A." *Scripta philologica* 1 (1977) 117–34.

Dean, Ruth J., "The Dedication of Nicholas Trevet's Commentary on Boethius," *Studies in Philology* 66 (1966), 593–603.

"Nicholas Trevet, Historian," in J. J. G. Alexander and M. T. Gibson, eds., *Medieval Learning and Literature: Essays Presented to Richard William Hunt* (Oxford 1976) pp. 328–52.

Delhaye, Philippe, *Christian Philosophy in the Middle Ages* (London 1960).

Delisle, L., *Recherches sur la librairie de Charles V* (3 vols., Paris 1907, repr. in 2 vols., Amsterdam 1967).

Doglio, Federico, *et al.*, *La rinascità della tragedia nell'Italia dell'Umanesimo: Atti del IV Convegno di Studio, Viterbo, 15–16–17 giugno 1979* (Viterbo 1980, repr. 1983).

Doležel, Lubomír, *Occidental Poetics: Tradition and Progress* (Lincoln, Nebr. 1990).

Donaghey, B. S., "Nicholas Trevet's Use of King Alfred's Translation of Boethius, and the Dating of His Commentary," in Minnis, ed., *The Medieval Boethius*, pp. 1–31.

Dronke, Peter, "A Note on *Pamphilus*," *Journal of the Warburg and Courtauld Institutes* 42 (1979) 225–30.

Dunn, Peter N., *Fernando de Rojas* (Boston 1975).

Bibliography

Dwyer, Richard A., *Boethian Fictions: Narratives in the Medieval French Versions of the Consolatio Philosophiae* (Cambridge, Mass. 1976).

Else, Gerald F., *Aristotle's Poetics: The Argument* (Cambridge, Mass. 1963).

Faral, Edmond, "Le fabliau latin au moyen âge," *Romania* 50 (1924) 321–85.

Flamini, Francesco, "Leonardo di Piero Dati, poeta latino del secolo XV," *Giornale storico della letteratura italiana* 16 (1890) 1–107; *ibid.*, 22 (1893) 415–17.

Fleischer, Ulrich, "Zur Zweitausendjahrfeier des Ovid," *Antike und Abendland* 6 (1957) 27–29.

Fontaine, Jacques, *Isidore de Séville et la culture classique dans l'Espagne wisigothique*, ed. 2, 3 vols. (Paris 1983).

Fothergill-Payne, Louise, *Seneca and Celestina* (Cambridge 1988).

Fowler, Alistair, *Kinds of Literature: An Introduction to the Theory of Genres and Modes* (Oxford 1982).

Frye, Northrop, *Anatomy of Criticism* (Princeton 1957).

Gabriel, Astrik, L., "The Source of the Anecdote of the Inconstant Scholar," *Classica et mediaevalia* 19 (1958) 152–76.

Gascón Vera, Elena, *Don Pedro, Condestable de Portugal* (Madrid 1979).

Gentilini, Graziella, *Il teatro umanistico veneto: La commedia* (Ravenna 1983).

Glendinning, Robert, "Pyramus and Thisbe in the Medieval Classroom," *Speculum* 61 (1986) 51–78.

Godefroy, F., *Dictionnaire de l'ancienne langue française*, 10 vols. (Paris 1881–1902).

Golenistcheff-Koutouzoff, Elie, *L'histoire de Griseldis en France au XIVe et au XVe siècle* (Paris 1933).

Haas, Renate, "Chaucer's *Monk's Tale*: An Ingenious Criticism of Early Humanist Conceptions of Tragedy," *Humanistica lovaniensia* 36 (1987) 44–70.

Halliwell, Stephen, *Aristotle's Poetics* (London and Chapel Hill 1986).

Harbert, Bruce, "Matthew of Vendôme," *Medium aevum* 44 (1975) 225–37.

Herrick, Marvin T., *Tragicomedy: Its Origin and Development in Italy, France, and England* (Urbana 1955).

Hillgarth, J. N., "The Position of Isidorian Studies: A Critical Review of the Literature since 1935," Manuel C. Díaz y Díaz, ed., *Isidoriana* (León 1961), pp. 11–74.

Hunt, R. W., "The 'Lost' Preface to the *Liber derivationum* of Osbern of Gloucester," *Mediaeval and Renaissance Studies* 4 (1958) 267–82.

Hunter, G. K., *Dramatic Identities and Cultural Traditions* (New York 1978), "Seneca and the Elizabethans," pp. 159–73; "Seneca and English Tragedy," pp. 174–203.

Iung, N., "Pierre de Blois," *Dictionnaire de théologie catholique*, 16 vols. (Paris 1903–72), vol. 12, cols. 1884–89.

Jenaro-MacLennan, Luis, *The Trecento Commentaries on the Divina commedia and the Epistle to Cangrande* (Oxford 1974).

Jorga, N., *Philippe de Mézières, 1372 –1405, et la croisade au XIVe siècle* (Paris 1896).

Jürgens, Heiko, *Pompa diaboli: Die lateinischen Kirchenväter und das antike Theater*, Tübinger Beiträge zur Altertumswissenschaft 46 (Stuttgart 1972).

Kelly, Henry Ansgar, *Love and Marriage in the Age of Chaucer* (Ithaca 1975).

"Aristotle–Averroes–Alemannus on Tragedy: The Influence of the *Poetics* on

Bibliography

the Latin Middle Ages," *Viator* 10 (1979) 161–209.

"Tragedy and the Performance of Tragedy in Late Roman Antiquity," *Traditio* 35 (1979) 21–44.

Canon Law and the Archpriest of Hita (Binghamton 1984).

"The Non-Tragedy of Arthur," *Medieval English Religious and Ethical Literature: Essays in Honour of G. H. Russell*, ed. G. Kratzmann and J. Simpson (Cambridge 1986), pp. 92–114.

"The Varieties of Love in Medieval Literature According to Gaston Paris," *Romance Philology* 40 (1986–87) 301–27.

"Lawyer's Latin: *Loquenda ut vulgus?*" *Journal of Legal Education* 38 (1988) 195–207.

Review of Marjorie Curry Woods, *An Early Commentary on the Poetria nova of Geoffrey of Vinsauf* [New York 1985], *Manuscripta* 32 (1988) 54–58.

"Chaucer and Shakespeare on Tragedy," *Leeds Studies in English* 20 (1989) 191–206.

Tragedy and Comedy from Dante to Pseudo-Dante, University of California Publications in Modern Philology 121 (Berkeley 1989).

Kottler, Barnet, "The Vulgate Tradition of the *Consolatio Philosophiae* in the Fourteenth Century," *Mediaeval Studies* 17 (1955) 209–14.

La Favia, Louis M., "Il primo commento alla *Divina commedia* in Spagna," *Hispano-Italic Studies* 1 (1976) 1–8.

Latham, R. E., *Revised Medieval Word-List from British and Irish Sources* (London 1965, repr. with Supplement, 1980).

Le Clerc, Victor, *Histoire littéraire de la France*, vol. 24 (Paris 1863).

Lenormand, Silvie, "Guillaume de Conches et le commentaire sur la *De consolatione Philosophiae* de Boèce," *Positions des thèses*, Ecole Nationale de Chartes (Paris 1979), pp. 69–74.

Lenz, Friedrich Walter, ed., Ovid, *Amores* (Berlin 1965).

Leo, Friedrich, "Varro und die Satire," *Hermes* 24 (1889) 67–84.

Lesky, Albin, *Greek Tragedy*, tr. H. A. Frankfurt from the third German edition of 1964 (London 1965, corr. repr. 1967).

Lida de Malkiel, María Rosa, *La originalidad artística de La Celestina*, ed. 2, ed. Yakov Malkiel (Buenos Aires 1970).

Loomis, Laura Hibbard, "Secular Dramatics in the Royal Palace, Paris, 1378, 1389, and Chaucer's 'Tregetoures,'" *Speculum* 33 (1958) 242–55.

Lucas, Robert H., "Mediaeval French Translations of the Latin Classics to 1500," *Speculum* 45 (1970) 225–53.

Lumiansky, Robert M., "The Alliterative *Morte Arthure*, the Concept of Medieval Tragedy, and the Cardinal Virtue Fortitude," in John M. Headley, ed., *Medieval and Renaissance Studies* 3 (Chapel Hill 1968), pp. 95–118.

MacFarlane, Katherine Nell, *Isidore of Seville and the Pagan Gods (Origines 8.11)*, Transactions of the American Philosophical Society 70.3 (Philadelphia 1980).

MacGregor, Alexander, "L'Abbazia di Pomposa, centro originario della tradizione 'E' delle tragedie di Seneca," *La bibliofilia* 85 (1983) 171–85.

Manitius, Max, *Geschichte der lateinischen Litteratur des Mittelalters*, 3 vols. (Munich 1911–31).

Bibliography

Marshall, Mary Hatch, "Boethius' Definition of *Persona* and the Mediaeval Understanding of the Roman Theater," *Speculum* 25 (1950) 471–82.

"*Theatre* in the Middle Ages: Evidence from Dictionaries and Glosses," *Symposium* 4 (1950) 1–19, 366–89.

McMahon, A. Philip, "On the Second Book of Aristotle's *Poetics* and the Source of Theophrastus' Definition of Tragedy," *Harvard Studies in Classical Philology* 28 (1917) 1–46.

"Seven Questions on the Aristotelian Definitions of Tragedy and Comedy," *Harvard Studies in Classical Philology* 40 (1929) 97–198.

Meiss, Millard, *et al.*, *French Painting in the Time of Jean de Berry*, part 2: *The Limbourgs and Their Contemporaries*, 2 vols. (New York 1974).

Mengaldo, Pier Vincenzo, "Stili, dottrina degli," in *Enciclopedia dantesca*, 6 vols. (Rome 1970–78), 5:435–38.

Mercati, Silvio Giuseppe, "Intorno al titolo dei lessici di Suida-Suda e di Papia," *Atti della Accademia Nazionale dei Lincei* 8.10 (Rome 1962) 1–50.

Messina, Nicolò, "Le citazioni classiche nelle *Etymologiae* di Isidoro di Siviglia," *Archivos leoneses* 34 (1980) 205–65.

Minnis, A. J., *Medieval Theory of Authorship: Scholastic Literary Attitudes in the Later Middle Ages* (London 1984).

Minnis, A. J., ed., *The Medieval Boethius: Studies in the Vernacular Translations of De consolatione Philosophiae* (Cambridge 1987).

Chaucer's Boece and the Medieval Tradition of Boethius (Cambridge forthcoming).

Moos, Peter von, *Consolatio: Studien zur mittellateinischen Trostliteratur über den Tod und zum Problem der christlichen Trauer*, 4 vols. (Munich 1971–72).

Morreale, Margherita, "Apuntes bibliográficos para el estudio del tema 'Dante en España hasta el s. XVII,'" *Annali del Corso di Lingue Letterature Straniere della Università di Bari* 8 (1967) 90–134.

Müller, Wolfgang, P., "Huguccio of Pisa: Canonist, Bishop, or Grammarian?" *Viator* 22 (1991) 121–51.

Naumann, Hans, *Notkers Boethius* (Strasbourg 1913).

Nicoll, Allardyce, *Masks, Mimes, and Miracles: Studies in the Popular Theatre* (New York 1931).

Novati, Francesco, "Un umanista fabrianese del secolo XIV, Giovanni Tinti," *Archivio storico italiano* 2 (1885) 103–57.

Ogilvy, J. D. A., "*Mimi, Scurrae, Histriones*: Entertainers of the Early Middle Ages," *Speculum* 38 (1963) 603–19.

The Oxford Companion to Film, ed. Liz Anne Bawden (New York 1976).

Paduano, Guido, "La prototragedia e le categorie del discorso drammatico," in Doglio *et al.*, *Rinascità della tragedia*, pp. 99–118.

Paetow, Louis John, *The Arts Course at Medieval Universities with Special Reference to Grammar and Rhetoric* (Urbana 1910).

Paolazzi, Carlo, "Le letture dantesche di Benvenuto da Imola a Bologna e a Ferrara e le redazioni del suo *Comentum*," *Italia medioevale e umanistica* 22 (1979) 319–66.

Dante e la "Comedia" nel Trecento (Milan 1989).

Paratore, Ettore, "L'influsso dei classici, e particolarmente di Seneca, sul teatro

Bibliography

tragico latino del Tre e Quattrocento," in Doglio *et al.*, *Rinascità della tragedia*, pp. 21–45.

Parent, J. M., *La doctrine de la création dans l'Ecole de Chartres*, Publications de l'Institut d'Etudes Médiévales d'Ottawa 8 (Paris 1938).

Pastore-Stocchi, Manlio, "Un chapitre d'histoire littéraire aux XIV^c et XV^c siècles: *Seneca poeta tragicus*," in Jean Jacquot, ed., with Marcel Oddon, *Les tragédies de Sénèque et le théatre de la Renaissance* (Paris 1964), pp. 11–36.

Penney, Clara Louisa, *The Book Called Celestina in the Library of the Hispanic Society of America* (New York 1954).

Pérez Priego, Miguel A., "De Dante a Juan de Mena: Sobre el género literario de 'comedia,'" *1616: Anuario de la Sociedad Española de Literatura General y Comparada* (1978) 151–58.

Perocco, Daria, "Albertino Mussato e l'*Ecerinis*," *Miscellanea di studi in onore di Vittore Branca*, 5 vols. (Florence 1983), 1:337–49.

Preti, Paolo, "Correr, Gregorio," *Dizionario biografico degli Italiani* 29 (1983) 497–500.

Quadlbauer, Franz, *Die antike Theorie der Genera dicendi im lateinischen Mittelalter*, Österreichische Akademie der Wissenschaften, Philosophisch-historische Klasse, Sitzungsberichte 241.2 (Vienna 1962).

"Die poetischen Gattungen und die rhetorische Theorie der drei Genera dicendi," unpublished paper given at Bressanone in 1978 and scheduled for publication in the *Quaderni del Circoli filologico-linguistico padovano.*

Raby, F. J. E., "Fulgentius, Fabius Planciades," *Oxford Classical Dictionary*, ed. 2 (Oxford 1970), p. 449.

Revell, Elizabeth, "Peter of Blois," in *Dictionary of the Middle Ages*, 13 vols. (New York 1982–89) 9:517–18.

Richie, Donald, *Japanese Cinema: Film Style and National Character* (Garden City, N.Y., 1971).

Riquer, Martín de, *Història de la literatura catalana, Part antiga*, 3 vols. (Barcelona 1964).

Ristori, R., "Dati, Leonardo," *Dizionario biografico degli italiani* 38 (1987) 44–52.

Roques, Mario, *Recueil général des lexiques français du moyen âge*, part 1: *Lexiques alphabétiques*, 2 vols. (Paris 1936–38).

Rotolo, Vincenzo, "*Cantare ad manum*: Ancora su Liv. 7.2.10," *Studi italiani di filologia classica* 2.32 (1960) 249–53.

Round, Nicholas G., "Las traduciones medievales, catalanas y castellanas, de las tragedias de Séneca," *Anuario de estudios medievales* 9 (1974–79) 187–227, 816 (English summary).

Rouse, Richard, "New Light on the Circulation of the A Text of Seneca's Tragedies," part 1, *Journal of the Warburg and Courtauld Institutes* 40 (1977) 283–86.

Roy, Bruno, "Arnulf of Orleans and the Latin 'Comedy,'" *Speculum* 49 (1974) 258–66.

Rubió Balaguer, Jorge, "Lituratura catalana," in Guillermo Díaz-Plaja, ed., *Historia general de las literaturas hispánicas*, 6 vols. (Barcelona 1949–68), 3:730–932.

Bibliography

Rufini, Sergio, " 'To Make that Maxim Good': Dryden's Shakespeare," in Piero Boitani, ed., *The European Tragedy of Troilus* (Oxford 1989), pp. 243–80.

Ruiz i Calonja, Joan, *Història de la literatura catalana* (Barcelona 1954).

Sabbadini, Remigio, "Biografi e commentatori di Terenzio," *Studie italiani di filologia classica* 5 (1897) 289–327.

Sanford, Eva Matthews, "Lucan and His Roman Critics," *Classical Philology* 26 (1931) 233–57.

"The Manuscripts of Lucan: *Accessus* and *Marginalia*," *Speculum* 9 (1934) 278–95.

Schiff, Mario, *La bibliothèque du Marquis de Santillane* (Paris 1905).

Schmidt, Peter Lebrecht, "Rezeption und Überlieferung der Tragödien Senecas bis zum Ausgang des Mittelalters," in Eckhard Lefèvre, ed., *Die Einfluss Senecas auf das europäischen Drama* (Darmstadt 1978), pp. 12–73.

Schmitt, Charles B., "Theophrastus in the Middle Ages," *Viator* 2 (1971) 250–70.

Silk, Edmund Taite, "Was Pseudo-Johannes Scottus or Remigius of Auxerre a Plagiarist?" in Margot H. King and Wesley M. Stevens, eds., *Saints, Scholars, and Heroes: Studies in Medieval Culture in Honor of Charles W. Jones*, 2 vols. (Collegeville 1979), 2:127–40.

Smits, E. R., "Helinand of Froidmont and the A-Text of Seneca's Tragedies," *Mnemosyne* 36 (1983) 324–58.

Southern, R. W., *Medieval Humanism* (New York 1970), chap. 5: "Humanism and the School of Chartres," pp. 61–85; chap. 7: "Peter of Blois: A Twelfth-Century Humanist?," pp. 105–32.

Stadter, Philip A., "Planudes, Plutarch, and Pace of Ferrara," *Italia medioevale e umanistica* 16 (1973) 137–62.

Stäuble, Antonio, *La commedia umanistica del Quattrocento* (Florence 1968).

"L'idea della tragedia nell'Umanesimo," in Doglio *et al.*, *Rinascità della tragedia*, pp. 47–71.

Thomas, Antoine, and Mario Roques, *Histoire littéraire de la France*, vol. 37 (Paris 1938).

Trillitzsch, Winfried, "Die lateinische Tragödie bei den Prähumanisten von Padua," in Alf Önnerfors *et al.*, eds., *Literatur und Sprache im europäischen Mittelalter: Festschrift für Karl Langosch zum 70. Geburtstag* (Darmstadt 1973), pp. 448–57.

"Seneca tragicus – Nachleben und Beurteilung im lateinischen Mittelalter von der Spätantike bis zum Renaissancehumanismus," *Philologus* 122 (1978) 120–36.

Troncarelli, Fabio, "Per una ricerca sui commenti altomedievali al *De consolatione* di Boezio," *Miscellanea in memoria di Giorgio Cencetti* (Turin 1973), pp. 367–80.

Villa, Claudia, *La lectura Terentii*, vol. 1 (Padua 1984).

Vindel, Francisco, *El arte tipográfico en España durante el siglo XV*, 9 vols. (Madrid, 1945–61), vol. 1: *Cataluña*.

Walsh, James Joseph, *The Thirteenth, Greatest of Centuries* (New York 1907).

Watling, E. F., Introduction to *Seneca: Four Tragedies, and Octavia*, Penguin Classics (Harmondsworth 1966).

Weismann, Werner, *Kirche und Schauspiele: Die Schauspiele im Urteil der lateinischen*

Bibliography

Kirchenväter unter besonderer Berücksichtigung von Augustin, Cassiacum 27 (Würzburg 1972).

Weiss, Julian, "Juan de Mena's *Coronación*: Satire or *Sátira?*" *Journal of Hispanic Studies* 6 (1982–83) 113–38.

Wessner, Paulus, "Isidor und Sueton," *Hermes* 52 (1917) 201–92.

Wetherbee, Winthrop, *Platonism and Poetry in the Twelfth Century: The Literary Influence of the School of Chartres* (Princeton 1972).

Whinnom, Keith, "Interpreting *La Celestina*: The Motives and the Personality of Fernando de Rojas," in F. W. Hodcroft *et al.*, eds., *Medieval and Renaissance Studies on Spain and Portugal in Honor of P. E. Russell* (Oxford 1981), pp. 53–68.

Willard, Charity Cannon, "El Condestable Don Pedro and the *Tragedia de la insigne Reyna Isabel*" (Abstract), *La Corónica* 17.1 (Fall 1988) 143–44.

Wilmart, André, "Grands poèmes inédits de Bernard le Clunicien," *Revue bénédictine* 45 (1933) 249–54.

"Préface de Guillaume de Conches pour la dernière partie de son *Dialogue*," *Analecta reginensia*, Studi e testi 59 (Vatican City 1933), pp. 262–65.

Wittig, Joseph S., "King Alfred's *Boethius* and Its Latin Sources: A Reconsideration," *Anglo-Saxon England* 11 (1983) 157–98.

Zwierlein, Otto, *Prolegomena zu einer kritischen Ausgabe der Tragödien Senecas* (Mainz 1983).

"Spuren der Tragödien Senecas bei Bernardus Silvestris, Petrus Pictor, und Marbod von Rennes," *Mittellateinisches Jahrbuch* 22 (1987) 171–96.

Index

Index

Arnaldi, Giralomo, 135n.
Arnulf of Orleans, 95
Arthur, King, 86, 210, 216; Arthurian
literature, 111; as tragedies, 85–87, 110,
215–17, 220
Atherton, Béatrice, 162n.
Atkinson, J. Keith, 158, 159n., 160n.
Atreus, 21n., 59, 132
Augustine, Pseudo-, 49, 82n.
Augustine, St., 17–18, 23, 25n., 30–31, 39,
45–46, 80n., 113, 126, 140–41, 166; as
performer of tragedy, 18, 30
Augustus, Caesar (Octavian), 8, 29, 83–84, 210
Averroes, on Aristotle's *Poetics*, 3n., 5, 118–25,
132, 137, 147, 157, 201–02, 208, 219; Arabic
text, 119n.
Avicenna, on Aristotle's *Poetics*, 120
Avignon, 126, 129, 130n., 158, 195n.

Babin, Raymond, 180
Babio, 103
Bacchus and Bacchantes, 188
Bacon, Roger, 109n.
Baker, Howard, 191n.
Balbus Januensis, John, *Catholicon* (1286), 102,
107–09, 131, 148, 155; in French, 167
Baldwin, John W., 95n.
Baldwin, William, *A Mirror for Magistrates*, 175
Balthasar (Belshazzar), 172
Bambaglioli, Graziolo de', 149
Barbi, Michele, 206n.
Bartholomew of Bruges, 124
Bassano, Castellano da, 141n.
battles, see tragedy: subjects (war)
Bavaria, 83, 87
Beare, W., 42n.
Beatrice, Dante's, 148–49, cf. 145–46
Bede the Venerable, St., 40, 62
Belgium, 169, 196
Bellomo, Saverio, 153n., 157n.
Benedict XIII (Pedro de Luna), pope
(1394–1417; d. 1422), 207
Benediktbeuren, 84–85
benshi, in Japanese cinema, 44
Benvenuto da Imola, 125, 154–55, 204, 206–08
Berengar of Poitiers, 89–90, 92
Bernard of Chartres, 69, 74
Bernard of Clairvaux, 89–90, 92
Bernard of Cluny, *De contemptu mundi*, 88
Bernard Silvester, see Silvester
Bernard of Utrecht, 61–64, 70
Berrigan, Joseph R., 135n., 136n., 186n.,
191n., 193
Bible, 122; 1 Corinthians, 23; Lamentations,
25n.; Matthew, 71n.; Proverbs, 79–80; see
also Adam, Abraham, Antiochus,

Apocalypse, Balthasar, Cain, Christ,
Habacuc, Herod, Holofernes, Job, Joseph,
Judas, Judith, Nabuchudonosor, Nimrod,
Paul, Pharaoh, Rebecca, Samson, Sodomites,
Solomon, Song of Songs, Susanna,
Syro-Phoenician woman
Bieber, Margarete, 12n., 41n., 49n.
Bigongiari, Dino, 42n., 82n.
Billanovich, Giuseppe, 130n.
Billanovich, Guido, 135n.
Bishop, T. A. M., 64n.
Blanc, Mel, 44
Blois, see Peter, Vitalis, William
Boas, Frederick S., 190n.
Boccaccio, Giovanni, on Dante, 149, 154, 195;
on tragedy, 134n., 170–71; as character in
tragedy, 203; *Comedia delle ninfe fiorentine*,
157; *De casibus*, no tragedies in, xiv, 171–72,
205n., 210; seen as tragedies by Chaucer,
Lydgate, Santillana, 171–72, 175, 203, 210;
Filostrato, 174
Boethius, sufferings, 70; *Consolatio Philosophiae*,
33–34, 49, 52–57, 68–75, 78, 93, 104, 107,
123, 126–29, 137, 142–43, 153, 157, 177,
195, 205n., 209, 211, 218–21; in English
(Chaucer), 171–72; in French, xiii, 158–64,
175, 185; elegies of, 151; meters of, 81, 186;
style and form of, 204n., 210; *Contra
Eutychen et Nestorium*, 24, 32–33, 50–52, 56,
74–76, 81, 113, 114n. (*De duabus naturis*), 115
(*De trinitate*)
Boggess, William, 118n.
Bolton, Diana K., 50n., 53n.
Bolton-Hall, Margaret, 158n.
Boniface VIII, pope (1294–1303), 212n.
Born, Bertran de, 146
Bornelh, Giraut de, 146
Borso d'Este, duke of Ferrara, 192–93
Bradner, Leicester, 190n.
Brito, William, 102, 109
Brugnoli, Giorgio, 58n., 144n.
Brutus, 215
Bubwith, Nicholas, bishop of Bath and Wells,
207n.
bucolic poetry, 99
Burley, Walter, 165n.
buskin (*cothurnus*), used by actors of tragedy, 8,
18, 20–22, 26, 41, 42n., 48, 53, 60, 77; made
of goatskin, 143; used by authors,
figuratively, 25, 28, allegedly, 53, 66, 142, cf.
48, 60, 93; used by hunters, 53
Buti, Francesco da, 156–57, 207
Butterworth, Charles E., 119n., 120n.
Byblis, 214

Cadmus, 210

245

Index

Index

Index

Index

Index

Index

Index

St. Louis Community College
at Meramec
LIBRARY

Printed in the United States
47284LVS00004B/215